Governing at Home

Governing at Home

The White House and
Domestic Policymaking

Edited by Michael Nelson and Russell L. Riley

University Press of Kansas

Published by the University Press of Kansas (Lawrence, Kansas 66045), which was organized by the Kansas Board of Regents and is operated and funded by Emporia State University, Fort Hays State University, Kansas State University, Pittsburg State University, the University of Kansas, and Wichita State University

Library of Congress Cataloging-in-Publication Data

Governing at home : the White House and domestic policymaking / Michael Nelson and Russell L. Riley, editors.
    p. cm.
  Includes bibliographical references and index.
  ISBN 978-0-7006-1810-1 (cloth : alk. paper) — ISBN 978-0-7006-1811-8 (pbk. : alk. paper)
  1. Presidents—United States. 2. Political planning—United States. 3. Political leadership—United States. 4. Policy sciences. I. Nelson, Michael, 1949- II. Riley, Russell L. (Russell Lynn), 1958-
  JK516.G68 2011
  320.60973—dc22   2011014244

British Library Cataloguing-in-Publication Data is available.

Printed in the United States of America

10 9 8 7 6 5 4 3 2 1

Contents

Preface and Acknowledgments

Fifty years ago, when Richard E. Neustadt first published his classic *Presidential Power*, he pioneered a new way of thinking about his subject, urging readers to "try to view the Presidency from over the President's shoulder." "This is not," he claimed, "the way we conventionally view the office; ordinarily we stand outside, looking in." Neustadt's pathbreaking work bore the indelible marks of his own experience alongside President Harry S. Truman, and so taught by example the value of looking over the president's shoulder. But while Neustadt's new orientation was indeed revealing, and revolutionary, his method left scholars with a practical conundrum: How can those of us outside the privileged confines of the Oval Office actually look "out and down from the perspective of [the president's] place"?

Apart from the fictional encounters of *The West Wing* television series, probably the closest most people will come to achieving this valuable habit of mind is through the secret White House recordings of the Kennedy, Johnson, and Nixon years. Those recorded conversations of presidential meetings and telephone calls still possess a fly-on-the-wall quality, allowing outsiders to listen in as these presidents and their advisers deal with the problems of the day, in real time and without the listener's knowledge of how things turned out. The most recent of those recordings, however, is approaching forty years old, with little prospect, because of Nixon's fate, of future presidents giving us a similar chance to listen in.

Another alternative—which is at the core of this book—is presidential oral history. If we cannot peer over the president's shoulder to see the world as he (or, eventually, she) sees it, we can ask those who were in such positions to recount for us their best memories of what they saw and heard—and what those recollections might mean for understanding presidential behavior and Washington politics. This is what presidential oral history allows. Such spoken recollections provide a front-row seat to history, or, in the language of the computer generation, a virtual look into the life of the White House that only a lucky few can experience first-hand.

This book originated in a two-day symposium of oral history conversations, held at the University of Virginia's Miller Center of Public Affairs, in Charlottesville, on June 12–13, 2009. The purpose of the symposium was to gather a cross-section of recent White House domestic policy advisers, from Democratic and Republican administrations, to reflect together on their experiences in helping presidents achieve their domestic policy goals. This event followed closely the pattern of two earlier Miller Center symposia, one each on White House–congressional relations and presidential speechwriting. The former was published as Russell L. Riley, ed., *Bridging the Constitutional Divide: Inside the White House Office of Legislative Affairs* (Texas A&M University Press, 2010). The latter was published as Michael Nelson and Russell L. Riley, eds., *The President's Words: Speeches and Speechwriting in the Modern White House* (University Press of Kansas, 2010).

These group symposia provide a valuable supplement to the core work of the Miller Center's Presidential Oral History Program, which primarily involves interviews with key individuals from every administration since Jimmy Carter's, conducted always under a veil of confidentiality. Yet because of the open nature of these group oral histories, we are able to get the collective wisdom of the participants into the public domain much more quickly than is possible with the main course of our core interviews.

Notwithstanding their public nature, these symposia typically produce a frank and fascinating set of exchanges, providing a remarkable window into the most private inner sanctum of American politics. In the present case, we had the good fortune of attracting nine White House alumni, representing every administration from Richard Nixon through George W. Bush. These discussions were moderated by a group of highly accomplished scholars, who probed and pushed these former White House aides to deal with the kinds of questions, large and small, that typically occupy the attention of political scientists and historians interested in the president's leadership when governing at home. The discussions were open-ended, but each session of the symposium dealt with one of a set of core questions: What role does the presidential campaign have in shaping the subsequent activity of the White House? How are domestic policies and priorities established once a president is elected? Who, and what, is routinely involved in trying to sell domestic policy proposals to the American people? And what lessons can be learned from past successes and failures to enhance the ability of future presidents to succeed?

Each of the participating scholars produced a draft paper on their session topic before the symposium, to help frame questions for the discussions. Their revised papers, informed by their exchanges with the assembled guests, appear in this book as the odd-numbered chapters. Each of those authored chapters is then followed by an edited transcript of the symposium discussions. These oral histories are rich, original source materials on the presidency and the process of domestic policymaking, and as such are provided here in their entirety for further mining by others who wish to do more work on these topics.

It should be noted here that the editors have taken as their principal goal accessibility—and so these spoken discussions have been edited to the extent necessary to make them relatively easy to read. This is a departure from the usual conventions of oral history, where strict fidelity to the spoken word is expected. Anyone who has ever used an unedited transcript, however, recognizes that the idiosyncrasies of spoken English can actually obscure the speaker's meaning when the words are literally converted to print. In this volume we have made every effort to avoid that outcome. For anyone who wishes to access the verbatim record of the proceedings, it is freely available in audio and video form on the Miller Center's Web site, at http://millercenter.org/scripps/archive/conference/detail/5471.

Finally, the editors wish to direct the reader's attention to the fact that the transcripts have been extensively annotated, including factual elaborations, scholarly references, and explanatory matter to clarify sometimes obscure allusions—all intended to enrich the content of the original discussions. These annotations appear in endnotes at the end of each transcribed chapter.

This book has genuinely been a team effort. Our greatest indebtedness is to those nine White House alumni who agreed to take two days from their busy schedules to come to Charlottesville and recount for us their experiences: Egil "Bud" Krogh, James Cannon III, Roger Porter, James Pinkerton, Stuart Eizenstat, Bertram Carp, Bruce Reed, William Galston, and Margaret Spellings. We could not have asked for a more luminous, engaged, or cooperative group. Most of the wisdom that appears in these pages can be either directly or indirectly attributed to their generosity. We also, of course, benefited enormously from the participation of a set of top-flight scholars on the presidency, who helped give shape to the discussions, brought to them their own learned insights, and, in this volume, crafted valuable lenses through which to view the subjects under discussion. This book itself is a testament to what can happen when political practitioners and academics deeply engage with one another to further public understanding of the nation's political life.

The entire enterprise would not have been possible without the financial support and endorsement provided by the Miller Center's leadership, including the director, Governor Gerald L. Baliles, and associate director W. Taylor Reveley IV. Moreover, the support staff of the center was indispensable, especially in handling the logistics for the original symposium. Oral history program administrator Katrina Kuhn took care of the lion's share of the planning until her husband's appearance at the College World Series drew her away—when Stephanie Cencula stepped up as our closer. Others who played valuable roles in the symposium were Michael Greco, Robert Canevari, Sean Gallagher, and Kevan Holdsworth, all involved in managing the audiovisual aspects of the event. Their jobs were happily complicated by the presence of C-SPAN cameras for the run of the session (thanks in large part to the efforts of Lisa Porter)—which we were delighted to welcome. We also owe a debt of gratitude to Martha Healey for transcribing the proceedings and to both Jane Rafal Wilson and Claiborne Lange for copyediting the original transcript so the editors and authors would have a usable document to get into shape for publication. At every step of the way these chores were handled with their usual aplomb and professionalism.

We again wish to express words of sincere thanks to the director of the University Press of Kansas, Fred Woodward, both for his continuing confidence in a book project of this unusual nature and for his superb efforts in showcasing the words of his authors and editors. He and this press continue to do remarkable work. Too, we want to acknowledge the key role Professors James P. Pfiffner and Andrew Rudalevige played in reviewing the original manuscript for Kansas. We thank Jim and Andy for their enthusiastic reaction to the project and for their characteristically insightful commentary on the substance of the text.

As always, our personal support networks helped us to keep body and soul together through both the symposium and the book-preparation process. For this, and also for their healthy, if surely underappreciated, diversions, we are grateful to Monique, Joseph, and Cathryn in Charlottesville and Linda, Michael, Sam, and McClain in Memphis.

Michael Nelson and Russell Riley

Chapter 1

Domestic Policy, Domestic Policy Advisers, and the American Presidency

Michael Nelson

Two themes animate this chapter. The first is that for nearly a half-century the president's domestic policy—every president's domestic policy—has been primarily a White House production, with the departments and agencies of the executive branch consigned to a distinctly secondary role. The second is that how domestic policy is made within the White House and who makes it have varied greatly in this period from administration to administration.

White House–Centered Domestic Policymaking

The seeds of White House–centered domestic policymaking were planted by the Committee on Administrative Management—the Brownlow Committee—in 1937. Franklin D. Roosevelt's first term as president had been marked by an explosion of legislative activity aimed at combating the Great Depression. Cumulatively, these new laws created a large and active role for the federal government in the nation's economy.

Because Roosevelt doubted the loyalty and competence of most of the existing departments and agencies, which had been created in less active times and were staffed mainly by Republican employees, he persuaded Congress to authorize new agencies to carry out his new programs. By adding so many components to the executive branch, however, Roosevelt created an administrative nightmare. He was frustrated by his inability to get the information he needed from the bureaucracy, to coordinate the activities of its old and new agencies, and to communicate his desires for action effectively.

On March 20, 1936, Roosevelt created the Committee on Administrative Management, with political scientist Louis D. Brownlow as chair, and charged it to design and recommend an overhaul of the executive branch that would make it more efficient and responsive to the president. On

January 8, 1937, Brownlow and his colleagues issued their report, which Roosevelt accepted wholeheartedly.

Arguing that "the president needs help," the Brownlow Committee recommended that the president be authorized to hire six personal assistants "possessed of high competence, great physical vigor, and a passion for anonymity." Their task would be to help the president "in obtaining quickly and without delay all pertinent information possessed by any of the executive departments so as to guide him in making his responsible decisions; and then when decisions have been made, to assist him in seeing to it that every administrative department and agency affected is promptly informed."[1]

In addition to these White House staff positions, the Brownlow Committee recommended that the Executive Office of the President (EOP) be created to serve the long-term interests of the presidency as an institution. The main components of the EOP would be the Bureau of the Budget, then housed in the treasury department, and the Civil Service Commission, long an independent agency.

After receiving the Brownlow Committee's report, Roosevelt immediately asked Congress for authorization to implement its recommendations. Angry over the president's recent effort to "pack" the Supreme Court, Congress did not approve his request until April 1939. (Even then, it left the Civil Service Commission independent and rejected proposals to bring several other agencies under direct presidential control.) On September 8, 1939, Roosevelt issued Executive Order 8248, and some of the Brownlow Committee's major proposals took effect. The president hired 6 new staff members and inherited a budget bureau with 35 employees. By 1946 the White House staff had grown to about 60. Since then it has risen as high as 542 under Richard Nixon, eventually settling into the 350–450 range in subsequent administrations. The BOB staff expanded to more than 600, where it has remained.[2]

Newly staffed, Roosevelt began to rely heavily on certain White House assistants for advice on domestic policy, especially Samuel Rosenman, Thomas Corcoran, Benjamin Cohen, and Harry Hopkins. Roosevelt's first three successors turned to Clark Clifford and Charles Murphy (Harry S. Truman), Gabriel Hauge and Sherman Adams (Dwight D. Eisenhower), and Theodore Sorensen and Myer Feldman (John F. Kennedy) for the same purpose. But the role of these staff members was generally "limited to advising the president on the merits of departmental recommendations" rather than devising and initiating policy proposals of their own.[3] Similarly, the expanded budget bureau assumed new responsibilities in domestic policy. Starting with Roosevelt, BOB began performing "central clearance"—that is, reviewing all proposed departmental recommendations to Congress to evaluate their consistency with the president's program.

As important as these innovations were, the president's domestic program still consisted almost entirely of proposals generated by the departments and agencies. Lyndon B. Johnson, who succeeded to the presidency when Kennedy was assassinated in 1963, grew frustrated with this process, both the slow pace with which departments developed new proposals and the necessarily narrow approaches to domestic problems that individual departments were able to offer. He charged White House staff members Bill Moyers and, after Moyers became press secretary in July 1965, Joseph A. Califano to form a series of task forces for domestic policy innovation. These task forces—145 in all during Johnson's five-and-a-half years as president— were dominated by departmental outsiders, mostly academics, businessmen, labor leaders, and state and local officials, with liaisons from BOB and Califano's own staff.[4] As political scientists Norman Thomas and Harold Wolman found, "the manifest intent of outside task forces was to bypass the departments and agencies as major instruments of policy formulation."[5] The departments were allowed to evaluate task force proposals, but even at this late stage of the process the judgments of BOB and White House staff evaluators—usually the same individuals who served as liaisons to the task forces in the first place—carried more weight. In Califano's brusque assessment, "We got most of our stuff from academics and quite frankly, a lot of stuff we just did and handed it to the department concerned."[6]

In 1968, both major party candidates for president faced the challenge of distancing themselves from Johnson: Republican Richard Nixon because he was the opposition-party nominee and Democrat Hubert H. Humphrey because, as vice president, he needed to emerge from Johnson's shadow. Both chose the domestic policymaking process as one vehicle for demonstrating their independence. In a national radio address, Nixon promised that policy in his administration would be made through a "reorganized and strengthened Cabinet." "The President's chief function is to lead, not to administer," he said; "it is not to oversee every detail but to put the right people in charge."[7] For his part, Humphrey declared to a Los Angeles audience: "A National Domestic Policy Council should be established to provide the same comprehensive, systematic, and reliable analysis of domestic problems which the National Security Council and its staff produce on foreign policy and national defense issues."[8]

Nixon was elected but, ironically, something resembling Humphrey's proposal eventually prevailed. Any hope that Nixon's "cabinet government" approach would succeed vanished when he appointed a cabinet consisting mostly of people he did not know, several of them liberals, and then gave them the freedom to appoint their own assistant secretaries and other sub-cabinet officers without White House clearance. In short order, Nixon came to view his cabinet members as captives of their departments' permanent civil servants, most of whom were Democrats. (Famously, Nixon aide John D. Ehrlichman said of the cabinet: "They go off and marry the natives.")[9] Nixon also was frustrated, as Johnson had been, by the slow pace with which the departments generated policy proposals. The "magic time" for introducing new policies to Congress was the president's first few months in office, Nixon believed.[10] But during Nixon's own first months, the only significant legislative proposals he was able to pull from the departments were to reorganize the post office and improve coal mine safety.[11]

As frustrated as Nixon was by his cabinet government approach to domestic policymaking, that is how happy he was in the realm of foreign policy with the National Security Council and, in particular, with the NSC staff. Formally, the NSC, created by law in 1947, consists of high-ranking officials, including the president, the vice president, the secretaries of state and defense, the chair of the Joint Chiefs of Staff, and others. In practice, Nixon generally ignored the council and relied instead on its staff, headed by national security adviser Henry A. Kissinger. In 1970 Nixon created the Domestic Council (DC) as a device to shunt the domestic department heads aside as well. The council itself was modeled on the NSC (it included the president, vice president, and the heads of the domestic cabinet departments), and in like manner the president treated it as window dressing. The real work was done by the DC staff under the direction of domestic policy adviser Ehrlichman.

Starting with Nixon, every president has centered domestic policymaking not in the cabinet departments or in Johnson-style outside task forces, but rather in one or more White House staff units. (These are discussed in the next section of the chapter.) The reasons presidents have done so emerge clearly from the discussions among White House domestic policy advisers from the Nixon through the George W. Bush administrations that took place at the Miller Center of Public Affairs at the University of Virginia on June 12–13, 2009. These reasons involve matters of trust, loyalty, priority, time, and coordination.[12]

Trust

Trust between the president and the staff develops during the election campaign and carries over into the White House. As Jimmy Carter staff member Stuart Eizenstat observes, "The people who start with the president during the time he's first running, the loyalists, when he's barely known, and go through the snows of Iowa and into New Hampshire—you build a bond with the president, a bond of loyalty and trust that can't be substituted for by others."[13] The result, according to Bruce Reed, who served under Bill Clinton, is that the White House staff "is heavily laden with people who have been on the campaign and are keepers of the campaign flame." Reed adds that "one of the reasons why, over time, policy development has become more and more concentrated in the White House, [is] because the White House aides by definition tend to know the president better, to know his preferences better. They've been with him longer. Cabinet members often have a lot of catching up to do."

Importing campaign loyalists into the White House entails costs. "Very frequently, loyalists are inexperienced" in government, says Clinton staff member William Galston. In addition, the skills that are of greatest value in a campaign staff member may not translate well into the new challenges of governing. The nominating and general election campaigns place a premium on skills of political combat. One succeeds in an election by defeating a series of opponents until they all are driven from the field. These are not the skills of governing, which require compromise and conciliation with the other constitutional branches of government. (Fondly though they may wish it, no president can defeat Congress and make it go away.) But the costs of surrounding themselves with an inappropriately skilled staff are costs that most presidents are willing to pay. According to Ronald Reagan staff member Martin Anderson, the president "wants loyalty, total, absolute loyalty and enthusiasm [from the staff]. Then if they know something about Washington, that's nice but not that critical."[14]

Loyalty

The White House staff's loyalty is undivided. Once in office, staff members have one constituent: the president. Presidents do not doubt the loyalty of staffers whose jobs in the White House are gifts that are as easily withdrawn as given. In contrast, the political scientist Richard Fenno has observed, cabinet members have "a great multiplicity of external relationships."[15] In addition to serving the president, they must serve legislators and a host of interest groups. The departments they head owe their existence to laws passed by Congress and continue to rely on Congress for the annual appropriations that sustain them. Department heads are required to testify before congressional committees, which may freely investigate their activities. For this reason, presidents worry constantly about departmental loyalty within the government, especially when the opposition party controls one or both houses of Congress, a situation that nearly every president from Nixon to Barack Obama has faced for at least part of his administration.[16]

As for interest groups, some domestic departments were formed for the purpose of representing them in the executive branch, including farmers (the agriculture department), westerners (the interior department), workers (the labor department), business (the commerce department), teachers (the education department), and veterans (the veterans affairs department). No department head can avoid the responsibility of advancing some, and usually several, group interests whether or not the president cares about or even shares them. In addition, cabinet members must cultivate their departments' career civil servants, on whom they depend for information, advice, and expertise.

White House staff members sometimes come to conceive of their role as protecting the president from cabinet officers whose perspective is shaped by their departments. James Cannon, an aide to President Gerald R. Ford, observes that "the worst thing a president can do" is have a cabinet member come to the White House, "and as he's leaving he says, 'Oh, by the way, Mr. President, I would like to do A, B, or C.' The president nods, or whatever he does; he doesn't say no." Cannon cites the "tragic" occasion when Secretary of Labor John Dunlop took Ford aside and asked him to support a union-backed proposal to allow common situs picketing. "The president didn't say no, so John went up to the Hill and working with labor people and so forth, got a deal on situs picketing. When it was about to be culminated, ten people in the White House said, 'Mr. President, you can't do that. It violates everything you've ever done, said, and believed in.' So President Ford had to tell John, 'I can't do this now.' John resigned and we lost a very good cabinet member because of this instance of, 'Oh, by the way, Mr. President.'"

Priority

Presidents usually are elected—and will or will not be reelected—chiefly on the basis of domestic issues. According to Bruce Reed, Clinton's "view was that running for president was the ultimate job interview. The agenda he laid out represented the terms of his contract." As a result, the Clinton staff's "strongest weapon in internal debates within the administration and in debates with Congress" was "to be able to say, 'This is what the president promised. We have to keep this promise.'" Because the executive departments cannot be expected to share the president's intense concern about keeping campaign promises, the staff becomes the trusted keeper of the flame. To be sure, performing this role can take a variety of forms. The process of converting campaign promises into government action does not always mean passing new laws. As George W. Bush staff member Margaret Spellings says, "there are places where you say, okay, there's not a piece of legislation, but there are executive orders, regulatory process issues, commissions, various other ways to scratch the policy itches."

Campaigns tend to overpromise, creating problems in office if they succeed on Election Day. "People often say, 'to govern is to choose,'" says Galston. "It is much less frequently said, 'to campaign is to choose.'" In addition, campaigns are much more about making promises than about how these promises will be fulfilled. Egil Krogh, who served on Nixon's domestic policy staff, recalls that one of Nixon's main pledges in 1968 was to "'cut the crime in the District [of Columbia], the crime capital of the world.' During the transition we were trying to figure out, What does that mean?" In Krogh's first meeting with the president, Nixon repeated: "We've got to cut the crime." Krogh ruefully recalls, "So I wrote in my pad, 'Cut the crime,'" wondering all the while how the president expected him to do that.

When a presidential candidate's campaign promises do not align with the president's policies in office, problems arise. According to George H. W. Bush adviser James Pinkerton, as a presidential candidate Bush listened when campaign strategist Lee Atwater said, "Look, you've got to win over the conservatives" by pledging not to raise taxes. But when Bush became president, he preferred advice "not to help me keep my campaign promises, but to help me do what I really want to do," which ultimately included the politically disastrous decision to negotiate a budget agreement with Congress that raised taxes. Other White House staff members note the problems that arise when a president introduces a new policy without having laid the groundwork during the campaign, as Carter did when he tried to repeal a number of water projects that were popular on Capitol Hill, Clinton did when he proposed to issue an executive order allowing gays and lesbians to serve in the military, and George W. Bush did when he tried to reform immigration policy. In every case the president was unsuccessful.

Time

The White House staff shares the president's fierce urgency about time, which the departments, with their much longer-term perspective, do not. Lyndon Johnson spoke for many presidents when he told his aide Harry McPherson, "You've got to give it all you can that first year. Doesn't matter what kind of majority [in Congress] you come in with. You've got just one year when they treat you right, and before they start worrying about themselves. The third year, you lose votes. . . . The fourth year is all politics."[17] Not just Congress, but also the executive departments, which have been around much longer than the president and expect to be there long after the president is gone, are in much less of a rush. They especially do not like being asked to tack dramatically right or left by one president only to be asked to tack in the opposite direction by the next.

Aggravating this contrast in time perspective is that many months are required for the president to appoint and win Senate confirmation for the departments' numerous subcabinet positions. The White House staff, appointed solely by the president, is in place and ready to go at the outset of the president's term while the departments' leadership is still taking form. According to Reed, "There is a huge advantage that goes to people in White House staff, particularly during the first six months, arguably the first year, before you start filling out people in departments and agencies and they are then in a position to be a little more effective in countering what the White House is doing. But the initiative and drive is always coming right out of the White House."

The gap between when the White House staff is formed (essentially during the transition period) and when the subcabinet is formed is both great and growing. Nixon needed only an average three-and-a-half months to get his subcabinet appointees nominated and confirmed by the Senate—itself an increase over the two-and-a-half months Kennedy required. That number has been rising ever since: to four-and-a-half months under Carter, five-and-a-half months under Reagan, eight months under George H. W. Bush, eight-and-a-half months under Clinton, and ten months under George W. Bush. In April 2009, one hundred days into Obama's term, not a single cabinet department had even one-third of its Senate-confirmed appointees in place, and the figure for eight departments was less than 10 percent. The explanation lies at both ends of Pennsylvania Avenue. In an era of ideologically polarized political parties, often aggravated by divided government, senators of the opposition party are primed to attack a presidential appointee who is vulnerable in any way, and presidents are reluctant to nominate someone who may be subject to such an attack.

The result is a talent pool of presidential appointees depleted by what Secretary of State Hillary Rodham Clinton described as a "clearance and vetting process [that] . . . is frustrating beyond words," "ridiculous," and "a nightmare."[18] In 2000, the Presidential Appointee Initiative surveyed a highly credentialed group of 580 corporate and nonprofit executives, college and university presidents, think-tank scholars, state and local officials, and leading lobbyists about the prospect of receiving a presidential invitation to be nominated for a leading position in the administration. As political scientist Paul C. Light summarized their responses, these "potential appointees viewed the nomination and confirmation process as unfair, confusing, and embarrassing." Many also were dismayed about the number and severity of the legal restrictions placed on their income and investments when taking office and their employment opportunities after leaving.[19] Former White House counsel C. Boyden Gray described the process as one in which appointees are "innocent until nominated."[20]

Coordination

Important issues seldom fit squarely within the domain of a single department or agency, which means that central coordination of the efforts of multiple executive branch units is necessary. In response to what Roger Porter, who served in three Republican White Houses, has described as "the interrelatedness of the substantive problems that government is expected to address," presidents necessarily turn to the White House staff to shape the ideas of various departments and agencies into policy proposals that are expansive enough to cover a problem's many facets.[21]

Although presidential staff members are aware of all the reasons why domestic policymaking has become a White House–centered process, not all of them are entirely comfortable with that development. Stuart Eizenstat notes that the campaign promises the White House staff is wedded to are "often slapped together under enormous political pressures" and as a consequence are "without the kind of interagency review you have when you're president, and without the kind of economic and budget data you would like to have." Bertram Carp, who served with Eizenstat on Carter's domestic policy staff, adds, "The great ideas we dream up all have to be implemented by GS-12s and GS-13s and GS-16s, and these White House–driven policy development efforts are not always as friendly to those people as they ought to be. Even if they don't have any good ideas, in the end we're going to move on and they're going to be there."

Changing Methods of White House Domestic Policymaking

The president's domestic policy is largely a White House production, no longer centered in the departments and agencies of the executive branch as it generally was prior to the 1960s. The enduring nature of this transformation is best evidenced in the administrations of several recent presidents—specifically, Nixon, Ford, Carter, Reagan, and George H. W. Bush—who entered office declaring their intention to devolve policymaking from the White House to the cabinet and the individual departments only to abandon that approach when it yielded unsatisfactory results. Their successors—Clinton, George W. Bush, and Obama—have known from the start that, for all the reasons discussed in the preceding section of this chapter, cabinet government is no longer a path worth exploring. To this extent, domestic policymaking has developed in the same way as foreign policymaking, an endeavor that for most of American history was the province of the state department but that gradually was drawn into the White House, starting with the creation of the National Security Council and, more importantly, the national security staff.

The crucial difference between modern White House–centered foreign policymaking and domestic policymaking is that the former has become institutionalized in form as well as in fact and the latter has not. Since the Nixon administration, every president's national security adviser and staff have comprised the hub of executive decision making in the international arena. No similar White House staff position or unit has become the standard template for policymaking in domestic affairs. Instead, each president has invented and reinvented the domestic policy apparatus, often changing course one or more times during his tenure in office. As one indicator of the contrast between the foreign and domestic domains, the NSC staff has been called the NSC staff for decades. The corresponding domestic policy unit has operated under a variety of names as individual presidents have searched for the ideal approach: Domestic Council, Domestic Policy Staff, Office of Policy Development, Domestic Policy Council, and Policy Coordinating Group.

Richard Nixon

Nixon is best remembered for creating the Domestic Council and the council's much more influential domestic policy staff headed by Ehrlichman. The DC consisted of the president, vice president, every cabinet member except the secretaries of state and defense, and assorted officials such as the postmaster general and the director of the newly renamed Office of Management and Budget (OMB). But the real work of domestic policymaking was done by groups of subcabinet officials directed by one or another of Ehrlichman's six specialized associate directors, with support from about seventy additional DC staff members.[22] Essentially, Ehrlichman, an associate director, and the support staff told the departmental members of each working group what the White House wanted to do, and the departmental members told the staff how they would do it. "Domestic policy making was woven by the White House, with input from the departments," writes political scientist Shirley Anne Warshaw. As for the actual Domestic Council, "when the council met, it was primarily a show-and-tell exercise."[23]

Less well remembered is that this arrangement prevailed only for the middle third of Nixon's five-and-a-half year presidency. Before creating the Domestic Council, Nixon had appointed what amounted to two White House domestic policy advisers: the liberal political scientist Daniel Patrick Moynihan to provide staff support to a new cabinet-centered Urban Affairs Council and the conservative economist Arthur Burns to serve as a wide-ranging counselor on domestic and economic affairs. The result, according to Egil Krogh, was that Burns and Moynihan would "lob memos at each other," with Nixon reluctantly forced to resolve their disagreements, a role with which he was temperamentally uncomfortable. "Nixon did not like it," says Roger Porter. "He did not like that at all." Within a year, the Urban

Affairs Council was dissolved, Burns left the White House to become chair of the Federal Reserve Board, and Nixon created the Domestic Council with Ehrlichman in charge of the staff.

Bracketing the DC staff's period of supremacy at the other end of the Nixon presidency was Ehrlichman's April 1973 resignation in response to growing evidence of his involvement in the Watergate scandal. In theory, the staff, now headed by Ehrlichman's deputy, Kenneth Cole, remained intact and in charge of domestic policymaking. In practice it became a shadow of its former self. Cole lacked Ehrlichman's close relationship with Nixon, and Nixon himself was preoccupied with trying to save his presidency from the growing scandal. Ironically, until Nixon resigned in August 1974, the domestic departments and agencies briefly became, by default, the centers of policymaking that Nixon had promised to make them during the 1968 campaign.

Gerald R. Ford

The Domestic Council and staff remained nominally in place when Ford succeeded Nixon, with Cole as domestic policy adviser and the cabinet departments exercising uncharacteristic leeway within their individual policy domains. But soon after becoming president Ford began restlessly experimenting with his domestic policymaking apparatus in ways that diminished both staff and cabinet. Initially, Ford pledged "to reverse the trend and restore authority to my Cabinet."[24] Facing an economy plagued by an unusual combination of rising inflation and growing unemployment, however, he created the White House–centered Economic Policy Board (EPB) in September 1974, less than two months into his presidency. In doing so, Ford separated his economic policy staff from the domestic policy staff and cabinet alike. Further, because, as Roger Porter has written, "almost any issue involves budgetary matters, and most issues can be defined as economic," the DC staff's role quickly shrank to insignificance.[25] Cole, who seldom had access to the president, resigned three months after the EPB was created.

On December 19, 1974, the same day that Cole resigned, Congress confirmed Ford's nomination of former New York governor Nelson A. Rockefeller as vice president. Determined to play a major role in the administration, Rockefeller persuaded Ford to let him head the Domestic Council. "At that point Ford had not really understood yet how to run the White House . . .," reflects James Cannon, a close Rockefeller associate who was appointed as the DC's executive director. "He did not understand, apparently, what he was promising to Rockefeller when he gave him that assignment." Determined to pursue a liberal agenda that included national health insurance and a host of new urban programs, Rockefeller was undermined at every step of the way by Ford's chief of staff, Donald Rumsfeld, and by the Economic Policy Board.[26] On October 6, 1975, the EPB persuaded Ford to offer a budget for the coming fiscal year that, far from funding Rockefeller's policy initiatives, proposed to reduce spending on existing domestic programs. Rumsfeld saw to it that Rockefeller was not even consulted about this decision. Less than a month later Rockefeller, with a push from Ford, announced that he would not be a candidate for vice president in the 1976 election; he also withdrew from the Domestic Council. Cannon became domestic policy adviser for the remainder of the Ford presidency with what he described as a very limited charge: "to deal with putting out brush fires, to move paper back and forth between the departments and the White House."[27]

Jimmy Carter

As a candidate for president in 1976, Carter repeatedly promised to devolve domestic policymaking from the White House to the departments. Meeting with the cabinet on the day he was inaugurated, Carter affirmed, "I believe in cabinet administration of government. There will never be an instance while I am president when the members of the White House staff dominate or act in a superior position to the members of our cabinet." He subsequently promised that "Cabinet officers . . . will be free to set their own priorities, . . . free to choose their own staffs, . . . and able to administer their own departments without White House interference."[28] Carter abolished the Domestic Council and renamed its White House component the Domestic Policy Staff (DPS), with Eizenstat as domestic policy adviser and a much-reduced staff. "Every single thing that was written by a cabinet officer went to the president," recalls Eizenstat's deputy, Bertram Carp. Eizenstat's main assignment was to shepherd proposals from the cabinet to the president with an accompanying memorandum that evaluated each proposal's advantages and disadvantages.

In time, all of these initial plans and intentions were diluted or abandoned. Carter appointed people he barely knew to the cabinet while staffing the White House with close associates from the election campaign and from his tenure as governor of Georgia, including Eizenstat. Cabinet members incurred the president's wrath by pursuing policies of which he disapproved. Taking Carter at his word that department heads were supreme in their own domains, for example, Secretary of Agriculture Bob Bergland lobbied Congress for greater farm price supports than the president favored, Secretary of Transportation Brock Adams pushed for additional spending on mass transit, and Secretary of Health, Education, and Welfare Joseph Califano independently promoted a politically controversial antismoking agenda. In July 1979 Carter fired nearly half the heads of the domestic cabinet departments. The Domestic Policy Staff doubled in size, and Eizenstat's memorandums to the president became much more overtly advisory in nature.

Ronald Reagan

Like all of his recent predecessors, Reagan campaigned for president in 1980 pledging that "cabinet government can and will work."[29] Like Nixon in the middle years of his administration, once in office Reagan organized the heads of the departments into working groups whose activities were for the most part directed by members of the White House staff. Unlike Nixon, Ford, and Carter, however, Reagan fostered harmony between cabinet and staff by appointing cabinet (and subcabinet) officials with the same emphasis on loyalty that presidents traditionally apply to the selection of the staff.

Reagan named Edwin Meese, who had been chief of staff during his tenure as governor of California, as his chief policy adviser with the title Counselor to the President. Meese persuaded Reagan to rename and restructure the domestic policy staff. As Roger Porter recalls, "Those of us in the economic and domestic policy arena wanted to be able to claim international economic policy as not national security but economic. Therefore Ed Meese said, 'Okay, let's get "domestic" out of the title. We'll call it the Office of Policy Development [OPD]. We can claim almost anything under that heading,' which ultimately successfully we did."

At Meese's suggestion, Reagan created six cabinet councils in addition to the National Security Council: economic affairs, human resources, legal policy, natural resources and the environment, management and administration, and commerce and trade. Each council was chaired by a cabinet member but largely controlled by the OPD staff. According to Martin Anderson, who was Reagan's first policy development adviser, "The White House controlled what time the meeting would take place, where the meeting occurred, and the agenda."[30] The result, observes Warshaw, was that "all the policy initiatives that emerged from the cabinet council process . . . were initiatives that the White House itself had crafted."[31]

During Reagan's second term, the domestic policy process became even more White House–centered when the president's new chief of staff, Donald Regan, reduced the number of cabinet councils to two: the Economic Policy Council and the Domestic Policy Council. Regan also engineered the appointment of a protégé, Alfred Kingon, to head the White House's cabinet affairs office, and charged Kingon to direct the cabinet councils. In doing so, Regan created yet another variation on the theme of White House–centered domestic policymaking, one that diminished cabinet and OPD alike and elevated the cabinet office.

George H. W. Bush

Although he never used the term during his successful 1988 election campaign, Bush was the only recent president other than Carter to try hard to make cabinet government work. Bush thought he would succeed where Carter failed because, unlike Carter's cabinet of strangers, nearly every one of Bush's department heads was a close friend of the president with long and varied Washington experience.

Because Bush's initial focus was on the cabinet (and, more generally, on foreign policy), he gave less attention to the White House staff's role in domestic policymaking. Structurally, Bush simply kept Reagan's OPD and the two second-term councils: economic policy and domestic policy. As OPD head with the title Assistant to the President for Economic and Domestic Policy, Bush chose Roger Porter, now serving in his third consecutive Republican administration. As Porter recalls, Bush "said, 'Brent Scowcroft is going to do foreign policy [as national security adviser] and I want you to do everything else.' I said, 'Well, I think we ought to divide it between economic and domestic as it had been previously.' He said, 'No, I just want to have the two of you.' So I ended up in the first Bush administration, being over both economic and domestic policy."[32]

Porter decided to add a policy planning office to OPD headed by James Pinkerton and charged it to focus on longer-term issues. Porter himself assumed an "honest broker" role on matters requiring more immediate attention, seeing to it that all points of view within the administration were fairly presented to Bush before decisions were made.[33] But Porter did not report directly to the president, unlike national security adviser Scowcroft and, more to the point, unlike domestic policy advisers Ehrlichman in the Nixon administration, Eizenstat in the Carter administration, and Meese in the Reagan administration.

In practice, cabinet secretaries, only loosely reined by the White House, succumbed to the tendency to promote new or expanded programs that were important to their departments but inconsistent with Bush's overall agenda of restraining government activity and reducing domestic spending. While Porter concentrated on the details of certain issues, such as the Clean Air Act, and on "ensuring the integrity of the process," Bush's chief of staff, John Sununu, and OMB director Richard Darman aggressively took charge of domestic policymaking.[34] At the same time, Sununu and Darman cracked down on Pinkerton, who was using the policy planning unit to promote a variety of bold conservative approaches to fighting poverty that they regarded as distractions from deficit reduction.

Bush's original decision to rely on his department heads for policy development and his accompanying neglect of the White House domestic policy process caused him no end of woe. Before leaving office the president went through a series of chiefs of staff and domestic policy advisers and structures, each less successful than the last. For example, in January 1992 Bush brought Republican National Committee chair Clayton Yeutter into the White House with the title Counselor to the President for Domestic Policy and replaced the Domestic Policy Council and Economic Policy Council with a unified Policy Coordinating Group. Porter was not fired, but he was stripped of his West Wing office, which Yeutter moved into.[35] In truth, on matters of domestic policymaking, Bush was in many ways the exception who demonstrates the rule—namely, that cabinet government, even when sincerely attempted, no longer offers a viable alternative to a White House–centered policy process.

Bill Clinton

Unlike his predecessors, Clinton made no pretense during the 1992 election campaign of planning to form a cabinet government. He knew from the start that he wanted to formulate domestic policy within the White House. In an innovation consistent with this intention, Clinton appointed a Domestic Policy Council that included not just cabinet secretaries but also a number of White House staff members. Staff-led working groups were formed within the council for the purpose of fleshing out the details of policies that the president and staff would originate.

At the outset of the Clinton presidency, however, individual cabinet members, several of whom had been appointed because of their close association with major Democratic constituencies, tried to use the working groups to pursue departmental goals for new programs and increased funding. In the wake of the Reagan and Bush presidencies, these goals represented twelve years of pent-up Democratic demands. Although the cabinet members' efforts were generally unsuccessful (Secretary of Labor Robert Reich later expressed his frustration in the title of his memoir: *Locked in the Cabinet*), they slowed the progress of domestic policymaking.[36] As Bruce Reed points out, "Particularly for your own supporters, who have been waiting a long time for your party to get back in power, saying to them when you come right into office, 'Don't worry, we're not going to do double funding in the first year; it's going to take us four years or eight years,' that's a tough message for them."

An additional source of problems in Clinton's first-term domestic policymaking process originated with the president himself. During the postelection transition period, Clinton had spent a frustratingly large amount of time seeking and finding enough women and minority cabinet members to fulfill his campaign promise to appoint "a cabinet that looks like America." When critics then pointed out that Clinton's senior White House staff consisted almost entirely of white men, Clinton selected Carol Rasco, who had worked for him on health and welfare policy while he was governor of Arkansas, as domestic policy adviser. Reed, who was Clinton's leading domestic policy aide during the campaign, was relegated to deputy adviser, along with fellow deputy William Galston. Under Rasco's weak leadership, concludes political scientist James Pfiffner, "a domestic policy staff existed in the White House, but did not function as a major force in policy making."[37]

The weakness of the domestic policy staff during Clinton's first term required others to fill the void. Three of the president's major initiatives—health-care reform, national service, and reinventing government—were assigned to First Lady Hillary Rodham Clinton, staff member Eli Segal, and Vice President Al Gore, respectively. None of the three reported to Rasco. Other important domestic issues became the province of Clinton's newly formed National Economic Council (NEC), with strong leadership from White House economic adviser Robert E. Rubin. A further dilution of the domestic policy staff's influence came in 1995 when, facing a difficult reelection campaign, Clinton secretly turned for advice to political consultant Dick Morris, who was a fount of policy ideas all by himself.

Rasco stepped down as domestic policy adviser after the 1996 election and Reed, who had shepherded the development of one of Clinton's major first-term achievements, welfare reform, took her place, with Galston remaining as deputy.[38] But the combination of the president's relatively substance-free 1996 reelection campaign and, from January 1998 on, the distractions of the Monica Lewinsky scandal and impeachment took the steam out of domestic policymaking throughout the second term.

George W. Bush

Bush, like Carter, Reagan, and Clinton (indeed, like every recent president except his father and Barack Obama) campaigned in 2000 as a state governor chiefly interested in domestic policy. He preserved the Domestic Policy Council and National Economic Council structure that he inherited from Clinton and, like Reagan, oversaw a highly centralized cabinet and subcabinet appointment process that insured loyalty to the president and deference to the White House staff among the departments and agencies.[39]

Bush selected Margaret Spellings, a trusted associate from his first gubernatorial campaign in 1994 and his six years as governor of Texas, as domestic policy adviser. Spellings's expertise was in public school reform, a major achievement of Bush's governorship that he promised during the election to make one of his major first-term goals. With Spellings in the driver's seat, Bush forged a bipartisan coalition in Congress to pass No Child Left Behind legislation.

Far from relying on Spellings and her staff for all domestic policy matters, however, Bush formed other White House units to develop and promote his HIV-AIDS, voluntarism, and faith-based service initiatives, the latter through a newly created Office of Community and Faith-Based Initiatives (OCFBI). He charged NEC to secure the enactment of major reductions in federal income taxes. He asked Vice President Richard Cheney to form and lead an energy policy task force. He assigned OMB general counsel Jay Lefkowitz to oversee his review of federal policy concerning stem cell research. The relevant cabinet members in all of these matters—the secretary of education on No Child Left Behind, the secretary of health and human services on stem cell policy, the secretary of the treasury on tax cuts, and the secretary of energy on energy policy—played distinctly secondary roles.[40] In addition, throughout his presidency, Bush's chief political aide, Karl Rove, influenced almost every aspect of domestic policymaking, with Cheney also weighing in episodically, usually on matters of environmental regulation that were of concern to the business community.[41] As Bradley W. Patterson has observed, "Rule One" of Bush's domestic policymaking process was: "Every important policy issue will have a home—*in the White House*."[42] Exactly where in the White House each issue would find that home was less predictable.

Bush attempted at various times to make the domestic policy process more coherent. In 2002 he brought Lefkowitz into the White House as deputy domestic policy adviser to play a coordinating role. In 2005, at the beginning of the second term, Bush moved several White House staff members to cabinet positions, including Spellings as secretary of education. He replaced her as domestic policy adviser with Claude Allen, who resigned a year later when he was arrested for shoplifting, and then Karl Zinsmeister of the American Enterprise Institute. But with Bush intensely focused on the wars on terrorism and in Iraq from September 11, 2001, until the end of his presidency, the domestic policymaking process necessarily took a back seat. Bush records in his memoirs that in 2006, when he asked an aide to "sketch the organizational chart of the White House," the resulting drawing "was a tangled mess, with lines of authority crossing and blurred."[43]

Barack Obama

Domestic policymaking during the Bush presidency remained centralized in the White House but was decentralized within it, reflecting a trend that has persisted and accelerated since Reagan's second term. Not just the domestic policy adviser and staff, but also other individuals, such as Regan (Reagan), Darman (George H. W. Bush), Morris (Clinton), and Cheney and Rove (George W. Bush), and other staff units, including most recently NEC, the cabinet office, and the Office of Community and Faith-Based Initiatives, have been major domestic policy players in various administrations.

From the start of his presidency in January 2009, Obama accelerated the trend toward intra–White House decentralization in domestic policymaking. Although he named Melody A. Barnes as domestic policy adviser, Obama preserved NEC, kept OCFBI while renaming it the Office of Faith-Based and Neighborhood Partnerships, and created the White House Office of Health Reform to formulate and promote new health-care legislation. The last of these decisions was especially surprising since Barnes had come to the White House from the staff of Sen. Edward Kennedy, the leading health-care reform advocate in Congress for several decades.

Nancy-Ann DeParle, who headed the health reform office, was one of several so-called White House "czars" whom Obama appointed to coordinate major areas of administration policymaking, transcending both the domestic policy staff and the departments and agencies. Obama also appointed czars in policy domains such as climate change, auto industry restructuring, urban affairs, and financial bailouts—by one count, a total of thirty-two during his first nine months in office.[44] Notwithstanding Obama's unprecedented embrace of czars, they are not an entirely new phenomenon. Presidents from FDR to Clinton filled a total of thirty-eight czar-like positions over a sixty-eight-year period, and George W. Bush appointed thirty-one in eight years.[45] As Pfiffner has written, "this proliferation of czars reflects the reality that functions that used to be performed by cabinet secretaries have, over the past half-century, been drawn into the White House."[46] It also illustrates how varied and decentralized recent presidential approaches to domestic policymaking within the White House have been.

Conclusion

"Every president gets the White House he deserves . . . ," observes William Galston. "The way that staff is organized reflects the president's character, personality, and predilections."

Galston's insight is not one that political scientists, with their emphasis on regularities rather than idiosyncrasies and institutions rather than individuals, will readily embrace. Nor should they embrace it entirely. The long-term rise of the White House staff and decline of the cabinet are aspects of the institutional presidency so entrenched that even recent presidents who intended to govern through their cabinets abandoned the idea. Within the White House, on matters of foreign policy the degree of institutionalization of the national security adviser and staff is especially great. Every president since Nixon has relied on the national security staff and, aside from occasional minor tinkering, has accepted the staff structure that he inherited.

As this chapter has shown, domestic policymaking is in some ways different. Nixon abandoned both the traditional department-centered approach and Johnson's task forces, but the apparatus he created went through three permutations in less than six years. Ford experimented for a time with a domestic policy process led by the vice president, only to abandon it after less than a year; he also separated economic policymaking from domestic policymaking. Carter's sincere effort to devolve responsibility to the departments ended in a mass firing of his cabinet and a return to a White House–centered policymaking process. Reagan tried to integrate staff with cabinet in cabinet councils, mostly for the purpose of keeping the departments moored to his conservative agenda, but eventually the reins of control were drawn back into the White House. George H. W. Bush, who like Carter made a real attempt at cabinet government, ended up lurching from one domestic policy process to another, none of them successful. Clinton, George W. Bush, and Obama each created several White House units to handle particular domestic policies, and all three relied on the Clinton-created National Economic Council instead of the domestic policy adviser and staff for economic policymaking.

Explaining the variability of White House–centered domestic policymaking is beyond the scope of this chapter. But certainly one explanation lies embedded in the insight offered by Karen Hult and Charles Walcott in Chapter 4. "'Domestic' policy," they observe, "is an elusive concept. . . . When one strips away foreign policy, military policy, economic policy, foreign economic policy, and homeland security policy, domestic policy can be defined as the residual." The ambiguity attending domestic policy allows, even invites, each president to mix and match particular policies with a variety of policymaking units in the White House virtually from scratch. Variability in how presidents make domestic policy is as likely to characterize the future as is the consistency with which such policy will be made somewhere, somehow in the White House.

Notes

1. "Report of the Brownlow Committee," in *The Evolving Presidency: Landmark Documents, 1787–2010*, ed. Michael Nelson (Washington, D.C.: CQ Press, 2012).

2. John P. Burke, *The Institutional Presidency*, 2nd ed. (Baltimore, Md.: Johns Hopkins University Press, 2000), ch. 1.

3. Shirley Anne Warshaw, *Powersharing: White House–Cabinet Relations in the Modern Presidency* (Albany: State University of New York Press, 1996), 32. See also Patrick Anderson, *The President's Men: White House Assistants of Franklin D. Roosevelt, Harry S. Truman, Dwight D. Eisenhower, John F. Kennedy, and Lyndon B. Johnson* (New York: Doubleday, 1968).

4. William W. Lammers and Michael A. Genovese, *The Presidency and Domestic Policy: Comparing Leadership Styles, FDR to Clinton* (Washington, D.C.: CQ Press, 2000), 75.

See also Charles E. Walcott and Karen M. Hult, *Governing the White House: From Hoover through LBJ* (Lawrence: University Press of Kansas, 1995), 152–154.

5. Norman C. Thomas and Harold L. Wolman, "Policy Formulation in the Institutionalized Presidency: The Johnson Task Forces," in *The Presidential Advisory System*, eds. Thomas E. Cronin and Sanford D. Greenberg (New York: Harper and Row, 1969), 124–143.

6. Andrew Rudalevige, *Managing the President's Program: Presidential Leadership and Domestic Policy Formulation* (Princeton, N.J.: Princeton University Press, 2002), 49.

7. E. W. Kenworthy, "Nixon Promises to Heed Dissent in Making Policy," *New York Times*, September 20, 1968. See also "Nixon on the Presidency," *Time*, September 27, 1968.

8. Hubert H. Humphrey, "Citizen Advice and a Domestic Policy Council," in *Presidential Advisory System*, eds. Cronin and Greenberg, 312–317.

9. Richard P. Nathan, *The Administrative Presidency* (New York: John Wiley and Sons, 1983), 30.

10. Daniel Patrick Moynihan, *The Politics of a Guaranteed Income: The Nixon Administration and the Family Assistance Plan* (New York: Random House, 1973), 74.

11. Warshaw, *Powersharing*, 54.

12. For a thoughtful discussion of these same matters, see Anthony J. Bennett, *The American President's Cabinet: From Kennedy to Bush* (New York: St. Martin's Press, 1996), ch. 8.

13. Unless otherwise noted, all quotations from domestic policy advisers are from the transcripts of the Miller Center symposium reported in Chapters 3, 5, 7, and 9.

14. Martha Joynt Kumar, "The White House Is Like City Hall," in *The White House World: Transitions, Organization, and Office Operations*, eds. Martha Joynt Kumar and Terry Sullivan (College Station: Texas A&M Press, 2003), 81–93.

15. Richard P. Fenno, *The President's Cabinet: An Analysis in the Period from Wilson to Eisenhower* (Cambridge, Mass.: Harvard University Press, 1959), 6.

16. Among these seven presidents, the sole exception was Jimmy Carter.

17. Harry McPherson, *A Political Education: A Journal of Life with Senators, Generals, Cabinet Members, and Presidents* (Boston: Little, Brown, 1972), 268.

18. "Hillary Clinton Rips 'Vetting' Process," *Washington Times*, July 14, 2009.

19. Paul C. Light, "Our Tottering Confirmation Process," http://www.brookings.edu/articles/2002/spring_governance_light.aspx

20. Ibid.

21. Roger B. Porter, *Presidential Decision Making* (New York: Cambridge University Press, 1980), 6.

22. Stephen Hess, *Organizing the White House*, 3rd ed. (Washington, D.C.: Brookings Institution Press, 2002), 108; and Karen M. Hult and Charles E. Walcott, *Empowering the White House: Governance under Nixon, Ford, and Carter* (Lawrence: University Press of Kansas, 2004), 142.

23. Shirley Anne Warshaw, *The Domestic Presidency: Policy Making in the White House* (Boston: Allyn and Bacon, 1997), 54–55.

24. Gerald R. Ford, *A Time to Heal* (New York: Harper and Row, 1979), 132.

25. Porter, *Presidential Decision Making*, 90.

26. Michael Nelson, "Nelson A. Rockefeller and the American Vice Presidency," in *Gerald R. Ford and the Politics of Post-Watergate America*, eds. Bernard J. Firestone and Alexej Ugrinsky, (Westport, Conn.: Greenwood Press, 1993), 139-159.

27. Warshaw, *Domestic Presidency*, 77.

28. Warshaw, *Powersharing*, 106.

29. Quoted in ibid., 132.

30. Ibid., 146.

31. Ibid., 152.

32. Warshaw suggests that Porter persuaded Bush to combine domestic and economic affairs in his title. Warshaw, *Domestic Presidency*, 164.

33. This was the role Porter had performed as executive director to Ford's Economic Policy Board, as explained and defended in Porter, *Presidential Decision Making*.

34. Charles Kolb, *White House Daze: The Unmaking of Domestic Policy in the Bush Years* (New York: Free Press, 1994), 29.

35. John Podhoretz, *Hell of a Ride: Backstage at the White House Follies, 1989–1993* (New York: Simon and Schuster, 1993), 125-126.

36. Robert B. Reich, *Locked in the Cabinet* (New York: Alfred A. Knopf, 1997).

37. James P. Pfiffner, *The Modern Presidency*, 3rd ed. (Boston: Bedford/St. Martin's Press, 2000), 101-102.

38. Bradley H. Patterson, *The White House Staff: Inside the West Wing and Beyond* (Washington, D.C.: Brookings Institution Press, 2000), ch. 4.

39. Andrew Rudalevige, "'The Decider': Issue Management in the Bush White House," in *The George W. Bush Legacy*, eds. Colin Campbell, Bert A. Rockman, and Andrew Rudalevige (Washington, D.C.: CQ Press, 2008), 135-163.

40. James P. Pfiffner, *The Modern Presidency*, 6th ed. (Boston: Wadsworth, 2011), ch. 4.

41. Michael Nelson, "Richard Cheney and Power of the Modern Vice Presidency," in *Ambition and Division: Legacies of the George W. Bush Presidency*, ed. Steven E. Schier (Pittsburgh: University of Pittsburgh Press, 2009), 172-189. See also Shirley Ann Warshaw, *The Co-Presidency of Bush and Cheney* (Palo Alto, Calif.: Stanford University Press, 2009), ch. 6.

42. Bradley W. Patterson, *To Serve the President: Continuity and Innovation in the White House* (Washington, D.C.: Brookings Institution Press, 2008), 109.

43. George W. Bush, *Decision Points* (New York: Crown, 2011), 95.

44. Michael Nelson, "The Appointment and Confirmation Process for Federal Executive Officials," unpublished background paper prepared for the Miller Center of Public Affairs, University of Virginia, October 2009.

45. Ibid.

46. Pfiffner, *Modern Presidency*, 6th ed., 89.

Chapter 2

Domestic Policy from Campaigning to Governing

Andrew E. Busch

President Barack Obama came into office on January 20, 2009, having run an election campaign in which he pledged to raise taxes on families making $250,000 or more per year, reduce the federal deficit, push through cap-and-trade environmental legislation and a comprehensive health-care reform that included a "public option" and no individual mandate, close the Guantanamo Bay terrorist detention facility within a year, and devote more resources to the war in Afghanistan. A year and a half later, he had devoted more resources to Afghanistan; pushed through a wide-ranging health-care reform, but one that included an individual mandate and no public option; broke the tax pledge; presided over a significant increase in the national debt; and had not yet closed Guantanamo or obtained passage of cap-and-trade. Obama had merely discovered what all presidents discover sooner or later: Moving from campaigning to governing is no easy matter.

An important question framing the development of domestic policy in any administration is the relationship between that policy domain and the election campaign that brought the president into power. Administrations do not operate in a vacuum, as if sprung into existence on January 20 of every fourth year. As Jeff Fishel and others have shown, presidents take their campaign promises seriously and more often than not make a serious attempt to realize them. According to Fishel, presidents from 1961 through 1984 took action to fully or partially fulfill their campaign pledges anywhere from 53 percent to 67 percent of the time and made "token" efforts to fulfill another 5 to 11 percent of their pledges. Presidents totally failed to take action on an average of only 11 percent of campaign pledges.[1]

At the same time, the public standing of the president is affected by contemporary interpretations of whether he is accomplishing his stated goals or at least is making a sincere effort to do so. Presidents George H. W. Bush and Bill Clinton both suffered from adverse reaction to their decisions to reverse campaign pledges to block new tax increases and to provide a middle-class tax cut, respectively. Unforeseen events or revised political calculations can conflict with promises made during the president's election campaign. Sometimes presidents also conclude, reluctantly, that their promises conflict with sound policy. Many analysts argue that the Bush and Clinton tax increases contributed to federal surpluses later in the decade, and Obama failed to close Guantanamo partly because no superior alternative emerged.[2]

The formal presidential transition—the eleven-week period between election day and inauguration day—is one obvious aspect of moving from campaigning to governing. As one scholar observed, the transition

> is a brief and unique period, one in which those who are about to take over the largest, most complex and important institution in the world must consider in much more concrete and specific terms than is possible in a campaign what they want to accomplish and how, when, and with whom they want to accomplish it. . . . Although presidents make changes in policy, personnel, and organization as they go along, they usually prefer adjusting course to reversing it, so the course they set initially must be chosen well.[3]

But the formal transition is not the only one, or even the most important. One must take a broader look at how campaigns affect governing after the formal transition is over. Indeed, since, strictly speaking, no "governing" takes places until inauguration day, the formal transition provides a framework that is much too constrained to adequately address the broader issues.

The relationship of campaigning to governing in domestic policy can be considered in light of four central topics: the context created by the campaign; the president's rhetoric; presidential appointments in the White House and executive departments and agencies; and actual policymaking, including the establishment of legislative priorities and the use of executive orders, especially (though not exclusively) early in the term.

The Context Established by Campaign Commitments

Once the central document of presidential campaigns, the national party platform is now much longer but less widely read than in the past. It nevertheless continues to serve as a point of contention between party factions and an important means of promoting a winning coalition of constituencies.[4] The candidate's own utterances offer another—probably more important —formulation of his policy commitments. These come most notably in his nomination acceptance speech, in the presidential debates, and in campaign advertising. The campaign's position statements, long available as printed handouts, are now easily accessed online, perhaps increasing the visibility of the candidates' second-tier promises.

The transition period is "the time to translate campaign promises into policy priorities and begin to establish a legislative agenda."[5] After inauguration day, that plan has to be effected. Fishel postulates a number of potential tradeoffs involved in the formulation of policy commitments, including tradeoffs:

1. Between the electoral incentives to fudge and the coalitional incentives to deliver;
2. Between the coalitional incentives to deliver and the unwillingness or inability of presidential candidates to specify the magnitude of how much will be delivered;
3. Between the coalitional incentives to deliver and the practice of mobilizing mass support, through symbolic appeals, for past or future presidential behavior; and
4. Between what campaign decision makers consider politically acceptable and the demands of influential group leaders who are interested in expanding or limiting the range of acceptability.[6]

Policymakers in the administration have to navigate the political and policy landscape established by how these tradeoffs were handled during the campaign. They may also have to contend with backlash fomented by the winning presidential candidate's campaign. For example, negative reaction to use of the Willie Horton issue in the 1988 campaign may have constrained George H. W. Bush's options when Congress passed the Civil Rights Restoration Act.

William Galston of the Clinton White House alludes to these tensions, arguing that "campaigning is about addition, and governing is about selection."[7] It is not always clear during the campaign how the two might be in conflict; only the process of governing brings out the tensions. Until then, the candidate is not even fully aware of the context in which he will be governing. Or, as Galston's Clinton White House compatriot Bruce Reed puts it, "Campaigning is something like falling in love, and governing is something like marriage"—more fulfilling but more challenging, not least because many supporters of the campaign see "what they want to see, and tend to ignore the other parts" of the candidate's campaign agenda until the process of governing reveals the president's real commitments and priorities.

Domestic policy advisers from the Nixon administration to the George W. Bush administration agree that campaign promises—at least on major issues that receive significant attention—set public expectations for the president and must be kept. Domestic policy discussions, especially during the transition and early in the administration, were heavily influenced—if not dominated—by policy commitments made during the campaign. Indeed, several advisers refer to campaign pledges as the standard against which their bosses hoped to be judged. Reed contends that in the Clinton Administration, "We treated the campaign promises as gospel. That was the only scripture to guide us." These sentiments are echoed by others. Failure to keep—or worse yet, outright reversal of—high-profile pledges are universally deemed to be highly damaging to the president as he seeks to govern. These advisers echo Richard Nixon's private advice to George H. W. Bush, which outlined a possible two-step move toward a deficit-cutting tax increase but cautioned that "to roll over [on Bush's well-known 'no new taxes' pledge] would guarantee oblivion."[8]

A variation of this problem is the difficulty that presidents face when they come to office promising to change the atmospherics of governing in Washington. George H. W. Bush's "kinder, gentler" rhetoric, Bill Clinton's "New Democrat" promises, George W. Bush's pledge to be "a uniter, not a divider," and Barack Obama's promise to bring together Red and Blue America, while appealing to many Americans on the campaign trail, led to disappointments and recrimination when the partisan impulses of Washington inevitably reasserted themselves.

The mirror-image problem, less noted by the public and scholars alike, is that presidents must be very careful when seeking to introduce new priorities that had not been thoroughly discussed in the campaign. The domestic policy advisers agree that issues such as the water projects "hit list" for Jimmy Carter and gays in the military for Bill Clinton created enormous controversy partly because they took the public and Congress by surprise, along with some of the president's own advisers. Bruce Reed says, "I traveled with Bill Clinton for the better part of two years and I don't think I'd ever even heard" about the promise to lift the ban on gays in the military. One could add Ronald Reagan's proposed 1981 Social Security cuts and, perhaps, George W. Bush's proposed 2005 Social Security reform, which he had discussed in the campaign but which was eclipsed by national security issues.

Thus, both failure to keep campaign commitments and the introduction of new issues not thoroughly vetted during the campaign are problematic for presidents as they govern. The campaign serves as a crucial place to lay policy groundwork, and what is said (or not said) at that time sets the parameters for much of the president's subsequent domestic policymaking. Stuart Eizenstat, who served both the Carter campaign and White House, argues that governing is consequently affected by the severe shortcomings of policymaking during a presidential campaign. "The problem with campaign promises," he notes, is that "they're made under suboptimum conditions for policymaking"—that is, under serious time and political pressures, often with inadequate staffing, information, and analysis. Yet the policymaking done during the campaign severely constricts the president's freedom of action once in the White House. Bert Carp of the Carter administration points to the difficulties faced by his boss when Congress proved recalcitrant. Although it might have made sense to recalibrate his approach, Carter could not even if he had wanted to: "If you run on comprehensive, I don't know how you can move from Blair House to the White House and turn into Mr. Incremental." As George W. Bush adviser Margaret Spellings emphasizes, if policy development in the campaign is going to bear fruit later, members of Congress and other important players have to be brought in.

Despite these caveats, the advisers tend to agree that it is better for presidents to know what they intend to do in policy terms, and to specify to the American people what they intend to do in the crucible of the campaign. As Reed explains, "One of the reasons why ideas need to be central to campaigns [is] . . . because you want to be in a situation where, when the president is elected, he is claiming a mandate that the country is actually aware of." Reed's point was illustrated by the breach from 1988 to 1989: as one scholar noted, the process of translating campaign promises into policy priorities under George H. W. Bush was significantly complicated by the character of Bush's campaign, which largely relied on a combination of vague appeals to "a thousand points of light" and a "kinder, gentler nation," with specific but narrow issues such as Willie Horton and the Pledge of Allegiance.[9] Bush's 1988 campaign has been unfairly maligned as trivial or cynical; it can hardly be argued that crime and taxes were unimportant issues or that the vision of a free society that solves many of its own problems through voluntary action rather than reliance on centralized government was a grossly unworthy one. Nevertheless, the execution of Bush's campaign clearly did not provide fertile ground for a broad and concrete policy agenda.

Furthermore, there is wide agreement among the policy advisers that the president's campaign promises were often a powerful weapon in internal administration debates and in discussions with Congress. This certainly seemed to be the case with George W. Bush's education and prescription drug programs, Clinton's welfare reform, Reagan's tax and spending cuts, and even Nixon's 1968 promise to curtail crime in the District of Columbia.

Finally, as scholar Carl M. Brauer has noted, "Although all new administrations enter office well stocked with campaign promises of dramatic change in national policy, continuities, not discontinuities, between administrations tend to be more striking. . . . There are a variety of restraints to actual shifts in national policy, most of which find expression in law and are based in the Constitution."[10] Eizenstat, Roger Porter (who advised three Republican presidents), and others agree, emphasizing the degree to which other factors besides the campaign intrude into the president's domestic policymaking trajectory. As Porter says, "One of the things that presidents discover when they get into office is what might be called reality." In particular, the political and ideological orientation of Congress and external events such as the Iranian revolution, Watergate, and 9/11 often combine to make it difficult if not impossible for the president to carry out his domestic campaign agenda, no matter how much Americans may expect him to fulfill it. The dire straits of the economy early in his presidency forced Reagan to deemphasize the social issues important to a large part of his base. Similarly, school vouchers were dropped by George W. Bush early in the negotiations for the No Child Left Behind Act for the simple reason that, as Spellings noted, they could not pass. Obama's administration illustrated the other side of this two-edged dilemma when the president suffered considerable criticism for neglecting the economy to focus on health care, an issue beloved by his base.

Rhetoric about Domestic Policy

As is often observed, campaigning is one thing; governing is something else. Yet, as scholars such as Jeffrey Tulis and Samuel Kernell have noted, presidents have become increasingly likely to blur the distinction between campaigning and governing.[11] This is particularly true when they go "over the head" of Congress, soliciting public support for their agenda through campaign-style events and oratory. As Kernell notes, "Forcing compliance from fellow Washingtonians by going over their heads to enlist constituents' pressure is a tactic that was known but seldom attempted during the first half of the century"; now the practice is routine, a "strategic adaptation to the information age."[12] Undergirding this practice has been a theoretical shift in which, according to Tulis, "the doctrine that a president ought to be a popular leader has become an unquestioned premise of our political culture. . . . Today it is taken for granted that presidents have a duty constantly to defend themselves publicly, to promote policy initiatives nationwide, and to inspire the population. And for many, the presidential 'function' is not one duty among many, but rather the heart of the presidency—its essential task."[13]

Although most scholarly attention has been focused on the stylistic component of this "permanent campaign," another important question concerns the degree to which the substantive content of campaign rhetoric is transferred into the governing realm. That content presents the president with a dilemma. On one hand, one might be skeptical of a president who issues a certain kind of rhetorical appeal on behalf of his policy agenda as a candidate and then abruptly drops such talk upon entering office. On the other hand, it might be at least as disconcerting for the president to repeat campaign slogans, some of which might be divisive or even demagogic, throughout his presidency, regardless of context and insensible of his new station. Of course, presidents often seek to incorporate the election results into a rhetoric stressing a popular "mandate" for their policies. Although there are good reasons to be skeptical of mandate claims, presidents can use them quite effectively.[14]

Woodrow Wilson argued that there should be an integral connection in the modern presidency between campaign commitments, campaign and presidential rhetoric (including mandate claims), and policymaking. Wilson's proposal, which is now a commonplace, was then a major departure from previous norms that looked with suspicion on the "popular arts" of charismatic, policy-specific leadership. It advanced an understanding of the parties and the presidency in which presidential candidates lead their parties, the candidates (and their parties) put forward detailed policy programs communicated directly to the voters, and the winners use their victory as evidence of a popular mandate for those policies. That "mandate" is conceived of as a means to overcome the obstructions resulting from the constitutional separation of powers.[15] Hence, presidential rhetoric is not a peripheral matter, to be dismissed as "mere rhetoric," but is arguably central to the advancement of a domestic policy program.[16]

There is a general consensus among domestic policy advisers that the presidents they served maintained significant rhetorical continuity when discussing domestic policy on the campaign trail and in the Oval Office. It is surely no coincidence that most recent presidents have incorporated campaign themes on domestic policy even into their inaugural addresses, which are typically among the least policy-oriented (that is, the most symbolic) of any form of presidential rhetoric. Obama mentioned the economy, education, health care, and energy. George W. Bush talked about reclaiming our schools, reforming Social Security and Medicare, cutting taxes, and promoting compassion. Clinton emphasized economic growth and responsibility, George H. W. Bush drugs, crime, the federal deficit, and civil society (the "thousand points of light"), and Reagan economic recovery, taxes and spending, limited government, and federalism. At the other extreme, John F. Kennedy, after running on a platform that included extensive and detailed domestic promises, delivered an inaugural address in which he made almost no mention of domestic policy. In between these extremes, substantively as well as chronologically, Nixon and Carter repeated a handful of vague domestic themes mentioned in their campaigns.[17]

When one turns to more policy-specific genres of presidential rhetoric, the connection between campaigning and governing is also clear. Most recent presidents have appeared before the American people from the Oval Office and before a joint session of Congress early in their terms to promote their programs. All have used the occasion to advance proposals that had their genesis in the themes and positions of their victorious campaigns. Some have gone beyond their campaigns and all have filled in details that the campaigns lacked. At least one (Clinton) had to publicly back away from a campaign pledge (the promised middle-class tax cut). Nevertheless, in his February 15, 1993, Oval Office address, Clinton used his campaign slogan, "putting people first."

The transcripts of the presidents' first press conferences show a more complicated dynamic, with the president often attempting to remain rhetorically aligned with his campaign but sometimes struggling to do so against the combined forces of circumstance and an adversarial media. In his January 29, 1981, press conference, Reagan reaffirmed fidelity to campaign pledges on dairy price supports and the abolition of the Departments of Energy and Education, saying more generally, "The clear message I received in the election campaign is that we must gain control of this inflation monster." On January 27, 1989, George H. W. Bush was pressed on his no-taxes pledge, saying only that he would like it to be a four-year pledge, and was repeatedly asked about the sincerity of his campaign's anti-drug stance. Obama, in his first press conference (February 9, 2009), devoted his remarks to the economic stimulus plan, but had to answer questions about Iran, Afghanistan,

Pakistan, and performance-enhancing drugs in sports. Perhaps the best example of press and events driving a president off-message was Clinton's first
press conference, which was devoted almost wholly to the issue of gays in
the military, forcing the president to deal with the ramifications of a real,
though obscure, campaign promise.

Not least, presidents will occasionally engage in national tours promoting a policy initiative in a series of campaign-style events, including the
equivalent of stump speeches before supportive crowds. During the past
three decades, such campaigns have included Reagan's budget push in 1981
and tax reform push in 1986, Clinton's budget campaign in 1993, Bush's
stumping for tax cuts and education reform in 2001 and Social Security
reform in 2005, and Obama's health-care push in 2009. Obama may have
been a latecomer to the behind-the-scenes legislative crafting of health-care
reform, but he was not slow to use the bully pulpit to put the issue on the
agenda or to engage in public persuasion. In most cases, these campaigns
developed to advance issues that had been a major part of the president's
election campaign. Such campaigns are sometimes linked to election results
in another way. When Bush went on the road to promote tax cuts and Social
Security reform, he targeted states that he had won but that had Democratic
Senators.

Although they generally agree that campaign themes continue into the
administration, domestic policy advisers are somewhat divided over the importance of rhetorical salesmanship. On one side, Stuart Eizenstat strongly
emphasizes how important policy promotion is for a president. To Margaret
Spellings, "The person with the biggest microphone in the country needs to
take it and use it to advance the legislative and other policy agenda. . . . If
that is a permanent campaign then we're all guilty as sin." Bruce Reed
contends that, after the disastrous midterm elections of 1994, the Clinton
White House came to realize that "The only way we could govern effectively
was to govern the way we had campaigned." Nevertheless, Reed discerns
limits to the permanent campaign: no amount of rhetorical skill can rescue
a "bad product." Moreover, facing a hostile Congress, Clinton turned to
administrative action to pursue his agenda.

Bert Carp extols the use of the presidency in campaign mode, but warns
that it is a two-edged sword. "You can't deal effectively with Congress unless
you can demonstrate an ability to go over their heads to some degree. There
is nothing worse than going over their heads and not making a connection."
You need to "move the needle. . . . I believe that members of Congress are

the most effective political polling organization there is in this country." If the president campaigns across the country and members of Congress fail to notice a change in opinion at their town hall meetings or in their mail, the campaign will be counterproductive. There is nothing worse, Carp argues, than running a "permanent campaign" that fails to "move the needle." And, as George C. Edwards points out in *On Deaf Ears*, it is actually very difficult for the president to "move the needle" with such rhetoric.[18]

Campaign rhetoric can force movement in a policy direction. But once the president takes office, imprecise campaign rhetoric—that is, almost all campaign rhetoric—has the potential to fuel significant squabbles within the administration once the time comes to make it concrete. As Reed contends, Clinton's pledge to "end welfare as we know it" was a case in point on both scores. The statement was so bold and so central to Clinton's campaign that it was impossible to imagine him backing away from it completely once in office. (Galston notes that only welfare reform ads were run in swing states for the last ten days of the 1992 race.) At the same time, it was a vague enough pledge that debates raged within the administration about what it meant in policy terms, and how far one had to reform the system to qualify as having "ended" it.

Personnel and Appointments

An old adage has it that "personnel is policy." To the extent that this is true, the connection of campaigning to governing will partially depend on whether the president has the assistance, in the White House and executive branch, of individuals who substantially share his policy commitments. As G. Calvin Mackenzie points out in *The Politics of Presidential Appointments*:

> Sound and thoughtful personnel management is essential to the achievement of a President's policy goals. Getting laws enacted is only one step in the policy-making process; implementation is quite another. If the people responsible for implementing the laws are out of tune or out of touch with those who sponsor them, a high probability exists that the actual effect of the law will differ from the intended effect. . . . The President's formal control of the selection process is only one of his several forms of political capital, but an important one. Wisely spent, it can contribute significantly to the achievement of presidential policy goals.[19]

At the same time, in Brauer's view, "Most former Presidents and their top aides would probably agree that personnel is the single most time-consuming, frustrating, and difficult part of transitions."[20] As James P. Pfiffner notes, generally speaking, "presidents choose their White House staffs primarily from among those individuals who have worked with them on their campaigns and who understand best their personality and values. . . . The natural choice of campaign aides, however, may lead to problems because the nature of governing is different in important ways from the nature of political campaigns."[21]

When it comes to executive branch appointments, some presidents (such as Ronald Reagan) have also expended considerable effort to ensure conformity with their agenda down to the subcabinet level.[22] Others (for example, Richard Nixon early in his presidency) gave broad discretion to cabinet secretaries to staff their own departments.[23] Despite variations, Thomas J. Weko has shown how presidents since Truman have centralized the appointment process through the Presidential Personnel Office in the White House.[24] At issue as well is the decision whether to centralize policymaking in the White House, as Nixon did in his second term. Reagan pursued this course to complement an aggressive appointment strategy, emphasizing, for example, central clearance of new regulations through the Office of Management and Budget. Such a strategy is based on the presumption that the Executive Office of the President is more consistently loyal to the president's policy agenda than the departments are.

Altogether, Reagan probably exerted more effort than any recent president to shift the direction of the bureaucracy, although some analyses have generally held that Republican presidents since Eisenhower have been more active in this domain than their Democratic counterparts—undoubtedly because of the Republicans' view that the bureaucracy is more naturally resistant to retrenching government than to expanding it.[25] Reagan's director of the Office of Personnel Management, Donald J. Devine, reported that Reagan assigned him to "establish policy control over the bureaucracy. The mission was to make the bureaucracy respond to his new political mandate."[26] To carry out this mission, Devine briefed Reagan's "incoming cabinet members and other political leaders on the new political theory of administration" espoused by Reagan and made possible by the Civil Service Reform Act of 1978, which had never fully been used by Jimmy Carter.[27]

Of course, loyalty to the president's agenda is not the only criterion for appointment. Other criteria include experience, expertise, competence, and reputation; coalition-building potential; patronage; and demographic or other symbolism. Indeed, the goal of ideological or policy conformity can sometimes operate in tension with the other criteria, as when an appointee of a previous president of the opposite party is held over in a gesture of bipartisanship. Furthermore, the president rarely has a completely free hand in making appointments. Bureaucracies, interest groups, parties, and members of Congress often play a major role, even before the Senate has its say in the confirmation process.[28]

Domestic policy advisers make two interesting points regarding personnel. First, Roger Porter observes that in the crucial early months of the administration, White House staff have the edge in policymaking because appointed executive branch positions often remain unfilled for months due to delays in the appointment or confirmation process. Consequently, the initiative in a new presidency lies with the White House staff and the Office of Management and Budget. This situation gives "a huge advantage to the White House staff," which is "heavily laden with people who have been on the campaign." It is precisely these people, Bruce Reed notes, who serve as the strongest "keepers of the flame" of the campaign's promises. (Clinton, on the other hand, invited troubles by filling his cabinet while White House positions sat open.) More generally, it is clear that delay in making appointments, whether in the White House or the departments, can have serious policy repercussions. Jimmy Carter's failure to move quickly during the transition to name cabinet secretaries made life difficult for transition staffers working on policy option papers, who reported that "We really can't go ahead much further until we know who the cabinet secretary is going to be." Likewise, George H. W. Bush's delay in appointing Roger Porter as chief domestic and economic policy adviser until ten days before the inauguration caused significant problems for policy planning during that transition.[29]

Second, Stuart Eizenstat notes a dilemma faced by presidents at the beginning of their administrations. On the one hand, their natural preference is to fill the White House with loyalists from the campaign, people with whom the president is familiar and comfortable. On the other hand, presidents need some high-level advisers who have experience in Washington and who bring a different perspective to the inner circle. It is crucial for presidents to have such advisers—the Carter presidency was seriously damaged by its lack in this area during its first year—but telling someone who sacrificed during the campaign that he is going to be passed over in favor of an outsider is hard. As Reed notes, "you have to share this thing that you helped build with . . . [the] whole party," many of whom did not support "your guy." Eizenstat credits Ronald Reagan with bringing in James Baker, an experienced Washington hand who had actually managed the nomination campaign of Reagan's chief rival. Spellings notes that George W. Bush deliberately brought in a combination of Washington people and trusted stalwarts from the campaign. The difficulty of finding the right balance is obvious. Although Reagan benefitted from Baker's broad perspective, he was not always well served by other outsiders in his administration, including Terrel Bell, his first secretary of education, who was not committed to Reagan's main education promise (to abolish the education department) and made no effort to advance it. Yet Bell oversaw the writing of the report *A Nation at Risk*, which spawned a call for greater rigor in the classroom accompanied by conservative reforms such as merit pay for teachers.

Direct Policymaking

The Constitution specifies that the president, when dealing with Congress, shall "recommend to their consideration such measures as he shall judge necessary and expedient." Although presidents have always done this to some degree, the progressive and New Deal transformation of the presidency resulted in a system in which the president is now widely considered, in the words of Clinton Rossiter, to be the "chief legislator" of the republic.[30] Woodrow Wilson's theory of the presidency, coupled with Franklin Roosevelt's assertive use of the office, succeeded in establishing an expectation that the president would enter office with a wide-ranging program of legislative proposals. The closest thing to an exception in recent times was the presidency of George H. W. Bush, who was largely reactive in domestic policy and whose chief of staff famously remarked partway through his term that Congress could go home because Bush didn't need any more legislation. To the extent that Bush did have a legislative agenda, it was scattered and not held together by a coherent theme. His political fate when he sought reelection will probably discourage a repetition of this experiment for the foreseeable future, and it was notable that his son took a much more activist approach to legislating. Whatever else they may achieve, presidents are judged at least partially on the basis of their ability to persuade Congress to enact significant new laws.

It is not difficult to discern in general outline that a president's top legislative priorities are generally connected closely with his campaign commitments, especially early in his presidency. Some examples stand out, such as Reagan's tax and spending cuts, Clinton's economic package and health-care reform, George W. Bush's education program and tax cuts, and Obama's health-care reform. Some presidents focus on a small number of high-priority items, while others choose to take a more diffuse approach. Yet in some fashion every president must set priorities among a multitude of campaign commitments on domestic policy.[31] These strategic choices about priorities can be momentous. Clinton's decision to push health-care reform ahead of welfare reform and George W. Bush's decision to lead his second term with Social Security reform rather than tax reform or (as Spellings suggests) immigration reform, arguably had enormous effects on the president's standing, the political environment in the country, and the course of public policy.

An instructive comparison has often been made between Carter, who threw forward a multitude of proposals in his first year without a clear sense of priorities, and Reagan, who approached his first year committed to a handful of high priorities. John P. Burke details the transition processes that led to those approaches. The initial Carter transition efforts, led by Jack Watson and begun long before election day, "had noted the need to identify ten to fifteen high-priority policy items, second-level items, and remaining policy issues." Over time, however, "proposed policy initiatives grew, and a recognition of the political realities requiring some setting of priorities faded." By October 1976, the list had grown to twenty issues; on November 3, Watson gave Carter a total of fifty policy option papers. Post-election policy efforts added more major proposals to the roster, including the water projects hit list and a $50 tax rebate.[32]

According to Burke, Reagan was the only incoming president in recent times "to both undertake policy development and link it to a broader strategic plan" during the transition. Issues task forces working during the campaign had already done much of the policy work, especially in the economic arena; thus, transition work could focus on implementation and tactics. An Office of Policy Coordination was established to bring together the products of the working groups and to educate incoming administration officials about Reagan's policy preferences. At the same time, pollster Richard Wirthlin, assisted by Roger Porter and Richard Beal, ran an Office of Planning and Evaluation, which put together an "Initial Actions Report" with a detailed strategy for the first three months of the term.[33]

According to a study by Patrick J. Fett of presidents' first year in office, the revealed preferences of presidents in the legislative process—what they say are their top legislative priorities or, conversely, what they say are unacceptable outcomes—accurately reflect their real preferences. In other words, presidents engage in less strategic calculation when describing their legislative preferences than many participants or observers assume—they generally mean what they say.[34] The process of revealing their preferences begins well before inauguration day, during the campaign itself.

Mark A. Peterson, examining presidents from Eisenhower to Reagan, has identified three maxims controlling presidential relations with Congress:

> First, no matter how astute the politician, what we generally perceive as successful leadership requires a consonance between the politician and the setting. . . . Second, nothing an individual president can do breeds success like clear priorities. . . . Third, nothing fails quite so dramatically as ignoring the first two maxims.[35]

The possible connections between the election campaign and governing are multiple. Most directly, presidents will seek legislative action on their campaign commitments because they believe those commitments represent good policy; that is why they make the pledges in the first place. Additionally, as one Lyndon Johnson aide put it, "Every President has a set of issues which he believes holds the key to the first victory. . . . And that faith propels the issue to the agenda" out of both a sense of obligation and a view that failure to do so could prove fatal in a reelection bid.[36] Welfare reform, which had proven such a powerful issue for Clinton in the 1992 campaign, had the potential to hurt him seriously four years later if he did not fulfill his pledge to "end welfare as we know it." At any rate, Clinton concluded that was the case, as did his chief political adviser, Dick Morris, who later related that in the summer of 1996 "I told him flatly that a welfare reform veto would cost him the election."[37] Even in the second term, presidents may see the issues that were vital to their electoral victories as essential to their public standing, which itself is essential to their continued effectiveness in Washington and their long-term appraisal by historians.

One survey of 126 former White House aides found that "electoral benefits"—including the attractiveness of an issue to past or future campaigns and the perceived importance of the issue to the president's electoral coalition—was one of three key categories of reasons that drove programmatic priorities (the others were "historical benefits" and "programmatic benefits"). Indeed, in all but one presidency between Kennedy and Carter, electoral benefits was the most frequently cited factor driving policy priorities.[38] More indirectly electoral victory can produce "political capital" that can be used to promote the agenda on which the campaign was fought, although as George W. Bush discovered in his second term, it is not always easy for presidents or their advisers to correctly estimate exactly how much political capital is gained in an election.[39]

Finally, it is also clear that the campaign itself can affect the winner's subsequent relations with Congress. Campaigns emphasizing policy proposals were said by Woodrow Wilson to bind parties together across the separation of powers, and sometimes they do, as with the Republicans in 1980. They may, however, drive a wedge between fellow partisans if members of the president's party in Congress feel that his campaign deliberately distanced him from them or simply neglected their interests. Nixon, Reagan, and Clinton were all accused by some in their party of having run a personalistic reelection campaign that made for short congressional coattails. Successful presidential campaigns almost invariably anger members of the opposition party in Congress, but the question is how much they are angered—and how much it matters.

The ability of the president to convince Congress to focus on his priorities ultimately depends on his skills as well as the political situation. One (highly simplistic) way to measure this influence is by examining which bills are assigned the designation H.R. 1 or S. 1. In recent years, when there was unified government and a new president, presidential priorities—generally established in the crucible of the campaign—were highlighted in Congress. Examples include family leave, which had been vetoed by Clinton's predecessor, in 1993, and the No Child Left Behind Act in 2001. The Democratic Congress coming into office with Obama put the American Recovery and Reinvestment Act—the fiscal stimulus bill—first, consistent with Obama's pledge to try to tackle the economic crisis. When there was divided government, or when the president was returning for a second term, competing priorities were more likely to crowd in (see Table 2.1). As Porter points out, Nixon, Ford, Reagan, and George H. W. Bush all took office without unified party control of Congress.

An alternative to legislation can be executive orders, which presidents often use to enact a portion of their domestic policy agenda. As Adam L. Warber has pointed out, executive orders can be efficient tools because "they allow presidents to establish policy in a relatively short period of time while circumventing the cumbersome policy process that occurs in Congress."[40] They also give presidents an additional means to build a record for themselves and their party, as well as to change the direction set by a predecessor.

Scholars disagree about whether there has been a general trend toward more aggressive use of executive orders by presidents.[41] In any event, it is clear that presidents vary considerably in the number of the executive orders they

Table 2.1   Bills Designated H.R. 1 or S. 1, 101st Congress through 111th Congress (post–presidential election congresses only)

Congress	President	House majority/	Senate majority/
		H.R. 1	**S. 1**
101st	Bush (41)	D/HUD reform	D/Integrity in postal employment
103rd	Clinton	D/Family leave	D/Family medical leave
105th	Clinton	R/Overtime reform	R/Safe and affordable schools
107th	Bush (43)	R/No Child Left Behind	R/Better education
109th	Bush (43)	R/Medicare cost credibility Congressional Gold Medal	R/Margaret Thatcher
111th	Obama	D/Recovery & Reinvestment	D/Recovery & Reinvestment

Highlighted indicates congruence between president and Congress

issue in the first month and first year in office, as well as in the proportion of those executive orders that they direct toward domestic policy concerns (see Table 2.2). Some presidents (Kennedy, Carter, Clinton, and Obama) begin issuing executive orders immediately, while others (Eisenhower, Nixon, and G. H. W. Bush) are much more cautious in their use of executive orders during the opening stages of their presidency.[42] In general, presidents issue slightly more executive orders in their first year in office than in subsequent years, but the difference is not statistically significant.[43] All but Eisenhower and Reagan devoted the vast majority of their first ten executive orders to domestic concerns and governance issues.

Executive orders, especially early in the administration, can carry not only substantive but symbolic importance. For example, Carter's first executive order gave amnesty to Vietnam War draft evaders, Reagan's ended oil price controls, George H. W. Bush's and Clinton's emphasized executive branch ethics, and George W. Bush's promoted faith-based initiatives. Obama's first executive orders, issued the day after he was inaugurated, had to do with release of executive records and ethics; the next day, another three dealt with issues of detention and interrogation of terrorists. All of these underlined important themes in Obama's 2008 campaign.

Executive orders can also result from difficulty obtaining legislative agreement from Congress and, if seen as a means of bypassing Congress, may further harden congressional resistance. Furthermore, one advantage of executive orders—that presidents can make law without going through the difficult process of building legislative coalitions—is also a disadvantage. Since they are often not deeply rooted in the political process or in public

Table 2.2 Executive Orders Issued in the First Year, Eisenhower through G. W. Bush (not including Johnson or Ford)

President	First executive order	First 30 days	First 10 executive orders	First year
Eisenhower	2/4/53 Admin. of Defense Production	2 of 3 domestic	6 of 10 domestic (incl. end wage & price controls)	13 of 29 domestic (45%)
Kennedy	1/21/61 Food to needy families	6 of 7 domestic	9 of 10 domestic (incl. Pres. Com. on labor-mgmt.)	59 of 72 domestic (82%)
Nixon	2/14/69 Asst. to Pres. for liaison w/ former presidents	1 of 1 domestic	9 of 10 domestic (incl. EEO and environment councils)	16 of 18 domestic (89%)
Carter	1/21/77 Vietnam draft pardon	5 of 7 domestic	7 of 10 domestic (incl. energy & Pres. Com. on mental health)	50 of 66 domestic (76%)
Reagan	1/28/81 Decontrol oil	3 of 5 domestic	4 of 10 domestic (incl. regulatory reform, ethics, federalism)	28 of 50 domestic (56%)
G. H. W. Bush	1/25/89 Ethics	1 of 2 domestic	7 of 10 domestic (incl. more ethics, com. on handicapped)	21 of 31 domestic (68%)
Clinton	1/20/93 Ethics	6 of 6 domestic	8 of 10 domestic (incl. economies in govt, Natl. Econ. Council, Dom. Policy Council, labor, sustainability)	40 of 57 domestic (70%)
G. W. Bush	1/29/2001 Faith-based initiatives	7 of 7 domestic	8 of 10 domestic (incl. labor-management)	38 of 54 domestic (70%)

Domestic excludes foreign affairs, trade, intelligence, defense, and miscellaneous national security issues.

opinion, executive orders are particularly vulnerable to reversal by Congress or by future presidents. Indeed, some presidents issue more than a few executive orders revoking executive orders issued by a previous president.

Altogether, presidents who face an opposition Congress, or who are challenging the dominant strain in their own party (such as Carter, Clinton, and George W. Bush), face the dilemma of deciding how hard to push their campaign promises. Not everyone in Congress, even in the president's party, places as high a value on his campaign promises as he does. Further, Bert Carp argues that, at least during the Carter administration, congressional Democrats did not understand the degree to which their fates were tied to the president's success. As Bruce Reed suggests, without some legislative achievements, the president loses the leverage needed to enact anything, and compromise in that environment is often a requisite to legislative success. Presidents must answer the question, "Where are you going to accept political reality and where are you going to try to change it?" In Reed's view, campaigns provide an opportunity to begin testing both the limits of reality and its malleability.

The White House often struggles against the need to prioritize its campaign commitments. Spellings makes a distinction between the "must haves"—those items that were integral to the campaign—and the mere "nice to haves," which can go by the wayside. To her, the key questions include how "ripe" is the issue, what are the president's greatest strengths, and what are the chances of passage? Some advisers noted the difficulties posed at times by structural constraints. For example, in 1977 Carter was deterred from pursuing welfare reform and health-care reform simultaneously because the same congressional committees (House Ways and Means and Senate Finance) would have had to tackle both; both also would have been processed by the same cabinet department: Health, Education, and Welfare. In 1993–1994, Clinton faced similar structural constraints, despite the desire of his staff to "flood the circuits" early in the administration. (By then, HEW had been split into the Department of Education and the Department of Health and Human Services, but one department—HHS—would still have processed both welfare and health care.)

Although some domestic policy advisers emphasize the importance of getting as much done as early as possible before the president's political capital declines, Reed offers a different interpretation: "Our experience was, you start off with [political] capital, and when you spend it well, you get more. If you make a bad bet you end up with less." Indeed, after the midterm election of 1994, Bill Clinton did replenish some of his political capital with a mix of strategic confrontation, legislative successes on welfare and the minimum wage, and emphasis on a number of symbolic "micro-issues," such as school uniforms and the "v-chip" allowing parents to block violent television programming.

More broadly, several advisers address the need for a long-term perspective when attempting to carry out a president's campaign agenda. Carp laments that the White House often does not follow up with incremental action on an issue if a large-scale reform goes awry; instead, the natural tendency is to move on to the next item on the agenda. Reed concurs that "One of the hardest things to get used to is the need to take the long view." However, "you can accomplish a lot over a long period of time" if you remain in office. Spellings notes that presidents can use executive orders, regulatory actions, and commissions as a backup strategy if Congress rebuffs important campaign pledges. Unfortunately, the president's supporters are often impatient, and the "issue and identity groups" within the president's party often work to obstruct the compromises and delays necessary to govern over the long run.

Themes for Consideration

Domestic policy advisers point to a number of additional questions for future consideration.

In terms of rhetoric, coalition-building, and development of programmatic proposals, the campaign is a prelude to domestic policymaking. Although scholars have paid substantial attention to each of these areas, they have not given deep attention to the question of how the pieces operate together. Within the domestic policy context established by the president's campaign, how do rhetoric, appointments, executive orders, and the president's legislative agenda work as parts of a whole? And do administrations come to power with a coherent strategic vision of how the pieces should fit?

The evidence is incomplete, but it suggests that the answer to the latter question is often no. In his account of the Reagan transition, Edwin Meese III pointed to exactly such a vision, referring to a January 15, 1981, meeting in which "Reagan reviewed plans for advancing [his] priorities through executive initiatives, projecting his legislative program, and developing a communications strategy."[44] On the other hand, Margaret Spellings discusses executive orders, regulatory actions, and other uses of executive prerogatives as backup options, rather than as parts of a comprehensive strategy. Bert

Carp bemoans the frequent failure of presidential administrations to have a "Plan B" in the event that initial efforts fall short.

That forming a comprehensive strategy is difficult should not be surprising. The structure of the modern presidency works against such coherence, which would require the longitudinal coordination of campaign and administration as well as the temporal coordination of units including the White House communications office, the Office of Personnel Management, the president's domestic policy staff, the office of congressional liaison, and large swaths of the executive branch (not to mention critical portions of the House and Senate). Also working against coherence is the nation's constitutional character, which, due to the separation of powers and federalism, is populated by competing political figures of independent standing who have their own campaign promises to keep. They are under no obligation to help the president keep his, though some of them may from time to time find it in their interest (or the country's) to do so. Not least, coherent strategy is undermined by the nature of politics, in which events large and small and the vicissitudes of "political time" frequently intrude.[45]

One particular subset of (mostly) domestic policy—constitutional issues—has undergone particularly significant change in campaigns. The weight given to constitutional issues in campaign rhetoric has declined significantly over time, and the character of the constitutional issues that are discussed has shifted in the direction of individual rights and the federal judiciary and away from structural concerns such as federalism and the enumeration of powers.[46] Yet some presidents, as with Nixon's and Reagan's "New Federalism" proposals, have put large-bore constitutional initiatives on the domestic policy agenda as a means of attempting to realize campaign themes, and others (like Reagan and G. W. Bush) have paid particularly close attention to judicial appointments. Even though they play no formal role in the process, presidents also may champion (or, less often, oppose) constitutional amendments. Good examples are George W. Bush's vain push for a Federal Marriage Amendment in 2004 and Jimmy Carter's equally futile drive for the Equal Rights Amendment in the late 1970s. What are the pressures for or against taking on such issues in campaigns, as opposed to focusing on more mundane matters of economic or social policy? To what extent should these initiatives be seen merely as symbolic politics, and to what extent should they be seen as involving hard policy as well?

Constitutional issues are a subset of a broader concern—whether the president will elect to "go long" by tackling some domestic issues of grand

importance or to build capital by fighting and winning on the field of "micro-issues." (As noted, some presidents, such as Bill Clinton, do both.) How
the campaign sets up the president for that choice is a crucial question. It is
often assumed that the margin of the president's election victory, and the
length of his congressional coattails, matter a great deal. But is this true?
Spellings, Reed, and Carp all deny that their presidents' less-than-landslide
wins made any difference to the policy agenda subsequently promoted by the
president. And what other variables affect presidential agenda formation?

Even the president's second term seems to be conditioned by, or to operate within the parameters set by, the campaign that led to the first term.
Most successful reelection efforts are built around a retrospective endorsement of the president's first term rather than a prospective, detailed discussion of the next set of domestic policy pledges. A few exceptions stand out,
notably Reagan's second-term tax reform push, which was part of the 1984
campaign. Even then, the Treasury Department did not release its tax reform proposal until December 1984, and discussion on the campaign trail
was relatively vague.

Conclusion

In domestic policymaking, presidents are both constrained and empowered
by their campaign promises. Despite the importance of campaign commitments to the presidency of the successful candidate, policymaking during
the campaign is a highly problematic affair. Domestic policy advisers are in
remarkable agreement about major points regardless of their party or the
president they served. As Bruce Reed suggests, "I always divide the world
into two real parties: hacks and wonks. We here are all wonks."

Clearly, some of the more difficult aspects of translating campaigning
into governing involve managing the tradeoffs required by the different char-
acters of campaigning and governing: keeping the president's policy agenda
safely within the framework established by the campaign; appointing enough
campaign loyalists to keep alive the "flame" of the campaign while leavening
those loyalists with enough experienced Washington hands to broaden the
president's perspective; and setting legislative priorities. Occasionally, someone like Karl Rove may seek to bridge the gap between the "hacks" and the
"wonks," although his defenders and his critics are deeply divided over how
successfully he did so. Failure to navigate these challenges can severely damage the prospects for success of the president's policy agenda.

Nevertheless, domestic policy does happen, and it often bears the stamp of the president and his electoral campaign. Whatever cynics may say, one can tell a great deal about what the president will do—or at least what he will try to do—by listening carefully during the campaign.

Notes

1. Jeff Fishel, *Presidents and Promises: The Campaign Pledge to Presidential Performance* (Washington, D.C.: CQ Press, 1985), 37–45. Full, partial, and token fulfillment of pledges combined ranged from 62 percent to 76 percent.

2. The actual role of the tax increases in the later surpluses is not easy to untangle. Economic growth probably played the biggest role, and spending restraint after 1994 was also crucial. Indeed, the deficit actually doubled in the years immediately following the 1990 Bush tax increase, and the 1993 Clinton budget plan anticipated reducing the deficit to only a bit over $200 billion before resuming an upward climb after 1996.

3. Carl M. Brauer, *Presidential Transitions: Eisenhower through Reagan* (New York: Oxford University Press, 1986), 256.

4. L. Sandy Maisel, "The Platform Writing Process: Candidate-Centered Platforms in 1992," *Political Science Quarterly* 108, no. 4 (Winter 1993–1994): 671–698.

5. John P. Burke, *Presidential Transitions: From Politics to Practice* (Boulder: Lynne Rienner Publishers, 2000), 205.

6. Fishel, *Presidents and Promises*, 18–22.

7. Unless otherwise noted, all quotations from domestic policy advisers are from the transcripts of the Miller Center symposium reported in chapters 3, 5, 7, and 9.

8. Related in Burke, *Presidential Transitions*, 207–208. This assessment may have been overdrawn, since a number of factors ultimately contributed to Bush's defeat in 1992, but the breaking of the tax pledge was undoubtedly one of them.

9. Burke, *Presidential Transitions*, 205.

10. Brauer, *Presidential Transitions*, 266.

11. Jeffrey K. Tulis, *The Rhetorical Presidency* (Princeton, N.J.: Princeton University Press, 1987); Samuel Kernell, *Going Public: New Strategies of Presidential Leadership*, 4th ed. (Washington, D.C.: CQ Press, 2007).

12. Kernell, *Going Public*, 2.

13. Tulis, *Rhetorical Presidency*, 4.

14. Robert A. Dahl, "Myth of the Presidential Mandate," *Political Science Quarterly* 105, no. 3 (Autumn 1990): 355–372.

15. James Ceaser, *Presidential Selection: Theory and Practice* (Princeton, N.J.: Princeton University Press, 1979).

16. Karlyn Kohrs Campbell and Kathleen Hall Jamieson, *Deeds Done in Words: Presidential Rhetoric and the Genres of Governance* (Chicago: University of Chicago Press, 1990). It should be noted that it is an open question whether this development is a good thing

or a bad thing. Tulis leans toward the latter view, as does Kernell, who blames it for the decline of deliberation and bargaining in Washington.

17. See www.presidency.ucsb.edu, accessed June 9, 2009.

18. George C. Edwards, *On Deaf Ears: The Limits of the Bully Pulpit* (New Haven, Conn.: Yale, 2006).

19. G. Calvin Mackenzie, *The Politics of Presidential Appointments* (New York: The Free Press, 1981), 86.

20. Brauer, *Presidential Transitions*, 262.

21. James P. Pfiffner, *The Strategic Presidency: Hitting the Ground Running* (Chicago: Dorsey Press, 1988), 21.

22. See Richard Nathan, *The Administrative Presidency* (New York: Wiley, 1983); Donald Devine, *Reagan's Terrible Swift Sword* (Ottawa, Ill.: Jameson Books, 1991).

23. Nathan, *Administrative Presidency*.

24. Thomas J. Weko, *The Politicizing Presidency: The White House Personnel Office, 1948–1994* (Lawrence: University Press of Kansas, 1995).

25. David E. Lewis, *The Politics of Presidential Appointments: Political Control and Bureaucratic Performance* (Princeton, N.J.: Princeton University Press, 2008), 3.

26. Devine, *Reagan's Terrible Swift Sword*, 2.

27. Ibid., 5.

28. Pfiffner, *Strategic Presidency*, outlines approaches to this issue taken by a number of recent presidents; 68–89. See also Lewis, *Politics of Presidential Appointments*; Brauer, *Presidential Transitions*, 262–266; Mackenzie, *Politics of Presidential Appointments*.

29. Burke, *Presidential Transitions*, 34, 209, 219.

30. Clinton Rossiter, *The American Presidency* (New York: Harcourt, Brace, 1960).

31. Pfiffner, *Strategic Presidency*, 145–147.

32. Burke, *Presidential Transitions*, 33–34.

33. Ibid., 108–116. See also Edwin Meese III, *With Reagan: The Inside Story* (Washington, D.C.: Regnery Gateway, 1992), 56–70.

34. Patrick J. Fett, "Truth in Advertising: The Revelation of Presidential Legislative Priorities," *Western Political Quarterly* 45, no. 4 (December 1992), 895–920.

35. Mark A. Peterson, *Legislating Together: The White House and Capitol Hill from Eisenhower to Reagan* (Cambridge, Mass.: Harvard University Press, 1990), 267.

36. Cited by Paul Light, *The President's Agenda: Domestic Policy Choice from Kennedy to Clinton*, 3rd ed. (Baltimore, Md.: Johns Hopkins University Press, 1999), 65.

37. Dick Morris, *Behind the Oval Office* (New York: Random House, 1997), 300. According to Morris, pollster Mark Penn had found that a Clinton veto of welfare reform would transform a 15-percentage-point win over Bob Dole into a 3-percentage-point loss.

38. Light, *President's Agenda*, 62–74.

39. Light, *President's Agenda*.

40. Adam L. Warber, *Executive Orders and the Modern Presidency: Legislating from the Oval Office* (Boulder, Colo.: Lynne Rienner, 2006), 14–15.

41. Warber, *Executive Orders and the Modern Presidency*; Kenneth Mayer, *With the Stroke of a Pen: Executive Orders and Presidential Power* (Princeton, N.J.: Princeton University Press, 2001); Steven A. Shull, *Policy by Other Means: Alternative Adoption by Presidents* (College Station: Texas A&M Press, 2006), 103.

42. This pattern corresponds with a general observation made by Carl M. Brauer that Democratic presidents after Roosevelt, driven by FDR's "activist legacy," "got rolling more quickly" than their Republican counterparts. Brauer, *Presidential Transitions*, 267.

43. Shull, *Policy by Other Means*, 104–105.

44. Meese, *With Reagan*, 70.

45. Stephen Skowronek, *The Politics Presidents Make: Leadership from John Adams to Bill Clinton* (Cambridge, Mass.: Belknap Press, 1997).

46. Andrew E. Busch, *The Constitution on the Campaign Trail: The Surprising Political Career of America's Founding Document* (Lanham, Md.: Rowman & Littlefield, 2007).

Chapter 3

Making the Transition from
Campaigning to Governing

Featured participants in this session are Bertram Carp (on Jimmy Carter);
Margaret Spellings (on George W. Bush); and Bruce Reed (on Bill Clinton).
This panel was moderated by Professor Andrew Busch
(Claremont McKenna College).

Busch: The theme of this particular panel is moving from campaigning to governing in domestic policy. This could be thought of narrowly, as just the transition period from Election Day to Inauguration Day, but I think it makes much more sense to think about this more broadly: How do you turn what the campaign talks about into policy after January 20th, and more generally, how does the campaign affect domestic policy after January 20th?[1]

Just by way of very brief introductory comments, it seems to me that there are several ways to approach this topic. One of them is, what sort of context is established for domestic policy by the campaign in a general way? The second is, how does campaign rhetoric about domestic policy translate into the sorts of things that the president talks about as president—or does it? What sorts of continuities or discontinuities are there rhetorically when it comes to talking about domestic policy? The third is appointments. How does commitment to the president's campaign agenda translate into appointments in the domestic realm, and what other sorts of factors come into play? Then there is policymaking itself, in terms of executive orders and the legislative agenda. How do you go about targeting the first executive orders, setting the legislative priorities originally, to try to fulfill the campaign's commitments? And what other sorts of things get crowded in that, maybe, move some of the campaign agenda out of the picture?

But let's start with this: During the transition and early stages of the presidency, to what extent were policy discussions influenced by the president's domestic policy commitments during the campaign, and what other sorts of factors came in to disrupt that focus?

Reed: In Clinton's experience we treated the campaign promises as gospel. That was the only scripture to guide us. He loved all aspects of politics, but he loved the policy part of it best, and his view was that running for president was the ultimate job interview. The agenda he laid out represented the terms of his contract.[2] Now when we got to Washington, that's not necessarily how the Congress regarded it, and even some in our own party, who had followed the campaign closely and listened to what he said, weren't necessarily convinced that everything he promised was a good idea. So there was an enormous amount of back-and-forth and a lot of pressure from people who weren't part of the campaign, in our party or in the other party, to selectively edit the campaign promises.

From Clinton's standpoint, he always felt that that was the way he should keep score. For those of us who had been on the campaign, and I'm sure Margaret had the same experience, that was our strongest weapon in internal debates within the administration and in debates with Congress. We were able to say, "This is what the president promised. We have to keep this promise." That's a hard thing for a president's allies to dismiss.

Spellings: I absolutely concur. In fact I still travel with my *Renewing America's Purpose: Policy Addresses of George W. Bush, July 1999 to July 2000*.[3] It informed the second campaign as well. Bush really had a very dense policy agenda with lots of specifics, more so than had been the practice, at least in our party, particularly to the extent that he had talked about being a different kind of Republican, which not everybody on my side of the aisle was wildly enthusiastic about. Things like, literally, a different kind of Republican—compassionate conservatism, education, immigration, faith-based initiatives—all those sorts of things that had a good bit of an edge to them.[4] That's why, not only did these promises inform our first work, but we knew that we had to get them done quickly.

When I see President [Barack] Obama tackling health care right away, I see a lot of similarities—that his popularity is as high as it is ever going to be.[5] I assume that that is probably the case generically, but some of the scholars here would know better.[6] That's the time to do the things that are maybe the most difficult to do. We lived by our promises absolutely, to the extent that there were specifics laying out a series of principles or ideas or a core philosophy or orthodoxy, which I believe the president did. It had a guiding effect into multiple iterations. Those keystones continued to inform our point of view throughout the administration.

Carp: I'll never forget being picked during the transition by someone who was clearly an enemy [*laughter*] to present to President Carter the case for an incremental approach to welfare reform. This meeting did not go well.

You know, a presidential campaign is a huge effort, a huge labor. Nobody else may be listening, but these guys [the candidates] are very much listening to what they have said. By the time they have said these things for over two years, they believe them. We had a notebook that was personally edited by the president of the United States. He added a bunch of stuff to it that was the set of campaign promises. This thing was absolutely sacrosanct. At the same time, Carter was, even more than those who followed him, a kind of insurgent candidate. I worked in the Senate and he wasn't our candidate; Birch Bayh was our candidate.[7] Something happened to Birch. He [Carter] ran against Washington and he believed that too. He had a very difficult time making his agenda fit with their agenda. It never did really work out.

If I can say one more thing, I think Carter did a tremendous favor to his successors, or we all did together. We had a failure of leadership to some extent and a failure of followership to some extent. We lost a ton of Senate seats when we lost in 1980, including members that nobody ever thought would leave—titans of the Senate like Gaylord Nelson, George McGovern, who were not thought to be in trouble, who had been in there for a long time.[8] I believe that's when members of Congress began to realize that if things didn't work out for their president, they might just not work out for them, either. There has been, ever since then, much more of a driven effort to work things out because there is a fear factor there that was not there until that unpleasant experience.

Busch: Okay, so it's a given that you come in and you do your best to pursue the plan that is set out in the president's campaign. Obviously, however, cases are going to arise from time to time when that is not possible—either you have to back off, or, sometimes in some cases, even backtrack and reverse yourself. When those cases came, how much discussion was there about the problems caused by the fact that this was a campaign commitment? Was that a central part of the discussion?

Spellings: In my experience it varied by degree, particularly for those of us who were working in the campaign setting. I always thought about things that were our must-haves and our things that were nice-to-have. The must-haves, I knew, the president knew, because they were created around a set of core ideas, principles, beliefs or whatever. Other things were up for grabs. So there are actually two scorecards: First, there is the scorecard of what is integral to the president. For one example, No Child Left Behind annual assessment[9]–all the stuff we stole from the DLC [Democratic Leadership Council].[10] Just kidding–but that's how we got eighty-seven votes for it in the Senate, I'll say that! And then there are the things that were less important, which ultimately did fall by the wayside because of various ensuing events, like 9/11, because of budget issues, and on and on and on. So there are really two groups of issues in this kind of context.

Reed: And those of us in the White House are not the only ones paying attention, obviously. The day we took office, the *Washington Post* ran a full-page list of every major promise that we had made. I put it up on my wall, and as Margaret suggested, I had a separate list of the ones that were, I thought, essential. But even in the transition, even before we'd taken office, whenever there was a hint that we were going to deviate in any possible way, it was front-page news. In fact, I can remember people who had not been on the campaign leaking that we were going to break a campaign promise long before a decision had been made to break a campaign promise, because they thought that would increase their leverage.

So by the time we took office, we already had a reputation for breaking some of these campaign promises that in the end we did not break. The biggest new piece of information that Bill Clinton inherited during the transition was a dramatic downturn in revenues coming in.[11] We were coming in at the tail end of a recession, and so the deficit he actually inherited turned out to be a lot larger than he had anticipated when he got into the campaign. In order to keep the campaign promises he made, he was forced to propose a bunch of painful cuts that he wouldn't otherwise have done.

He was actually not bummed out by this at all.[12] When we first told him, we were all terrified about breaking the bad news that the country had half as much money as we'd anticipated. He thought it would be an interesting challenge trying to balance the federal budget and keeping his campaign promises at the same time. It actually was a discipline-forcing mechanism. It made it easier to prioritize which campaign promises really mattered.

Nelson: Can I ask Bert Carp and then the others–during the campaign, you're talking about what you hope to do as president in the present tense.

In other words, "When elected, here's what I hope to do." Once you take office you've got four years. Is there a process by which you try to educate voters that, even though we're not going to try to keep every promise the first year—it is a four-year term—that we have a sense of the order in which we intend to proceed, and that we will get to everything. Having not preached patience, it seems like now in office you've got to preach patience. How do you do that and how well does it work? Bert?

Carp: Most presidents are in a big hurry to get the things that they most care about done, partly because we all believe presidents have more clout at the beginning. But one thing I want to say is there is a tendency that I certainly look back on with some regret, which is we tend to have big ideas in political campaigns. We submit these big ideas and then, sometimes, when the big idea isn't adopted—when, for example, comprehensive welfare reform isn't adopted—we just move past it, riding the horse away. There's not that tendency to stay with the thing and, if you can't get the big thing, to put some building blocks together for the future. So when things don't work out, we tend to leave these kinds of ruins behind that discourage other travelers. They then say, "Oh, I don't want to go there." That's one of the bad things—you've dashed those smaller ideas. That's too bad. I think that's too bad. Among other things, it wastes a lot of expertise that is built up on congressional committees and among people in administrations, when you just saddle up and ride down the hill.

Spellings: I want to add to that for a second. I agree with that in part. That was our experience with immigration. One of my great disappointments is that we left the place worse than we found it with respect to immigration.[13] That notwithstanding, I do think there are places where you think, *Ugh*, and move on, and then there are places where you say, okay, there's not a piece of legislation here, but there are executive orders, regulatory process issues, commissions, various other ways to scratch the policy itches. In these pronouncements that we lay out in campaigns, it doesn't always say we're going to pass a bill that does this or that. There are other ways to scratch the itches, and that's part of the game plan that you have to consider.

Nelson: Can you think of an example of doing that? Doing an executive order, for example, or a commission instead of seeking a law?

Spellings: I'm thinking about postal reform. The post office was in bad shape. We needed legislation. It was overdue for reauthorization, but we needed to build some more ideas, we needed to build some consensus, we needed to get a bipartisan group, and so the president appointed a commission. It did its work and ultimately we enacted legislation. The point is we needed all that lead-up. So for all the people who cared most desperately about postal reform, we said, "Wait, we've got this commission over here and we'll see you later."[14]

Reed: I do think that one of the hardest things to get used to is the need to take the long view. As long as you hold onto the job, you can accomplish a lot over a long period of time. We were able to double education funding over an eight-year period, even though in any given year we were just making an incremental change. Particularly for your own supporters, who have been waiting a long time for your party to get back in power, saying to them when you come right into office, "Don't worry, we're not going to do double funding in the first year; it's going to take us four years or eight years," that's a tough message for them.

But in Washington it's as important to preach *impatience*. You've got an entire Congress that is counseling patience, particularly on the things that you want to do that may very well have gotten you elected, on the kind of changes to Washington that you want to make. I can remember after Clinton took office, the congressional leadership met with him and said, "We know that you said that we should cut our staffs, but we don't really want to. We know you want to reform the campaign finance laws and the lobbying laws, but really you can't do that, because if you do campaign finance reform, that's taking away our current jobs, and if you do lobbying reform, that's taking away our next job." [*laughter*] Clinton deferred to them on their staffs but ended up pressing campaign and lobbying reform anyway.[15]

The country doesn't expect that much, but the key is for the president and the White House to recognize which issues are better dealt with one step at a time, and which issues require going long on first down, otherwise you're not going to get another chance.

Busch: This brings up the importance of message, the talk about domestic policy. My next question is: Out of all of the areas of domestic policy, what were the areas where the president's message or his rhetorical content remained more or less the same from the campaign, and were there any where there was a significant difference between how he had to talk about something while governing, and how he had to talk about something when he was running for president?

Reed: I can give you an example of presidential rhetoric that was treated as sacrosanct, which led to an enormous debate within the administration over what it meant. One of the central promises of Bill Clinton's '92 campaign was to "end welfare as we know it," and he laid out in some specific terms what that meant: Everybody who was able to work had to go to work, and they had to do so within two years.[16] This was going against the grain of his party. It was not a promise that Washington wanted to get to any time soon. So there was a lengthy internal debate about what did it mean to "end welfare"? If we just did this in a couple of states, would that count? If we let people stay on welfare forever, would that count?

What was interesting about it, in part because the phrase itself was so ambitious—it was very difficult to walk back from that promise. It would have been difficult to go halfway. I remember the welfare commissioner from Connecticut actually printed out the acronym EWAWKI, "End Welfare As We Know It," and posted it in every welfare office. She tried to instill in her workers that promise even before we'd figured out exactly how to keep it.

Spellings: Well, 9/11 of course introduced a set of circumstances that obviously had the effect of recalibrating our game. Certainly in the domestic agenda, there are more that got done, maybe with the exception of social security. And the way we ended up handling that was more of "We didn't get it done," as opposed to "We changed directions." We had a commission, obviously.[17] But it remains undone by us—and everybody.

Carp: I don't recall a case on a major issue where we really changed direction in any respect.

Busch: Then let me ask this: Were there examples of cases where on a particular domestic policy issue it actually proved counterproductive for the president to remain in campaign mode when he was talking about issues?

Spellings: I don't know that it's counterproductive to remain in campaign mode. I think circumstances dictate how you react to particular things and what your point of emphasis is. Obviously it would have been ridiculous for President Bush to continue to talk solely about education and the faith-based initiative in October of 2001. That's where the reactive part of this gets into it. It's not that you've abandoned your agenda or are less committed to it. There does get to be, just as we're seeing right now with President Obama and the economy, a point where you're playing the cards that you're dealt. Obviously, Bruce, you had a lot—I mean, everybody had a lot of that.

Carp: If there was one word that President Carter repeated throughout his primary and general election campaigns it was "comprehensive." The word on the other side was "incremental." In those speeches, Washington was a place of incrementalism, and that was what was wrong with Washington.[18] I think he was elected because he believed it. He believed it. Because Washington at that time, especially, was an incremental place, it created the conflict that characterized the Carter years. On the other hand, if you run on comprehensive, I don't know how you can move from Blair House to the White House and turn into Mr. Incremental.[19]

Reed: One of the interesting tensions that all three of our presidents faced is that in each case the president was elected from outside Washington, had an agenda that was somewhat at odds with his own party, and had, to some degree, a mandate for the changes that he was seeking. So when you get to Washington you're faced with a reluctant Congress that, if it had wanted to do what you were coming to do, probably would have done it already. What kinds of compromises are in your interest and in the country's interest, and what ones aren't?

I think that Bill Clinton was influenced by Jimmy Carter's experience: If you push Congress too hard, they'll just give up on you. He was quickly cured of that approach by the '94 midterm results, because we found that really the only way we could govern effectively was to govern the way we had campaigned.[20] Through some trial-and-error we got to that point. But it is an important debate that the party has to have, because if you don't make any incremental progress on your agenda, then the country is going to regard you as a failure.[21] The most successful presidents with their domestic agendas have found a way to keep speaking past the Congress, past Washington, directly to the country on the items that they want to get done. And eventually Congress is more likely to bend to the will of the people and a popular president than to stick to their guns.

Carp: I do think there's a point to be made here to defend the guy who only got four years. Carter came into office right after the Nixon and Ford administrations, which were probably the best period of time for Democratic members of Congress in the history of the world. Everything you think was passed under Lyndon Johnson was in fact passed under these two guys, and our guys didn't even have to take responsibility for the part that wasn't perfect.[22] It's just like, "Well, that's EPA [Environmental Protection Agency]. Best we could do. Would have been better, but best we could do."

Unlike your situation [nodding to Reed] where the parties are in different hands and not getting along, this was a secret political love fest. Then comes Carter, who is like a sane guy and is saying "No." It's like, *whoa.* I do think that the big electoral defeats, especially in the Senate in 1980, made the lives of subsequent presidents easier than they would have been otherwise. I mean Congress is still opposed, they're supposed to be antagonists, but there was a sense after that 1980 election that "We may all hang separately here if we don't hang together," which was not present before then.

Nelson: I wonder, in talking about how campaigning translates into governing—there is the intervening event of the actual election and the size of the victory that the incoming president wins. Carter, Clinton, and Bush all campaigned by talking about either comprehensive changes they wanted to bring about or something equally big. They won victories that were not landslides.[23] Carter was very narrowly elected, really no coattails in the form of new Democratic members of Congress.[24] Bush is famously a minority president in terms of the popular vote. Clinton won a significant victory but far from a landslide, 43 percent of the popular vote. Do you all, in helping the president make that transition, take into account that they weren't elected with a Reagan-style or even an Obama-style landslide, and adjust accordingly, in terms of what you put on your domestic agenda?

Spellings: No, and to the contrary even. I think Bush redoubled his efforts to educate and talk about the reason for his message. He felt like he had maybe more work to do to continue to get those numbers up. But far from saying, "Oh, my God, I'd better turn in a different direction."[25]

Reed: In our case, Clinton got 43 percent of the vote but Ross Perot got 19, so there was a huge groundswell for change, more or less of the same kind.

We felt like the country wanted things to change in a hurry. I do think this is one of the reasons why ideas need to be central to campaigns, why the domestic promises you make need to have a high profile in the campaign, because you want to be in a situation where, when the president is elected, he is claiming a mandate that the country is actually aware of, not one that just happens to be in some campaign literature that reporters might have read or that a few wonks on the campaign are familiar with. The more the country is aware of the fine print, the better off they are.[26] It varies from time to time how much the country wants to get to the fine print. Sometimes they just want a new president and they're not even going to get to the bottom of the contract.

In our cases, because the country wanted a lot of change but was skeptical of government's ability to deliver on that change and had some doubts about our party, they scrutinized everything we did and were quite aware of the promises that we had made.

Carp: I think presidents, at least certainly President Carter, felt that he had to implement this agenda he'd laid out in the campaign. To the degree that he campaigned on something, he really wasn't interested in how enactable it was, or he was much less interested in how enactable it was. But if you get past that initial stuff and get to programs that were designed later inside the administration, then you could at least get congressional relations concerns to move up the list of things that were taken into consideration. As we moved through the years, it was increasingly possible, early in the process to ask, "Where are we going to put our priorities, or what exactly is this program going to look like?"—to have how enactable it was be a factor. Not how popular it was, but how enactable it was—once you moved past the stuff that he campaigned on.

Spellings: We've all been involved in the development of the policy on the campaign trail, and the other thing that is really important is how good a job you do in bringing in members of Congress and local officials and whomever else you can to be part of that and feel some ownership of those policies. Obviously I'm most familiar with education stuff. Judd Gregg and John Boehner—the only thing they liked about the health committee was the pension stuff, and maybe a little of the health care.[27] But education was not their thing. So George Bush had to do, and did do, a lot of teaching them on, What is this about? Then they bought into it. It became their deal as much as his. So how you spread around the equities is really important and helps predict whether you're going to be successful or not.

Busch: Okay, so you come into office, you have to deal with Congress, you've made a lot of campaign commitments. Congress gets overloaded to a certain extent if you try to do too much at once, or at least that's what they claim. How do you decide? How do you decide which of the campaign commitments to put on top and which ones to say, "Well, we'll wait 'til the second round. We'll wait 'til next year"?

Spellings: Ladies first? It's a series of things: How ripe it is legislatively? Is it in queue? Was it up for reauthorization? Is it a leftover? Is there any general appetite for moving forward on that issue? Is it something that the president considers personally important? I know when we put education first, the president was most comfortable with that issue. His facility around that issue was strong and it was a good, strong place to start. What are the prospects for bipartisanship and passage? All those sorts of things. It is a series of elements on how you decide.

Reed: We wanted to flood the circuits. We figured that Congress would slow-walk enough things as it was, so that we didn't have to make it any easier for them. One of the areas where we ran into the most difficulty was that the congressional system is not well set up to handle a couple of high priorities at the same time. Bill Clinton actually wanted to pursue welfare reform and health care at the same time, because he felt that they were intrinsically related as policy and that they spoke to different anxieties of the electorate. Unfortunately, they went through the same committees. And even worse, the House wanted to do health care and not welfare reform, and the [Senate] Finance Committee wanted to do welfare reform and not health care.[28]

At a certain point, any White House makes the calculation that "this is what we can get done and we'll have to pursue it, and we'll come back later." I do think that White Houses are often wrong in assuming that you start with a lot of political capital and it has a half-life and it all goes away. That was not our experience. Our experience was, you start off with capital, and when you spend it well, you get more. If you make a bad bet you end up with less.

Carp: That's right. Basically, we had to pick between doing welfare first or doing health care first. We felt that you couldn't do both at the same time for two reasons: One was that you had one Department of Health, Education and Welfare, and it was really not capable of designing two major programs at the same time. The other was that you had these two committees in the Congress, the Finance Committee in the Senate and the Ways and Means Committee in the House, who would have the dominant role in dealing with both of those programs, and you just couldn't possibly ask them for both simultaneously. We kind of flipped a coin, and I guess we're good Democrats so we put the poor people first. But it could have come out the other way.[29]

I must say this [Obama] administration does not seem to have that problem. They've got different cabinet departments and bureaucracies involved in their big initiatives, but they certainly are jamming these congressional committees. It never would have occurred to us—I don't think anybody ever spent two minutes thinking about sending a welfare reform proposal and a health-care reform proposal up there at the same time to these committees, but that is exactly what this administration is doing, and maybe we're going to learn something here.

Busch: Okay, I think we're going to open it up.

Nelson: Just one more thing because we've been talking about this transition in the very serious and grand terms of public policy, but here's what I want to know: Coming out of the campaign, how did you get your job? [*laughter*] And what did you think your job was going to be?

Riley: Mike, if I could put a modifier on that, do the policy fights get transposed on who gets the jobs, both in the White House and in the cabinet?

Nelson: But don't give them that out of talking about grand public policy. I want to know how the campaign resulted in Bruce Reed and Bert Carp and Margaret Spellings in the domestic policy office.

Reed: Two things: First, we were in an unusual situation because a Democrat hadn't been in the White House in twelve years, so almost no one on the campaign even knew anyone who had worked in the White House. We had very little idea what these jobs were. We had a general sense, and we knew Stu Eizenstat, so he told us a little bit about how the place worked. But really, even with people who were older than I, more senior than I, they didn't really know how a White House worked. You can see a dramatic difference in how the Obama administration hits the ground running and what we had to do in our first couple of years, because they've got people who have done it before, and we had almost no one like that.[30]

I imagine that most campaign workers feel the same anxiety the moment that their candidate wins, in realizing that now you have to share this thing that you helped build with everybody else: with a whole party full of people who either weren't helpful, were actively unhelpful, didn't root for your guy, or opposed what you were trying to do. And now they were in as good a position to get an influential role in the administration as you were, even though you'd given up your life for a couple of years and you actually believed in the guy you just elected.

It's difficult and important for a White House to figure out how to integrate the rest of the world that it's going to have to live with and make sure that people from the campaign are in a position to fight for the promises that they helped make.[31] One of the roles that Gene Sperling and I played in the first Clinton term was as kind of keepers of the flame. We were the ones who reminded the more senior people, the older people who hadn't been part of the campaign, that actually we did promise this and the American people signed off on this. This is really what the president believes in, what he wants to do.[32]

Bill Clinton completely empowered us to do that because he wanted to make good on those promises. He didn't want to have to sacrifice them. I think it's just all part of the moving-to-Washington aspect of governing. People on the Hill thought that because they'd been doing domestic policy for the last ten or fifteen years, they were as natural a candidate to do the kinds of jobs that we were doing as we were.

Spellings: We had not a dissimilar experience with respect to the eight-year period. Republicans maybe were pretty united because we had been in the wilderness. The president, I know, wanted a combination of D.C. people—the Andy Cards of the world, the Josh Boltens, the Mitch Danielses—and people that he had worked with and had known and could trust.[33] Not that he couldn't trust those people, but he knew us better. And to the extent that I grew up around a state legislature and worked on behalf of local governments and whatnot, there was a lot of alignment between that and the domestic agenda. I'll never forget when Andy Card called me—this is kind of a personal—this is closed to the press, right? He called me and said, "The president wants to talk to you about being the domestic policy adviser," and I went, "What?! Are you kidding me?" I was mystified by the mighty Washington. I had just been in Austin or Houston, Texas.

I thought, my God, could I do that? All those sorts of things. Karen Hughes and I talked about this and how we were going to manage.[34] I was a single mother at the time. Of course Andy went through the whole thing about, "You'll never see your children. It's hell, and it's really hard work, and the people are evil and mean." It just sounded about as bad as possible.

Karen Hughes and I had a talk about that and she said, "I don't think we can go. I can't go under those circumstances." The next thing I knew, the president was calling Andy and saying, "Are you running off the mothers?" Needless to say, neither of the mothers was run off and we agreed to do the jobs. That's how I got my job.

Carp: Well, I worked for Mondale in the Senate and then I went down to Atlanta for the campaign where I worked on his speechwriting and tried to make sure that the policy stuff was all coordinated. I came up here [to Washington] and I did some things on the transition, but I didn't have a job. It might have been that welfare briefing I gave the president, I don't know. Mondale had a Christmas party and he walks up to me at the Christmas party and he says, "Well, how are you doing?" I said, "I'm doing pretty good for a guy who has absolutely no job." He picked up the phone, called Eizenstat, and the next day I had a job.

Busch: Very good. So we've had a chance to chew on quite a few things here and I think we should just open it up to the other participants.

Jacobs: I've got a question to get some background here. There's kind of a folk wisdom about whether it makes good sense to develop policy during a campaign, whether it identifies what it is voters are voting for and that's a mandate, or if it is a bad idea because candidates running in a competitive environment over-promise. They may not understand the tradeoffs, or they do understand the tradeoffs but decide not to give them airing. We can see this dynamic in the current administration in Iraq and health care and a whole slew of other areas. Is the campaign a good place to develop policy? And if it isn't, does it then make sense to look to the campaign to inform policy during the governing period?[35]

Reed: I feel pretty strongly that anybody who runs for president needs to know before they get into the race why they're doing it, why they want to be president, and what they want to do as president. As a practical matter, once the campaign gets going, you can still make policy and you should, and you can still search for ideas and new ideas come up. But if you don't know why you're doing it and what the most important things you want to accomplish are before you seek the job, you probably won't get it, for starters, but you'll also be completely at the whim of your political operation.

I always divide the world into two real parties: hacks and wonks.[36] We here are all wonks. We speak hack, but we aren't hacks. Both of those personality types are necessary in a campaign, but the country will get a much better result if a presidential candidate has an agenda that he or she has thought about, is serious about, and has thought through all the different aspects of the agenda so that it makes some intellectual sense. And for that matter I think that the best candidates are ones who actually run on something, as opposed to just run on a phrase, run on a theme, run on a mood. Our system was, as I said, designed to be a job interview that negotiates the terms of the job contract, and what you are going to do for the country ought to be foremost on that list.

Spellings: I completely agree with that and would add only one P.S. to it. To all that string of reasons that Bruce stuck together, I'd also add a track record, experience that substantiates that philosophy and that agenda.

Porter: One of the things that presidents discover when they get into office is what might be called reality. Campaign promises are very valuable in setting a path and charting a course, but ultimately you have to deal with the situation in which you find yourself. Now curiously enough, Bruce and Margaret and Bert all worked for presidents who came into office with their party in control of both houses of Congress. I ended up working for three Presidents: Ford, Reagan, and the first Bush, none of whom had a majority in both houses of Congress. Reagan did have a majority in the Senate when he first came, but not in the House.

Given that, you have to figure out what your strategy is going to be to deal with the context you face. It is one thing if you've got your own party to work with; it's another thing if you're Gerald Ford, or George H. W. Bush, who came into office with larger opposition majorities facing him than any elected president in United States history. So the first thing you have to take into consideration in how you treat your campaign promises is, what is the composition of the Congress and what can you do?[37]

The second thing is, what is the reality that I face in terms of the real world? When Reagan came in we'd had two years of back-to-back, double-digit inflation, the only time in the nation's history. The prime interest rate was 21.5 percent. Federal spending the previous year had increased 17 percent. We had rising unemployment.[38] And because we had a graduated income tax with the lowest bracket at 14 and the highest bracket at 70, every taxpayer had been pushed into a higher tax bracket, so we had the phenomenon of bracket creep, because we had not yet indexed the tax code.

When he [Reagan] came in he had no alternative but to focus his attention on the economy. This was a source of intense irritation to many of his supporters who were very interested in the set of social issues that they thought were important, that had animated their support for him during the campaign. I can remember being in a number of meetings with him where they were excoriating him for ignoring their issues. But Reagan discovered what all presidents discover, which is, "I cannot focus on multiple things simultaneously; I have to decide what are the priorities now." Those priorities are in part driven by what you have said, but they're also driven by the context you face with respect to the Congress. And they're also driven by the reality of what is happening in the country.[39]

We went through a campaign just recently in which the number-one issue was going to be Iraq. If you had looked at the primary campaign of the Democratic Party, the thing that was dividing candidates was what was going to happen on that. Well, the reality is that we now have a president who is facing a very challenging economic environment that didn't receive a lot of attention during the early part of the campaign, but which now, of necessity, has got to consume an enormous amount of his time, attention, energy, and political capital, simply because you cannot ignore the economic realities we face now.[40]

I'm interested in what other people's experiences are with respect to the extent to which campaign promises can assist you—because I think Reagan's campaign promises on the economy did assist him in pushing through his tax and spending initiatives—and the extent to which they can prove to be an albatross around your neck—because you have made the promise in good faith, partially because you believe in it and partially because it is going to engender support from groups that are important to you. Then reality changes and you get into office and you now have to decide what you are going to do.

George H. W. Bush faced this with respect to a promise that he had made about taxes, and how he was going to be able to produce a balanced budget through what he called a "flexible freeze." When that did not work, because Congress would not go along with it and deficits were rising and mounting, he was now faced with a campaign promise that proved to be very difficult to keep.[41]

Likewise, most presidents have come into office with one or more commitments to the steel industry, which tends to be enormously successful in using Section 201 of the Trade Act to present presidents with an escape-clause case in their first six months in office that they're going to have to deal with.[42] I know this caused an enormous amount of consternation in the most recent President Bush's administration.[43] How are we going to deal with this campaign promise we made, when internally large numbers of administration officials thought this is not the direction that we really want to take policy? I would be interested in other people's experiences as to how you deal with a situation where you made a promise that has now been effectively overtaken by events.

Reed: I'd say in the albatross department we had "Don't ask, don't tell," right out of the box in the Clinton administration.[44] I traveled with Bill Clinton for the better part of two years and I don't think I'd ever even heard that promise made. It was there in *Putting People First* somewhere, and he had in fact made it, but it was not one that had been emphasized.[45] No one had thought through how you were actually going to convince the joint chiefs of staff to go along with this. That was one where there just wasn't any way to get it done, and he folded his hand. It was an example—you have to be careful in making your campaign promises you don't promise things that you have no possibility of delivering. Or if you make those kinds of promises, you have to level with people that it is going to be extremely difficult and you may not be able to do it. The hardest thing for a candidate to decide—one of the most important decisions is where they're going to accept reality and where they're going to try to transform it. The best example of a promise we made that opened doors that wouldn't open otherwise is that Clinton made such an ambitious, audacious promise on welfare reform. It never would have happened otherwise. All of our own side would have watered it down to nothing if they could. But because he promised so much, we had to make good on it.

Something that Bill Galston worked on, national service—if Clinton hadn't made as big a campaign promise as he had, it wouldn't have come out of Congress on its own.[46] The luxury of a campaign or the possibility of a campaign is that it is not entirely bound by existing reality in Washington, CBO [Congressional Budget Office] scoring, all kinds of things. It is important for campaigns not to promise what is mathematically impossible, or to pander in ways that are fundamentally dishonest. But it is important to try to raise the sights of American politics because a presidential campaign is the one chance you have to do that.

Carp: I agree with Bruce. I just want to make the point that that is why it is so important that he is doing what he is doing. To a large degree, the presidential campaigns are going to be what they're going to be and the speechwriters are going to write the speeches. The intellectual content that lies behind that is they're not think-tank presidents. Our parties go through various cycles in terms of how intellectually prepared we are for these—and these cycles you would think would correspond with who gets elected. [laughter] But they don't always.

So on both sides of the aisle, having a really vibrant intellectual backpinning is critically important.[47] There are times when each of these groups has gotten into real trouble because that part of it wasn't quite up to the speeches.

Spellings: The other thing, Roger, I'd observe is—you mentioned steel, then Yucca Mountain.[48] But when I sit here and try to inventory those things, my observation is that they were all things that were very important to a subset of folks. So to the extent that you end up maneuvering or disappointing on some of those issues, they're not so macro.[49] As I said, immigration is my personal biggest disappointment domestically—it overtakes everything. Yes, you can make a lot of people mad. School vouchers—that's another one. People are still writing about why we capitulated so early.

Nelson: Why did you?

Spellings: Why did we? We couldn't pass it.

Galston: There probably are no generalizations about American politics that hold true of all cases to the same degree without exception, but there are some broad tendencies. This question of campaigning versus governing and the transition from one to the other does bring to the surface a real structural difference between campaigning and governing. To a first approximation, campaigning is about addition, and governing is about selection. It is no accident that people often say, "to govern is to choose." It is much less frequently said, "to campaign is to choose." There's a reason for that. What that means is that in the transition you're going from something broader and more capacious to something that in the nature of events is going to be narrower.[50]

That carries with it two imperatives that are very difficult inside a White House. One is the struggle, and it frequently is a struggle, for the control of the sequence of major initiatives. Bruce and I both remember the first twelve months when we had health care, welfare reform, a major change of direction on economic policy, and a very controversial decision to proceed with a couple of votes on trade issues that were quite divisive within the Democratic Party.[51] And so the question of what comes before what—because you can't do everything at once with any hope of success—is very important.

But secondly, circumstances can highlight the tensions or even contradictions between or among equally serious presidential campaign promises. It is no accident that during the transition and the first month of the Clinton presidency there was the famous "Battle of the Bobs." Bob Rubin authentically represented an important promise that Bill Clinton had made, and Bob Reich authentically represented a different set of genuinely important promises that Bill Clinton had made.[52] The president as president decided that he had to decide, and he made, as history reported, a clean decision. It was a brave, fateful, ultimately productive decision that paved the way for a subsequent partial redemption of the original promise of *Putting People First*. But it certainly was not manifest during the campaign that there would be some tension between these two pieces of *Putting People First*. Circumstances forced the president's hand in a very difficult way.

Virtually every administration can probably, by the end of the day, record instances in which there is a tension between two equally important, equally sincerely intended promises that have got to be resolved with a choice rather than a compromise.

Reed: To Bill's point, I think that campaigning is something like falling in love, and governing is something like marriage. In campaigning it's all wooing, and in governing it's a lot of arguments, purposeful and ultimately more satisfying, but more difficult. The interesting thing about the early days of an administration is that, as Bill suggested, there's a lot of willful disbelief that goes on in campaigns, so a new president's supporters see in him or her what they want to see, and tend to ignore the other parts.

There were plenty of battles of the Bobs that went on where people who fundamentally disagreed with some major promise that Bill Clinton had made just sort of selectively ignored it and thought, Well, really he's for this; he's just saying that on the campaign trail. But for the president himself, keeping all these people happy who have fallen in love with him for different reasons is a challenge.

Krogh: Richard Nixon in 1968 ran on a law and order platform.[53] One of his main points was, "I'm going to cut the crime in the District, the crime capital of the world." During the transition we were trying to figure out, what does that mean? "We're going to cut the crime"? In my first meeting with the president he said, "Now, Bud, you know that crime has gotten up very high here in the District. Katharine Graham has been over to see me, and Edward Bennett Williams, and we've got to cut the crime."[54] So I wrote in my pad, "Cut the crime."

I went back to my office and I called Mayor Walter Washington, one of the great Americans, and I said, "Mr. Mayor, my name is Bud Krogh.[55] I've just come from a meeting with the president. He'd like to cut the crime in the District, so would you go ahead and cut it and call me back?" [*laughter*] There was this long pause on the phone. As I mentioned, the crime rate was about 169 FBI index crimes per day and I sort of set that aside.[56] Okay, crime is going to go down. I'll check into that three months later. Three months later it was up to 202 per day, which was not progress.

At this point we had to figure out, what do we really do to cut the crime? That was a campaign promise. The president had repeated it several times. Then we had a brilliant man, Robert DuPont, in the District of Columbia— you might remember him.[57] He had done a study that showed a correlation between heroin addiction and the crimes that we were specifically trying to address: armed robbery, burglary and the rest. So I called the mayor and I said, "We've got this data here. I think we need to support you with some drug treatment programs." This is where I think Bert Carp said that the Nixon and Ford White Houses were the Democrats' best years.

We looked around to see who did drug treatment and there weren't any Republicans that did that. [*laughter*] We then had to look around the country. Who can do this? Who can address this problem? We found another brilliant person in Chicago, Dr. Jerome Jaffe.[58] We brought him to Washington and we set up drug treatment programs all over the District of Columbia. Methadone maintenance was a huge thing for us because—can we possibly support making an opiate available to addicts? These were very tough policy questions for us, driven by the campaign promise to cut the crime in the District. That was our scorecard all the way through—how are we doing.

Well, we got to the point where we were able to reduce the rate of increase. That led to a metaphysical discussion. If you reduce the rate of increase, are you really reducing the crime? It is very difficult to come up with an answer.[59] But after four years had ended, to show you just how broad-minded we were, we went down and hired Peter Bourne, who headed Governor Carter's drug treatment program down there in Georgia.[60] He came up and did yeomen's service for us. We didn't care what party people came from. "Do you know about this? Because we don't, and we need to learn." But that campaign commitment that Nixon made in 1968 was a very important part and we were checking to see how we were doing, not just in the District, but in cities all over the country.

Quirk: There's an aspect of connections between campaigning and governing that hasn't come up that I'd be interested in hearing about. That's the idea of the permanent campaign, which is the idea that campaigning doesn't stop when it ought to, that the attitude and the activities of the campaign have too much influence on what goes on in government.[61] I'd be interested in what people think about whether there was too much campaigning in their White Houses, or whether it was just something that just has to be done, that it was somewhat beneficial.

Spellings: Permanent campaigning is obviously pejorative, but the truth of the matter is, the person with the biggest microphone in the country needs to take it and use it to advance the legislative and other policy agenda that is going on. If that's a permanent campaign, then we're all guilty as sin. How the president uses his time is the most valuable commodity that you have, and how you use that to enforce what you're trying to do is the name of the game. So yes, it's a permanent campaign, but this one is just like the last one and the one before, and the one before.

Reed: As long as it's a permanent campaign for ideas. If the next election is what's driving everything and it's just the politics of it, then that can be destructive. But Margaret is exactly right. The president got elected on ideas and he should spend all his time fighting for them, because if he doesn't, they won't happen.

Carp: I think it's a two-edged sword. You can't deal effectively with the Congress unless you demonstrate an ability to go over their heads to some degree.[62] There's nothing worse than going over their heads—I'm an expert in this—there's nothing worse than going over their heads and not making a connection. They all know it. They all go out there and they hold their town hall meetings. You don't need a poll. Congress is the most sophisticated poll we have in this country. The presidents who have been the most effective have been the ones who managed that the best, who have not gone out there too many times and proved they couldn't deliver, because as soon as that happens then you're the lion tamer, they're the lions, and you're not having a good time.

Milkis: I just wanted to pursue a little bit more something Roger brought up about parties. It's not only significant whether you have unified government or divided government, but also how sharp the line is between the parties. And as Bert suggested, we've moved from a situation in the country where party politics was fairly flexible and pragmatic to a situation where that's much less so, where it's much more polarized and rancorous. Each of you had different experiences with party politics. I'd like to hear how the party lines and the way party politics operated in Congress and the country affected your lives in the White House.[63]

Carp: I think this is a fairly simple phenomenon. When I first came to Washington in the early '70s as an elementary school intern, the South had still not gotten over [Abraham] Lincoln. What that meant was that you had a Democratic Party here, a national Democratic Party, that governed through a coalition that went from the Deep South to Wisconsin and Minnesota. But these people disagreed about most things except the identity of the speaker [of the House] and who the [Senate] majority leader ought to be. In order to legislate, whether you were from Mississippi or whether you were from Wisconsin, you had to go find some friends in the other party. No wonder everybody was nice to everybody. Whether you were a Democrat or Republican, you were running with one set of people and you loved them, and then you were legislating with another set of people and you loved them, and we had a golden age of civility.[64]

But the South did get over Lincoln, and we have just an ideological lineup now. That magic moment is just over. I believe this is the new reality and I don't think there is any point in bemoaning the old days. We're just not going to have real liberal people in the Republican Party and we're just not going to have real conservative people in the Democratic Party. That may be a good thing or a bad thing, but it's just something that's happened.

Spellings: I have a little variation on that. Obviously, the president has a strong degree of influence over who the national chairman is, so the RNC [Republican National Committee] or the Democratic Party, its own self, is not problematical. It is all the subset of issue-identity groups that are more problematical and less affiliated with you or anybody that you're connected to. I don't fundamentally disagree with you, Bert, that we are where we are and that's changed and it's going to have an effect on our country and it's going to be a vexing thing for President Obama, as it was for Bush.

Reed: I don't think it is insurmountable. In spite of the efforts of all our respective bosses to try to change the tone in Washington, it has gotten progressively worse. But it is possible to make progress where there are areas of common interest. We found—as Bert was alluding to, what Nixon had found with the Congress of the other party—that where there were general goals that both parties were interested in working on, even if they didn't start from the same spot, it was possible to find common ground.

We actually had a pretty productive period of a couple of years before the other side went off the deep end, working on balancing the budget and reforming welfare and doing things in areas where there were broad, common interests, and it was just a question of working out details we could agree on.[65] Actually where we ran into trouble was when we got to the end of the list of common things on our to-do list and there really weren't any more. When we got around to proposing a big expansion of child care in early 1998, congressional Republicans looked at us and said, "We don't have any interest in that. We can negotiate forever but we're not going to do it." So they decide to launch impeachment hearings.

The challenge is not the partisanship in and of itself; it's whether there are people in either party who are willing to go out on a limb and break with the orthodoxy in their own ranks to make it possible to reach agreement across party lines. There are plenty of areas where it happens. In state government it happens all the time. It is the expected model in most state capitals. In Washington, it's not. It's frowned on, partly because, as Margaret said, there are all kinds of interests that raise a red flag any time you move toward progress.

Members of Congress run in districts—on the House side anyway—that are very narrow ponds, so they are accurately reflecting their constituencies by being more ideological than the country is as a whole.

Spellings: To me the thing that is really critical here is that there is really nobody in the Congress that feels accountable for passing legislation, and they're not going to go home and suffer the consequences if a health-care bill doesn't get enacted. President Obama is. President Fill-in-the Blank is. That's why, I think about my friend Ted Kennedy, who is a legislator and wants to do some things at least as important as all this *yada yada* that is going on in the interest groups. Nobody on the Hill feels very accountable to execute a play.

Nelson: You know, there are three presidents represented at this end of the table, but also three vice presidents, and probably the three most influential vice presidents in history: Mondale with Carter, Gore with Clinton, and Cheney of course with George W. Bush. I wonder, during the campaign and then the transition, and then into governing, to what extent was the vice presidential candidate steering you toward certain promises and then maybe holding your feet to the fire to try to achieve those promises? Bert, you worked for Mondale before he became vice president.

Carp: He always said he wanted to meet the guy that we had hired to work in OMB [Office of Management and Budget] who had studied his career and would go down there and try to cut every single program he'd ever funded.

Spellings: In my case, as is famously known, the vice president's primary interests were not necessarily in the domestic agenda, so while his staff would weigh in from time to time, he had other interests.[66]

Carp: I think, seriously, if there is a frustration that the Carter White House staff had with the vice president, it was that we could get him to engage a lot less than we wanted him to, because he was certainly our most effective staff lobbyist. But he didn't like people knowing what he was doing or what his conversations were with the president, and you just couldn't dial him up, sometimes on things we thought were quite important. Or if we had dialed him up we could never prove it, even to ourselves.[67]

Then there were other issues like the *Bakke* case, where he was basically senior lawyer in the government, where he really did go out there and take an open position.[68] He might have helped to build this model, because of course he was a protégé of Hubert Humphrey, and I think he had studied the vice presidency as a hobby for a long time before he was in it, and he brought a lot of thought to it.[69] But of all these vice presidents, he was hardest to really smoke out. You knew he was doing something but you didn't necessarily know what it was.

Reed: Al Gore was a very passionate advocate for the promises that he worked on in the campaign. Actually, even before Clinton picked him as vice president he had consulted Gore on his environmental policy. Gore helped write the environmental policy speech that Clinton gave in the primaries.[70] Luckily for them, Clinton and Gore had different interests that they were especially passionate about. Clinton hadn't spent that much time on environmental policy as governor, so he was happy to give Vice President Gore some running room on that issue. That was true on science and technology policy. It might have been more difficult if you'd had two guys who were such young hard-chargers who had worked on all the same issues and had made different promises over the course of their career that were at odds with one another, but it worked out quite well for us.

Porter: Andy raised earlier the question of these early months when you come into office and how you go about translating campaign promises into some form of initiatives or reality. One thing that we haven't mentioned but that I think is worth noting since we all came out of the milieu of the White House and the Executive Office of the President, is that when a president first comes into office, he's got a large number of people, at least positions in departments and agencies, that require Senate confirmation. People cannot act in those positions until they've been confirmed. In fact, there are lots of good reasons for them not to be involved in the making of decisions beforehand.

So the initiative inevitably swings to the White House and the Office of Management and Budget, because the director has to be confirmed, but he will always get confirmed along with the rest of the cabinet officers. But the associate directors at OMB don't have to go through Senate confirmation.

So when you're putting together that first program that the president is going to deliver at a joint session of Congress—Reagan did it on the 18th of February; Bush I did it on the 9th of February; I can't remember when Clinton did it, but it was February—it's very shortly after you come into office. That's the first opportunity that a president really has to address the Congress and the country as to what his priorities are now going to be and what specific proposals he is going to advance.

There is a huge advantage to the White House staff and the Executive Office of the President because they're the ones who are already there. It is heavily laden with people who have been on the campaign and are keepers of the campaign flame, and that is a very powerful argument: "We promised this during the campaign and we want to be known as an administration that keeps its promises." There is a huge advantage that goes to people in the White House staffs, particularly during the first six months, arguably the first year, before you start filling out people in departments and agencies and they are then in a position to be a little more effective in countering what the White House is doing. But the initiative and drive always is coming from right out of the White House.

Notes

1. The end of the presidential term on the 20th day of January is provided for in Section 1 of the 20th Amendment to the Constitution.

2. A detailed governing agenda is presented in their campaign manifesto, Bill Clinton and Al Gore, *Putting People First: How We Can All Change America* (New York: Times Books, 1992).

3. *Renewing America's Purpose: Policy Addresses of George W. Bush, July 1999 to July 2000* (Austin, Tex.: Bush for President, Inc., 2000), available in its entirety at http://campus .murraystate.edu/academic/faculty/mark.wattier/Purpose.pdf (accessed October 27, 2010).

4. See Marvin Olasky, *Compassionate Conservatism: What It Is, What It Does, and How It Can Transform America* (New York: Free Press, 2000).

5. See Lawrence R. Jacobs and Theda Skocpol, *Health Care Reform and American Politics: What Everyone Needs to Know* (New York: Oxford University Press, 2010).

6. The pattern of decline in popularity over time in the presidential term is addressed in Lee Sigelman and Kathleen Knight, "Why Does Presidential Popularity Decline? A Test of the Expectation/Disillusion Theory," *Public Opinion Quarterly* 47, no. 3 (Autumn 1983): 310–324.

7. Birch E. Bayh II was a U.S. senator from Indiana, serving from 1963 to 1981.

He ran for the Democratic presidential nomination in 1976, the race that produced Carter.

8. The Republicans picked up twelve seats in the Senate in the 1980 Reagan landslide, giving them a 53–46 majority (with one independent, Virginia's Harry F. Byrd, Jr., caucusing with the Democrats). Gaylord A. Nelson (1916–2005) represented Wisconsin in the Senate from 1963 to 1981, and had been a two-term governor of that state. George S. McGovern served from 1957 to 1961 in the House, and from 1963 to 1981 in the Senate, from South Dakota. He was also one of the party's liberal standard bearers and its 1972 presidential nominee.

9. No Child Left Behind was President George W. Bush's signature education initiative, aimed at improving schools nationwide partly through a regimen of testing, or annual assessment. See Patrick J. McGuinn, *No Child Left Behind and the Transformation of Federal Education Policy, 1965–2005* (Lawrence: University Press of Kansas, 2006); Maris Vinovskis, *From a Nation at Risk to No Child Left Behind: National Education Goals and the Creation of Federal Education Policy* (New York: Teachers College Press, 2009).

10. The Democratic Leadership Council was formed in the 1980s by moderate and conservative Democrats, primarily from the South, who wanted to steer the party in a different direction after the ascendency of the Reagan presidency and the failure of Walter Mondale's 1984 campaign. Education was one of the DLC's major domestic interests. Bruce Reed had a longtime affiliation with the DLC, which Bill Clinton once headed, and at the time of the symposium he was the organization's chief executive officer. For more on its origins and development, see Kenneth S. Baer, *Reinventing Democrats: The Politics of Liberalism from Reagan to Clinton* (Lawrence: University Press of Kansas, 2000).

11. On this unexpected development, see Bob Woodward, *The Agenda: Inside the Clinton White House* (New York: Simon & Schuster, 1994), 79–92.

12. Labor secretary Robert B. Reich records of this discussion that "Bill isn't upset. In fact, he seems buoyed by the challenge. 'We certainly have our work cut out for us!' he says enthusiastically. At the end of the meeting he virtually leaps out of his chair." Bob Woodward's reporting indicates, however, that there were unhappy moments, including a profane barb about the extent to which his future was hostage to bond traders. See Reich, *Locked in the Cabinet* (New York: Alfred A. Knopf, 1997), 28; Woodward, *Agenda*, 84.

13. President Bush did move to support comprehensive immigration reform in 2006, including a nationally televised address from the Oval Office on the issue. But he confronted major resistance in his own party to many of the provisions he supported, including a "temporary worker" proposal that critics tagged as a form of amnesty. See Matthew Cooper, "Inside Bush's Compromise Strategy in the Border War," *Time*, May 16, 2006, at http://www.time.com/time/nation/article/0,8599,1194524,00.html?cnn=yes (accessed October 27, 2010).

14. For one opinionated account of the reform effort, see Murray B. Comarow, "The Strange Story of Postal Reform," unpublished paper, National Academy of Public Administration, February 2007, available at http://www.ftc.gov/os/comments/USPS%20

Study/529332-00004.pdf. The final report of the commission can be seen at http://www.ustreas.gov/offices/domestic-finance/usps/pdf/freport.pdf. The president's substantive position on postal reform is detailed in the July 26, 2005, "Statement of Administration Policy: HR 22—Postal Accountability and Enhancement Act," addressed to the House sponsors. This document is available at http://www.presidency.ucsb.edu/ws/index.php?pid=24836 (accessed October 27, 2010).

15. An account of the debate over campaign finance reform in the early Clinton presidency can be found in Michael Waldman, *POTUS Speaks: Finding the Words That Defined the Clinton Presidency* (New York: Simon & Schuster, 2000), ch. 4. Waldman was a longtime advocate of such reform.

16. See R. Kent Weaver, *Ending Welfare as We Know It* (Washington, D.C.: Brookings Institution Press, 2000).

17. Bush named the sixteen-member bipartisan commission on May 2, 2001. It was charged with studying the program's long-term viability and examining the feasibility of privatizing some aspects of it. The commission issued its final report, entitled "Strengthening Social Security and Creating Personal Wealth for All Americans" in December 2001. The full text of the report is available at http://govinfo.library.unt.edu/csss/reports/Final_report.pdf (accessed October 27, 2010).

18. Scholars Scott A. Frisch and Sean Q. Kelly offer a similar conclusion: "Once at work in the Oval Office . . . Carter also made clear that he was equally impatient with what might be termed 'public policy incrementalism;' unfortunately, from a strictly political point of view, this was not a value shared by many of the people's representatives in Congress, especially its more senior and powerful members." *Jimmy Carter and the Water Wars: Presidential Influence and the Politics of Pork* (Amherst, N.Y.: Cambria Press, 2008), p. xx.

19. Blair House is an official guest residence across Pennsylvania Avenue from the White House, often used to accommodate visiting dignitaries. It is also where the president-elect usually stays just before moving into the White House—thus Carp's reference here.

20. The 1994 midterm elections produced a complete reversal in partisan dominance of Congress, including a Republican majority in the House of Representatives for the first time in forty years. A chastened Bill Clinton tacked considerably to the political center, but also struck a more confrontational tone when the Republican congressional leadership sought to push him too far. See David Maraniss and Michael Weisskopf, *Tell Newt to Shut Up!* (New York: Simon & Schuster, 1996).

21. One of the consequences of the 1994 elections was a turn by Clinton toward modest initiatives that were achievable in a time of divided government. Although some critics derided Clinton's efforts as "small ball," these modest but popular changes did, as Reed suggests here, allow the president to accumulate a record of accomplishments to offset the failures of health-care reform and the loss of Congress. They helped to secure his re-election in 1996.

22. For a more thorough argument on this point by a sympathetic author, see Joan Hoff, *Nixon Reconsidered* (New York: Basic Books, 1994).

23. Carter won 50.1 percent of the popular vote, and 297 electoral votes (with 270 needed to win). Clinton won 43.0 percent of the popular vote, but 370 electoral votes. George W. Bush lost the popular vote contest to Al Gore, 47.9 percent to 48.4 percent (Ralph Nader taking most of the balance)—but Bush won the electoral vote with 271.

24. Carter picked up only a single House seat and the partisan balance in the Senate was unchanged. Moreover, his vote totals trailed those of all but a single Democratic senator and all but twenty-two House Democrats in their districts. Also, he had just defeated in the 1976 nominating contest some of the key Democratic congressional leaders he would have to work with in Washington, so those personal relations were a bit frayed from the outset. See congressional liaison Frank Moore's comments in Russell L. Riley, ed., *Bridging the Constitutional Divide: Inside the White House Office of Legislative Affairs* (College Station: Texas A&M University Press, 2010), 74, 125–126, 177 n. 25.

25. For an extended treatment of this question, see John P. Burke, *Becoming President: The Bush Transition, 2000–2003* (Boulder, Colo.: Lynne Rienner, 2004). Burke reports (131), "What is interesting and significant about the agenda of this presidency is that Bush and his associates not only resisted the post–December 13, 2000, call of some Democrats that he establish a coalition government in light of the election outcome, but instead quickly devised a set of legislative proposals based on Bush's chief campaign themes, prioritized them, and made the decision to pursue a fairly ambitious policy agenda." (That mid-December date refers to the final decision issued by the U.S. Supreme Court in *Bush v. Gore* and Gore's withdrawal from the race).

26. See Patricia Heidotting Conley, *Presidential Mandates: How Elections Shape the National Agenda* (Chicago: University of Chicago Press, 2001).

27. Judd A. Gregg served in the U.S. Senate from New Hampshire from 1993 to 2011. He was a senior member, and then chair, of the Senate's committee on health, education, labor, and pensions during the Bush years. John A. Boehner has been a member of the Ohio congressional delegation since 1990 and served as chair of the House's education and workforce committee from 2001 to 2006, when he became the House majority leader. He was chosen speaker of the House in January 2011, when the Republicans reassumed control of the chamber. His personal history and political career are chronicled in Peter J. Boyer, "House Rule," *New Yorker*, December 13, 2010, 58–69.

28. On the decision to pursue health-care reform first and the political fall-out from that decision, see John F. Harris, *The Survivor: Bill Clinton in the White House* (New York: Random House, 2005), 233–236.

29. See Lawrence E. Lynn and David Whitman, *President as Policymaker: Jimmy Carter and Welfare Reform* (Philadelphia: Temple University Press, 1981).

30. Because of the public image of the Carter presidency as a failure, previous experience in that administration was, for some people, a positive disqualifier for returning to the White House with Bill Clinton. This was evidently more the case on the domestic

side than in the area of foreign policy, where those with Carter experience were drawn back in—including Warren Christopher and Madeleine Albright. The contrast with the next Democratic White House was indeed striking. President Obama drew from a very experienced Democratic bench when he took office, including such seasoned hands as chief of staff Rahm Emanuel and his own secretary of state, Hillary Clinton. Many other former Clinton staffers returned in other capacities to the White House and the upper reaches of the executive departments.

31. These pressures are addressed in Stephen Hess and James P. Pfiffner, *Organizing the Presidency*, 3rd ed. (Washington, D.C.: Brookings Institution Press, 2002).

32. As early as the day of his announcement for the presidency in 1991, Clinton had informed Reed that "You're here to keep me honest." Accordingly, he was viewed by Clinton as a compass both for himself and for the staff he surrounded himself with in the White House. Quote appears in Harris, *Survivor*, 235.

33. Andrew H. Card was George H. W. Bush's deputy chief of staff before being named secretary of transportation in 1992. He then became the first White House chief of staff for President George W. Bush. Joshua B. Bolten initially served as deputy chief of staff under Card, then was named director of the Office of Management and Budget (OMB), before returning to the White House as chief of staff in 2006. Mitchell E. Daniels, Jr., currently serves as governor of Indiana, but was the younger President Bush's first director of OMB, from 2001 to 2003. Earlier, he did intergovernmental relations work for Ronald Reagan.

34. Karen Hughes is a longtime associate of George W. Bush, serving as his communications director in Austin, from 1995 to 2000. She was also one of Bush's senior advisers in the 2000 campaign. During the first two years of the Bush presidency she was his counselor, and from 2005 to 2007 was undersecretary of state for public diplomacy. Her account of her years with Bush is *Ten Minutes from Normal* (New York: Viking, 2004).

35. On these questions, see Stephen J. Wayne, "Presidential Elections and American Democracy," in *The Executive Branch: American Institutions of Democracy*, eds. Joel D. Aberbach and Mark A. Peterson (New York: Oxford University Press, 2005), ch. 4; Jeff Fishel, *Presidents and Promises: From Campaign Pledge to Presidential Performance* (Washington, D.C.: CQ Press, 1984).

36. Bruce Reed elaborates on this theme in "Bush's War against the Wonks: Why the President's Policies Are Falling Apart," *Washington Monthly*, March 2004, available at http://www.washingtonmonthly.com/features/2004/0403.reed.html (accessed October 28, 2010).

37. Those charged with managing the president's program on Capitol Hill—the head of the legislative affairs office—do not universally agree that unified party control is an enabling context. See the discussions in Riley, ed., *Bridging the Constitutional Divide*, 64–97.

38. These poor economic factors contributed greatly, however, to Reagan's 1980 campaign victory over Jimmy Carter, who four years earlier had bludgeoned Gerald Ford because of an intolerably high "misery index" (calculated from the kinds of economic

statistics Porter cites here). By 1980, the index was over 50 percent higher than when Carter entered office, hitting a historic high in June of that year.

39. Reagan's longtime domestic policy aide and first assistant for policy development, Martin Anderson, has recorded similar observations about social policy: "I remember early on in the Reagan years, 1981, we had a very powerful staff that came that was working for me. They were very excited people and they all wanted to do what they were particularly interested in. One person wanted to save the cities. Another person wanted to do something about school prayer. Another person wanted to do something about abortion. Basically my view was, 'Look, those are all interesting issues. However, that's not what the President wants to do first. The first thing the President wants to do is get the economy straightened out, because that allows him to do what he wants to do in military affairs. The two go together. Everything else, while very important to a whole lot of people, is secondary to what he wants done.' So basically what we did was I turned the shop into—instead of policy development on a broad scale, it was implementation of economic policy. Now, my staff did not like that. That was one of the main reasons to have the working groups. I remember, take one case, typical. I sat down—I think it was Gary Bauer. Later on he was giving me credit for his start, but I remember him raising his hand and saying, 'We've got to do something about abortion and about school prayer.' I said, 'Fine, that's your issue and we'll set up a working group. Go work on it.' And he's worked on it ever since. You have to deal with that." Martin Anderson Interview, Miller Center, University of Virginia, Ronald Reagan Presidential Oral History Project, December 11-12, 2001, 76-77.

40. A sympathetic account of President Obama's grappling with the difficult realities he inherited is Jonathan Alter, *The Promise: President Obama, Year One* (New York: Simon & Schuster, 2010).

41. The core idea of the flexible freeze was to cap overall increases in federal spending to a set limit (for example, at the rate of inflation), and then to force decisions on growth in specific programs to fit within that overall limit by requiring off-sets elsewhere. This idea was the core of Bush's deficit reduction program as a candidate in 1988, but it never materialized in any significant way once he was elected. See Timothy J. Naftali, *George H. W. Bush* (New York: Henry Holt, 2007), 54, 63, 73.

42. "A 'Section 201' action is one of the strongest fundamental trade remedy actions under U.S. law. This provision of the Trade Act of 1974 [commonly known as the 'escape clause'] authorizes the U.S. International Trade Commission (ITC) to examine whether a given import is causing or threatening to cause injury to the domestic industry. If the ITC determines that it is, Section 201 provides the President with a range of remedies to restore fair competition to the marketplace. . . . Once the ITC issues its recommendations, the President has 60 days to 'take all appropriate and feasible action to facilitate efforts by the domestic industry to make a positive adjustment to import competition and provide greater economic and social benefits than costs.' The actions that the President may authorize include increasing or imposing duties, imposing a tariff-rate quota,

modifying or imposing quantitative restrictions, implementing adjustment measures, withdrawing or modifying concessions provided to U.S. trading partners, and commencing negotiations with foreign governments to limit exports into the United States." Daniel B. Pickard, "The Future of Section 201: Safeguard Actions in International Trade Law in Light of WTO Review," *Metropolitan Corporate Counsel*, June 1, 2006, available at http:/www.metrocorpcounsel.com/current.php?artType=view&artMonth=July&artYear =2009&EntryNo=5136 (accessed October 29, 2010).

43. On Bush and steel, see Douglas A. Brook, "Meta-Strategic Lobbying: The 1998 Steel Imports Case," *Business and Politics* 7, no. 1 (2005), Article 4, available at http:// www.bepress.com/bap/vol7/iss1/art4/ (accessed October 29, 2010).

44. See Bill Clinton, *My Life* (New York: Alfred A. Knopf, 2004), 483–486; George Stephanopoulos, *All Too Human: A Political Education* (Boston: Little, Brown, 1999), 122–129; Nigel Hamilton, *Bill Clinton: Mastering the Presidency* (New York: PublicAffairs, 2007), ch. 5.

45. See Clinton and Gore, *Putting People First*, 64: "Prohibit discrimination in federal employment, federal contracts, and government services; issue executive orders to repeal the ban on gays and lesbians from military or foreign service."

46. For an account of this story, see Stephen Waldman, *The Bill: How Legislation Really Becomes a Law: A Case Study of the National Service Bill* (New York: Penguin, 1995).

47. See on this topic David M. Ricci, *The Transformation of American Politics: The New Washington and the Rise of Think Tanks* (New Haven, Conn.: Yale University Press, 1993); Andrew Rich, *Think Tanks, Public Policy, and the Politics of Expertise* (New York: Cambridge University Press, 2004).

48. Yucca Mountain is a site in remote Nevada that has been considered, with great controversy, as a potential repository for nuclear waste. All three branches of government have been entangled in the contest.

49. Spellings's claim here about the distribution of costs and benefits shaping the politics of an issue hearkens to the scholarly work of Theodore J. Lowi. See his classic, "American Business, Public Policy, Case-Studies, and Political Theory," *World Politics* 16, no. 4 (1964): 677–715.

50. A concrete example of Galston's point arose in the development of education policy in the 2000 campaign, when George W. Bush's welter of proposals left careful observers wondering which he really meant to pursue once in office. One contemporaneous account noted, "Chester E. Finn Jr. . . . suggests that many of those proposals serve to cloud Mr. Bush's original agenda. Early on, '[Bush] laid out a comprehensive package grounded in a pretty coherent set of principles,' Mr. Finn said. That agenda emphasized flexibility, accountability, testing, and school choice. 'But for reasons of daily tactic, [the campaign] lapsed often into a new-program-a-day approach,' added Mr. Finn, who was an assistant secretary of education in the Reagan administration. 'I [then] worried that they were planting trees instead of designing a forest.'" Erik W. Robelen, "Bush Promises Swift Action on Education," *Education Week*, January 10, 2000, 1.

51. Clinton's major decision on trade was to endorse the North American Free Trade Agreement (NAFTA), which was vigorously opposed by significant segments of the Democratic Party, especially organized labor. That vote was a cliffhanger, which Clinton won by adding to a substantial Republican base Democrats won through extraordinary personal lobbying. Clinton speechwriter Michael Waldman, who came to Clinton from a traditional Democratic background, records the ambivalence of some in the White House about this effort in a chapter in *POTUS Speaks* entitled "NAFTA, 'Cause We Hafta" (56-68).

52. That debate is detailed in Woodward, *Agenda*, especially chs. 11-12. Reich's version appears in his *Locked in the Cabinet*. Robert E. Rubin's account is found in Rubin and Jacob Weisberg, *In an Uncertain World: Tough Choices from Wall Street to Washington* (New York: Random House, 2003).

53. The backdrop of Nixon's 1968 law-and-order campaign is discussed by his speechwriter Raymond Price, with references to cities on fire and bomb threats, in Michael Nelson and Russell L. Riley, eds., *The President's Words: Speeches and Speechwriting in the Modern White House* (Lawrence: University Press of Kansas, 2010), 123-124.

54. Katharine M. Graham (1917-2001) led the *Washington Post* newspaper from 1963 to 1979, serving formally as publisher for the last ten of those years. She took over the paper after the death by suicide of her husband Philip Graham, who had served as publisher from 1946 to 1961. Graham led the paper through its greatest journalistic triumph, the investigative work on the Nixon White House's Watergate scandal, and her Georgetown home was a longtime center of social life in the nation's capital. Edward Bennett Williams (1920-1988) was a high-powered Washington trial lawyer best known to the public for his ownership of two professional sports franchises, the Baltimore Orioles baseball team and Washington Redskins football team.

55. Walter E. Washington (1915-2003) served as the elected mayor of Washington from 1975 to 1979, and for seven years before had been the presidentially appointed mayor-commissioner of the city.

56. "Index crimes are the eight crimes the FBI combines to produce its annual crime index. These offenses include willful homicide, forcible rape, robbery, burglary, aggravated assault, larceny over $50, motor vehicle theft, and arson. In order to compare statistical information on a national basis it was necessary to come up with a common definition for crime comparison. The index seeks to overcome differences in individual state statutes, that would ignore how the individual is charged, and create a standardized definition of crime classification." USLegal.com, at http://definitions.uslegal.com/i/index-crimes/ (accessed October 29, 2010).

57. Robert L. DuPont is a prominent national public health expert on drug abuse, who headed the National Institute on Drug Abuse from 1973 to 1978, and for much of that time also was the White House drug czar for Presidents Nixon and Ford.

58. Jerome H. Jaffe is a psychiatrist who was appointed in 1971 to head the Nixon White House's drug control efforts, making him the nation's first "drug czar." He was an influential voice in promoting methadone treatment for heroin addicts.

59. The crime index for the District of Columbia actually peaked in 1969 and 1970, declining significantly in 1971 and 1972, escalating again in the late 1980s.

60. An English-born physician, Peter Bourne led Georgia's first statewide drug treatment program under Governor Jimmy Carter, before being brought to Washington by Nixon to work on the national drug abuse problem. Bourne later played an influential role in Carter's bid for the presidency in 1976 and joined the Carter White House as an adviser on health-care issues.

61. See Thomas E. Mann and Norman J. Ornstein, eds., *The Permanent Campaign and Its Future* (Washington, D.C.: American Enterprise Institute and The Brookings Institution, 2000).

62. The classic scholarly treatment of this phenomenon is Samuel Kernell, *Going Public: New Strategies of Presidential Leadership*, 4th ed. (Washington, D.C.: CQ Press, 2007). There is, however, a sizeable literature in political science now questioning the real extent to which presidents can successfully go "over the heads" of members of Congress. A leading voice for this view is George C. Edwards III—see *On Deaf Ears: The Limits of the Bully Pulpit* (New Haven, Conn.: Yale University Press, 2003).

63. The University of Virginia's Miller Center of Public Affairs hosted, under the direction of Sidney M. Milkis, panel discussions on the subject of partisan rancor and its roots—among political scientists, historians, and sociologists—at a one-day conference in October 2007. Video of those panels, under the heading "Partisan Rancor and American Democracy," can be found at http://millercenter.org/scripps/archive/conference/detail/3854 (accessed October 30, 2010).

64. William A. Galston addresses this subject of partisan polarization in "Can a Polarized American Party System Be 'Healthy'?" *Issues in Governance Studies*, no. 34, The Brookings Institution, April 2010. See also Sean M. Theriault, *Party Polarization in Congress* (New York: Cambridge University Press, 2008).

65. For more discussion of this period of cooperation between Clinton and the Republican Congress, see commentary by the Clinton congressional liaison at the time, John Hilley, in Riley, ed., *Bridging the Constitutional Divide*, 65–68.

66. Cheney's interests are detailed in Barton Gellman, *Angler: The Cheney Vice Presidency* (New York: Penguin Press, 2008).

67. Carter congressional liaison Frank Moore reported of this relationship: "They had a weekly lunch, private; nobody knew what they talked about. Vice President Mondale never said anything; President Carter never said anything. He was totally loyal." Quoted in Riley, ed., *Bridging the Constitutional Divide*, 110.

68. *Regents of the University of California v. Bakke* was an affirmative action case that was ultimately decided by the U.S. Supreme Court in 1978. The justices ruled that racial quotas were unconstitutional. Race could, however, be used as one factor in institutional attempts to create a diverse student body. President Carter would later claim that "by a 5-4 vote, the Court agreed with our position," which had been presented to the Court by the solicitor general. Quote taken from Jimmy Carter, *White House Diary* (New York:

Farrar, Straus and Giroux, 2010), 88. Details about the origins of the case and the Court's decision can be found in Howard Ball, *The Bakke Case: Race, Education, and Affirmative Action* (Lawrence: University Press of Kansas, 2000).

69. Hubert H. Humphrey (1911–1978) was, like Mondale, from Minnesota and served in the U.S. Senate from 1949 to 1964, and again from 1971 to 1978. In between those terms, he was vice president under Lyndon Johnson and in 1968 was the Democrats' presidential nominee.

70. Gore's book on the environment, *Earth in the Balance: Ecology and the Human Spirit* (Boston: Houghton Mifflin) was published originally in June 1992, just when Gore's name was actively in consideration by Bill Clinton for the vice presidential nomination.

Chapter 4

Domestic Policy Development in the White House

Karen M. Hult and Charles E. Walcott

"Domestic" policy is an elusive concept. Perhaps it is most easily defined by what it is not. When one strips away foreign policy, military policy, economic policy, foreign economic policy, and homeland security policy, domestic policy can be defined as the residual. But even that does not quite satisfy, because all of the preceding policy areas have domestic implications, in that they interact closely with standard domestic concerns—economic growth with environmental protection, for instance. So not only is domestic policy hard to nail down conceptually, it also permeates practically everything else including, obviously, electoral politics. As a consequence, it is not hard to see why the creation of a stable set of White House structures and processes for dealing with domestic policy—as has more or less occurred in the areas of national security and economic policy—has been a challenge for modern presidents. As we wrote more than twenty years ago, "the problems posed by the ill-definition of domestic policy have persisted. Both within and across presidencies domestic policy units have varied considerably in their structuring, activities, and status within the White House."[1]

Nonetheless, some continuities of organizational structuring and processes have been achieved in recent administrations. Since Richard Nixon created the Domestic Council in 1970, all White Houses have featured staffs devoted to the development and monitoring of domestic policy, relatively broadly defined. All the while, the political and institutional environment surrounding domestic policy has changed in ways that have required presidents to continually adjust and rethink not only policy substance but also policy processes.

In this chapter we will briefly trace this pattern of change, focusing on three related issues. The first is the sources of the president's domestic agenda—where the ideas come from, and what makes them attractive or important enough to be actively considered. The second is how the White House has been structured to cope with these ideas and demands. Finally,

we will examine the ways that the interplay of agendas and structuring af-
fects interpretations of the policymaking process. These three foci are not
distinct from one another. For instance, the people who first promote ideas
tend to remain involved in the processes of formulation and adoption in the
White House and beyond; similarly, some policy concerns in effect cause
structures to be created to house them. Yet for the sake of clarity we will look
at these three analytical issues in sequence, allowing us in each case to focus
on how White House involvement has evolved.

Where Do the Ideas Come From?

Robert Wood, a scholar as well as a White House veteran, has offered a
useful typology of the "intervening elites" whose advocacy of ideas and programs supplies the initial dynamic of the policy process.[2] Wood defines these
elites primarily as elected officials, senior administrators, and intellectuals.
Each, he notes, brings a different set of goals, talents, and expectations to
the policy debate.

Elected Officials

During any presidential campaign year, myriad elections are taking place on
every level of the American political system. Wood regards this total process, one of "self-starting" politicians who "run scared" nearly all the time,
abetted by an apparatus of pollsters and consultants, as a key source of information about the issues that play well (or poorly) with the electorate at
any given time.[3] At the same time, however, the pressurized, hectic world of
campaign politics draws attention to a multiplicity of issues while precluding
serious development or analysis of any of them. Thus, "good, doable ideas
left entirely to professional politicians with all the good intentions in the
world will emerge at best so grossly transformed as to become the roughest
approximations of feasible policy."[4]

Nevertheless, promises and proposals made during the presidential campaign have a powerful presence in a newly elected administration. As Bruce
Reed puts it, "we [the Clinton White House] treated the campaign promises as gospel."[5] Those promises provide much of an administration's early
agenda during the "honeymoon" phase in which the president's public approval and political momentum are uncharacteristically high. Margaret Spellings notes that the George W. Bush White House "knew that we had to get

them done quickly," although she adds that even promises that were not met "continued to inform our point of view throughout the administration."

A similar source of policy ideas and commitments—in effect prefabricated campaign promises—is the platforms produced by the national party conventions. Although not all platform planks represent meaningful or feasible commitments, many do, which is why interest groups and party factions struggle so vigorously over them. Moreover, presidents know that journalists will use the platform at some point as the basis for "did he keep his promises?" stories.

Administrators

Senior career executives collectively comprise a powerful, experienced, and informed elite. A key to their influence is their knowledge of and participation in webs of issue networks that bind together the principal policy actors who populate every substantive area.[6] Unlike elected officials, administrators are issue experts, but their relationship with their political superiors is complex and marked "rarely, if ever, by trust."[7] Although frequently policy entrepreneurs, administrators typically operate through indirection, giving advice seasoned by experience and cautioning against the pursuit of ideas previously found to be flawed. Career officials and government agencies typically contain accumulated agendas, "good" ideas awaiting a champion and the circumstances necessary to gain them full consideration.[8]

Intellectuals

Presidents have long drawn on university-based academics for policy advice, a practice that predates even Franklin D. Roosevelt's "Brains Trust." Panels of experts have been mobilized before and during presidential administrations to help staff commissions or task forces focused on particular policy issues, such as drugs in the Nixon administration and health care under Clinton. Academics often have played the role of advocate, bringing to bear not only knowledge but also normative goals. As John Kessel has pointed out, however, many see themselves as policy scientists, providing politically and ideologically neutral (or at least nonpartisan) analysis.[9]

Another, probably more important trend has been the institutionalization of policy advice in think tanks such as the Heritage Foundation and the Center for American Progress. Once a relatively rare species, think tanks began to proliferate in the 1970s.[10] As Tevi Troy has shown, the growth of the think-tank industry was driven in substantial part by wealthy conservatives who despaired of the entrenched liberalism of the academy and sought an alternative platform for scholarship and advocacy.[11] Ideological think tanks are important as sources not only of ideas but also of personnel for new administrations. Ronald Reagan, for instance, leaned heavily on the Heritage Foundation as a source of "movement conservatives" to staff his early administration.

Interest Groups

At about the same time that the number of think tanks was beginning to grow, the "advocacy explosion" was multiplying the number of interest groups spectacularly. No more were "the interests" comprised mainly of the traditional business, labor, agriculture, and professional organizations. The first wave of new groups, which hit the policy shore in the 1970s, was comprised largely of public interest or "citizen" groups, positioned mostly on the left. The 1980s saw a reaction in the form of business-based groups along with conservative public interest groups, some of which marked the emergence of the religious right as a political force. Many of these newly formed groups have focused narrowly on a small range of issues and are frequently unbending in their views. For presidents as well as members of Congress, such groups have tended to make bargaining and coalition formation more challenging.

Other Sources

Presidents themselves bring policy issues to the agenda, often reflecting their personal experiences and beliefs. This was the case, for instance, for John F. Kennedy and mental retardation, and George W. Bush and faith-based social services. The mass media are also sources of ideas, although more likely as conduits than as originators. Meanwhile, the Internet and social media are excellent vehicles for transmitting enthusiasms, gaining publicity, and mobilizing support and opposition.

How Has White House Structuring Evolved?

Whatever the sources of policy ideas or proposals, they must be incorporated into the president's program through a process driven by the White House.

As the size and activity of the federal government have grown over the course of the twentieth and early twenty-first centuries, the older practice of leaving primary responsibility for policy development in the departments and agencies of the executive branch has given way to a White House–centered process. As much as anything, this is a consequence of the nature of contemporary issues. Lester Salamon wrote in 1981 that "modern problems are so complex that most public issues cross departmental lines and therefore call for some integrating influence."[12] Only the White House, broadly defined to include units of the Executive Office of the President such as the National Security Council, Domestic Policy Council, and National Economic Council staffs, has the perspective and the authority to perform this task of integration. On the most important matters, decisions ultimately need to be made by the president. As James Cannon observes about Gerald Ford, "there was no way a president could give up control over domestic policy."

The task of pulling together policy options is sufficiently daunting that no single approach to structuring has proven entirely satisfactory. To some extent, though, a process of trial and error has yielded a degree of consensus about what works.

Central Clearance

As Richard Neustadt first made clear to the scholarly community, the watershed event in presidential assumption of policy integration occurred under Franklin Roosevelt, when the Bureau of the Budget began clearing legislative policy proposals from the departments.[13] This process, which became a regular institutional feature of the presidency under Harry S. Truman and Dwight D. Eisenhower, gave the president's staff a degree of leverage over the departments unknown before that time.

External Task Forces

Central clearance provided a degree of order, but it did not meet presidents' need for new policy initiatives, a particular concern for John Kennedy and Lyndon B. Johnson. Both turned to task forces comprised of outside (and, under LBJ, executive branch) experts, in part because both presidents lacked sufficient in-house expertise.[14]

Domestic Policy Staffs

Lyndon Johnson can be credited with setting up the first White House policy staff when he established a small group under Joseph Califano that was primarily charged with generating ideas for the Great Society. The first systematic, comprehensive effort to bring a strong policy competency to the White House was Richard Nixon's creation of the Domestic Council in 1970. A cabinet council modeled after the National Security Council with a White House–based staff, it was continued in the same form under Gerald Ford. Subsequent presidents modified the form, especially the degree of involvement by cabinet members, but all have retained the idea of a staff to coordinate, oversee, and on occasion formulate domestic policy.

Interagency Task Forces

Gerald Ford and especially Jimmy Carter supplemented their policy staffs with interagency task forces focused on particular issues. These allowed a better opportunity to tap the expertise of the departments and agencies, although they also provided room for interagency rivalry and dissension. As Salamon comments, "These defects were the mirror image of those that afflicted the domestic council approach, but they produced a negative political reaction nonetheless."[15]

Structural Design: Criteria and Tradeoffs

The approaches that presidents have developed for domestic policy formulation are not mutually exclusive. Indeed, recent presidents have tended to deploy an array of them. This is probably the best way to overcome what Salamon stresses are the limitations of any one approach. Salamon's analytical scheme is useful. He begins by discussing three major "design issues" that confront presidents as they contemplate domestic policymaking. The first is how to divide responsibility between the agencies and the White House. The White House staff has four possible roles: reactive (agencies retain initiative), facilitative (White House and agencies cooperate), stimulative (White House initiates), and controlling (White House dominates and supervises).[16]

The second issue involves the use of "institutional" (the EOP, especially the OMB) versus "personal" (White House Office) presidential staff. The options are simple: either may dominate, or there can be some sort of mixed approach. Salamon observes that the trend through the 1980s was toward increasing the power vested in the White House Office. More recently, scholars have traced the growing centralization of policy (and other) tasks in the EOP.[17]

The third design issue is whether the White House staff at the center of the process should be consolidated or compartmentalized. Here Salamon notes the trend toward compartmentalization—the emergence of specialized White House units for tasks such as domestic policy.[18] In light of the interdependence of policy and political issues, however, it is not obvious that compartmentalization is the best strategy. Some support for this concern may be gleaned from Roger Porter's account of the Reagan administration's decision to define broadly the mandate of the Office of Policy Development. Porter recounts that the growing recognition of the importance of international economic policy led those designing White House structures for domestic policy to look for ways to encompass international economic concerns. Counselor Edwin Meese suggested they "get rid of 'domestic'" in the policy unit's title, producing the Office of Policy Development. Along with the NSC staff, OPD sought to "play the role of coordinator" of ideas, expertise, and advice from throughout the executive branch.

Salamon then specifies nine evaluative criteria and applies them to the options available for resolving the design issues he identifies. Although there is not room here to elaborate on each, their meaning and relevance are relatively straightforward. They are:

1. substantive soundness of policy;
2. identification of and responsiveness to national needs;
3. responsiveness to national priorities;
4. coherence (overcoming institutional fragmentation and integrating policy and resource allocation);
5. accountability and political sensitivity (toward Congress, groups, the states, etc.);
6. representation and orderliness (a predictable process allowing multiple advocacy);
7. timeliness in reaching closure on decisions;
8. manageability and selectivity (ability to prioritize, avoid bottlenecks);
9. institutional and organizational sensitivity (to implementers and institutional memory).[19]

Salamon's conclusions follow logically from these criteria. Briefly, he finds that facilitative or stimulative White House roles are most satisfactory. A reactive role scores too low on responsiveness and timeliness, while a more controlling role fares poorly on the criteria of accountability and representativeness as well as on manageability and sensitivity. On the whole, his advice comports with the decisions made by presidents and their advisers when setting up domestic policy staffs.

When it comes to staffing patterns, although Salamon tends to favor dominance by institutional staff to personal dominance, he considers a mixed version (albeit one somewhat vaguely specified) as being better than either institutional or personal dominance. A more mixed approach (such as, for example, "the establishment of a core secretariat of careerists who would staff at least the procedural parts of the policy development function"[20]) would permit the balancing of the "enhanced substantive soundness, orderliness, managerial and institutional sensitivity" of an institutional staff with the "greater responsiveness to national needs and presidential priorities, the greater political sensitivity, and the superior timeliness of the personal staff."[21] Finally, Salamon tends to favor consolidated structures, mainly because more specialized (compartmentalized) ones do poorly on the managerial criteria of coherence, orderliness, timeliness, selectivity, and sensitivity. His overall prescription counsels moderation: either upgrade OMB relative to the White House Office staff or consolidate the White House policy staffs.[22]

The greatest utility of this scheme, however, is less Salamon's relatively modest conclusions than his identification of the issues involved in staff design. These parallel closely the considerations that have motivated presidents and their aides to innovate and modify policy decision structures in the presidency since 1970.

A Brief Survey of Structuring for Policy Decision Making

Although it is impossible in a single chapter to describe and discuss all aspects of domestic policy evolution in the seven presidencies from Nixon to George W. Bush, we can at least sketch the broad outlines and indicate the kinds of trade-offs each president was willing to make.[23] Table 4.1 summarizes our conclusions about which of Salamon's roles these presidents' domestic policy staffs assumed.

Table 4.1   Roles of Domestic Policy Staffs: Richard Nixon through George W. Bush

Possible staff roles*	White House domestic policy staffs
Controlling	Nixon
	Early 2nd term Reagan cabinet secretary
Stimulative	Early G. W. Bush Office of Faith-Based and
	Community Initiatives?
Facilitative	Carter
	1st term Reagan OPD
	Clinton 1994–1996
Reactive	Ford
	2nd term Reagan OPD
	G. H. W. Bush
	Clinton 1993, 2nd term
	G. W. Bush, especially post-9/11

* Possible roles are drawn from Salamon, "The Presidency and Domestic Policy." Unless otherwise noted, classifications are of the formal domestic policy staff.

Nixon

Richard Nixon did not initially create a centralized domestic policy structure; instead, he had two staffs that competed fiercely. One, under Arthur Burns, was nominally accountable for domestic as well as economic policy and took on the conservative outlook of Burns, a noted economist. The other, under Democrat Daniel Patrick Moynihan, was given dominion over urban policy, a Nixon point of emphasis. The result was "two distinct and conflicting structures for managing domestic policy."[24] Each reported to Nixon through White House Counsel John Ehrlichman. This situation produced little in the way of progress or consensus, so Nixon determined in the fall of 1969 to reorganize his administration, appointing the Advisory Council on Government Organization chaired by Roy Ash to deliver recommendations.[25]

The Ash Council produced a recommendation that resulted in broadening the responsibilities of the Budget Bureau, rechristened the Office of Management and Budget (OMB), and laying the groundwork for the replacement of both Burns's and Moynihan's operations with the Domestic Council (DC). Ehrlichman, who had supported this idea, was named head of the DC staff.[26] The council itself, following the National Security Council model, initially was to be composed of the secretaries of all departments with significant domestic responsibilities. To that membership Nixon later added seven others, including top White House advisers, the two highest-ranking executives in OMB, and the head of the Office of Economic Opportunity. In fact, the unwieldy council contributed little, meeting infrequently: "When the council met, it was primarily a show-and-tell exercise. Policy was not debated."[27]

The real influence over most domestic policy came to be wielded by Ehrlichman and the Domestic Council staff. As Egil Krogh characterizes it, the DC was "primarily staff driven." Ultimately, the staff was organized according to policy areas, with Ehrlichman's deputies in charge of as many as six areas. In time, Ehrlichman transferred day-to-day responsibility for the DC to his deputy, Kenneth Cole, who became DC head in December 1972. The scope of the DC's responsibilities was not limited to integrating policy ideas; "it was also involved in the advocacy, monitoring, and evaluation of policy . . . with substantial policy discretion and de facto ability to direct and oversee the performance of department and agency executives."[28]

In keeping with decision making throughout the Nixon White House, the DC's processes emphasized thorough staffing through circulating proposals and ideas widely throughout the White House and relevant parts of the administration for comment. Of course, this did not always work perfectly. Krogh recalls that special assistant for consumer affairs Virginia Knauer called him to check on her upcoming testimony before the House Agriculture Committee on the fat content of hot dogs, which she supported reducing from 32 percent to 30 percent. Busy with other tasks, Krogh readily approved. Following her testimony, newspapers proclaimed a "major administration shift on wieners." Meatpackers complained loudly. Fortunately for the White House aides, the president saw the story and telephoned Knauer, telling her to "stick to your guns." Nixon noted that he "c[a]me from humble origins. We were raised on hot dogs and hamburgers. We've got to look after the hot dog." For his part, Krogh quickly learned that much can potentially go wrong when proper staffing is not performed.

In contrast, James Cannon's tale of inquiring into the need for a presidential science adviser illustrates how the process worked when done right. President Ford asked Cannon to prepare materials on the history of presidential science advisers, on the views of others in the administration about the need for and the responsibilities of such an adviser, and on what previous science advisers and an independent science writer believed were their major accomplishments. Following a meeting with administration officials to hear their advice and perspectives, the president withdrew to his office to put his decision in writing.[29]

By the outset of Nixon's second term, the DC staff had grown to about eighty and was the hub of ambitious plans for change. Structurally, the DC now was organized into fourteen committees, reflecting the contours of Nixon's proposed (although never adopted) reorganization of the cabinet. But a central role for domestic policy and the DC in the second Nixon term never materialized: Watergate pushed nearly everything else off the table until the president's abrupt resignation.

Nixon in effect consolidated policy responsibility, at least to the extent of bringing the diverse strands of domestic policy together. He also empowered the OMB, although mostly in the area of management oversight. The experiment with the DC was not an unqualified success. Most observers would agree with Margaret Wyszomirski that the DC staff, although highly responsive to the president, "seemed to breed misunderstanding and distrust with others—Congress, the bureaucracy, the party, and the media."[30] These difficulties are consistent with Salamon's concern about the White House controlling policy. That is what Nixon's staff tried to do, although initially something more like a stimulative role was envisioned. Nonetheless, Nixon firmly implanted the idea of a domestic policy staff in the modern presidency.

Ford

In his brief tenure as president, Gerald Ford tried, without much success, to innovate in the organizational structuring of domestic policy. While maintaining the DC structure—there was, after all, little opportunity to overhaul the organizational arrangements in the short time he served—Ford sought to carve out a powerful role for his vice president, Nelson Rockefeller, as the overseer of domestic affairs. But things did not work out as planned.

The fundamental problem lay in disagreement about the direction of domestic policy. Rockefeller was an activist who sought, as Warshaw says, "to forge a domestic agenda and to develop major domestic initiatives for the administration."[31] He confronted a formidable opponent in Ford's de facto chief of staff, White House "coordinator" Donald Rumsfeld. Procedurally, Rumsfeld insisted that domestic policy issues run through his office, while Rockefeller sought a direct line to Ford. Substantively, the vice president's preference for activism clashed with the views of Rumsfeld and his deputy,

Richard Cheney. Cheney succinctly expressed his and Rumsfeld's position in a memo suggesting that Ford urge all DC task forces to "consider doing nothing as an option, and also the possibility of doing less as an option. . . . Many of our problems are caused by previous misguided efforts to fix something."[32]

Ultimately, Rumsfeld and Cheney prevailed, not least because their position was closer to Ford's. The president, preoccupied with economic problems and more interested in the work of his innovative Economic Policy Board, had little desire for domestic policy innovation.[33] Rockefeller, whom Ford did not invite to run for vice president in 1976, finally asked to be relieved of his domestic policy assignment, leaving the DC without major policy responsibility. Certainly, this was a significant change from Nixon's day. Under Ford, the White House role is hard to characterize in Salamon's terms. Perhaps it is most accurate to see it as reactive, and slow to react at that.

Ford's domestic policy structuring was most notable for his attempt to find a major role for the vice president, which itself was a clear break from precedent. Had Rockefeller's plans for domestic policy been followed, his DC staff might well have played a stimulative role. Surely there is some irony in the fact that the effort was blocked in part by Cheney, who in time would become the most powerful vice president in history.

Carter

Jimmy Carter's decision to maintain a domestic policy staff went a long way toward institutionalizing Nixon's innovation, thereby creating a bipartisan precedent. Carter's main structural change was to eliminate the cabinet council feature of Nixon's Domestic Council, creating instead a Domestic Policy Staff (DPS) in the White House. Functionally, Carter saw the staff as principally advisory. Domestic policy assistant Stuart Eizenstat drew a contrast between the DPS and the DC when he expressed the president's intention that the DPS "would not get involved consciously and purposively in any implementation of policy."[34] In other words, in contrast to Nixon's White House Domestic Council staff, the DPS was expected to defer to the departments rather than oversee their interpretations of their mandates and the laws they applied. Deputy domestic policy assistant Bertram Carp characterizes the Carter staff as "too reactive" in restricting its involvement to issues on which cabinet officers disagreed, again reflecting Carter's determination to empower his cabinet.

Although in many ways the DPS worked well in the Carter administration, it had a difficult existence. At the outset the DPS experienced some upheavals before Eizenstat's role and authority were firmly established.[35] Then a period ensued in which the White House seemingly lost control of the departments, culminating in Carter's dismissal of four cabinet secretaries in July 1979. A subsequent White House reorganization placed the DPS under the newly designated chief of staff, Hamilton Jordan, a move that evidently enhanced the DPS's effectiveness in gaining control of the policymaking process.[36] Meanwhile, many of the problems attending White House relations with the cabinet were addressed successfully through an interagency task force approach, which the DPS participated in but did not always drive. By the time White House structuring became stable, however, the administration's reputation already was scarred, and its attention soon turned to more urgent issues, such as the Iranian hostage crisis and the president's bid for reelection.

As Table 4.1 indicates, Carter's DPS ultimately fit well with Salamon's preference for a facilitative rather than a controlling role. But the staff's early struggles illustrate the problems that accompany organizational fragmentation. Like much of the Carter administration, the DPS was notable for its capacity to learn and adjust, and it eventually seemed to get things right, albeit too late in the game of politics, in which the reputations of presidential administrations tend to be established early and are difficult to change.

Reagan

Ronald Reagan named his policy staff the Office of Policy Development (OPD). He had it report to him through Counselor to the President Edwin Meese, and sought to address the problem of relations with the cabinet by having the OPD staff support a newly created system of cabinet councils, each of which concentrated on a specific policy area. This approach, along with the strategy of appointing established Reagan loyalists to executive positions in the departments, sought to ensure close and compatible working relationships between the White House and the agencies.[37] The OPD typically stayed away from policy implementation, leaving that to the Legislative Strategy Group, chaired by chief of staff James A. Baker III. Instead, as Roger Porter has indicated, OPD sought to bring together the two primary considerations involved in deciding on a policy: issue substance and the politics of the issue. The OPD's role essentially was facilitative, although one might characterize the White House staff's overall approach as more nearly controlling.

Reagan's design sought to integrate various policy streams, placing all policy initiatives under Meese and assigning both domestic and economic policy to the OPD. As Porter recounts, one important motive for this broadening of the domestic staff's jurisdiction was to include international economic policy within its purview, rather than that of the National Security Council staff. Nonetheless, the OPD experienced competition from the OMB, whose emphasis on restraining spending sometimes clashed with spending priorities formulated by OPD head Martin Anderson.[38] In Warshaw's analysis, the OPD under Anderson tended to be overshadowed by David Stockman's OMB, but when Edwin Harper replaced Anderson in 1982, the worm turned. Stockman had been embarrassed by a too-candid interview with the *Atlantic Monthly*, undermining his credibility and allowing Harper to assert the influence of the OPD. OPD's influence and participation stalled, however, under Harper's successor, John Svahn.[39]

Much changed in Reagan's second term. With Meese gone to head the Justice Department, new chief of staff Donald Regan undertook a reorganization. The Office of Cabinet Affairs, which had not been a policy unit in the first term, reappeared as the Office of the Cabinet Secretary and, with a new Regan ally in charge, was given control of the cabinet councils. Roger Porter, now the head of OPD, was most involved with economic policy issues, and a new White House senior aide, Charles Hobbs, was brought in to take primary responsibility for social policy. Ultimately, Regan dissolved the cabinet council structure, replacing the seven councils with two, one for domestic policy and one for economic policy. Porter "focused most of his activities on his role as executive secretary of the economic policy cabinet council," clashed with John Svahn (who remained in the White House as an adviser), and left at the end of 1985.[40] As a result, the OPD was not by that time a major policy player. That role fell to the Cabinet Secretary's office, a unit fully accountable to Regan. The OPD had become more reactive than facilitative, as cooperation both in the broader executive branch and within the White House became harder to achieve.

Yet another change in OPD's mission and fortunes occurred in 1986 when Gary Bauer was named as its head and given a mandate to focus on developing broad positions on basic conservative issues such as welfare reform. Bauer's influence was felt in the departments, but overall "agenda setting for domestic policy was moved to a back burner in the White House as

[Reagan's] second term began," limiting the possible influence of any White House staff unit.[41] Soon the Iran-Contra affair forced Regan's resignation, and the importance of domestic policy development in the White House receded even further.

The Reagan administration innovated in its creation of cabinet councils and use of the OPD to support them. But the multiplicity of influential actors and agendas led to instability. All of this, of course, occurred in an administration whose stated aim in the domestic policy arena was to reduce the role of the federal government. Thus it is unsurprising that no stable solution to the puzzle of the most appropriate structural arrangements for domestic policy development emerged.

George H. W. Bush

George H. W. Bush organized his administration around a powerful chief of staff, John Sununu. Roger Porter, who headed Bush's policy staff and had responsibility for policy development, reported to Sununu and also shared responsibility with the cabinet secretary, who handled policy initiatives originating in the departments. Porter's job description included economic as well as domestic policy. But Cabinet Secretary David Bates also oversaw the domestic and economic cabinet councils, which continued from the Reagan administration. Thus the cabinet secretary again was a major domestic policy player.

The influence of the cabinet secretary and councils, however, was limited. Warshaw contends that Bush's minimal objectives in domestic policy led department and agency heads to focus more on management than on policy innovation. In any event the efforts of OMB, under Richard Darman, to limit spending effectively squelched many initiatives.[42]

Meanwhile, Porter's aides came to work closely with the departments. He divided his staff into an Office of Policy Development and an Office of Policy Planning (OPP). The OPD focused on forging consensus and acting as an honest broker among the executive departments.[43] The OPP, under the energetic and provocative leadership of James Pinkerton, sought to push an innovative agenda, but, according to Pinkerton, received little backing because support for domestic initiatives was lacking at the top.[44] Pinkerton's arguments for a conservative "New Paradigm" fell mostly on deaf ears, and, in his words, "people got tired of hearing me sputter: 'We have to have a plan. This is my plan. If you hate my plan, fine. But what's your plan?'"[45]

For his part, Porter concentrated on a few issues, most notably the Clean Air Act, for which he was primarily responsible. Yet, Warshaw argues, Porter's personal emphasis on a handful of issues meant that "other policy issues fell by the wayside. White House staff within the Office of Policy Development became reactive rather than proactive."[46]

A later effort to regroup in the domestic policy area occurred when Clayton Yeutter, and later Dennis Ross, came to the White House to oversee it. Yeutter abolished the cabinet councils, replacing them with a single Policy Coordinating Group. Essentially, this effort was too little, too late. Perhaps the lesson of the first Bush administration is that no structure can compensate for a dearth of ideas and leadership at the top.

Clinton

Bill Clinton's formal policy development structure deviated little from that of his predecessors. The OPD remained at the core, but it was divided into three policy councils: domestic (directed by Carol Rasco), economic (Robert Rubin), and environmental (Kathleen McGinty). None of the directors reported to Chief of Staff Mack McLarty; instead they reported directly to the president. Yet in the absence of a clear presidential policy agenda, these councils were more or less left to create their own directions and strategies. The Domestic Policy Council (DPC) was formally established as a cabinet council, although in practice it "rarely met and its function was served by its own staff of approximately thirty Presidential appointees who specialized in the areas that fell under its purview: education, welfare, crime, children and families, and health care."[47]

The DPC did much of its business through "working groups," ad hoc groupings of DPC staff and personnel from relevant agencies that focused on developing and passing legislation.[48] In that sense, the arrangement resembled the task forces assembled by the Carter White House. Indeed, DPC's structure reflected a gradual trend toward greater uniformity from one administration to the next. In Warshaw's judgment, however, Clinton's DPC continued another, more problematic trend: it tended to be outshone by economic advisers in the newly created National Economic Council.[49] The task force convened under First Lady Hillary Rodham Clinton to develop a comprehensive plan for health-care reform also bypassed the DPC. Throughout 1993, journalist Elizabeth Drew reported, White House staffers complained about the "separate fiefdoms" in policy and the lack of a "domestic policy coordinator."[50] Based on her interviews and observations, Drew concluded that the DPC "foundered, in part because the economic team ran over [Rasco], in part because the health care policy was made elsewhere, and in part because [Rasco] didn't assert herself in the near chaos."[51]

Nor were these difficulties immediately altered when the White House underwent a reorganization after Leon Panetta was appointed as a much more powerful chief of staff than McLarty had been. The new chief of staff turned to fighting immediate fires. For example, he shifted two deputy domestic policy directors—William Galston and Bruce Reed—to overseeing the administration's proposals in Congress, including placing responsibility for health-care reform with Reed.[52]

After the politically disastrous 1994 midterm elections, as the administration trimmed its policy ambitions and learned to deal with a more hostile Congress, the latitude for domestic policy innovation shrank considerably.[53] Even so, domestic policy aides pursued a number of initiatives. These included deputy policy director Bruce Reed's work on welfare reform, as well as on a range of "small-bore" issues such as requiring V-chips in new televisions, promoting competency tests in public schools, and encouraging more stringent enforcement of laws for collecting child support from "deadbeat parents."[54]

Nonetheless, the domestic policy staff operation never became central in the Clinton administration. Warshaw contends that, confronting divided government and working with a "politically diverse" cabinet, the domestic policy office often failed both "to establish narrow objectives for policy development" and to fashion ways to formulate credible policy proposals.[55] The contrasting success of the National Economic Council has been well documented.[56] That the domestic and the economic policy units took different approaches to performing their tasks is not necessarily a criticism. Once again, however, Salamon's concern about the consequences of fragmented policy units in the White House appears to be relevant. Bill Clinton, a president who, by his own account, aspired to be "great," finally was consigned to a reactive role for his domestic policy and for its staff.[57]

George W. Bush

White House structuring for domestic policy changed little under George W. Bush. In most respects, the structures of the Clinton White House were retained, including the domestic and economic councils.[58] Specialized policy units such as those for drug control and for HIV/AIDS policy, also by this time a standard practice, continued, while another was created for the administration's community and faith-based initiatives.

Fragmentation persisted. Especially at the outset, the Office of Faith Based and Community Initiatives had few interactions with the Domestic Policy Council (DPC) or the rest of the White House staff. Other domestic issues were handled outside of the DPC staff. Vice President Richard Cheney, for instance, oversaw the administration's review of energy policy, and OMB general counsel Jay Lefkowitz directed its examination of stem cell policy.[59]

The Bush administration enjoyed early success despite a relatively modest domestic agenda, highlighted by the enactment of tax cuts and the No Child Left Behind education reform.[60] But the terrorist attacks of September 11, 2001, pushed domestic issues to the periphery of the policy agenda, where they tended to remain in an administration increasingly consumed by the "war on terror" and ground wars in Afghanistan and Iraq. Nonetheless, the White House sought to strengthen its domestic policy efforts, naming Lefkowitz as deputy assistant to the president for domestic policy in early 2002 and charging him to coordinate domestic policy. By the end of Bush's first term, some contended that the administration's domestic policy efforts were "prone to capture by the ideological right," and that in any event domestic policy was "dominated by [Karl] Rove and the political side of the White House."[61]

In the second term, Bush's major domestic initiative, Social Security reform, never gained political traction. This illustrates another common theme in domestic policy development: domestic issues tend to give way to national security issues (which grew in the Bush years to encompass "homeland security") or to economic crises and concerns. Even presidents who enter office principally focused on domestic policy, such as Reagan and Clinton, frequently see those aims eclipsed by events.

How Are Policy Decisions Made?

From the outside, policy choices conventionally are viewed as the outcomes of a rational process in which goals are posited, alternatives are examined, and the option that maximizes goal achievement is chosen. But as Graham Allison and others have pointed out, this rational choice model is only one, and not necessarily the best, way of looking at decision making.[62] The usefulness of such a simple characterization is limited by two factors that almost always are present in decision making.

The first of these can be roughly called "politics." Decision makers are not neutral evaluators of options. Rather, whether they are elected officials, lobbyists, senior appointees, or White House aides, they tend to be partisans who bring both their values and their understanding of how the world works to the task of making or influencing decisions. Any difficult choice entails multiple values and multiple sources of uncertainty concerning outcomes. Thus, participants have leeway about which of many goals they will emphasize as well as about how they estimate the likelihood of various possible outcomes. The result is less a rational calculus than something closer to a struggle with multiple ambiguities.[63] Decisions may reflect the views of a winning coalition, although not necessarily the first choice of any member of it. In the White House, of course, the president has the ultimate say, no matter how the opinions of advisers may array. This is the aspect of policy development of greatest interest to journalists, since conflict sells, and it is thus the part of politics that citizens best understand and frequently claim to deplore.

The second limitation is less obvious. Yet, according to Paul Light, it is the key to understanding White House policymaking.[64] Not only is there no workable formula for fully rational decision making, but there also is simply no time to try to make such decisions. If decisions are to be made at all, analytic shortcuts must be found. Among these may be cues from external political actors such as interest groups and congressional leaders, prior presidential commitments such as campaign promises, or already formulated proposals from, for example, think tanks. Faced with competing priorities, often ambiguous information, and limited time and attention, the search for alternatives will be limited, and typically will focus on finding something that is "good enough."[65] Stuart Eizenstat underscored the "very tough judgment call" involved in balancing the "right policy" with "how much the public will [accept]." In some cases, the search among options will focus on ideas that have been bandied about and advocated before, perhaps as solutions to problems other than the one at hand. This process, sometimes dubbed a "garbage can" approach to decision making, envisions such solutions being attached to problems that arise and prevailing because they are already known and already have advocates.[66]

Under time pressure, presidents also may be vulnerable to special pleadings that occur outside the usual channels of advice and decision. Thus

James Cannon cautions that presidents need protection against "oh, by the way" decisions, those in which supplicants such as cabinet members make requests in private, perhaps at the end of a meeting, for which the president is unprepared. In Egil Krogh's words, such decisions can leave the president "exposed, and he can get into a terrible amount of trouble."

The main implication of these ideas about decision processes is that, given the plurality of aims and evaluative criteria Salamon's analysis offers, one may expect that however the White House Office and the Executive Office of the President are structured for domestic decision making, policy debate will be driven as much by circumstance as by anything else. Attempts to master the political environment are worthwhile, but seem doomed to frustration. Nonetheless, policy experts and White House veterans are clear in their belief that policy structures and processes designed to encourage rationality are valuable, if not perfect. Domestic policy is, as we noted at the outset, an elusive concept, filled with uncertainties and ambiguities in its very definition as well as in political practice.

Despite these challenges, over the course of presidential administrations from Richard Nixon through George W. Bush, and now Barack Obama, there has been a gradual process of coming to consensus about the sorts of arrangements that tend to work best. This has led to a growing stability of structural design and process in administrations of both political parties. Unsurprisingly, the conventional wisdom on how to organize the domestic policy process comports well with the analysis and prescriptions advanced by Lester Salamon and largely confirmed by the experiences of White House veterans. The once-elusive conundrum of domestic policy structuring has become a relatively predictable element of the institutional presidency.

Notes

1. Charles Walcott and Karen M. Hult, "The Conundrum of Domestic Policy Organization in the White House: From Hoover to Johnson," paper presented at the Annual Meeting of the American Political Science Association, Atlanta, Georgia, September 1989, 33–34. See also Shirley Anne Warshaw, *The Domestic Presidency: Policy Making in the White House* (Boston: Allyn & Bacon, 1997), ch. 1.

2. Robert C. Wood, *Whatever Possessed the President? Academic Experts and Presidential Policy, 1960–1988* (Amherst: University of Massachusetts Press, 1993), ch. 1.

3. Ibid., 13–15.

4. Ibid, 14.

5. Unless otherwise noted, all quotations from domestic policy advisers are from the transcripts of the Miller Center symposium reported in chapters 3, 5, 7, and 9.

6. Wood, *Whatever Possessed the President?*, 17.

7. Ibid., 18. See also, for example, Joel D. Aberbach and Bert A. Rockman, *In the Web of Politics: Three Decades of the U.S. Federal Executive* (Washington, D.C.: Brookings Institution Press, 2000); Hugh Heclo, *A Government of Strangers: Executive Politics in Washington* (Washington, D.C.: Brookings Institution Press, 1977); Robert Maranto, *Politics and Bureaucracy in the Modern Presidency: Careerists and Appointees in the Reagan Administration* (Westport, Conn.: Greenwood, 1993); Robert Maranto and Karen Hult, "Right Turn?: Political Ideology in the Higher Civil Service, 1987-1994," *American Review of Public Administration*, 34 (June 2004): 199-222.

8. Such circumstances may include major disruptions such as the terrorist attacks of September 11, 2001. These, for a time at least, enhanced the participation of federal agency bureaucrats in testifying before Congress. See Peter J. May, Joshua Sapotichne, and Samuel Workman, "Widespread Policy Disruption and Interest Mobilization," *Policy Studies Journal* 37 (November 2009): 793-815.

9. Paraphrased in Wood, *Whatever Possessed the President?*, 21.

10. See, for example, Andrew Rich, *Think Tanks, Public Policy, and the Politics of Expertise* (New York: Cambridge University Press, 2005).

11. Tevi Troy, *Intellectuals and the American Presidency: Philosophers, Jesters, or Technicians?* (Lanham, Md.: Rowman & Littlefield, 2003).

12. Lester M. Salamon, "The Presidency and Domestic Policy Formulation," in *The Illusion of Presidential Government*, eds. Hugh Heclo and Lester M. Salamon (Boulder, Colo.: Westview Press, 1981), 178.

13. Richard E. Neustadt, "Presidency and Legislation: The Growth of Central Clearance," *American Political Science Review* 48 (1954): 641-647.

14. Salamon, "Presidency and Domestic Policy," 180-181.

15. Ibid., 184-185.

16. This discussion of "design issues" can be found in ibid., 186-186.

17. See, for example, Terry M. Moe, "The Politicized Presidency," in *New Directions in American Politics*, eds. John E. Chubb and Paul E. Peterson (Washington, D.C.: Brookings Institution Press, 1985).

18. See, for example, Karen M. Hult and Charles E. Walcott, *Empowering the White House: Governance under Nixon, Ford, and Carter* (Lawrence: University Press of Kansas, 2004).

19. Salamon, "Presidency and Domestic Policy," 186-188.

20. Ibid., 193. The NSC staff, of course, has long had many longer-term staffers.

21. Ibid., 192.

22. Ibid., 198-199.

23. In discussing presidencies through Clinton, we rely especially on Shirley Anne Warshaw's comprehensive descriptions in her book *The Domestic Presidency: Policy Making*

in the White House. On domestic policy staffs in the Nixon, Ford, and Carter administrations, see also Hult and Walcott, *Empowering the White House*, ch. 7.

24. Warshaw, *Domestic Presidency*, 32. Egil Krogh agrees that this arrangement worked poorly.

25. On the Ash Council, see, for example, Peri E. Arnold, *Making the Managerial Presidency: Comprehensive Reorganization Planning, 1905-1996*, 2nd ed., rev. (Lawrence: University Press of Kansas, 1998), ch. 9 and *passim*.

26. See Warshaw, *Domestic Presidency*, 26-38, for a relatively detailed account.

27. Ibid., 45.

28. Margaret Jane Wyszomirski, "The Roles of a Presidential Office for Domestic Policy: Three Models and Four Cases," in *The Presidency and Public Policy Making*, eds. George C. Edwards III, Steven A. Shull, and Norman C. Thomas (Pittsburgh: University of Pittsburgh Press, 1985), 134.

29. Margaret Spellings warns, however, that the process can become too cumbersome and "stall out" before producing desired decisions.

30. Ibid., 135.

31. Warshaw, *Domestic Presidency*, 66.

32. Richard Cheney, quoted in Warshaw, *Domestic Presidency*, 72.

33. Warshaw, *Domestic Presidency*, 64-66.

34. Quoted in Wyszomirski, "Roles of a Presidential Office," 138-139.

35. See Warshaw, *Domestic Presidency*, 99-101. The main issue was clarifying that Eizenstat's office, not cabinet secretary Jack Watson's, had primary responsibility.

36. Ibid., 107-109.

37. This sought to blend the strategies of centralization and politicization that Terry Moe introduced in "The Politicized Presidency." See also David E. Lewis, *The Politics of Presidential Appointments* (Princeton, N.J.: Princeton University Press, 2008); Lewis and Moe, "The Presidency and the Bureaucracy: The Levers of Presidential Control," in *The Presidency and the Political System*, 9th ed., ed. Michael Nelson (Washington, D.C.: CQ Press, 2010), 367-400.

38. Warshaw, *Domestic Presidency*, 124.

39. Ibid., 129-133.

40. Ibid., 137.

41. Ibid., 139.

42. Ibid., 163.

43. Ibid., 164-167.

44. Ibid., 166-167.

45. Quoted in ibid., 167-168. For another perspective on these dynamics, see Charles Korb, *White House Daze: The Unmaking of Domestic Policy in the Bush Years* (New York: The Free Press, 1994).

46. Ibid., 171.

47. *A History of the White House Domestic Policy Council 1993–2001*, prepared for the Clinton Administration History Project, Miller Center, University of Virginia., 7.

48. Warshaw, *Domestic Presidency*, 195.

49. Ibid., 198–200. Description of the National Economic Council (created in 1993) is available at http://www.whitehouse.gov/administration/eop/nec.

50. Elizabeth Drew, *On the Edge: The Clinton Presidency* (New York: Simon & Schuster, 1994), 240.

51. Ibid, p. 348. Cf. Warshaw, *Domestic Presidency*, 207ff.

52. Warshaw, *Domestic Presidency*, 207.

53. Examination of specific policy initiatives can be found, for example, in Paul J. Quirk and William Cunion, "Clinton's Domestic Policy: The Lessons of a 'New Democrat,'" in *The Clinton Legacy*, eds. Colin Campbell and Bert A. Rockman (New York: Seven Bridges Publishers of Chatham House Press, 2000); David Stoez, *Small Change: Domestic Policy under the Clinton Presidency* (White Plains, N.Y.: Longman, 1996). See also Paul Light's examination of "the derivative presidency" in *The President's Agenda: Domestic Policy Choice from Kennedy to Clinton*, 3rd ed. (Baltimore, Md.: Johns Hopkins University Press, 1999), ch. 12.

54. See, for example, George C. Edwards III, "Campaigning Is Not Governing: Bill Clinton's Rhetorical Presidency," in *Clinton Legacy*, eds. Campbell and Rockman; Stoez, *Small Change*.

55. Warshaw, *Domestic Presidency*, 210.

56. On the NEC, see, for example, Kenneth I. Juster and Simon Lazarus, *Making Economic Policy: An Assessment of the National Economic Council* (Washington, D.C.: Brookings Institution Press, 1997).

57. Cf. William W. Lammers and Michael A. Genovese, *The Presidency and Domestic Policy: Comparing Leadership Styles, FDR to Clinton* (Washington, D.C.: CQ Press, 2000), ch. 11.

58. Andrew Rudalevige, "'The Decider'": Issue Management in the Bush White House," in *The George W. Bush Legacy*, eds. Colin Campbell, Bert A. Rockman, and Andrew Rudalevige (Washington, D.C.: CQ Press, 2008), 143.

59. See, for example, Karen M. Hult, "The Bush White House in Comparative Perspective," in *The George W. Bush Presidency: An Early Assessment*, ed. Fred I. Greenstein (Baltimore, Md.: Johns Hopkins University Press, 2003).

60. The No Child Left Behind legislation was stalled in a conference committee until Senator Edward Kennedy joined forces with the administration to secure final passage in December 2001. The bill was signed into law on January 8, 2002. See Robert A. Maranto with Laura Coppeto, "The Politics behind Bush's No Child Left Behind Initiative: Ideas, Elections, and Top-Down Education Reform," in *George W. Bush: Evaluating the President at Midterm*, eds. Bryan Hilliard, Tom Lansford, and Robert P. Watson (Albany, N.Y.: SUNY Press, 2004).

61. Gary Mucciaroni and Paul J. Quirk, "Deliberations of a 'Compassionate Conservative': George W. Bush's Domestic Presidency," in *The George W. Bush Presidency:*

Appraisals and Prospects, eds. Colin Campbell and Bert A. Rockman (Washington, D.C.: CQ Press, 2004), 161, 163. That Lefkowitz reportedly also was a link to Christian conservatives is consistent with this interpretation (see, for example, Dana Milbank, "A Hard-Nosed Litigator Becomes Bush's Policy Point Man," *Washington Post*, April 30, 2002).

62. Graham T. Allison, *Essence of Decision: Explaining the Cuban Missile Crisis* (Glenview, Ill.: Scott, Foresman, 1971), especially chs. 5 and 6.

63. See, for example, Hult and Walcott, *Empowering the White House*, ch. 1, for a discussion of how organizational processes and design adapt to uncertainty and controversy over both means and ends.

64. Light, *President's Agenda*.

65. This, of course, is what Herbert Simon famously called "satisficing." See his *Administrative Behavior: A Study of Decision Making Processes in Administrative Organizations*, 4th ed. (New York: The Free Press, 1997), 118–120. For a similar application to the Clinton presidency, see Bert A. Rockman, "Cutting with the Grain: Is There a Clinton Leadership Legacy?" in *Clinton Legacy*, eds. Campbell and Rockman, 277ff.

66. Light, *President's Agenda*, 175–176. John W. Kingdon applied similar reasoning to the emergence of congressional agendas in *Agendas, Alternatives, and Public Policies*, 2nd ed. (New York: HarperCollins, 1995).

Chapter 5

Developing Domestic Policy in the White House

Featured participants in this session include James M. Cannon III (on Gerald Ford); Bertram Carp (on Jimmy Carter); Egil "Bud" Krogh (on Richard Nixon); and Roger Porter (on Gerald Ford, Ronald Reagan, and George H. W. Bush). The session is moderated by Professors Charles Walcott and Karen Hult (Virginia Tech).

Hult: The theme of this panel is developing domestic policy in the White House; that is, moving beyond the campaign and even to some extent the transition period. How is domestic policy fashioned and then moved toward enactment or in some cases implementation, once the president-elect is finally in the White House itself?

I thought we might get started by asking each of you how you came to be a domestic policy staff person, and, perhaps along with that, what you thought the job entailed when you first accepted the position as domestic policy adviser for the president.

Krogh: I could start with how I got to the White House and then became a domestic policy person. I was in John Ehrlichman's law firm in Seattle and had to stay there during the campaign while he was tour director, because I was working on his cases.[1] He said, "Elections have two outcomes: one wins, one loses. If we lose, I'd like you to have run my cases well so you get to stay in the firm." Right after the election, John came to Seattle, came to my office, and said, "Do you like your job here?" I said, "Yes, I do." He said, "Would you consider changing your job here?" I said, "Yes sir, I would." He said, "Would you consider leaving Seattle, coming to Washington, D.C. to be staff assistant to the counsel to the president?" "Yes." There was no gap between the question and my answer. I just said "yes" immediately.

Three days later I was in the transition headquarters. I came down to Washington on January 20. Our transition was in New York City at the Pierre Hotel, which is a very unusual federal facility, to be working out of the Pierre. I started working right at the start on full field investigations getting people prepared for their hearings for various committees. It was about seven months in when I started more seriously working on domestic policy. Then, when they formed the Domestic Council, I became an associate director. I was first a deputy assistant for domestic affairs. So it all took place during that first year.[2]

Cannon: Well, I began by coming down with Governor Rockefeller, who was nominated to be vice president.[3] When President Ford, a few weeks into his presidency, asked Rockefeller to be his vice president, he gave him some serious work to do. The background for that was that Ford had hated the vice presidency. He hated being vice president. He hated having to zigzag, as he put it, by defending Nixon one day and saying the next day in public that he ought to deliver the tapes to the House Judiciary Committee, and so on.[4] It was an unhappy time for Vice President Ford. He told Dick Cheney, when Dick became vice president, that it was the most unhappy period of his life.

So with that as background, he wanted Rockefeller to be his vice president and he had to promise him he would not just be a mouthpiece or go and do funerals and so on. So he made him several specific promises. He told him he would be involved in national security affairs and that he would be in charge of domestic policy. At that point Ford had not really understood yet how to run the White House. It was days into his administration and he still thought he could run it in what he called a "spokes of the wheel" arrangement, which is the way he had run his office as minority leader in the House. He did not understand, apparently, what he was promising to Rockefeller when he gave him that assignment.

It took Rockefeller four months to get confirmed.[5] It was a difficult and embarrassing and expensive job assignment for him. But in December, just before Christmas of '74, we came down, the governor and several of his staff members, including me, to get his assignments. Ford reiterated what he had promised him before, that he would be in charge of, among other things, domestic policy.

We didn't know this then, but by that time [Donald] Rumsfeld had come into the White House, and Rumsfeld was a superb organizer. He knew how to manage; he knew how to run an organization. He had organized President Ford's White House and he saw right away that this was a mistake, because there was no way a president could give up control over domestic policy; it was too great a part of his responsibility. But the promise had been made and we tried to make the best of it, and after a tussle between Rockefeller and Cheney over who should be the domestic policy adviser, the president appointed me, and that's how I came to have the job.

We had no idea what it did. We hadn't studied it. We tried to understand it. The domestic policy staff—you [nodding to Krogh] and the others were gone by that time. We couldn't ask them what they had done. So I got into the job thinking we were doing high-level policy, and that's what Vice President Rockefeller thought it was going to be.

It didn't work out that way. I got my first assignment, and I think this is a fair example of how President Ford addressed issues and policy. This issue was whether there should be a science adviser to the president.[6] Rumsfeld gave me this assignment to—"staff this out" was the expression he used. I thought, I've never done this before. I better ask President Ford what he wants in this kind of thing. So I went down to see him. He said, "Well, I want it stated in clear, crisp English what the issue is, what the background is, who stands where, what the history of it is, who stands on what side. I want to have tabs with this brief summary you're going to give me, a complete account of what everybody thinks his position is on this issue."

He said, "Now I want you to do two other things. I want you to call up every science adviser to the president thus far and ask him what he thinks he accomplished. Then I want you to have some outsider, some good science writer, tell me what he thinks each one of them accomplished."

I went through these. If you're in the White House, you can get anybody on the phone. Eisenhower's science adviser said he thought he had calmed the public to some extent after *Sputnik* went up. Jerry Wiesner said he never really got very far with Kennedy because he'd try to explain something to him and Kennedy would say, "Jerry, tell me how radio works. Tell me how it gets from over there to over here." Nixon's adviser told me, "I never got to see him after I took a stand on Vietnam. I never saw the president again." At any rate, I reported all this to the president and he said, "Let's have a meeting on this."[7]

He got everybody concerned—OMB [Office of Management and Budget] never wants to expand anything—and so we got the meeting. Everybody had his say. President Ford went around the whole table and everybody got a chance to talk. He ended by saying, "Does anyone else have an observation he wants to make?" Then he would go into the office and write out his decision.

He called me in and he said, "Now I've written this out because I learned a long time ago that if you don't write it out, people hear what they want to hear. So I'm writing this out and I'm going to say we're going to do this, but I want you to have Congress authorize this because Congress will pay a lot more attention to it if they have voted on it." Then he said, "I'm putting you in charge of getting this done." That was really my first assignment and that was a fair illustration of how President Ford addressed an issue and how we served to help him make policy.

Porter: Well, the first president that I worked for, President Ford, was the one that Jim had described. I came to this job quite by chance or good fortune. I'd been selected as a White House Fellow in the spring of 1974.[8] When the Fellows are selected they have the opportunity to express preferences as to where they would like to work. I called some people in Washington and asked them what was the furthest place that you could get from the Nixon White House and still be in the executive branch. I was told by all four of them, "The Ford vice presidential staff," because they weren't on speaking terms. Eight of us interviewed with the vice president's office and they narrowed it down to two and then two of us got an interview with Vice President Ford.

I had about half an hour with him. I of course had never met him before, but we seemed to hit it off. So on the 31st of July he called me and offered me a position on his staff. I told him I would see him bright and early the morning of September 1, which was when the fellowship year began. He said, "What I want you to work on I would like you to get started on right away. I'd like to have you come as soon as possible." I left Cambridge the morning of August the 8th and arrived at 8:30 in the morning to begin my work for Vice President Ford on August the 9th, and he was sworn in as president at noon. So I technically spent three-and-a-half hours in the Nixon administration.

And I had the good fortune of linking up with Bill Seidman, who had been his assistant for economic affairs as vice president and whom he appointed as assistant to the president for economic policy.[9] Jim [Cannon] and Bill were officed in the same suite. Those of you who worked on the second floor of the West Wing will know that suite and I was in one of the others. There are four offices there and I was in one of them, serving as the Deputy to Bill Seidman and Jim Cannon.

We spent an enormous amount of time with one another during those days. I then went back at the end of the Ford administration and began an academic career and ended up writing a book on presidential decision making that came out in the summer of 1980.[10] Somehow it got to candidate Reagan, who liked it, and so three days after the 1980 election I got called and asked if I would be willing to come work on the transition, on how they were going to organize the White House. At the end of that stint I was asked if I would stay on to coordinate economic policy in what was called the Office of Policy Development. We took the domestic council staff and what had been known as the Economic Policy Board, and put them together. That office, which was called the Office of Policy Development, I worked in for the first five years of President Reagan's term.

In that process I got to know Vice President [George H. W.] Bush well, and so when he got elected in November of 1988 he called and asked if I would come down. I said, "How are you dividing the world?" He said, "Brent Scowcroft is going to do foreign policy and I want you to do 'everything else.'" I said, "Well, I think we ought to divide it between economic and domestic as it had been previously." He said, "No, I just want to have the two of you." So I ended up in the first Bush administration, being over both economic and domestic policy. I just happened to be there at the right place at the right time.

Carp: I worked for then-Senator Mondale for seven years in the Senate and I went down to Atlanta to coordinate the policy and speechwriting side of the vice presidential campaign with the presidential campaign. Then I came back to Washington and of course my job in the Senate disappeared, and I was working for the transition. There were no signs anybody was going to hire me. Mondale had a Christmas party—that was his mistake. I went to the Christmas party, he said, "How're you doing?" I said, "Well I'm doing about as well as you can do with two little kids and no job." So he picked up the phone, he called Stu Eizenstat, and I got a job.

When we looked at how he wanted to organize the White House, we got a lot of advice from Jim Cannon and his excellent staff. Our role in the Carter administration was a product of two things. One was his campaign commitment to cabinet government, which to him meant that the cabinet officers were going to be the big guys in the administration and the White House staff were not going to be the big guys in the administration,[11] and second was the fact that he was an engineer and a naval officer, a very organized guy, who certainly enjoyed a meeting and thought that was an important part of developing policy, but who wanted to make his decisions on paper, generally speaking at one o'clock in the morning, and all by himself.[12]

We thought that the thing we needed to do was to establish a position in the paper flow; that was going to be the key to our success.[13] We were very focused on that, and we did stand between the executive branch, including the Office of Management and Budget, and the president, in terms of the paper flow. We would try to make sure that everything was right. Every single thing that was written by a cabinet officer went to the president. Every cabinet officer could call the president. The president often would read the stuff, but as you guys know, one thing a cabinet agency cannot do is to write anything short.

So we were the decision memo people. Presidents do these things differently, but because of the way he wanted to make decisions, this was a system that worked. It was a very organized system and he was a very organized guy, and therefore it worked well. I wouldn't say it is necessarily a model for anybody else, but for him this system served him pretty well.

Walcott: One of the continuing themes of domestic policy is, How do you do this organizational division, how you put things into boxes? Bud, could you tell us a little bit about how it came to pass that President Nixon created a domestic policy council?

Krogh: Well, trial and error. Maybe I should say error and trial. At the beginning we weren't quite sure who was going to do domestic policy. I remember being at a meeting with Ed Morgan, Henry Cashen, and Wilf Rommel from the Office of Management and Budget, then the Bureau of the Budget.[14] We were reviewing all the legislation that was going from the executive branch to Congress and deciding whether or not it was consistent with the president's program, no objection.

After we'd done that for about five weeks, Morgan said, "I think we're running the government here. I don't think we're quite capable of doing that. There are just three of us." We went to Ehrlichman and said, "I think we need help, sir. We're signing off on all the major budgets." He said, "Well, just keep going. Keep doing it."

So we did it for a few more months. We were rookies in a lot of things. We weren't quite sure how to staff things out. I got a call once from Virginia Knauer, who was the consumer affairs adviser,[15] and she said, "Bud, I've been asked to testify tomorrow before a House agricultural committee on the fat content of the American hotdog." I said, "That sounds good." She said, "I'd like to support it. I'd like to reduce the fat content by 2 percent, from 32 to 30."

I'm busy. I'm doing full field investigations getting people ready for their hearings, so I said, "Go ahead and testify." So she went up the next day and she testified. And the headline that came out was something like, "Major Administration Shift on Wienies." [*laughter*] The meat packers from Colorado to Iowa started calling the Department of Agriculture and the question was usually, "Who was the idiot who approved the testimony of reducing the fat from 32 to 30?" All the vectors are coming into my office.

This could have made for a very short White House career, and in retrospect that would have been a good thing. [*laughter*] But the president saw that story. I'm not sure what he was thinking, but he picked up the phone and he called Virginia Knauer. I'm going to just tell it to you the way he told it to her and the way she told me, because she called me right after. I thought I would be going home to Seattle. The president said, "Stick to your guns, Virginia. I come from humble origins. We were raised on hot dogs and hamburgers. We've got to look after the hot dog." I said, "Would you repeat that for me?" She did. I said, "That's better than 'Ask not what your country can do for you. . . .'" [*laughter*] At that point in my career this was a very good thing. I was saved by that. I asked her to call *Newsweek* and *U.S. News & World Report* and *Time* and share this wonderful story. You can Google this, by the way. You can go on and find the *Time* magazine story.[16]

My point was I really hadn't quite figured out how to staff out something like that. You know, a hot dog is not very big, 2 percent is not much, go with it. There were a lot of misfires like that that led us to wonder how could we actually organize this better. It took us about six or seven months to think through how to do it.

Now, we had Daniel Patrick Moynihan in the basement, who was running the Urban Affairs Council, and Dr. Arthur Burns, who had his staff over in the Old Executive Office Building, and they would lob memos at each other.[17] Depending on where you were, if it was an incoming memo you would read it, but we weren't able to translate that into actual policy documents, into real specific programs, legislation, budgets, people, and the rest.

Toward the end of the summer, after some of these misfires, the idea of the domestic council came up through the Ash Council.[18] That was a group that was put together and they proposed basically expanding the function of the Bureau of the Budget to make it the Office of Management and Budget and to create the Domestic Council. I think there has been a domestic council in some form or other ever since. Before that, it was mostly ad hoc and the rest, people with specific tasks reporting to the president. Once the

Domestic Council was set up, there was a much more regularized organization. We knew who would have responsibilities for what. We all had our own staffs and it worked much better.

I would say the genius behind making it successful was John Ehrlichman, who was a very good organizer. We'd have a meeting every morning when the Congress was in session, at a large table in the Roosevelt Room, and at the head would be John Ehrlichman. The other side would be the head of the Office of Management and Budget and the associate directors. We'd all sit around at 7:30—that's early, by the way, to get to work in the morning. We'd talk through the issues of the day, make sure we were tracking with each other's issues. It kept us on top of things. It worked pretty well.

Porter: One of the features of government in general, and the White House in particular, is that policy is always the product of many hands. Presidents spend very little time with individuals one-on-one and they do this for a whole variety of reasons, because they recognize that there are a wide variety of different perspectives that they want to be informed about and they don't want to find themselves the prisoner of one person or one particular idea.

So the White House in part tries to pull everything together, across an executive branch of government that is very far flung and has lots of pockets of excellence where people have valuable pieces of information to help you understand what the consequences are of moving from 32 to 30 with respect to the fat content in hot dogs.

What presidents want is really two things. They want to make informed decisions so that they don't discover three months or six months later, "My gosh, why didn't somebody tell me this? If only I had known that, I would have made a different decision." The second thing they want is the likelihood or at least a good shot at the likelihood that the decisions that they take will actually get implemented, that there is some sort of structure in place that is going to translate the decision they make into an outcome. That involves dealing with the Congress and organized interest groups, and regulatory agencies, and the public, and the press, et cetera. Producing informed decisions that get implemented roughly in the way the president intended them to be does not happen automatically.[19] It is only the product of people working closely with one another, and that's what really led to the creation of the Domestic Council and ultimately its counterparts on the economic side. In the Ford administration we called it the Economic Policy Board; in the Carter administration it was called the Economic Policy

Group.[20] "Group" was considered to be less formal than "Board." Board was Republican and—

Hult: Group is Democrat.

Porter: Then when President Reagan came in we called it the Office of Policy Development.[21] There's a real interesting reason why the term "domestic" was dropped. That was because—and I was actually there when we were figuring this out—people had woken up in the late 1970s to the fact that international economic policy was big, that people were not very enthusiastic in a nuclear age of firing weapons at one another, but there were lots of ways in which nations could compete with one another and try to exercise political leverage, and economics was a big thing.[22]

So the State Department and other elements were trying to get engaged in this. Those of us in the economic and domestic policy arena wanted to be able to claim international economic policy as not national security but economic. Therefore Ed Meese said, "Okay, let's get 'domestic' out of the title. We'll call it the Office of Policy Development. We can claim almost anything under that heading," which ultimately successfully we did.

Then we created a whole series of cabinet councils.[23] We started with five and ended up with seven. That became a little too complicated so they got collapsed at the beginning of President Reagan's second term, into the Economic Policy Council and the Domestic Policy Council. That was continued during the Bush administration. Then when President Clinton came in they kept the form the same but changed the names and got the National Economic Council and the Domestic Policy Council.[24]

So you've essentially had these two collective groupings, economic and domestic, trying to play the role of coordinating and facilitating and bringing together the expertise that is scattered all across the government and the expertise that is scattered all throughout the Executive Office of the President. You've got the Office of Management and Budget, the Council of Economic Advisers, the Office of Science and Technology Policy, and a whole host of other entities there, all of whom are full of very talented people who want to play a role, want to have input. But it is very confusing and troubling for presidents to be trying to listen to large numbers of people on essentially the same issue. They need—I like to call them honest brokers—people who are skillful and adept in pulling together all of the interested parties so that the president gets a good feel for both the substance of an issue and the politics of the issue.

Cannon: I'd like to re-emphasize what Roger has said about the president not being a captive of one person. The idea really of the Domestic Council and the Economic Policy Board and NSC [National Security Council] is that any issue, any development, any problem, any new initiative, should be subjected internally to its natural enemy so that you make sure that you know everything that is wrong with this before you go public with it. The worst thing a president can do is have somebody come in, a cabinet officer or somebody else, and have a meeting on something and as he's leaving he says, "Oh, by the way, Mr. President, I would like to do A, B or C." The president nods, or whatever he does; he doesn't say no. The next thing you know you've got a WIN Program, which was an abomination and whispered in President Ford's ear by Bob Hartmann.[25]

Krogh: Was that "Whip Inflation Now"?[26]

Cannon: Yes, Whip Inflation Now. Ford went before Congress with a huge button, WIN.

Krogh: There was only one button at the time he launched it.

Cannon: But the other, in a way more tragic, was when John Dunlop, who was secretary of labor said, "By the way Mr. President, I think I can get a deal in Congress on situs picketing."[27] I never understood exactly what that was but maybe Roger does.[28] The president didn't say no, so John went up to the Hill and working with labor people and so forth, got a deal on situs picketing. When it was about to be culminated, ten people in the White House said, "Mr. President, you can't do that. It violates everything you've ever done, said, and believed in." So President Ford had to tell John, "I can't do this now." John resigned and we lost a very good cabinet member because of this instance of, "Oh, by the way, Mr. President."

Porter: He was an excellent cabinet member and I talked to him at great length about this, both at the time and later. He believed that he had fully informed President Ford in the meeting that they had in the Oval Office of what the consequences were. Dick Cheney, who was the chief of staff and was thirty-five and relatively new in the job—this was right after the so-called "Halloween Massacre" when Ford had reshuffled his cabinet—was there and didn't pick up on it.[29]

So this excellent cabinet secretary went up on the Hill, as you described. Once the full ramifications of what was happening came to people's attention, then Ford found himself in the very difficult situation of having essentially given a green signal to a cabinet officer who thought he had explained it to him. I've talked to him at great length and he didn't feel as if he was trying to pull the wool over his eyes, or not fully inform him, but common-situs picketing is a complicated issue and I'm fairly confident Ford didn't fully understand it.

As a result of that decision, Ford became very insistent that people not meet with him one-on-one. There used to be a little game. I don't know whether this is true in the other administrations. If you have been in the cabinet room, there is a big long table that seats twenty-two people around it. The president comes from a door at that end and he sits right there. Well, what would happen is, once the meeting is over, the president physically has to get from where he is out that door. People always try to intercept him. The staff—we're sitting there, across on this side of the room, watching to see who is trying to nab the president. "I just need thirty seconds of your time. Can we do this?"

I remember one day [Earl] Butz, secretary of agriculture, wanted to change some milk price support levels.[30] Technically this is within the authority of the secretary of agriculture, at least it was at that time, but traditionally it has been cleared by the White House and approved by the president. So he asked President Ford, "Oh, by the way, we're probably going to need to raise the milk price support level this quarter because of such-and-such." Ford turned to him and said, "Has this gone through the Economic Policy Board?" Butz said no. Fifteen minutes later I got a call from Dick Cheney who was the chief of staff and he said, "By the way, Secretary Butz caught the president on the way out and wants to have the milk price support level brought up at the Economic Policy Board meeting this next week." I thought I'd have some fun so I just waited for fifteen minutes. Fifteen minutes later, Secretary Butz called and said, "Could you help me out? I'd like to get on the agenda." He never said that he had tried to skirt the system. "I'd like to get this on the agenda."

Ford had learned, partially out of this common-situs picketing experience, that you need to force it through a regularized channel so that everybody is going to have the opportunity to have their say, and in order that the president can make an informed decision. Because it is those uninformed decisions that come back to really haunt you and we've all seen what can happen when those occur.

Krogh: Roger, where were you when I needed you on the hot dog issue? You could have spared me a whole lot of embarrassment. I think you've gotten a general point here that when the president is spoken to individually there's risk, or when he sets up a unit on his own and tells them they can't talk to anybody else—"You come up with it and go forward"—there's risk. You need to have a system in place where you can bring to bear all the different points of view. You do need an honest broker, no matter how sensitive or difficult they are. Otherwise, he's out and he's exposed and he can get into a terrible amount of trouble.

Porter: There is a very fundamental, analytical reason for this, it seems to me, and that is, a large number of disputes in government and in public policy are over forecasts of what will happen in the future. If we do X, what will be the stream of consequences? What will be the costs? What will be the benefits? Proponents of a proposal and opponents of that proposal are often going to have very different ideas about how to calculate that stream of benefits and those costs. A large part of what the White House mechanisms exist to do is to get the people in the room at the same time, so that you can hammer out, "Okay, why are you estimating this to be X, and why are you estimating it to be Y?" When this isn't done well, as it wasn't done in the mid-1960s for Medicare and Medicaid, you discover that within one year the costs of those programs were five times what had been estimated. The costs within a decade were ten times what they were estimated.[31]

No president, if he had known what the stream of actual consequences was going to be on that, would have made the same decision. But they were presented with a set of "facts" or analyses on which they based their decision, which turned out to be wildly inaccurate.

Hult: Could you all talk just a little bit about how well you thought the Domestic Council and the Domestic Policy Staff and the Office of Policy Development handled those activities during the times you were in the White House, or if that was the place where that kind of brokering was done?

Carp: We pretty much followed the Ford model—at least what I understood the Ford model to have been, except we had to get rid of something, so we got rid of the cabinet council, which I gather pretty much rarely met as a group anyway. The biggest difficulty that we had—where presidents tend to get involved is where cabinet officers disagree. If two cabinet officers disagree, somebody has to referee this.

Well, all of the most urgent questions are not questions on which cabinet officers disagree. And not all issues that cabinet officers disagree on really ought to be decided by the president of the United States. He might not want to be accountable for every single one of these things. The system that we set up, we found—and we struggled with it for four years—to be too reactive. It was especially difficult to do something given the great deference that the Carter administration paid to its cabinet officers.[32] No person in the White House with the exception of the president could tell a cabinet officer to do anything.[33]

We were finally able to come up with a system in which we ranked at least legislative issues. We gave them explicit priorities and we said, "If you didn't get to this priority, we're not going to work on it. The White House legislative staff isn't going to work on it; the president won't make phone calls." We were able to use that in a way to sort of discipline the process.

But the biggest weakness in the way we had the thing set up is that you could drive it just by creating a disagreement between the secretary of labor and the secretary of HEW [Health, Education and Welfare], and the next thing you'd know we'd all be in up to our elbows and there might be something else that was going to get us into even more trouble perking away somewhere. Maybe we were so busy doing this that we weren't saying, "You know, you really need to come in and talk to the boss about that before you decide what you want to do." Our life was a struggle not to be overly reactive.[34]

Walcott: Is that a common experience?

Krogh: No. Ours was quite different because for the first year there was an effort to make cabinet government work. President Nixon became increasingly dissatisfied with that, to the point that no cabinet member could call him up.

Carp: We were the opposite of that. That's why we were the way we were.

Krogh: That's right. Maybe we should have done what you did there, Bert. But ours became primarily staff driven after a while. We had associate directors for the Domestic Council working with their counterparts in OMB and we would bring together the work groups that included the departments, included the agencies. We would prepare the documents, which was probably consistent—we tried to be honest brokers there. We also tried to intercede when we would bring the cabinet together so we wouldn't get the president nabbed before he got to the door before he went out. Sometimes the president would say, "Well, this was a staff idea." "That was me, sir. I thought you liked it before we came in."

Over the last couple of years it worked pretty effectively. We were trying to do a lot of things. The environmental programs that came out of the Nixon White House—some people are surprised to know that we did support the National Environmental Policy Act.[35] I remember Ehrlichman asking me, "Now what's this about this 'EIS,' this Environmental Impact Statement?" I said, "It's a two-page check-off, sir. It's not a big deal. You just go through the thing. You can do it in an afternoon."[36] [laughter] That was not properly staffed, I can tell you that, because ten years later he said, "I think we've created the environmental-industrial complex, and you're at fault."

For the most part we tried to staff things out. John Whitaker was our associate director for the environment and natural resources.[37] He was very thorough, very careful in the papers he put together, and in a two-year period we passed the NEPA, the National Environmental Political Act, set up the Environmental Protection Agency, the Council for Environmental Quality, clean air, clean water, endangered species, solid waste. A lot of things were done because it was extremely well staffed. Now, was Nixon a passionate proponent of environmental legislation? Probably not. But he had staff people who were able to point out to him that there was a lot of support for this, that the mood in the country was different then, starting from 1970 to '72, different than it was even in '68. He was able to respond to that. So it worked pretty well the last couple of years, I'd say the end of '71, '72 and early '73.

Porter: It didn't work perfectly.

Krogh: Not perfectly.

Porter: By evidence to the following: Richard Nixon selected John Connally as his secretary of the treasury.[38] He became enormously enamored of John Connally, who for those of you—

Cannon: Infatuated.

Krogh: I wouldn't go that far.

Porter: He liked him a lot.

Krogh: Infatuated? I don't know, Jim.[39]

Porter: But John Connally is a very engaging individual, or was a very engaging individual, who could be enormously persuasive in a meeting where you were not being driven by these tightly crafted memos that Nixon used to like to get. One of the problems is that Nixon really did not like domestic issues as much as he liked the foreign policy stuff, so he became—I interviewed John Connally for over three hours on this and it was one of the most fascinating experiences that I had. He was the one who sold Richard Nixon on imposing wage and price controls on August the 15th of 1971.[40]

When you go back and look through the records, all the other advisers were recommending against this—George Shultz, Herb Stein, Paul McCracken.[41] John Ehrlichman was one of those who was opposed to it. I remember Herb Stein telling me, "We would just be terrified every time Nixon was alone with Connally because you never knew what the two of them were going to come up with."[42] That is why you really do need a process that subjects presidents to a wide variety of opinions, so that they can have a good feel for all the ramifications of an issue as opposed to getting captured by one strong, magnetic powerful personality.

Krogh: I think President Nixon was almost trying to groom Connally for the presidency at some point. He really felt that he had command presence—

Cannon: When he called Ford and said, "I'm going to appoint you as vice president, but you should know that I'm going to support John Connally in '76," Ford said, "That's fine with me. I'm getting out anyway."[43]

Porter: I will say that Ford and Reagan and Bush 41, the ones that I know best, all understood this well and were very comfortable hearing people argue in front of them. This is an important element for a president to have. He has got to be willing to—Nixon did not like it. He did not like that at all. He wanted it all on paper like a lawyer's brief, and he could sit down and go through it. If you go in the presidential archives, some of the best memoranda come from out of the Nixon administration, because you recognize that an enormous amount of decisions were going to be done from paper.

Krogh: He graded your paper almost every day. You didn't want to flunk out.

Porter: I happen to like a system that combines carefully crafted, well-thought-out papers with meetings in which people can convey to the president—

Cannon: Which is what Ford liked to do best.

Porter: Which is what Ford loved to do.

Cannon: He really liked to do that best. I remember with swine flu, President Ford insisted that David Matthews bring in every expert on this in any way.[44] He went around the room and listened to every one of them and at the end he said, "Does anybody else have something to offer?" Nobody said anything. He said, "I'm going to be in my office for thirty minutes, and if somebody else has a contrary view, I want you to come in. Just tell the secretary you want to see me and come right on in because I want to hear it." He decided that day.

Incidentally, when you said, "What is the Domestic Council? How good were we?" In my opinion we did our best to be an honest broker, and we were also a resource for finding out things that the president wanted to ask but might have been a little bit too embarrassed to ask. In the swine flu thing we got the decision, "We're going to go ahead with this and we're going to have to have millions of vaccines and they all have to be made with fertilized eggs." One of the duties that our agriculture expert had to do was find out if there were enough roosters alive at that point to fertilize all those eggs. We made an inventory of all the roosters in the United States.

Hult: It's a very difficult job.

Krogh: Somebody's got to do it.

Hult: Let's open it up to the broader audience.

Carp: I'm interested in something. We tried to be honest brokers, but we were always perfectly clear that we were going to make recommendations and that no one was going to know what our recommendations were. That is, everyone on the White House staff knew what our recommendations were, but nobody outside the White House staff ever knew what our recommendations were. People who participated in the process knew that we would make recommendations, although we would never tell them what those recommendations would be. And people made huge efforts to come in: "I want to see how you're writing that memo. I want to see what your recommendations are."

Walcott: Within the Domestic Policy Staff, how did you decide what the recommendation would be? What was the process of determining that?

Carp: Stuart [Eizenstat] decided what the recommendation would be. He was the assistant to the president. We had our people divided up by subject matter expertise. I wanted people to come in and talk to me but I wanted good people. If they came in to talk to me I would put a little slip on it that said, "Cleared by Bert," and their memo would go over to Eizenstat. And if they didn't talk to me then the thing wouldn't be there, so Stuart's secretary would send it back and I would put a memo on there saying what I thought about it. That system worked pretty well.

Krogh: But the president knew what your position was. Would you be identified on the memo itself?

Carp: Actually, my rule was—you'll find the memos all have Stuart's name on it and the memos all have the name of the staff person who wrote the memo. Except under unusual circumstances, they would not have my name on it.

Hult: On occasions, though, your initials indicated that you had seen the memos, is that correct?

Carp: Stuart always knew whether I had seen it. But it is very important for these hard-working, good people to get appropriate credit.

Porter: This practice has varied enormously across White Houses. We had a very transparent system [in the Ford White House] because there was such dissatisfaction in the departments and agencies about not knowing what White House offices and what White House staff were saying. So we had a rule, which was that everybody gets recorded and everyone gets a copy of the final memo that went to the president.

I'll give you a little anecdote in this connection. During his first year and two months, Henry Kissinger served simultaneously as Ford's secretary of state and national security adviser. We were preparing a memo on an international economic policy issue. The State Department had voted for option two, and the NSC staff had voted for option three. I went in to my boss and I said, "Gee, this is embarrassing. Kissinger is in charge of both the State Department and the NSC. This can't be right. He looks schizophrenic."

Krogh: That's easy for Henry.

Porter: Right. I thought, I'm going to have my head handed to me in this meeting. So I called up Bob Hormats, who was working at the NSC, and I said, "Got a little problem here. We're getting ready to send this memo in and the State Department is on two and the NSC is on three. Which is it that you want?"[45] The last thing I wanted was for Kissinger to go through the ceiling in the meeting, saying, "You guys can't even put together a memo. You can't even get people who are on—." So he checked, and sure enough, Kissinger wanted the State Department to be listed on option two and the NSC on option three.

Well, we got into the meeting with the president. I had pointed this out to my boss, who pointed it out to Ford beforehand. Ford thought he would have a little fun in the meeting. He said, "Henry, I see you haven't made up your mind." Kissinger says, [using accent] "Well, Mr. President, you will note that the State Department is voting for option two and the NSC staff is voting for option three. I try to keep my people happy. Now I will tell you what the right answer is." And he would lay it out.

It was a system in which everybody got to see. Now, the White House staff got to vote last because it had already been circulated around the others. But in the end we allowed the departments and agencies to see the memo that was going to the president because it would be circulated before the meeting with the president and they could see where everyone stood.

Carp: We were weak. So the only thing we had was this little mystery over—sometimes the cabinet got over staff. I was one day sitting innocently in my office and all of a sudden I had eight Catholic bishops in my office.

Krogh: Was this a scheduled meeting or they just came in?

Carp: It was scheduled for about an hour. Somebody had decided, "You're going to meet with these bishops." Congress had passed a summer jobs program and the summer jobs program had said that on a nonsectarian basis these summer jobs should be allowed to be in the programs in the religious schools as well as in the public school system. The ACLU [American Civil Liberties Union] had challenged this ruling, and of course they had challenged this in Madison, Wisconsin. The ACLU had won.

The Justice Department had then looked this over, decided that the district court was correct, and they were not going to appeal it. They were going to apply this ruling nationwide. Of course, the Catholic bishops were saying, "We should have known better, but because the Justice Department was in there we filed an amicus brief, but we did not become parties to the case, and now we cannot appeal." Eizenstat was out of the country or something so there I was; I was in charge. So I write my little memo to the president saying, "If you run into the attorney general, you might want to raise this with him because (a) they seem like they have a semi-meritorious position; and (b) they're really mad."

This was as we were moving into the later days of the Carter administration. So he took my memo and he wrote a note on my memo and sent it to the attorney general. It is in the attorney general's book as being one of the things that's wrong with the White House management of the Justice Department.[46] But what were we going to do?

Hult: I have kind of a flow question, flowing from that, however. Did you pass it by the White House counsel's office?

Carp: All those memos got circulated.

Hult: Okay, so that was—

Carp: I was just the person who had the meeting. It was just a piece of paper—

Porter: Bert's illustration raises a question on which I would be very interested in hearing everybody else's viewpoint. The president of the United States only has twenty-four hours in a day like everyone else. He doesn't just have to deal with domestic and economic policy issues; he's got to deal with foreign policy and all sorts of other issues as well. How did you go about deciding what were the issues that needed to be brought to his attention, what information he needed to receive, and whether, as Bert pointed out, this was an issue that you needed to get resolved, even if it was just bringing two cabinet officers into your office and saying, "We're not going to leave until you've come to some sort of resolution of this because it is not worth bothering the president at this time, because there's only so much that we feel that we can pass on to him."

Walcott: Do we have examples from any of the other administrations represented here in response to that question?

Cannon: In my case, with President Ford that decision was usually made by the chief of staff. If he sent the paper down to me and said, "The president wants you to staff this out," then I staffed it out and it went back to him. That was basically not my responsibility to decide.

Sometimes it did happen. I remember some time in '75, I guess, we had a junior economist who kept coming in to see me and saying, "We've got to meet with the president on electronic transfer." I said, "What the hell is that?" I didn't have any idea what it was. He kept pestering me about it. He said, "We've got to have this meeting." I said, "What is it?" He said, "Well, a bank is going to transfer money electronically." I said, "Nonsense, they're not going to do that without somebody signing a piece of paper." But he persisted. OMB had the regulations all drafted and so forth. So we set it up and President Ford came in and listened to both sides in the argument. President Ford, who had had some experience as a lawyer in banking, served on a banking board, understood it right away. He said, "No, this will work. If it can be a double code here, I think it will work." He said, "Go ahead with it." So today you have the ATM [automated teller machine].[47]

Spellings: To Roger's question I have four answers. One is, in the first term—Roger, you talked about how there's nobody home at the departments and agencies so there you are. So the kinds of decisions that under other circumstances might have been made in the cabinet agencies—and I was glad to have been at the White House in the first part and at the cabinet the second part [*laughter*]—that's the way to do that. That's point number one.

Point number two is—this is sort of the bridge from our last discussion—things that were in the campaign that the president really knew about, cared about, asked about—big or small, those were things that he wanted to be involved in and kept apprised of. Often, as you said, Bert, the accountability being elsewhere is highly desirable. And then the final two are just general newsworthiness and congressional interest. Those were the criteria, in my experience.

I did want to raise just one quick thing. My mother always told me that not to decide is to decide. One of the things that I really observed was how those people for whom a nondecision is a decision, is a burden, is a hurdle. I can think of a particular example in higher education, actually. President Bush had said some things about it during the campaign. There were some of us in the White House who wanted him to be more aggressive on it and others who did not. Try as we might, over and over, to have processes litigated, we just sort of never got there. We had all the stuff. But what I'm trying to say is the process can stall out.

Galston: In my experience, this is going to be a judgment call time after time that is driven sometimes imponderably by the way you size up the immediate situation in which you find yourself. I'll give you an example: Bruce and I were fellow deputies at the beginning of the Clinton administration, and like the pope drawing a line down the globe, he and I got together very early on and we quite literally divvied it up. It turned out that our hemispheres fit together perfectly, because what Bruce had a passion for, I didn't know much about, and vice versa.

Anyway, the education portfolio was part of my assignment. One of the things that candidate Bill Clinton had talked about during the campaign and that I worked on during the transition was the now-famous direct lending program for student loans. This turned into an enormous brouhaha in the Congress.

Spellings: Still is.

Galston: Still is, although the good guys are finally winning—but opinions differ. I did not expect my job to be vertically integrated, so to speak, to the extent that it was. But the Clinton administration was consumed with a lot of very high-profile items during that period and the education agenda did not enjoy the prominence in that time that it did from the very beginning of the George W. Bush administration. Basically I was out there on my own, to be blunt. I found myself in vote-counting meetings, everything from high policy to low chicanery.

One night I'm sitting in my office around 9:30, and Senator Nancy Kassebaum calls me up and she proposes a compromise on the direct lending program.[48] Well, the president is up to his eyeballs in health care and the controversy over trade, et cetera. I said to myself, I cannot get this to the president. I told her I'd get back to her in half an hour. I sat there thinking for half an hour. Then I picked up the phone, I phoned her back, and on my own hook, I rejected the compromise. I then put the phone down and I said, Oh, my God, I may now be responsible for the collapse of one of the pieces of education policy that the president of the United States really cares the most about. How am I ever going to live this down if things go badly? But I thought I had to do that because there were three or four other things going on simultaneously that I knew darn well were higher on the presidential radar screen.

I suspect that everybody in a medium-to-high position in the White House ends up making a series of judgment calls on a daily basis as to what rises to the president's level and what you just have to take a deep breath and take responsibility for yourself. And you're going to get it wrong sometimes. There is no magic algorithm that draws a bright line between the rises-to-the-level and doesn't-rise-to-the-level. That's why, Bud, I was listening to you. Your headline, "White House Changes Course on Wienie" could have been worse, because the headline could have been "White House Wienie Changes Course" [*laughter*].

Porter: I would be very interested in knowing to what extent people had regular time with the president.[49] For the last many administrations, presidents have typically gotten a national security briefing early in the day. Often this is double: one time it is with the director of central intelligence, or I guess it is called the national intelligence director now; then the next one is with the national security adviser and generally the White House chief of staff. To what extent did you have regular time with the president?

Let me just start off by saying that in the first Reagan administration we had this triumvirate at the top of the White House: Meese, [James] Baker, and [Michael] Deaver would regularly go in.[50] Meese was representing the policy side of the shop, so if you wanted to get something in to the president, that was an adequate channel.

In the George H. W. Bush administration, we had about half-an-hour after the national security briefing where the White House chief of staff, myself as the assistant for economic and domestic policy, and the OMB director would go in, and the OMB director and I were responsible for the agenda. The chief of staff was there but he wouldn't present what the issues were. We found that we could get through about three to four issues in that thirty-minute period a day. So we knew that we had roughly three to four issues a day that we could take up with the president, make sure he was informed on it, get his guidance.

With a huge array of issues, you've got to figure out which three or four we take in today. Which does he really need to know about? We had a rule that we would not try to circumvent the other process by extracting a decision, but we needed to get some guidance as to what direction he wanted to move so that we didn't find ourselves in the position of creating a problem for him that later would be embarrassing both to ourselves and to him. I would be very interested to hear what other people—

Krogh: Start with Nixon because we would have that early morning meeting with everyone and then [H. R.] Haldeman and Ehrlichman, sometimes Kissinger, would meet with the president. Haldeman was there a lot, I would say maybe four or five or six hours a day. Ehrlichman had—I don't know if you had it on your phone, your POTUS [President of the United States] thing, which would light up and that would mean go down the flagpole to go see the president of the United States. I'd be in meetings with Ehrlichman, we'd be talking about stuff and he'd say, "Oh, I've got to go down the pole and meet with the president." They spent a lot of time with him. When there were issues that we felt were critical, I was able to get to Ehrlichman regularly. "Here's something that we need to decide today or this week or next week," usually on paper.

Same thing for Haldeman's staff. Kissinger had his own link there, but usually Haldeman was present. When you go back and look at the transcripts [of the secret Oval Office recordings], Haldeman was usually the person who was going to be there for both Ehrlichman's meetings and Kissinger's meetings.[51] But they were there enough so they sensed what was important to the president and they had met with us early each day. When we didn't have those meetings we'd call them up wherever they happened to be—they might be traveling with the president—to let them know what was really critical. There was a lot of face-time with the president.

For myself, in the areas that I had responsibility for, I would have face-time with him. I would go in there. One time he had his feet up on the desk. I was right behind his shoes; he just V's his shoes. It was like, Oh, my God, there he is. I got past that. It was one of those initial scary moments. You had the opportunity to talk to him enough and explain things, why it was important, because Ehrlichman couldn't always do the background work so that he was articulate. He'd bring you in for that, but he was really our route to the president for the most part.

Spellings: We had time, probably two or three times a week, and filled it up with issues. Sometimes it was a single important topic and other times it was more of a smorgasbord, not unlike what Roger talked about. As things progressed through time, it was more a combination of paper plus continued meetings. Obviously 9/11 made for less domestic policy real estate all the way around.

Krogh: Are there people who go in with President Bush and just sit down and chat and talk and go on and on?

Spellings: No, we always staffed it. The meeting was the deadline for the culmination of the paper process on major decisions. So it wasn't, "Oh just FYI, we're coming to you in two weeks with such and such." Sometimes that happened if he brought it up.

Reed: Clinton started with having standing time for foreign, economic, and domestic policy, and quickly realized that it just wasn't the most efficient way to use his time and that it was actually terrifying to the people who had to go in front of him. One of the real dangers, especially in a young White House, is making sure you have people in the room who actually know the subject that the decision is being made on.[52] We would spend much of our day trying to undo a preliminary decision that had been made with incomplete information early in the day. Clinton much preferred to see us more or less every day when he was in town, but on a particular issue that was ripe for decision, rather than just having a standing appointment where he'd sit down—

Hult: Did that continue in the second term as well?

Reed: Yes, the longer he was in office, the more he could make decisions simply with—we were often just providing additional information on paper. We'd send him a weekly report. We'd see him on a regular basis and then we'd reserve his time for the most divisive issues, where you had a deep division among the White House staff.

Spellings: Yes, I think that's generally true. The process that you use on Day One really does change—it's organic over time.

Galston: I was at the deputy level, which is of course not the same thing as being the assistant to the president for anything. But above and beyond that, I will confess to you that Bill Clinton terrified me because he almost always knew a good deal more about the subject, or at least some aspect of the subject, than you did. So I came very quickly to prefer a paper relationship with him. I deliberately did not seek out face-time because I knew that I wouldn't be so over-awed if I sat down and wrote an orderly memo that presented the facts that he needed to know and the options that he needed to consider.

It is also the case that if you're writing a memo, he can't interrupt you. He can't divert the conversation. So you can actually get a balanced range of facts, arguments, and views before him in a way that is very difficult if you're doing it on a face-to-face basis. So the relationship that I had with him, such as it was—and it wasn't nearly as intimate as Bruce's—stemmed from the fact that I knew how to write memos and Bill Clinton liked to read them.

Porter: My sense is that this changes over time, for two reasons. My sense was that nobody wanted to pretend that they were the president and that they knew more and that they were going to make decisions. But you quickly become aware of how busy he is and you become more aware of what his preferences are on particular issues. So then you ask yourself the question, "If I can't get to him but we need a decision now, what would he say?" By your second term, you [Bruce Reed] and Gene [Sperling] knew an enormous amount about what his preferences were on that, so the notion that "we're going to decide this and inform him later" is much less of a leap of faith.[53]

Reed: I think that's one of the reasons why, over time, policy development has become more and more concentrated in the White House, because the

White House aides by definition tend to know the president better, to know his preferences better. They've been with him longer. Cabinet members often have a lot of catching up to do. Margaret is a rare exception. They're important figures in their own right but they don't really know where the president's heart is, and they're guessing.

In our experience, the decisions that most had to be brought to the president's attention weren't necessarily differences among cabinet members; they were when the White House staff was divided. When the people who knew the president best weren't sure where he would be or weren't sure what the right thing for him was, or who had watched him closely and still came to the conclusion that he could go either way on this, then you knew that it was a decision that really he had to hear.

Often in Clinton's case, he preferred to be the great synthesizer. You'd come to him with Option One, Option Two, and Option Three, and he would develop an Option Four, in part by hearing everybody's point of view, looking for other opinions—looking to see who was dissatisfied in the room, trying to bring them out some. Then he would come up with some perfect synthesis that usually turned out the best policy and the best politics and also gave his advisers on the White House staff and in the cabinet a chance to walk away feeling like they'd added something. They could save face even if they didn't totally win the argument.

Galston: Here's the problem. And I think in this conversation I'm gradually revealing how often I got it wrong. One of the judgments that you have to make is where the president would like to go. The question is, how far can you get down that road to what the president would really like to have happen, and if you can't get all the way down the road, is this good enough? Right? And not only is that good enough in principle and in practice, but will that be good enough for the president? In the nature of things, in the legislative process, you can't take all of those judgments to the Oval Office, either in person or on paper.

I'll give you an example. Somehow the issue of whether adoption ought to be carried out on a race-neutral basis fell onto my plate. There were all sorts of arguments involving HHS [Health and Human Services], the Justice Department, other interested parties, and it was clear to me that the president cared a lot about this issue. He cared a lot about it in part because a columnist who then had a regular *Wall Street Journal* column, namely Al Hunt, was passionate on the subject, having made several trans-racial adoptions himself, and he was outraged that race should be a factor in the adoption process.

I worked with Congress and there were a lot of interest groups that felt equally passionately on the other side. We moved the ball substantially down the field, but we didn't get all the way. I finally said, "Okay, this is good enough."[54] Then the administration's position surfaced. Al Hunt wrote a column denouncing the White House wienie for having wimped out, or words to that effect.

Krogh: There is no White House wienie.

Galston: I happened to find myself in the Oval Office on another matter that same day, by bad luck, and the president went ballistic. I tried to tell him, "Mr. President, there has been a lot of heavy lifting. This was the best we could do. It was this or nothing." He was having none of it. He was convinced that this "bad outcome" had occurred because I didn't care about this issue as much as he cared about this issue. In fact, my position was identical to his and at least as passionately espoused, but I had been working the issue for six weeks and I knew that that was the best we could do. But he would not believe it. Those are the sorts of judgments that get made all the time and I got a lot of them wrong.

Reed: Can I just interrupt? You were right more often than not. I would say that one of the reasons—it goes to the nature of the role of domestic policy adviser. We always describe it as an honest broker, but it isn't exactly that, because it isn't as though the job is to weigh the views of each respective cabinet department and put them all on the table and say to the president, "Well, there's five for Option Two and six for Option Three." It really is an attempt to make sure that, to the extent possible, the option the president wants considered is on the table. It is to force the government to deal with what the *president* wants to do, rather than force the president to deal with what the government wants to do.

Porter: But that is if the president knows what he wants to do, and on some issues he doesn't have a very clearly formed view. So he wants to know what everyone wants. But then he will turn to you and say, "What do you think?"

Krogh: Sometimes you almost have to protect the president from a cabinet member. Just a quick story. Just before the election in 1972, a very large number of Indians took over the Bureau of Indian Affairs, the "Caravan of Broken Treaties."[55] They proceeded to just settle in. I was called Friday night by Walter Washington, the mayor. "Bud, I see this and it's ready to blow. This is very dangerous. There's a recommendation here that we go in and pull them out by force. What would you do?"

John Dean was then counsel to the president, I was moving on to Transportation, and I said, "Gosh, I can't counsel you on this, Walter." Now it's a personal appeal: "Bud, you're my friend. What would you do?" I knew that the president had a very progressive Native American policy. He believed in it. He'd given a lot of land back. He was a deep believer in that policy.[56] I thought about it and said, "What are the risks if we do pull them out?" He said, "I think there will be bloodshed. I think they want to be martyred."

I said, "Well, you know, Walter, I can just give you a personal opinion. I'd send the police over." I got a call about fifteen minutes later from John, saying, "What's going on here? We were ready to move on the building and pull these folks out. This is now your problem to solve." I moved back down to the White House—this is Friday night, four days before the election—and proceeded to try and figure out how serious this problem is. It turned out to be extremely serious. This is when heroes and heroines arise. Bobbie Kilberg on the White House staff was able to get into the Bureau of Indian Affairs and find out that not only had the building been trashed, but they were welcoming an attack.[57]

The attorney general had gone to the district court and gotten an order to cease and desist their state of trespass, and set a deadline of six o'clock on Monday, the day before the election.[58] If they didn't come out, "We're going to go in and pull you out and we will gas you out." I went to a meeting in the Justice Department presided over by the attorney general [Richard Kleindienst] and they were talking about vertical envelopment. I said, "What's that term?" "It's from Vietnam. We land on the roof and we will gas them out through the building." I said, "That sounds a little scary to me." But that was the operative plan. Now they basically didn't use helicopters but they brought in enough marshals, they had enough metropolitan police, they were physically going to pull people out of the building.

I went back to the White House staff, to my staff: Bobbie Kilberg, Walter Minnick, Dick Nordahl, Len Garment.[59] I said, "What do you think we should do?" They said, "Well, the attorney general has gotten a court order.

He has gotten approval to go forward with this from San Clemente." San Clemente was where the president was waiting to fly back the next day after the election.[60] So you have a choice to make. If we actually attack that building, what is the likelihood of violence? It is very high. What's the likelihood that they'll burn the building? It's very high.

So we have a law enforcement imperative going forward, driven by the attorney general. I had worked with the president for four years. He knew exactly how I felt about demonstrations. We do the maximum not to have any provocation or to make things worse. So it came down to making a call to San Clemente. I talked to Ehrlichman, who was with him, with Haldeman. We were ahead in forty-nine states and we didn't want to win Massachusetts. [laughter]

Carp: I'd like to make a point here, though.

Krogh: Bert, let me just finish the story. So here's what happened: I told him, "You're going to come back tomorrow after a great victory and you're going to see an orange glow on the horizon. That's the Bureau of Indian Affairs on fire. Here are the headlines: 'So Many Indians Slain,' 'So Many Policemen Slain,' and the third one will be, 'Nixon Wins in a Landslide.'" So he went to see the president, who called me back. Ehrlichman called me back. He said, "The president agrees with you. Shut it down, no violence."

We had to move everybody away from the building. That was a discussion I had with the attorney general that was spirited. He said, "I hope you know what you're doing." I said, "I have no idea what I'm doing, General, but I know what we're not going to do. We're not going to attack right now." I felt that my job then was to be the steward of the president's policies. He had worked four years to try to establish good relationships. Secondly, the risks were too high. Human life was too important. It turned out that another genius, Frank Carlucci, came forward and he said, "They're destitute over there. Why don't we give them some money?"[61] We basically got $66,650 and we gave them money to go back to the reservations. They were all gone by Wednesday.

The building was trashed, that's true. We fixed the building. But the point was, on the domestic policy staff where I was, my job I thought was to protect the president's interests at all costs. Dick Kleindienst and I didn't talk for a while but we got over it after a couple of months.

Hult: Bert?

Carp: I was just going to say that these pendulums go back and forth between the cabinet and the White House in terms of where policy is going to be developed. I certainly worked in a White House that represented an extreme. But I think that things are lost when you move too far away from that. For one thing, the great ideas we dream up all have to be implemented by GS-12s and GS-13s and GS-16s, and these White House–driven policy development efforts are not always as friendly to those people as they ought to be.[62] Even if they don't have any good ideas, in the end we're going to move on and they're going to be there.

I do believe that the White House needs to be a place where you're not personally accountable to Congress. You can't be called up there to testify.[63] But the bigger and the more all-encompassing and the larger bureaucracy it becomes, then the harder it is to defend those protections, in terms of the accountability and the transparency that we all agree with. I've noticed in this current administration some czars are in jobs where they have to be confirmed by Congress; some czars are not.[64] I don't know. Everybody ought to work this out the way that it works out best for them. But the model that says that a cabinet are simply implementers and that policies all can be made over here has serious disadvantages to it, which need to be taken into account, and which academics need to look at.

Notes

1. John D. Ehrlichman (1925–1999) came to Richard Nixon through H. R. Haldeman, assisting with Nixon's 1960 presidential campaign and his failed 1962 attempt for the governorship of California. Ehrlichman became counsel to Nixon and then his domestic policy adviser. He served time in federal prison for his role in Watergate and the related break-in to the offices of Daniel Ellsberg's psychiatrist. See David Stout, "John D. Ehrlichman, Nixon Aide Jailed for Watergate Dies," *New York Times*, February 16, 1999, http://www.nytimes.com/1999/02/16/us/john-d-ehrlichman-nixon-aide-jailed-for -watergate-dies-at-73.html (accessed October 22, 2010). Ehrlichman's own account of his time with Nixon is *Witness to Power: The Nixon Years* (New York: Simon & Schuster, 1982).

2. On March 12, 1970, President Nixon signed Reorganization Plan 2, which established the Domestic Council to serve as the "domestic counterpart to the National Security Council." Quoted in Stephen Hess, *Organizing the Presidency* (Washington, D.C.: Brookings Institution Press, 1976), 131.

3. Nelson A. Rockefeller (1908-1979) was a leading liberal in the Republican Party, who served as governor of New York from 1959 to 1973. The following year he became vice president (1974-1977), a position that had opened when Gerald Ford rose to the presidency upon Richard Nixon's August 1974 resignation. Rockefeller was not, however, Ford's running mate in 1976.

4. During the period of congressional investigations into the Watergate scandal, it became known that the White House had been keeping comprehensive audio recordings of President Nixon's meetings. The contents of those recordings became the focus of an intensive legal and political battle between Nixon and his critics. The Supreme Court ultimately ruled, in *U.S. v. Nixon*, that the president could not keep secret these audio records. See Stanley Kutler, *The Wars of Watergate: The Last Crisis of Richard Nixon* (New York: W.W. Norton, 1990), ch. 19.

5. Rockefeller assumed the vice presidency on December 19, 1974.

6. Presidents had used science advisers since at least the time of Franklin D. Roosevelt, who consulted with Vannevar Bush on the development of the atomic bomb. Ford's question to Cannon was whether this arrangement should be further institutionalized. Subsequently it was. On May 11, 1976, Congress established, within the Executive Office of the President, the Office of Science and Technology Policy, the head of which would be the president's official science adviser. For more history on this, including an intimate account of the relationship between the science adviser and the president, see D. Allan Bromley, *The President's Scientists: Reminiscences of a White House Science Advisor* (New Haven, Conn.: Yale, 1994). Bromley served with President George H. W. Bush.

7. Eisenhower had four science advisers: Lee A. DuBridge, Isadore A. Rabi, James Killian, and George Kistiakowsky. Given the timing of the *Sputnik* launch (October 4, 1957), Cannon's source was probably Killian. Jerome Wiesner (1915-1994) served Kennedy and then Johnson, from 1961 to 1964. Nixon brought back DuBridge, and then replaced him in 1970 with Edward E. David, Jr.

8. The White House Fellows program was created in the Johnson administration to provide promising young professionals an opportunity to spend a year working closely with high-ranking government officials in the executive branch. It is a nonpartisan way for rising leaders to get experience in the upper reaches of Washington officialdom.

9. L. William Seidman (1921-2009) was an American lawyer and economist. He later rose to public prominence during the savings and loan crisis of the late 1980s, both as director of the Federal Deposit Insurance Corporation and head of the Resolution Trust Corporation, which was charged with cleaning up the debris from that industry's collapse.

10. That book is Porter's *Presidential Decision Making: The Economic Policy Board* (New York: Cambridge University Press, 1980).

11. On Carter and cabinet government, see Scott A. Frisch and Sean Q. Kelly, *Jimmy Carter and the Water Wars: Presidential Influence and the Politics of Pork* (Amherst, N.Y.: Cambria Press, 2008), 49-59; Charles O. Jones, *The Trusteeship Presidency: Jimmy Carter*

and the United States Congress (Baton Rouge: Louisiana State University Press, 1988), 101–103. For contemporaneous criticism of Carter for this preference, see "Nation: Curbing Cabinet Government," Time, May 15, 1978, at http://www.time.com/time/magazine/article/0,9171,948104,00.html (accessed October 22, 2010); and James Fallows, "The Passionless Presidency: The Trouble with Jimmy Carter's Administration," Atlantic Monthly, May 1979, 33–48.

12. Douglas Brinkley asserts, "If one had to sum up Carter's leadership style in a phrase, it would be 'hands-on engineering.' Among Carter's greatest flaws as president—and one the Republicans exploited without mercy—was his excessive micromanagerial style. For better or worse, Carter was a control freak who wanted to know exactly what was happening around him at all times." See Brinkley's The Unfinished Presidency: Jimmy Carter's Journey beyond the White House (New York: Penguin, 1998), 15–16. A more nuanced assessment appears in Erwin Hargrove, Jimmy Carter as President: Leadership and the Politics of the Public Good (Baton Rouge: Louisiana State University Press, 1988), 23–32.

13. Carter affirms in his memoir that he "preferred to receive questions and advice in writing." Jimmy Carter, Keeping Faith: Memoirs of a President (Fayetteville: University of Arkansas Press, 1995), 59.

14. Edward L. Morgan (1938–1999) was an attorney who served on the White House staff as a deputy to John Ehrlichman and then became assistant secretary of the treasury. He resigned from the latter post in 1974 and was convicted of felony charges associated with trying to generate a fraudulent tax deduction for President Nixon. Henry C. Cashen II was deputy counsel to the president (1969–1970), deputy assistant to the president for domestic affairs (1971–1973), and subsequently a prominent Washington lawyer. Wilfred H. Rommel was assistant director for legislative reference in the Bureau of the Budget.

15. Virginia Harrington Knauer, the first woman elected to the Philadelphia city council, was sworn in as special assistant to the president for consumer affairs on April 19, 1969. She held the same post under Presidents Ford and Reagan.

16. Contemporaneous accounts, confirming exactly the Nixon quote, do appear, both in Time (July 27, 1969), http://www.time.com/time/magazine/article/0,9171,900915,00.html, and in Life (October 3, 1969, p. 24), http://books.google.com/books?id=CFEEAAAAMBAJ&pg=PA24&lpg=PA24&dq=Virginia+Knauer+1969+hot+dog&source=bl&ots=j2_C7x70qR&sig=67Up1YJcZhPE0RN-RIcgHdJ2GU0&hl=en&ei=_ZTFTKyTAYt8AbYgrTYBg&sa=X&oi=book_result&ct=result&resnum=1&sqi=2&ved=0CBMQ6AEwAA#v=onepage&q&f=false (both accessed October 25, 2010).

17. Daniel Patrick Moynihan (1927–2003), formerly director of the Joint Center for Urban Studies at Harvard and MIT, was counselor to the president for urban affairs in the Nixon White House. He later had a distinguished diplomatic career, including service as U.S. ambassador to the United Nations during the Ford presidency, and was elected as a Democrat to the U.S. Senate from the state of New York, serving from 1977 to 2001. Arthur F. Burns (1904–1987) was an economist whose most prominent public service came as chair of the Federal Reserve Board (1970–1978). Before this appointment, he

served in the Nixon White House as counselor and as a member of the cabinet committee on economic policy.

18. The Ash Council, so called after its chair, industrialist Roy Ash, was formally
the president's Advisory Council on Executive Organization—designated by Nixon after
his 1968 election. Its broad-ranging final report was issued on January 31, 1971. David
M. Abshire has written that, as a result of the council's work, "Nixon sent to Congress
the most comprehensive structural reorganization of domestic agencies ever proposed
by any President. By proposing to consolidate seven departments and several independent agencies into four departments, the President courageously challenged many of the
most powerful special interest groups and Congressional committees. As a result of the
extensive lobbying work on Capitol Hill, major portions of the reorganization seemed to
be nearing congressional approval when the 1972 election and Watergate brought this
impressive initiative to a halt." *Triumphs and Tragedies of the Modern Presidency: Seventy-six
Case Studies in Presidential Leadership* (Westport, Conn.: Praeger, 2001). For another inside
account of the effect of the Ash Council's work, see Dwight Ink, "Nixon's Version of
Reinventing Government," *Presidential Studies Quarterly* 26, no. 1 (Winter 1996): 57–69.

19. This observation was at the core of Richard E. Neustadt's conception of the
presidency and his assertion that "presidential power is the power to persuade." Neustadt
claimed that there are few meaningful instances in the exercise of presidential power
when the president can command that something be done and know that it will happen.
Even implementation most typically involves the power of persuasion. One of Neustadt's
more colorful anecdotes illumines the point, with President Truman predicting an unhappy life for President Eisenhower: "He'll sit here [in the Oval Office] and he'll say, 'Do
this! Do that!' *And nothing will happen.* Poor Ike—it won't be a bit like the Army. He'll find
it very frustrating." *Presidential Power and the Modern Presidents: The Politics of Leadership
from Roosevelt to Reagan* (New York: Free Press, 1990), 10.

20. Porter's own *Presidential Decision Making* details the work of the Ford Economic
Policy Board. For a discussion of Carter's economic policymaking process, see W. Carl
Biven, *Jimmy Carter's Economy: Policy in an Age of Limits* (Chapel Hill: University of North
Carolina Press, 2001), ch. 3. On the broader institutional evolution Porter discusses here,
see Chris J. Dolan, John P. Frendreis, and Raymond Tatolovich, *The Presidency and Eco-
nomic Policy* (Lanham, Md.: Rowman & Littlefield, 2008), ch. 3.

21. For an additional inside account of domestic policymaking in the Reagan White
House, see Martin Anderson Interview, Miller Center, University of Virginia, Ronald
Reagan Presidential Oral History Project, December 11–12, 2001.

22. On the formation of the office, see Chester A. Newland, "Executive Office Policy
Apparatus: Enforcing the Reagan Agenda," in *The Reagan Presidency and the Governing of
America*, eds. Lester M. Salamon and Michael S. Lund (Washington, D.C.: The Urban
Institute, 1984), 135–168.

23. On the emergence and use of cabinet councils, see Ed Meese, *With Reagan: The
Inside Story* (Lanham, Md.: Regnery, 1992), 75–78; Shirley Anne Warshaw, "White House

Control of Domestic Policymaking: The Reagan Years," *Public Administration Review* 55, no. 3 (May-June 1995): 247-253.

24. There is still a surprisingly meager literature on the emergence and development of the National Economic Council. See Dolan, Frendreis, and Tatalovich, *Presidency and Economic Policy*, 88-93; Kenneth I. Juster and Simon Lazarus, *Making Economic Policy: An Assessment of the National Economic Council* (Washington, D.C.: Brookings Institution Press, 1996).

25. Robert T. Hartmann (1917-2008) was a longtime aide to Rep. Gerald Ford who became the president's counselor after Ford moved into the Oval Office in 1974. He is credited with having written Ford's most famous words, upon Nixon's resignation: "My fellow Americans, our long national nightmare is over." Hartmann also served as something of an enforcer for the mild-mannered Ford, once chiding his boss, "You don't suspect ill motives of anyone until you're kicked in the balls three times. As a human being, that's a virtue. As a president, it's a weakness." Reported in Robert Schlesinger, *White House Ghosts: Presidents and Their Speechwriters from FDR to George W. Bush* (New York: Simon & Schuster, 2008), 233.

26. For a brief account of the WIN episode, see Yanek Mieczkowski, *Gerald Ford and the Challenges of the 1970s* (Lexington: University Press of Kentucky), 132-144.

27. John T. Dunlop (1914-2003), a labor economist and former dean of Harvard's faculty of arts and sciences, served as secretary of labor in 1975 and 1976.

28. Common situs picketing is an expansion of labor rights, allowing unions to use a dispute with a single subcontractor as justification for protest action by all laborers at that site.

29. The so-called "Halloween Massacre" was a major reshuffling of the cabinet and White House staff by President Ford in late October 1975—occasioned by falling poll numbers and bitter in-fighting among some senior executive officials. The changes included the termination of Henry Kissinger as national security adviser (he kept his post as secretary of state), the replacement of defense secretary James Schlesinger with White House Chief of Staff Donald Rumsfeld, and the elevation to chief of staff of Rumsfeld's deputy, Richard Cheney. For a brief description, see Walter Isaacson, *Kissinger: A Biography* (New York: Simon & Schuster, 1992), 669-671.

30. Earl L. Butz (1909-2008) was dean of the college of agriculture at Purdue University from 1957 to 1967 and then served as secretary of agriculture for Presidents Nixon and Ford. He resigned in October 1974, because of a joke he told revealing his racial insensitivity, affinity for blue humor, and unchecked tongue.

31. On these initial cost projections, see H. J. Aaron and R. D. Reischauer, "The Medicare Reform Debate: What Is the Next Step?" *Health Affairs* 14, no. 4 (November 1995): 8-30; Richard L. Kaplan, "Taking Medicare Seriously," *University of Illinois Law Review* 1998, no. 3: 777-799.

32. James P. Pfiffner has remarked on this point: "Presidents must also set early ground rules for the role that cabinet members will play in the administration and the

appropriate relationship between the White House staff and the cabinet. It must be clear what is and is not delegated before cabinet secretaries get established in their departments. If this is not done it will be very difficult to call presumed delegations back in." He reports that Nixon and Carter both lived to regret the extent to which their cabinets frustrated their presidencies. "White House Staff versus the Cabinet: Centripetal and Centrifugal Roles," *Presidential Studies Quarterly* (Fall 1986): 666–690.

33. This problem is magnified by the fact that, in the words of Calvin Coolidge's vice president, Charles Dawes, "The members of the cabinet are a president's natural enemies." Quoted in Neustadt, *Presidential Power and the Modern Presidents*, 34.

34. Carter is not alone in having to referee disputes among cabinet members. Bill Clinton's congressional liaison, Lawrence Stein, has reported on another example "that drives me crazy to this day, and that's the needle exchange program. We had Barry McCaffrey [the drug control director], who was violently opposed to any kind of liberalization of needle exchange, and we had Donna Shalala [HHS secretary], who had a body of medical evidence demonstrating that it was the right thing to do. All of our political judgment—and the political judgment of anyone you could drag in off the street—would be, *stay away from that issue!* Well, guess what. The president wasn't allowed to stay away from that issue, partly because his people, who *are* his people, named by him, couldn't bring themselves to stay away from the issue." Quoted in Russell L. Riley, ed., *Bridging the Constitutional Divide: Inside the White House Office of Legislative Affairs* (College Station: Texas A&M University Press, 2010), 33.

35. See J. Brooks Flippen, *Nixon and the Environment* (Albuquerque: University of New Mexico Press, 2000).

36. See H. Paul Friesema and Paul J. Culhane, "Social Impacts, Politics, and the Environmental Impact Statement," *Natural Resources Journal* 16 (April 1976): 339–356.

37. John C. Whitaker was President Nixon's first cabinet secretary and then became deputy assistant for domestic affairs in November 1969. He later was named undersecretary of the interior, serving under Rogers C. B. Morton. Whitaker has an extensive record of insightful commentary on his experiences dealing with environmental and natural resource issues for Nixon, including the John C. Whitaker Exit Interview, May 4, 1973, Nixon Presidential Materials Staff, National Archives and Records Administration, at http://www.nixonlibrary.gov/virtuallibrary/documents/exitinterviews/whitaker.php (accessed October 26, 2010); and John C. Whitaker, "Nixon's Domestic Policy: Both Liberal and Bold in Retrospect," *Presidential Studies Quarterly* (Winter 1996): 131–153.

38. John B. Connally (1917–1993), a conservative Democrat, served three terms as governor of Texas before joining the Nixon cabinet as treasury secretary in 1971–1972. Although his career was closely entwined with Democratic Party presidential politics—he had been a member of Lyndon B. Johnson's inner circle and was in the president's car and was injured when John F. Kennedy was assassinated—he switched parties and sought, unsuccessfully, the Republican presidential nomination in 1980, famously spending $11 million to secure one convention delegate.

39. The exact extent to which Nixon was either "infatuated with" or "enamored of" John Connally emerges in the pages of H. R. Haldeman's private diaries. For example, in January 1972, Haldeman reported on a troubling conversation he had that day with OMB director George Shultz, who observed that the White House was now Connally's domain. "Looking at it realistically," Haldeman wrote, "we're moving to a position of Connally functioning as Deputy President for International Economic Affairs, [and] he is already Deputy President for Domestic Economic Affairs. Still he is also the Secretary of the Treasury, with vast responsibilities which he is not carrying out, and he's the Chairman of the Cost of Living Council." Nixon's great fear, however, was that Connally was preparing to leave to return to Texas. In April, Haldeman recorded a further conversation with Nixon, in which he speculated about the possibility of joining with Connally after the 1972 election to form a new party, and thus "make a truly historic change in the entire American political structure." *The Haldeman Diaries: Inside the Nixon White House* (New York: G. P. Putnam's Sons, 1994), 399, 444.

40. On this episode, see Daniel Yergin and Joseph Stanislaw, *The Commanding Heights: The Battle between Government and the Marketplace That Is Remaking the Modern World* (New York: Simon & Schuster, 1997), 60–64.

41. All three are economists. George P. Shultz was at this time director of the Office of Management and Budget, but had previously served in the Nixon administration as secretary of labor. He later was Nixon's treasury secretary, and from 1982 to 1989 was Ronald Reagan's secretary of state. Herbert Stein (1916–1999) was on the Council of Economic Advisers, later to chair that body. Paul McCracken was serving as chair of the CEA in 1971.

42. Yergin and Stanislaw claim that Connally had no fixed economic principles, quoting him as saying, "I can play it round or I can play it flat. Just tell me how to play it." *Commanding Heights*, 63.

43. Nixon has affirmed that his first choice to succeed Spiro Agnew as vice president was Connally. See Richard Nixon, *RN: The Memoirs of Richard Nixon* (New York: Grossett & Dunlap, 1978), 925.

44. The threat of a swine flu epidemic emerged early in 1976, prompting a major government effort to inoculate the American population against it quickly. Controversy emerged from this effort, partly because of the adverse physical reactions some had to the vaccine. See Richard E. Neustadt and Harvey V. Fineberg, *The Swine Flu Affair: Decision-making on a Slippery Disease* (Washington: U.S. Government Printing Office, 1978), available in full text online at http://books.nap.edu/openbook.php?record_id=12660&page=R1. F. David Mathews was, from 1975 to 1977, Ford's secretary of health, education, and welfare. He formerly served as president of the University of Alabama.

45. Robert D. Hormats served on the National Security Council staff, handling international economic affairs, from 1969 to 1977, including time under Kissinger, Brent Scowcroft, and Zbigniew Brzezinski. He later held several senior presidential appointments in the State Department and the office of the U.S. Trade Representative.

46. Carp's reference is to the account of this episode in Griffin B. Bell and Ronald J. Ostrow, *Taking Care of the Law* (Macon, Ga.: Mercer University Press, 1982), 24–28.

47. The Web site of the Gerald R. Ford Presidential Foundation affirms this claim: http://geraldrfordfoundation.org/gerald-r-ford-biography (accessed October 26, 2010).

48. Nancy Landon Kassebaum represented Kansas in the U.S. Senate from 1978 to 1997. She is the daughter of former Republican presidential nominee Alf Landon. During her final year in the Senate, she was married to former Tennessee Senator Howard Baker.

49. For those interested in the allocation of presidential time, and in who gets an audience with the president, the Presidential Daily Diary is an indispensable source. It is a conscientious effort by National Archives personnel, situated in the White House, to keep a minute-by-minute record of the president's activities. Many are now available online. Jimmy Carter's can be found at http://www.jimmycarterlibrary.gov/documents/diary/1979/ and George H. W. Bush's at http://millercenter.org/scripps/archive/documents/ghb/diary (both accessed October 26, 2010). For example, the Bush diary for Friday, July 7, 1989, indicates that, among other things, he had breakfast at 6 a.m. with Mrs. Bush, spoke by telephone with his son George W. Bush from 7:52 to 7:54, had a national security briefing with General Scowcroft and his deputy Robert Gates (along with chief of staff John Sununu and an unnamed CIA briefer) from 8 to 8:14, participated in a swearing-in ceremony for the new NASA director from 11:15 to 11:23, met with the new Miss National Teenager and her escorts from 11:35 to 11:37, hosted a lunch for unnamed baseball stars from 12:09 to 1:07, discussed the budget with Roger Porter, the vice president, and others, from 1:16 to 1:57, met again with Scowcroft and Gates from 2:33 to 2:45, and retired that evening at 9 p.m. The full schedule is available online.

50. James A. Baker III, a Texan, had been George H. W. Bush's campaign manager in 1980 when he unsuccessfully contested the Republican nomination with Ronald Reagan. But after his election, Reagan designated Baker to be White House chief of staff, serving with Meese and Deaver in what became known as the "Troika." In Reagan's second term, Baker became secretary of the treasury, and then was secretary of state under the first President Bush. Michael Deaver (1938–2007) was deputy chief of staff and the keeper of the Reagan image—as well as Nancy Reagan's unofficial eyes and ears within the West Wing.

51. For access to transcripts and audio of the Nixon recordings that have been processed and released by the National Archives, see the Web site of the Presidential Recordings Program at the Miller Center of Public Affairs, University of Virginia, at http:// whitehousetapes.net/tapes/nixon/chron (accessed October 26, 2010).

52. In the Clinton White House, a corollary problem in the early days was the tendency for meetings to be opened to just about any staff member who cared to attend—contributing to a lack of focus in the decision-making process. Budget director Leon Panetta, who was soon called on to rectify the problem, evidently told President Clinton in mid-1994 that "I don't think there's enough discipline. I think there aren't clear

lines of supervision. You've got too many free-floating people who are general counsels." Quoted in Nigel Hamilton, *Bill Clinton: Mastering the Presidency* (New York: PublicAffairs, 2007), 292. See also the description in John F. Harris, *The Survivor: Bill Clinton in the White House* (New York: Random House, 2005), 55–63.

53. Gene B. Sperling, a lawyer by training, was one of Bill Clinton's closest aides for domestic policy and economics during the 1992 campaign. He initially took a position working under Robert Rubin at the National Economic Council in Clinton's first term, and came to direct that body from 1996 to 2000. He later was a senior adviser in the treasury department and then director of the National Economic Council during the Obama presidency.

54. The resulting legislation was the Howard Metzenbaum Multiethnic Placement Act, signed into law by President Clinton on October 20, 1994. For details on the issue and policy, see Ezra E. H. Griffith and Rachel L. Bergeron, "Cultural Stereotypes Die Hard: The Case of Transracial Adoption," *Journal of the American Academy of Psychiatry and the Law* 34, no. 3 (2006): 303–314. This act outlawed the use of race as the sole factor in denying multiethnic adoption, but said that adoption agencies could take race into consideration as one factor in the process.

55. The Trail of Broken Treaties Caravan was organized by several Indian rights organizations, most prominently the American Indian Movement (AIM), to focus national attention on the plight of Native Americans. In the process of crossing by caravan from the West Coast, the Indians constructed a twenty-point position paper detailing their grievances against the U.S. government. One sympathetic account of this event is Vine Deloria, Jr., *Behind the Trail of Broken Treaties: An Indian Declaration of Independence* (Austin: University of Texas Press, 1974).

56. See, for example, Nixon's "Special Message [to Congress] on Indian Affairs, July 8, 1970," which began: "The first Americans—the Indians—are the most deprived and most isolated minority group in our nation. On virtually every scale of measurement—employment, income, education, health—the condition of the Indian people ranks at the bottom. This condition is the heritage of centuries of injustice." Text available (in abbreviated form) at http://www.epa.gov/tribal/pdf/president-nixon70.pdf (accessed October 26, 2010).

57. At the time Barbara G. Kilberg, a graduate of Yale Law School, was evidently a White House Fellow assigned to the Domestic Policy Council. She later served as the director of public liaison, and then head of intergovernmental affairs, for President George H. W. Bush.

58. The attorney general at this time was Richard Kleindienst (1972–1973), because John Mitchell had left earlier in the year to take over the Committee to Re-Elect the President (CREEP).

59. Walter C. Minnick is a Harvard-trained lawyer who served both as President Nixon's staff director for the Cabinet Committee on Narcotics Control and at the Office of Management and Budget. He resigned to protest Nixon's efforts to rid himself of the

Watergate prosecutors, the so-called "Saturday Night Massacre." He also served a single term in the U.S. House of Representatives, from 2009 to 2011, as an Idaho Democrat. Richard Nordahl was a Domestic Council staff assistant, who worked mainly on the demand-side of narcotics issues. Leonard Garment was, at this time, special consultant to the president for domestic policy, later replacing John Dean as White House counsel.

60. President Nixon maintained an oceanfront home in San Clemente, California, where he often vacationed as president and to which he retired after resigning the presidency. He later moved back to the New York City area.

61. In 1972, Frank Carlucci was deputy director of the Office of Management and Budget and then moved to become undersecretary of the department of health, education, and welfare. He later held several senior foreign policy positions, including secretary of defense (1987–1989), under Ronald Reagan.

62. Carp's reference here is to the permanent, senior civil servants in the federal departments and agencies, whose positions are ranked by GS levels.

63. Because of the separation of powers doctrine, nonconfirmed presidential aides cannot usually be compelled to testify before congressional committees—they may, however, agree to appear voluntarily. There was significant controversy, for example, over whether President George W. Bush's national security adviser, Condoleezza Rice, would offer testimony before the National Commission on Terrorist Attacks upon the United States (also known as the 9-11 Commission)—which was created by an act of Congress. Ultimately she cooperated, but only after White House counsel Alberto Gonzales sent to the commission co-chairs a letter formalizing ground rules, including "assurances from the Speaker of the House and the Majority Leader of the Senate that, in their view, Dr. Rice's public testimony in connection with the extraordinary events of September 11, 2001, does not set, and should not be cited as, a precedent for future requests for a National Security Adviser or any other White House official to testify before a legislative body." A copy of this letter can be found at http://www.msnbc.msn.com/id/4630900/ (accessed October 27, 2010).

64. President Barack Obama has made extensive use of "czars" as a means of assigning certain issue areas or problems to a single administrator with responsibilities that cut across the usual bureaucratic boundary lines of the executive branch. One September 2009 account found almost thirty such czars, on matters ranging from automobile industry recovery to global climate change. See http://www.politico.com/news/stories/0909/26779.html (accessed October 27, 2010).

Chapter 6

Irrational Exuberance: Selling Domestic Policy from the White House

Lawrence R. Jacobs

The president is often thought of as the salesman-in-chief owing to his un-paralleled access to the media and to public attention. No individual can rival the extraordinary capacity and capability of the president and White House staff to put issues on the agenda and to promote publicly the president's policy proposals with the American people and with his institutional rivals in Washington, ranging from Congress to the news media.

Such firepower breeds exuberance. As one communications staffer ex-plained during President Bill Clinton's second year in office, the White House can "get away with anything provided you believe in something, you say it over and over again, and you never change." Staff members promote the president's policy initiatives with the expectation that they will "achieve a large scale public response" by "using the power of the White House to control the message" and "market the plan."[1]

The candidate-centered system of selecting party nominees and contest-ing the general election tends to produce presidents who are skilled and confident public advocates. Ronald Reagan parlayed his Hollywood skills into service as the "Great Communicator" who sold tax cuts to Americans and to a House of Representatives controlled by Democrats. Bill Clinton and Barack Obama used their remarkable communications skills to over-come significant barriers to their elections and to promote their legislation in Washington. Presidents adept at salesmanship not only can make a per-suasive pitch, they also can single out a few priorities and persist in pro-moting them. Both Reagan and George W. Bush effectively focused their administrations on cutting taxes while Jimmy Carter was unable to stick with a disciplined agenda.

The personal gifts for communication are amplified by institutional advantages. The media are organizationally wired to cover the president, accounting for one of the primary "beats" in Washington. The press is a kind of slingshot for presidential authority and institutional capacity, catapulting the president's sales pitch into the country. Presidential advantage results from the compounding of the White House's unique media access with the president's extraordinary constitutional powers and organizational capacity. No other individual shares the president's ability to use his outreach offices to roll out a major new policy, to step up to the microphone in a cheering House chamber to deliver a nationally televised State of the Union address, or to launch a military operation. A defining feature of the modern presidency is force multiplication—namely, the combining of unparalleled media access, assertive presidential authority, and burgeoning White House operations.

The president's capabilities as a salesman, although important, are not sufficient to secure support from Americans, members of Congress, the media, and other critical components of the Washington community. Two hurdles face presidents who depend on salesmanship to advance themselves and their policies. First, presidential promotion involves multiple sellers and buyers and a number of issues over time. Although the president may give a speech, for instance, on tax reform, Cabinet officials and the White House staff will need to promote the proposal in the following months, as well as to shop around other policy initiatives important to valued administration constituents that the president supports but lacks the time to invest in. Advancing policy is a collective and institutional process rather than an individual exercise, and reliance on others dissipates the assumed power that presidents derive from personal engagement.

Second, presidential sales pitches rarely produce policy change on their own. The folklore among White House staffers as well as the standard scholarly approaches to studying presidential leadership play a trick by drawing our attention to success—for instance, Reagan returning from an assassination attempt to cajole a Democratic House to pass tax reform and Lyndon B. Johnson championing the Voting Rights Act in a stirring speech to a joint session of Congress. The reality, however, is that research on a wide range of cases of presidents making public appeals and attempting to trade on their popularity consistently demonstrates little effect on public opinion or congressional success.[2] The assumed causal relationship between presidential promotion and a successful outcome is often spurious, resulting from shared partisan or philosophical commitments, among other factors.

The sobering reality of presidential selling is that it relies upon and therefore is defined by a mutual dependence that delineates the terms of the exchange—its timing, content, and success. The president's sales pitch and its effectiveness are a function of the capabilities and characteristics of White House organization and outreach as well as of interactions with the broader political and informational environment, ranging from Congress to the political calendar to the dynamics of political reporting. Instead of dominating Washington through powerful sales pitches, effective presidents accept the limits and conditions of their promotional efforts, appropriately value the institutional nature of their powers, and focus on exploiting opportunities offered by the environment to serve their ends.

Defining the success of presidential salesmanship is an important step in introducing realism about the nature and extent of influence based on public promotion. Indeed, the modern White House's tendency to engage in grandiose exaggeration about the potential for success may well encourage an over-reaching beyond the president's political and institutional capital.

This chapter addresses three aspects of presidential promotion. First, it outlines the White House's sales force—offices and operations that project the president and his policies to Congress, the press, interest groups, and the mass public. Particular attention is devoted to the offices of the press secretary and communications and their often one-way link to the White House staff charged with formulating policy. The second component is the context and conditions that make nearly all presidential promotions contingent and often ineffective. The third element returns to the notion of success, challenging the heroic speech myth and warning that presidential sales often produce White Houses that suffer from "irrational exuberance," as Federal Reserve Chairman Alan Greenspan once characterized the Wall Street boom during the late 1990s. Effective presidential promotion capitalizes on the opportunities within the institutional environment and webs of mutual dependence that define American national governance.

Organizing for Presidential Sales: The Specialization of White House Operations

Woodrow Wilson famously complained that the fixation of the framers of the Constitution on a "Newtonian" system that divided and dispersed power depleted American government of the authority to develop and implement policies that were essential to the country's development. More recent research confirms that the national government is a "hapless giant," huge in size but crippled by multiple and competing lines of authority and insufficient capacity for governing.[3]

Wilson (both as scholar and president) and generations of successors latched on to the president's singular access to the public's attention as the key to enhancing the executive's power and the country's governing capacity. Stuart Eizenstat, who was Carter's domestic policy adviser, explains that "the president has very few real powers under the Constitution. . . . The president's real power on the domestic side is his power to mobilize [public] support, to use the bully pulpit of the presidency, and to be, in effect, the salesman-in-chief, to rally the public and ultimately Congress behind his initiatives." Clinton's second-term domestic policy adviser, Bruce Reed, agrees: "The White House is the center of the journalistic and political universe . . . and you might as well use that in the best possible way to roll out some ideas."[4]

Reflecting the centrality of presidential promotions, the president and his chief of staff actively participate in determining the tactics, timing, and content of administration sales. The president's unique and unmediated connection to the mass public is often singled out as the defining feature of presidential power.

The political importance attached to public promotion has generated an institutional redesign of the presidency during the past half century. The modern presidency responded to the incoherence of the American system of government by developing an organizational infrastructure for public sales. Reflecting on the mixed success of the administration's promotional capacities, Eizenstat reports that an effective president "make[s] sure that he has a White House staff that is organized to back his initiatives. . . . so [that] when the major policies are announced there is an outreach strategy." Reagan and Clinton were effective at this, Eizenstat explains, because each had a chief of staff and senior staff who were experienced in Washington and could "pull together policy and politics, salesmanship and substance, and organize the White House in that way." Both effectively used the White House's promotional capacity to frame the debate over their budgets and to win passage of key parts despite divisions within their own parties and stout resistance from rival partisans. By contrast, Carter unnecessarily ran into political trouble during his first year because he lacked a chief of staff who could set priorities and integrate policy and outreach in ways that would maximize the president's bully pulpit. Although well intentioned, Carter's efforts to scale back earmarks and special projects for members of Congress led to an ill-timed and poorly presented veto of waterway legislation that was overwhelmingly backed by Democrats. This action side-tracked higher priority initiatives and damaged the president's standing in his own political party.

Clinton domestic policy adviser Carol Rasco traces the skill of linking policy with promotion to "work[ing] in a very rough campaign . . . [which] give[s] you an appreciation for . . . how you'll go about presenting [administration policy initiatives] or building the base that it needs to get it enacted."[5] Margaret Spellings, who served both as George W. Bush's first-term domestic policy adviser and second-term secretary of education, agrees that campaign experience instills in the core staff "discipline" and a habit of following a "routine," planned strategy to publicly promote the president's priorities. Like a crowded campaign, the White House packages the president's presentation, according to Clinton campaign and White House adviser Anne Lewis, with a story and a headline to "break through" the heavy competition for the public's attention and to "cu[t] through the fog that so often shrouds the public's view of Washington politics and the president."[6]

The link between the White House's policy staff and its public outreach effort is uneven (Reagan and Clinton were more effective from the start than Carter) but the nature of this link does share a critical characteristic across administrations—it is often a one-way relationship. The policy shop hands off sales to the marketing department. The White House's specialists in public promotion are charged with retail sales while the policy staff focuses on product development.

The emergence of an institutional capacity for presidential promotion has produced functionally specialized offices within the White House. Even as political and institutional incentives motivated the turn to promotion, the operational reality of public promotion created internal challenges and risks. Ray Jenkins, who worked with the press during the Carter administration, emphasizes that "there is absolutely no margin for error whatsoever. . . . [When you] make errors, . . . you spend the rest of your time correcting [them]."[7]

One of the growth industries in Washington over the past four decades has been lobbying, with a particular focus on Congress. Although consumer and other community groups have expanded their presence in order to make their case to legislators, there has been a particular expansion in the representation of individual businesses and coalitions of firms.[8] Partly in response to this development, the White House developed its own lobbying capacity through the Legislative Liaison Office and the Office of Public Liaison, which have responsibility for building relations with Congress and interest groups, respectively. One of the most important contributions of the legislative liaison operation is information collection, which equips the White House to focus its agenda on issues most likely to win favor in Congress and to identify possible modifications in its proposals that will widen support. After failing to persuade members of Congress or recalcitrant interest groups, administrations often turn to public appeals as a last resort. Referring to the White House's capacity to link to Congress and interest groups, Eizenstat explains that they have to be "built into the policy process, not an afterthought to it. . . . to make sure that [the president's] outreach effort is . . . part and parcel of the development of policy."

Although presidential promotion encompasses nearly every staff unit within the White House, two offices were specifically developed to take the lead in structuring outreach to the mass public and other constituents: the Office of the Press Secretary and the Office of Communications. Presidential press secretaries have become familiar figures—literally, the face of the White House. Although each press secretary is different, the office itself has evolved to routinely perform a set of stable functions in trying to manage the media's coverage of the president. The press office's objective is to develop working relations with the media that both meet their needs and fulfill the White House's own need to disseminate the president's message.

As the press office adapted to the routines and norms of the press as the price for gaining access to Americans through the mass media, the Office of Communications engaged in a more unencumbered strategy to rally Americans and influentials in Washington. A key function of the communications office is to coordinate the numerous White House offices that convey information publicly in order to send a crafted, coherent message that advances the president's agenda. Its job is to link together the administration's policy experts with those charged to manage the press and Congress, sustain relationships with interest groups, manage intergovernmental affairs, write speeches, and plan presidential travel.

With the Office of Communications as the command center, words are treated as ammunition. The White House has built a veritable word factory to fashion the administration's language, arguments, and symbols in order to win the communications wars. Speech writers pound out the words for presidential pronouncement. In doing so, they collaborate with the president, policy experts, and other staff.

Public opinion polling has become a routine facet of White House operations and an important influence on speech writing and, more generally, White House communications.[9] One study of the Nixon through Reagan administrations found that polling data and analyses were most frequently exchanged at the top among the president, his chief of staff, and senior advisers, as well as among White House offices devoted to public outreach. In terms of the White House's promotional activities, "most poll exchanges took place within and between Communications, the Public Liaison, and the Political Liaison offices."[10]

Although many assume that presidential promotions are exclusively focused on the general public, the truth is that many are geared to specific audiences. Presidents devote an enormous amount of time and energy to selling their policies to business groups (from manufacturers to high-tech entrepreneurs), service providers (whether doctors, hospitals, and pharmaceutical manufacturers or educators), foreign policy organizations, and other specialized groups. Each presentation is carefully crafted to promote the president's initiatives and build support. For instance, Obama's public schedule is chock full of speeches projecting messages tailored to discrete groups in business (National Restaurant Association), politics (Black and Hispanic Caucus), labor (AFL-CIO Executive Council), military (Disabled Veterans of America), and others.

Although the White House has developed an enduring institutional commitment to communications, the scope and effectiveness of its efforts vary across administrations. Coordination and control over communications have ranged from quite effective during most of the presidencies of Reagan and George W. Bush to less effective during the Carter administration and the presidency of George H. W. Bush. Communications offices also vary in their aggressiveness in advocating a particular president's agenda to journalists, ranging from the active efforts on behalf of Bill Clinton by George Stephanopoulos and Mark Gearan to the more passive role in transmitting information and strategic planning played by Don Baer.[11] Administrations further differ in the degree to which they push press secretaries to serve as pitchmen, asking them to serve as both distributors of crafted messages and as sources of information that are trusted by reporters.

Outside the White House Bubble: The Conditionality of Presidential Promotions

Within the White House, the decision to launch a presidential promotion of a policy or initiative often rests on a presumption of dominance. Presidential archives overflow with plans to roll out new proposals and to bolster the president's approval ratings. These plans are premised on the capability of the White House to set the terms of debate and to neutralize opposition from members of Congress, interest groups, and the press. The White House's approach to communications may resemble a communications version of Sim City in which the presidential message is scripted to dominate, with legislators and other Washington players following their written parts.

The reality is that White House communications rarely follow the script and are often blunted or counteracted. Three factors condition the effectiveness of presidential promotions. The first is the president's commitment. Even with extensive stage-crafting, a president's failure to embrace publicly his core political commitments is a recipe for disaster. James Pinkerton, who worked for George H. W. Bush, looks back on the president's break from his "no new taxes" pledge as an unmitigated political disaster—a case in which the very publicness of presidential promotion multiplied the political damage of his reversal. Pinkerton describes Bush's original pledge as necessary to win the 1988 Republican nomination. But Bush "didn't believe it," which led him to agree to tax increases once in the Oval Office in order to reduce the budget deficit. Bush's decision to break his pledge was, according to Pinkerton, "no sales job." This episode illustrates a not uncommon tradeoff between political effectiveness in sustaining the president's electoral coalition and policy effectiveness. Bush was persuaded on policy grounds that breaking his tax pledge would generate revenues to reduce the government's ballooning deficits, and, indeed, his decision is credited with helping to create the later budget surpluses under Clinton.

Second, building a constituency is a prerequisite for effective presidential promotions—high-profile speeches are not enough. Eizenstat warns against any White House initiative that "wasn't part of your campaign [and that requires] you . . . to jerry-build a political constituency." Carter's decision to veto congressional water projects, according to Eizenstat, lacked a supportive coalition because it was "not part of the campaign [and therefore]. . . . caused a furor on Capitol Hill [that] diverted attention from the major priorities we were trying to sell [and] complicated our public outreach." Spellings singles out the efforts of George W. Bush to pass immigration reform as posing a similar challenge. Because it had not been a prominent campaign issue, "Build[ing] a constituency around [immigration reform] and against Rush Limbaugh was impossible."

The third and perhaps most durable challenge facing presidential promotions is the institutional environment surrounding the White House. Presidential promotions interact with independent institutions that are empowered by their own reservoirs of authority and guided by their own motivations, organizational priorities, and operating procedures. The result is mutual dependence rather than domination: the White House relies on the cooperation or deference of surrounding institutions just as these institutions rely on the White House for their own purposes. According to Don Baer, President Clinton's effort to use the public platform of a National Governors Association meeting required "negotiations with [the Association] over what the governors were willing to hear from him versus what we wanted to do."[12] This is a common experience for presidents. Faced with institutions that possess the authority and capacity to resist, White House staff must be "anchored at both ends" in order to "adapt to the president's way of doing business and . . . have secure relations with all presidential clientele."[13]

The Filter

The press is the institution that most directly conditions the White House's public communications strategies. White House efforts to impose its message run into the media's own norms, procedures, and organizational requirements. Rather than futilely attempting to impose the president's message, the press office structures its relations with the media to serve reporters and, in the process, to promote the president's message. "Weaving together" the interests of the White House and the press builds a "cooperative" relationship in which each relies on the other.[14] Clinton Press Secretary Mike McCurry explains that his job required him to "make sure [reporters are] taken care of in addition to taking care of our agenda."[15] This two-way relationship defines the president's persuasive task.

White House acceptance of the president's mutual dependence on the media introduces constraints and opportunities. The main opportunity is to use the airwaves to "get the president's story out." Reagan Press Secretary Marlin Fitzwater says that reporters are "not going to use [the information] just the way I gave it to them but . . . [that is] the price for getting my president's position out."[16] Providing reliable information to reporters builds trust, which provides "more credibility in the future" for the White House to trade on.[17] Trust and credibility provide leverage for managing potentially damaging news reports by steering reporters away from stories that are wrong or convincing them to address omissions and avoid one-sided accounts.[18]

The administration's dependence on news organizations does complicate the links between the White House's policy and promotional operations. While the press office and press secretary rely on mutual dependence and respect to advance the president's agenda among autonomous news organizations over whom they exert no control, a number of White House staff members seek to treat the media as veritable carrier pigeons for their message. In particular, the press secretary's effort to serve the president by serving the press regularly clashes with the short-term, win-at-all-costs approach of political advisers and staff in the Office of Communications, as well as of staffers preoccupied with winning a vote in Congress or launching a policy initiative. In contrast to the "us-them, we've got to defeat them" mentality of running a campaign, governing requires—according to a variety of administration officials, including Roger Porter who served under Ford, Reagan, and the first president Bush—"build[ing] coalitions and work[ing] with others because . . . in our system power is so widely distributed and fragmented that that's the only way you can effectively govern."[19]

The conflict between the press office's emphasis on working with and through the media and the short-term orientation of other staff is expressed in their divergent views about balancing persuasion and information. White House staff members who are devoted to winning votes in Congress and to advancing the administration's political position view facts as ammunition to be deployed selectively for the sole purpose of publicly demolishing a rival's challenge. By contrast, staff members devoted to working with the media treat facts as the currency of the realm, with persuasion flowing from fair factual presentation. Mike McCurry warns that pressure to "spin the politically attractive side of the [administration's case]. . . . diminishes the authority you need . . . so people understand that this is good information."[20] Although delivering truthful information is necessary to sustain the media's willingness to report the administration's stories, Ford Press Secretary Ron Nessen explains that "members of the [White House] staff don't want to do that [because] they don't understand it[s importance]."[21]

The reality, then, is that the White House enjoys extraordinary access to the media but at the cost of respecting the press's norms and routines. Efforts to manipulate the media by releasing inaccurate or significantly incomplete information diminish the White House's trustworthiness and therefore its effectiveness.

There are, of course, variations across administrations in the degree to which the symbiotic press-president relationship is mutually beneficial. Although the Clinton and second Bush presidencies excelled at "feeding" the press, the Obama media operation was openly and repeatedly criticized by White House reporters for not meeting their needs during its first two years—they complained about Press Secretary Robert Gibbs's demeanor and about not receiving adequate access to senior officials. This diminished the Obama team's ability to project its message and may have contributed to widespread public confusion about their domestic and foreign policy initiatives.

The Calendar of Presidential Sales

The timing and content of presidential promotions are conditioned by the congressional calendar and by the electoral cycle. The State of the Union address begins the calendar year and is the premier opportunity for the president to set the agenda and promote his primary initiatives. Clinton aide Bruce Reed explains (and George W. Bush adviser Margaret Spellings agrees) that the White House's policy and promotional strategy was "organized around [the State of the Union address] because that's our one chance . . . to set the agenda for the year."

Although the State of the Union Address creates an unrivalled opportunity for the president, the length, depth, and effectiveness of the speech is limited by its format (short enough to keep the attention of a large television audience), its setting (in front of Congress), and its aftermath, which is characterized by an avalanche of critical scrutiny from the opposition party and media commentators. The Clinton White House attempted to mitigate some of these constraints by starting to roll out its State of the Union agenda by the end of the preceding November, just after most members of Congress had left town. The dynamics of the legislative process continue to structure White House strategy after the State of the Union address, especially the budget process and the flow of bills from committee consideration to floor action and then to the president for signature or veto.

The timing of congressional and presidential elections also structures what presidents promote and where they promote it. As midterm elections approach, presidents typically hit the road to tout their accomplishments in bold and easily understood terms in politically competitive states and congressional districts. For presidential elections, the White House closely coordinates the president's travel and message with his party's campaign and the consultants and pollsters who are directing it. As Spellings explains, "the bulk of the sales job on policy was done not in Washington but out on the hustings . . . to influence . . . the Hill and [to win] battleground states."

President Obama aggressively hit the campaign trail in the lead-up to the 2010 midterm elections. Although Democrats suffered historic losses in the House of Representatives, his intensive campaigning is credited with holding the Democratic majority in the Senate and helping prominent liberals to keep their seats—including the highly competitive Nevada Senate seat retained by Majority Leader Harry Reid, who had spearheaded passage of the president's landmark legislation on health-care reform.[22]

Struggling to Translate Presidential Promotions into Increased Congressional Support

Presidents often turn to public promotions to build congressional support. In an era of sharp political polarization, the White House attempts to rally the public as its best available opportunity to build legislative coalitions that both maintain support from the president's fellow partisans and attract a small but often decisive number of votes from the opposing party. The White House calculates that members of Congress will avoid direct defiance of the president out of fear of retribution when they need a favor or because they anticipate grassroots outrage by voters.

In reality, the overriding calculation of legislators is based on the views and interests of their constituents, their own judgments about good policy, and pressure from colleagues, especially party leaders and fellow partisans. Presidential promotion may solidify support from legislators who are on the fence but it rarely converts members of Congress whose own interests and policy judgment push them in a contrary direction.[23]

Contrary to the hopes of White House communications staff, the constitutional separation of powers limits the effectiveness of presidential promotions. President Reagan's repeated public campaigns to win congressional support for funding anti-communist rebels fighting to overthrow the

Nicaraguan government not only failed but backfired: Congress overwhelmingly passed prohibitions against any administration effort to support the rebels. (The decision of some Reagan administration officials to circumvent the congressional prohibitions led to the "Iran-Contra" scandal that marred the president's second term and led to the conviction of senior officials.) Obama's energetic public promotion of energy and climate change legislation in 2009 could not even get the Senate—which was three-fifths Democratic—to put aside regional and constituent reservations and pass a heavily compromised bill.

Politically astute administrations redefine the purpose of presidential public appeals from converting opponents to solidifying potential supporters and encouraging compromise. Institutional reality forces the White House to "make accommodations," as Reagan aide Kenneth Duberstein explains.[24] Reflecting on his experience in the Ford White House, Donald Rumsfeld underlines the need for realism when dealing with Congress: "I want someone in congressional relations who can get Joe 2 out of 3 [times] . . . [so we can] have floating coalitions." Rumsfeld counsels against "dead-end[ing]" legislators who defy the White House by declaring them "the enemy . . . [whom the White House is] not going to talk to . . . [or] deal with."[25] Presidential promotions that fail to win over a legislator who is cross-pressured by constituent needs may help lure the same member on another issue.

The enduring challenge that the Constitution imposes on presidents is made harder by the recent growth of partisan polarization in Congress. In particular, the president faces two daunting challenges. First, he is dependent on the structural constraint created by congressional elections, which set the partisan parameters of what he can accomplish. White House legislative success is, in large measure, a function of whether his party enjoys majority status in both legislative chambers because he will get little or no support from the opposing party. He also needs to unify his party, which is difficult given intraparty regional and philosophical divisions. The odds of success are further lengthened by the recurrent use of Senate filibusters, which means that presidents often require the support of sixty members to move their legislation. Obama came into office with his party controlling both houses of Congress by the largest margins in years, and yet the confluence of unified Republican opposition, Democratic divisions, and institutional vetoes like the Senate filibuster defeated much of his agenda from labor reform to climate change and immigration legislation. Even where he achieved landmark legislative breakthroughs on health care and financial reform, the partisan and institutional booby-traps nearly took out there initiatives on more than one occasion and chewed up much of his first two years in office.

In short, the White House does not dictate legislative outcomes any more than it does press coverage. The reality is that the president depends on institutions with the capacity to resist and to redirect even the best-planned White House communications. The effect is to dissipate or counteract presidential promotions. The effectiveness of the president's efforts at public sales depends not simply on the quality and sophistication of the White House's communications strategy (as is often assumed by pundits) but also on the administration's realism in accepting its institutional vulnerability and in identifying and influencing the leverage points that can be used to move existing institutions.

The Snare and Delusion of Presidential Promotions

The temptation to give a prime-time presidential address is the political equivalent of the Greek Sirens who seduced sailors onto rocky shores. Cases of effective addresses enjoy a prominent place in the pantheon of heroic leadership. But these cases are rare.

Defining Success

In sorting out myth from reality, it is helpful to distinguish three criteria by which the success of these presidential appeals may be judged. The first is whether such appeals improve the public's evaluation of the president's job performance and policy proposals. Research does not find much evidence of such success. For example, political scientist George Edwards's analysis of George W. Bush's campaign to boost public backing for privatizing Social Security reveals little or no change in support of the administration's position.[26] In general, the public's basic policy preferences are quite stable and generally immune to prime-time speeches and other short-term efforts to alter them.[27]

Exaggerated and misguided conceptions of the president's capacity to direct public sentiment may backfire, diminishing the administration's standing. Pollster Pat Caddell fed Carter unsophisticated and biased survey data to bolster his claim that "all the [administration's] legislative initiatives, programs, [and] foreign policy efforts . . . are essentially irrelevant to solving its deeper, more fundamental, and more demanding problem."[28] At Caddell's urging and against the advice of Vice President Walter Mondale and senior domestic policy adviser Stuart Eizenstat, Carter delivered a nationally televised speech in July 1979 in an effort to end the country's "crisis of confidence." Contrary to Caddell's and Carter's hopes, the speech "did not produce long-lasting change in the public's perceptions of the Carter administration and may have even made matters worse with the malaise legacy it left behind."[29]

The second criterion for sizing up the success of presidential promotions is their effectiveness in shaping press coverage in ways desired by the White House. Clearly, the president can use his unparalleled visibility to focus press coverage on his policy agenda.[30] But sustained presidential promotions risk prompting journalists to seek out sources critical of the administration's policy in order to balance their coverage. Clinton's campaigns to reform health care and Bush's to reform Social Security generated more press use of opposition sources.[31]

Success in producing policy change and legislative enactment is the third criterion for evaluating presidential promotions. Although public appeals may fortify likely supporters in Congress, most members will be guided by their partisan loyalty and their personal policy views.[32] Research finds that presidential promotions often have limited effects on legislative success. In 2009 and 2010, for instance, Obama's energy and climate change initiative faced unified Republican opposition in the House and resistance from congressional Democrats who disagreed with its "cap-and-trade" approach and who defended their regions' interests, especially those who came from coal-reliant states like West Virginia.

Indeed, the White House's irrational exuberance in the transformational power of its communications capacities may seduce the president into offering proposals that lack sufficient legislative support. For instance, the supreme confidence of the Clinton and Bush White Houses in their ability to mobilize support for their soaring proposals to restructure health care and Social Security, respectively, far outstripped public and congressional support. The allure of public promotions that would reverse institutional obstacles led the Clinton and Bush White Houses to squander their political capital and, consequently, the opportunity to enact significant, if less extensive, reform.

Looking back on his time in the Clinton White House, Bruce Reed concludes that "the greatest power of the executive is not selling, it's doing. The president has the ability [through executive orders and other unilateral powers] to take actions that back up his policies and that sell his policies better than any speech or any press secretary or any spin operation can do." Although the use of executive authority may not achieve the long-lasting and comprehensive solutions of ambitious reform proposals, Reed's recommendation reflects a sober recognition of the limits of presidential promotions— namely, the reality that its "advantage . . . erodes over time" and its use does not go "unanswered" in America's media environment and separation of powers system.

Implications of Inflated Presidential Confidence in Public Promotions

Presidential reliance on public promotions may produce a paradox: a strategy of winning through salesmanship may end up impeding presidential success and effectiveness. Specifically, the reliance on public appeals can have two potentially detrimental consequences for the president.

The first consequence is that failure is persistently interpreted as confirming rather than undermining the political effectiveness of presidential promotions. The failure of the promotional strategy to enact Clinton's health-reform initiative and Bush's Social Security proposal was attributed by both administrations to flawed performances by the staff rather than to the inherent weakness of the strategy itself. Disappointment breeds turnover as the president regularly shuffles through communications staff in search of better performance. As Clinton communications aide George Stephanopoulos explains, "if the president isn't doing well, it's a communications problem . . . [making it the] natural place to make a change."[33] Obama interpreted the Democrats' crushing midterm losses in 2010 not as a repudiation of his policies but rather as an indication of flawed messaging by himself and his staff.

The second consequence is that the White House's drive to win public support often prompts a shift in administration strategy away from debates over policy and toward appeals based on evoking particular emotions, personal images, and misleading perceptions through carefully crafted presentations. This contradicts a core concept of democracy and the dominant theory of elections, which posits that electoral competition motivates candidates in two-party systems to converge toward the electorate's median policy preferences.[34] Presidential polling is expected to reliably identify these preferences so that politicians can faithfully respond to them.

The White House drive to dominate public opinion has led it to latch

onto three tactics for manipulating or shifting the nature of citizen evaluation. The first tactic is to use White House polling to try to change the preferences of Americans in support of the policy goals already embraced by the
president and his supporters. For instance, one study finds that the Johnson
White House used opinion data to fashion public positions on Vietnam
that were expected, as aides promised the president, to "change the public mood" and "marshal . . . American support for the Administration."[35]
Aides set out to change public sentiment by using White House polling data
to identify how to "affect . . . the tone, the content, and the form of what we
say publicly and privately on Vietnam." Future administrations expanded
Johnson's polling capacities in an attempt to enhance the effectiveness of
their messages and presentations in changing public preferences.[36]

The second tactic is to narrow-cast presidential appeals in order to win
over politically important groups instead of the entire, much-ballyhooed
"American people." Quantitative and qualitative evidence from the Reagan
White House points to a consistent pattern of calibrating the president's
policy statements to align with the views of individual groups.[37] In particular, Reagan's policy positions systematically corresponded with the views of
high-income earners who favored reducing government spending, lowering
taxes, and reforming Social Security to make the program voluntary. Reagan
also responded to social conservatives (especially Southern Baptists and Roman Catholics) on issues such as family values and crime and to hawkish
Republicans on foreign policy.

The third tactic is to craft a personal image of the president that appeals
to voters on nonpolicy grounds in order to build public support for him as
a leader even when Americans refuse to back the administration's policies.
John F. Kennedy focused on constructing and maintaining a public perception of himself as a vigorous agent of change.[38] The focus on nonpolicy,
image-based appeals was intensified under Nixon, whose White House staff
was the first to commission studies exclusively about presidential image.
Nixon systematically responded to negative evaluations of his personality
traits by emphasizing bold and aggressive foreign policies. Archival records
reveal that Nixon and his senior advisers calculated that such policies would
bolster his image as competent and strong.[39] Shifting the focus of public
evaluations from the president's policy positions to his personality offers a
strategically attractive approach to minimizing the electoral risk of pursuing
the policy goals that he and his allies desire.

Although the institutional apparatus of the White House has substantially enhanced its capacity to launch public appeals, the implications for presidential performance and American democracy are not uniformly positive. The siren song of presidential promotions invites over-reaching and a squandering of opportunities for policy innovation. Meanwhile, the single-minded focus on building and holding public support for the president as the linchpin of a functioning system of government has guided presidents to bypass the national constituency in favor of narrower ones, to rely on crafted presentations to mislead the American people, and to recast the nature of representation toward image and away from government responsiveness to the public's policy preferences.

Effective power requires self-restraint. Effective use of the presidency's promotional advantages requires realistic assessment of its institutional dependence on the broader political and constitutional environment. Power-savvy presidents will accept the limits and conditions of their promotional efforts, appreciate the institutional nature of their influence, and seek to exploit opportunities offered by the environment to serve their ends.

Notes

1. Lawrence R. Jacobs and Robert Y. Shapiro, *Politicians Don't Pander: Political Manipulation and the Loss of Democratic Responsiveness* (Chicago: University of Chicago Press, 2000), 106.

2. Jon Bond and Richard Fleisher, *The President in the Legislative Arena* (Chicago: University of Chicago Press, 1990); George C. Edwards III, *Governing by Campaigning* (New York: Pearson & Longman, 2007).

3. Stephen Skowronek, *Building a New American State: The Expansion of National Administrative Capacities, 1877–1920* (Cambridge: Cambridge University Press, 1982).

4.Unless otherwise noted, all quotations from domestic policy advisers are from the transcripts of the Miller Center symposium reported in chapters 3, 5, 7, and 9.

5. Quoted in Bradley Patterson, *The White House Staff: Inside the West Wing and Beyond* (Washington, D.C.: Brookings Institution Press, 2000), 85–86.

6. Quoted in Martha Joynt Kumar, "The Office of Communications," in *The White House World: Transitions, Organization, and Office Operations*, eds. Martha Joynt Kumar and Terry Sullivan (College Station: Texas A&M University Press, 2003), 259, 277.

7. Quoted in Martha Joynt Kumar, "The Pressures of White House Work Life," in *White House World*, eds. Kumar and Sullivan, 105.

8. Jack Walker, *Mobilizing Interest Groups in America* (Ann Arbor: University of Michigan Press, 1991).

9. Lawrence R. Jacobs and Robert Y. Shapiro, "Presidential Manipulation of Public

Opinion: The Nixon Administration and the Public Pollsters," *Political Science Quarterly* 110, no. 4 (Winter 1995): 519–538; Jacobs and Shapiro, *Politicians Don't Pander*.

10. Diane Heith, "Staffing the White House Public Opinion Apparatus," *Public Opinion Quarterly* 62, no. 2 (Summer 1998): 165–189, 176.

11. Kumar, "Office of Communications."

12. Ibid., 256.

13. John Kessel, "The Political Environment of the White House" in *White House World*, eds. Kumar and Sullivan, 64.

14. Martha Joynt Kumar, "The Office of the Press Secretary" in *White House World*, eds. Kumar and Sullivan, 232.

15. Quoted in Kessel, "Political Environment of the White House," 68.

16. Quoted in Kumar, "Office of the Press Secretary," 232.

17. Deputy Press Secretary Roman Popadiuk for George H. W. Bush, quoted in Kumar, "Office of the Press Secretary," 233.

18. Kumar, "Office of the Press Secretary," 233.

19. Martha Joynt Kumar, "The White House Is Like City Hall" in *White House World*, eds. Kumar and Sullivan, 84–85.

20. Quoted in Kumar, "Office of the Press Secretary," 235, 248–249.

21. Ibid., 226.

22. Lawrence R. Jacobs and Theda Skocpol, *Health Care Reform and American Politics* (New York: Oxford University Press, 2010).

23. Bond and Fleisher, *President in the Legislative Arena*; Charles Cameron, *Veto Bargaining: Presidents and the Politics of Negative Power* (New York: Cambridge University Press, 2000).

24. Quoted in Kessel, "Political Environment of the White House," 67.

25. Ibid., 68.

26. Edwards III, *Governing by Campaigning*.

27. Benjamin Page and Robert Shapiro, *The Rational Public* (Chicago: University of Chicago Press, 1992).

28. Quoted in Heith, "Staffing the White House Public Opinion Apparatus," 181.

29. Robert Strong, "Recapturing Leadership: The Carter Administration and the Crisis of Confidence," *Presidential Studies Quarterly* 16, no. 3 (Fall 1986): 636–650, 647.

30. Jeffrey Cohen, *Presidential Responsiveness and Public Policy-Making: The Publics and the Policies That Presidents Choose* (Ann Arbor: University of Michigan Press, 1998).

31. Lawrence R. Jacobs, "The Presidency and the Press: The Paradox of the White House 'Communications War,'" in *The Presidency and the Political System*, 9th ed., ed. Michael Nelson (Washington, D.C.: CQ Press, 2009); Jacobs and Shapiro, *Politicians Don't Pander*.

32. Bond and Fleisher, *President in the Legislative Arena*; George C. Edwards III, *The Strategic President: Persuasion and Opportunity in Presidential Leadership* (Princeton, N.J.: Princeton University Press, 2009).

33. Quoted in Kumar, "Office of Communications," 253.

34. Duncan Black, *The Theory of Committees and Elections* (Cambridge: Cambridge University Press, 1958); Anthony Downs, *An Economic Theory of Democracy* (New York: Harper Row, 1957).

35. Lawrence R. Jacobs and Robert Y. Shapiro, "Lyndon Johnson, Vietnam, and Public Opinion: Rethinking Realists' Theory of Leadership," *Presidential Studies Quarterly* 29, no. 3 (September 1999): 592–616.

36. Jacobs and Shapiro, *Politicians Don't Pander*.

37. James Druckman and Lawrence R. Jacobs, "Segmented Representation: The Reagan White House and Disproportionate Responsiveness," in *Who Gets Represented?* eds. Christopher Wlezien and Peter Enns (New York: Russell Sage, forthcoming).

38. Lawrence R. Jacobs and Robert Y. Shapiro, "Issues, Candidate Image and Priming: The Use of Private Polls in Kennedy's 1960 Presidential Campaign," *American Political Science Review* 88, no. 3 (September 1994): 527–540.

39. James Druckman, Lawrence R. Jacobs, and Eric Ostermeier, "Candidate Strategies to Prime Issues and Image," *Journal of Politics* 66, no. 4 (November 2004): 1205–1227.

Chapter 7

Selling Domestic Policy from the White House

*Featured participants at this session are Stuart Eizenstat (on Jimmy Carter);
James Pinkerton (on George H. W. Bush); Bruce Reed (on Bill Clinton);
and Margaret Spellings (on George W. Bush). The moderator is Professor
Lawrence Jacobs (University of Minnesota).*

Jacobs: We've been talking quite a bit about the making of policy. Obviously presidential campaigns matter a lot. There are important promises and commitments made during that campaign, so when you come into the White House they've got to be followed through on. You've got party interests and other sorts of interest groups in Washington pressing for different kinds of policy initiatives, and you have a whole host of other sorts of influences, of course, including real-world changes.

Once the president makes a policy decision, the next step is how to sell it, how to promote it, how to build support for that policy outside the White House. That's what this session is about. We want to think now about how this is done, who does it, who's the audience, and to what effect. Mr. Eizenstat, let's start with you. Who is it that takes the ball from those who design policy and then sells it?

Eizenstat: First of all, the president has very few real powers under the Constitution of the United States besides being commander in chief. It is no accident that Article I of the Constitution is about the powers of Congress. The president's real power on the domestic side is his power to mobilize support, to use the bully pulpit of the presidency and to be, in effect, the salesman-in-chief, to rally the public and ultimately Congress behind his initiatives.[1]

In order for that to be effective, the president has to make sure that he has a White House staff that is organized to back his initiatives. He has to have an Office of Public Liaison that is built into the policy process, not an afterthought to it.[2] For his chief priorities, he's got to make sure that his outreach effort is part and parcel of the development of the policy, so when the major policies are announced, there is an outreach strategy for it.

168 Stuart Eizenstat et al.

We had a number of flaws in the first year [of the Carter administration] that prevented that from occurring. They were corrected in the second year and we had much smoother sailing thereafter. But the first year is critical because that's when the public forms its impression of a president. Let me talk about the organization of the White House in that respect.

The first decision, which Jim Cannon, my close friend who was in this position with President Ford will remember—President Ford initially had no chief of staff when he came in, sort of a reaction against the centralization of power under [John] Ehrlichman and [H. R.] Haldeman. President Carter followed that practice. He adopted a "spokes-of-the-wheel" organization in which six or seven senior aides had equal access, but there was no chief of staff to organize and coordinate the policy and the politics, along with the outreach and the announcement of policy. This was a serious mistake. This was not, however, done by happenstance. Stephen Hess from Brookings had written a book arguing against the centralization of power in the White House.³ Hess and Carter, I put the two of them together.

President Ford actually learned in the second half of his presidency the importance of having a centralized chief of staff to organize outreach as well as policy, and a fellow named Dick Cheney became his chief of staff. One humorous anecdote is the day we came in from the inauguration there was in the chief of staff's office—occupied by Hamilton Jordan, but he was not given the title nor the responsibilities for it initially—a broken bicycle wheel. Dick Cheney put a note saying, "Don't follow the spokes of the wheel."⁴ We should have followed that advice. We did, ultimately, but by then it had cost us badly.

Indeed, because there was no setting of priorities by the chief of staff, we had a multiplicity of priorities and the salesmanship job therefore became more difficult, because we were at one and the same time trying to sell welfare reform, hospital cost containment, a major energy bill, the Panama Canal Treaty, and a whole host of other initiatives. A president, to be effective as salesman-in-chief, has to be able to have a very tight discipline on the priorities he is going to set, and the chief of staff is where that starts. Again, that was done later in the administration, and Vice President Mondale played a role at the end of the term in setting those priorities. It was not done initially. So your public outreach has to be coordinated by the chief of staff to be part and parcel of the policy development process, not as an afterthought.

Indeed, our first public liaison saw it as her job to represent the interest groups of the Democratic Party to the president, rather than the president to the interest groups.[5] That was changed by the end of the first year when Anne Wexler was brought over from the commerce department. Anne, who is a consummate professional, did a truly brilliant job. We actually ended up with a *Congressional Quarterly* rating of success in our legislation higher than John Kennedy's and almost equal to that of Lyndon Johnson, because we did learn.[6] Anne was excellent at creating the first modern outreach effort, getting constituency groups in for briefings that I would do on the domestic side, and [Zbigniew] Brzezinski did on the foreign policy side. The president would come in—we would have East Room events and these groups were given their mission to try to sell our programs.[7] It worked very effectively, but only after the very difficult first year in which none of that was in place. And we paid a frightful price in having too many initiatives without having the public salesmanship part built into the process at the beginning.

I would like, if I may, to talk for a minute about campaign promises, because really salesmanship starts in the campaign. Jimmy Carter was a Democratic president sandwiched in between eight years of Republican presidents on one side and eight years on the other.[8] He was not coincidentally a moderate Democrat. If he had been a liberal Democrat he wouldn't have gotten elected, even with Watergate.[9]

It is important to understand that when he came into office there was a mismatch between the expectations of a highly liberal Democratic Congress, who were looking for a revival of the Great Society after eight accidental years of Nixon and Ford, and instead they got this moderately conservative southern Democrat, who was in effect a New Democrat—the first New Democrat before Paul Tsongas, and if I may say so, before Bill Clinton. That is to say, he was fiscally moderate if not conservative, socially liberal on civil rights, on environment, and on a whole variety of other issues. This was a new type of Democrat.

Now the problem with campaign promises, which are a predicate for selling your program as president, is not what the public thinks. The public thinks that presidential candidates just promise whatever they have to to get elected and then ignore it when they come in.[10] It's the opposite. They are very serious about their campaign promises. The problem with campaign promises is not that they're so often ignored; it is that they're fulfilled. But they're made under suboptimum conditions for policymaking, under great time pressures, under great political pressures, with a small campaign staff, without the kind of interagency review you have when you're president, and without the kind of economic and budget data you would like to have. They're often slapped together under enormous political pressures and then you have to live with them when you come into office.

There are real implications for breaking campaign promises. Let me give you two examples, which all the salesmanship in the world couldn't handle. Toward the end of the '76 campaign, with the race tightening, as Jim again will remember, a very large lead we had, twenty-seven points, was withering to one point. Texas became a very key state, and oil and gas are very important issues in the state of Texas. I drafted, at the urging of then-Governor of Texas Dolph Briscoe,[11] a letter from President Carter, which was faxed back in that ancient time, from the campaign plane "Peanut One," which said very explicitly, "If elected president I will deregulate natural gas." This was a huge issue in Texas because natural gas had been regulated since the time of Harry Truman. I wouldn't say it was the only reason we won Texas, but it sure didn't hurt.[12]

When we put together the energy package, there was no department of energy at that time. Jim Schlesinger was energy adviser, and he convinced the president to abandon that campaign promise on the ground that John Dingell, the chairman of the energy and commerce committee in the House, and Scoop Jackson, his companion in the Senate, were dead against deregulation of natural gas, as were the Democratic interest groups.[13] It was an anti-consumer type of thing.

We had a meeting in the cabinet room, which I can, unfortunately, remember to this day. I was the keeper of the campaign promises and the president was serious about campaign promises, so much so that he said, "Your job during the transition is to organize them and publish them so that we can be held accountable." And indeed we were. This was published in a CCH [Learning Center] yellow book. We used to call it the "Yellow Book," a sort of Mao book.[14]

The president, at this meeting with Schlesinger, who was saying, "We really shouldn't do this deregulation; it will kill our whole energy bill," turned to me and said, "Stu, you're the keeper of the campaign flame. What shall we do?" I reminded him of the Dolph Briscoe letter and the importance of it. And then in a sentence I wish I had never uttered, I said, "Well, I guess if Jim feels so strongly about it, if there's one campaign promise you can ignore, perhaps it's this one."

Now this turned out to be a catastrophically bad decision—because in the House of Representatives, more than two-thirds of whom were Democrats, natural gas deregulation, offered as a substitute for the Dingell bill, failed by one vote. It would have passed by twenty-five or thirty votes if we had simply said this was what we believed in. When it went to the Senate, natural gas deregulation passed easily. That one item held the whole energy bill up, which had been our number-one priority for eighteen months.[15] It created a cloud over the president's capacity to handle Congress, and it is a good example of what happens when you abandon campaign promises.

A second example was the so-called "Fifty-Dollar Rebate," which was part of our stimulus package.[16] The president was persuaded, and here perhaps with better economic reasons, that with inflation beginning to rise, this is one that we should abandon as part of our stimulus package. The problem was that Senator [Edmund] Muskie, then head of the new Budget Committee, had created an extraordinary third budget resolution to fit this in after it had passed the House.[17] He learned about the president's decision to abandon the rebate, which was done at the insistence of the secretary of the treasury, by reading the ticker. If you're going to abandon a campaign promise, for goodness' sake lay the groundwork for it and have a very good explanation, because otherwise you'll pay a very stiff price.[18]

Jacobs: Ms. Spellings, let me pick up on one of the comments that Mr. Eizenstat made, which was about the importance that promotion and sales play in setting your priorities in policymaking. The administration of George W. Bush was very skilled in setting priorities and then following through with a sales plan. Who did that? What were the mechanisms within the Bush White House that created that coordination, the priorities, and what would seem, at least from the outside, to be a fairly effective handoff?

Spellings: Our watchword was "discipline." I'll credit my colleague Karl Rove with thinking through and routinizing a calendar that had such discipline to it that really selling the president's policies was everybody's job in the White House: the legislative shop, of course, public liaison, and all of us in the policy shop.[19] While we certainly had areas of responsibility, it was absolutely an all-hands-on-deck sort of approach.

The very first week of the presidency we spent the entire time talking about education, with events in and out of the White House, in and out of Washington. One of the things that we sometimes think about when we sell public policy is the public side of this, and strategic ways to message this, particularly out of Washington, in key states, with key members of Congress and the like, and what the president does with his private time.

A couple of the first things that Bush did when he came to office, literally in the first week, was to have George Miller and Ted Kennedy and John Boehner and Judd Gregg and the whole fam damily over to watch the movie— I can't remember the name of it—about the Cuban missile crisis.[20] It was a surreal moment for me to watch Senator Kennedy and President Bush sit in the front row of the White House movie theater watching this movie about Senator Kennedy's brother, literally feet away from the Oval Office, and the entirety of the movie virtually takes place in the Oval Office. These sorts of important personal moments, these relationship-building moments, are as important as the public campaign or public effort to engender support.

As I said, discipline. As much planning as is possible. The way we did it, the way Karl did it, was to look at a calendar of about two months, which in White House time is an eternity. We would sort of phase things so education would be on week one and week three and week six, and in the intervening period we'd do Anne Wexler–like activities, public liaison things and relationship-building and on and on. It was very much a tactical kind of exercise, not a haphazard sort of, "This is our priority, everybody do your thing." It was very much a planned out, disciplined operation.

Jacobs: Bruce Reed, when you think of your experience in the Clinton White House, would you describe it as disciplined and focused, following a strict calendar?

Reed: Yes, in this sense. President Clinton discovered when he got to the White House that the best organizing principle for his agenda was the state of the union. Our entire effort every year was organized around that speech. For months ahead of time, as he prepared, as the White House prepared, the president's budget, we had the state of the union in mind, because that's the one chance where the president gets to do what he could do in a campaign, which is to set the agenda for the year.[21] Our state of the unions ended up being quite long as a result. In 1995 we set the modern record with an 89-minute speech.[22]

It was important because it was a chance to speak in an unfiltered way directly to the voters, which is any president's greatest asset. If he can make a connection with the voters on his ideas, then that is something that he can sustain for quite some time. The great advantage of the state of the union is that Congress is generally down. Historically, they haven't done much work in January and February, so we always viewed that as our greatest opportunity to get a leg up.

Jacobs: One of the innovations from the Clinton years was the pre-state of the union rollout.

Reed: That's right. We realized that precisely because Congress was out of town and not doing anything, we didn't have to save the state of the union for the night of the formal address. So with each successive year, we started leaking out pieces of it earlier and earlier. By the end, we were taking advantage of the Christmas holiday. The White House is the center of the journalistic and the political universe, so you can get attention for whatever you're doing, and you might as well use that in the best possible way to roll out some ideas.

Jacobs: Mr. Pinkerton, there was a sense that George H. W. Bush was not so comfortable with the television camera, not on the Clinton level or the level of Bush 43. How did you all think about salesmanship with that president, or in terms of how to organize the White House to get the message out?

Pinkerton: We had one huge benefit back in the Bush 41 White House. We had Roger Porter, who was probably the only domestic policy adviser for a president who had written a book on domestic policy advising to a president, before he got there. I think it is fair to say that Bush 41 was not a natural television aficionado, but the real dilemma that the Bush 41 domestic policy operation had—I was charmed to hear Stu Eizenstat say that Jimmy Carter was preceded by eight years of Republican presidents and succeeded by *eight* years of Republican presidents. We were actually in there too—years nine through twelve. The story of our life—Rodney Dangerfield.[23]

I started working for Bush 41 in 1985 in his political action committee and then in his campaign. I was there for the entire period from '85 to '92 to observe these things. During that time, Bush 41 was called a wimp. That was a standard epithet in the media.[24] We always said that the real problem we have here—he's certainly no wimp by anybody's standard, he's a war hero, a family man, an oil man—is he had the dilemma that he was not entirely comfortable with his campaign and what he was saying.[25]

It's fair to say that Bush 41 was and is a conservative in the European sense of the word. He is sort of a custodian, sort of a steward, sort of an aristocrat. Again, he fought for his country at a young age, because that's what you did. It wasn't as if he was sitting around reading *Conscience of a Conservative*, or *A Choice Not an Echo*, or Ayn Rand or something.[26] He was very aware that his faction of the party, the [Nelson] Rockefeller wing of the party, the Prescott Bush wing, was in the minority.[27] He had been sort of beaten up in Texas by Harris County Republican ladies at one time or another.[28] Not literally—I realize we're speaking for the record here. I've got to emphasize this.

Spellings: But they could. [*laughter*]

Pinkerton: But they could. He had a terrible 1984 campaign, which was very demoralizing to him. Some political scientist did a study and said that Bush had the absolute worst press coverage of any national politician ever. The key factoid was he didn't have just a few positive stories; he had *zero* positive stories written about him in '84. I mean, Reagan was sailing off into the pantheon and the media would then turn on Bush and say, "Who is this runt coming along behind him?" I can remember joking, "Does anybody realize that Bush 41 is actually taller than Reagan?" Nobody would believe it. We'd say, "Look, here's a picture." They'd say, "Oh, you cheated. You Photoshopped it."

Into this context, Lee Atwater, who became the de facto head of his political operation, said, "Look, you've got to win over the conservatives."[29] So we made a real effort to get Bush 41 on the right side of the tax issue, the Grover Norquist "no tax increase" pledge.[30] Under extreme pressure and over the objections of the OVP [Office of the Vice President] back then, we persuaded Vice President Bush to sign the Grover Norquist pledge in April of 1987. That was a fight. Okay, that's the good news. We thought we had created sort of an exoskeleton, if you will, of campaign promises that would protect him. I don't think we would have gotten him nominated otherwise against Jack Kemp, running to his right, and Bob Dole, who had the moderate establishment Senate side of things. He wouldn't have gotten through. That's the good news.

The problem is, you have a situation like that where he gets nominated doing one thing and then the general election campaign was much more the true George H. W. Bush. It was "a thousand points of light" and "kinder, gentler." We had this program called YES, Youth Entering Service, which to my knowledge never had so much as a policy paper behind it. It was just sort of a notion, "We're going to do this." It became Points of Light and national service, all these things that are now familiar.[31] Then you get to the White House—and this is where I believe that the Bush 41 White House was destined to anticipate Professor Jacobs's very smart book of a decade or so ago, *Politicians Don't Pander*. When they get in they say, "Okay, what do I really think, and what really ought to be done here? Now it is your job not to help me keep my campaign promises, but to help me do what I really want to do."

John Sununu, and more to the point, Richard Darman, convinced President Bush that a budget deal with a tax increase was just decisive and necessary. If there's one phrase that people remember, it's "Read my lips." If there's one thing that we just beat in the political sense over and over again in 1988, it was "We're not going to raise taxes. Who knows what else we'll do, but we're not going to raise taxes." Then there we were. Talk about no sales job. The sequence of how this happened—Roger, if I remember this right, they posted a memo on the White House press office bulletin board saying that he will be open to tax revenue increases.[32] It was April of 1990.

Governor Sununu said, "Yes, we're for tax revenue increases but that doesn't mean a tax increase. See, we'll cut the capital gains tax and that will make revenues go up and that will be our tax revenue increase." Well, Speaker [Thomas] Foley and Majority Leader [George] Mitchell weren't going to sit still for this. They made us say, over a bloody month, "Say you're for a tax increase," so we did. The rest is history in terms of Louis XV's deluge descending on us.

Anne Wexler to this day is still seen as the ideal of what a public liaison operation should be. If your public liaison officer and your congressional affairs people are involved from the get-go in the formulation of the policy, then there's a decent chance you might get somewhere with it.[33] But if the policy just comes because the president and the chief of staff and the budget director decide to break the most sacred campaign promise you've ever made, then your chances of success for anything other than a tax increase, which you can get done—but your own political future is, shall we say, jeopardized. That's where we fall into the Eizenstatian category, disappearing from history. Because people don't even remember we were there.

Eizenstat: Well, I very much remember, because for one thing, when Bush was CIA director, he briefed President Carter-elect during the transition and

I was the only staff person involved, and he gave really world-class briefings.[34] I would say to Jim, with twelve years of Republicans after Carter, that it would have been sixteen even with that, had it not been for Ross Perot running. I say that, Bruce, knowing that Bill Clinton is the great political icon of our time. He has enormous political skills. But I think that the conservative tide in the country had still not exhausted itself and it's not at all clear, even with Bill Clinton's fantastic political skills, that if Perot hadn't divided the conservative vote that President Bush wouldn't have been reelected.[35]

But Jim emphasized again the point I was making in my presentation of the risks of appearing to back off of a campaign pledge. It was more visible for sure with the "no tax" pledge of President Bush than it was with natural gas deregulation.

I'd like to turn, Larry, to a similar situation, when you make as a major priority something that wasn't part of your campaign. The campaign really is the opportunity for the candidate to lay the groundwork for being the salesman-in-chief when you're elected. If you suddenly pop up with major initiatives at the beginning of your presidency that weren't part of that political landscape during the campaign, you also run into problems, because you have to jerry-build a political constituency that is not prepared for it, both in the public and in the Congress.

May I just give you two examples: One was the so-called "hit list" of water projects that very much fulfilled President Carter's notion of dealing with government waste.[36] He had been perhaps the only governor in history to block a Corps of Engineers project, the Sprewell Bluff Dam project, when he was governor.[37] He saw these as wasteful and inefficient, which in many cases they were. But this touched the nerve endings of almost every major member of Congress. And because it was not part of the campaign, when it popped up at the very outset of the presidency, it caused a furor on Capitol Hill and diverted attention from the major priorities we were trying to sell. It created a novel issue, which again complicated our public outreach.

The second and more significant was the first energy package, the moral equivalent of war. Looking back at that, it was prescient, prophetic when one looks at where we are in our energy picture today, and very courageous. But by making this the number-one domestic priority at the very outset of the presidency, with the fireside chat reminiscent of FDR, when that had not been a major issue in the Carter-Ford campaign—energy was not a major issue. The notion that there was an urgency about doing it was not part of that debate. Suddenly popping that onto the agenda was courageous but it was politically very difficult, and it is one of the reasons, among others, that it took eighteen months to get this very difficult package passed was because there hadn't been a public preparation for this. You had to jerry-build a public outreach strategy without at that point having Anne Wexler on board.

Jacobs: Ms. Spellings, I want to bring in another element to this discussion about how presidents sell their policy, and that's the press. There's kind of a two-way street between the White House and the press. On the one hand, the press is dependent on the White House for information. It's the number-one beat in Washington, and that dependence is an opportunity. On the other hand, the White House has, as you've eloquently put it, its own sense of the story it wants to tell. That's very different from the situation that Bruce Reed mentioned with the state of the union, where you're unfiltered.

President Bush famously described the media as "the filter."[38] How did your White House think of the press and how to manage that two-way street, how to both respect and earn the respect of the media by playing by their rules, while still using it to achieve the purposes that the White House needed?

Spellings: A couple of things, and I do want to credit Bruce and President Clinton—we stole a page from his book on the leak-your-state of the union-nuggets-before-you-go-in, and talk again in the aftermath. One of the things that we used most effectively was, "Get the heck out of Washington," for starters. You often got much more favorable response in regional media, big and small cities, taking members of Congress along, those sorts of things.[39] I would say that the bulk of the sales job on policy was done not in Washington but out in the hustings.

Jacobs: It's very interesting: If you actually look at the audience numbers on press coverage, the viewership of local news is higher than the viewership of national news.

Spellings: Absolutely.

Jacobs: Did you target particular local news people?

Spellings: Sure. I mean, it was not particular people so much as particular places where we knew we needed to be for a variety of reasons—influence on the Hill, battleground states. It's no accident that President Obama is going to Arizona and New Mexico, these swing states and key places. The purple states are the purple states and will continue to be and that's where they're going to spend their time.[40] That's where President Bush spent a lot of time; that's where President Obama is going to spend a lot of time, and so on. Places that matter and places that you need to be thinking about always. He didn't spend a lot of time selling the message in Texas, George W. Bush. He didn't need to.

I want to pick up for a second on something that Stu said about the issues that are not part of the campaign and how important that is. For us, that was immigration. In 2000, that was just something that was close to Bush's heart. As incendiary as that topic is now, it was virtually a sleeping dog then. Pete Wilson had gone through his thing in California, learned from it, and we did the total opposite in Texas.[41] I mean school—English-only and all of that stuff—we never had any of that sort of issue. We began to work on this very early in the administration. It's one of the most complicated policies because it implicates every single council—National Economic Council, the National Security Council, and of course domestic policy. Every single agency is implicated. Then 9/11 came and we stopped. Obviously in 2000 and in 2004 we didn't talk about it much on the campaign trail. Then, to try to build a constituency around and against Rush Limbaugh was impossible.[42]

Jacobs: Mr. Reed, the Clinton White House was very skilled in terms of its communications operations, very capable folks in the press room, press secretaries, a string of them who are well respected to this day. Was there a tension between both the energetic effort to push a political line, a spin coming out of the communications office, versus perhaps the need for a press secretary to earn the respect of the media, to give a Joe Friday, "just-the-facts-ma'am" sort of approach? Did you see a tension there, or not?

Reed: There's always a tension between the political advisers and the facts. [laughter] Let me make a couple of points about marketing in the White House. First, I have to take issue with Stu and correct the historical record. You forget that in the '92 campaign the anti-Washington mood was so strong. It wasn't all George H. W. Bush's fault. It was so overwhelming that without Perot in the race we would have won a Reagan-style landslide, and if Perot had stayed in the race the whole time, it is entirely possible that

President Bush would have finished third and Perot would have given us a run for our money.

I worked for the greatest presidential salesman of all time. But he would be the first to say that really at the end of the day it's all about the product. Because the White House and the bully pulpit is what everyone is watching, we assume that that is the White House's great advantage. But in my view, the greatest power of the executive is not selling, it's doing. The president has the ability to take actions that back up his policies and that sell his policies better than any speech or any press secretary or any spin operation can do.

It took us a while to realize that, but after the '94 elections when we didn't exactly have a compliant Congress, we realized that they weren't going to do anything that we wanted to do unless we forced them to pay attention. We developed an aggressive strategy doing executive orders and other kinds of executive actions to force their hand. The one that I worked on the most, welfare reform—we did I would say probably half-a-dozen executive orders on child support enforcement, and another half-dozen on welfare reform. And about the middle of 1996, Republicans who had been trying to stop us from being able to pass welfare reform, finally just threw up their hands and said, "Well, if you're going to do it anyway, we might as well go along so at least we can share some of the credit and be at the signing ceremony."

Jacobs: Let me just explore this idea with you about President Clinton deciding that "doing," using executive orders, is really what it is about. Because the notion that Stu Eizenstat mentioned about the bully pulpit presumes that you will be going through the usual legislative process. You put a proposal up, you work it through the usual legislative process where it is passed, and then the president signs it or vetoes it. What you're suggesting is really circumventing that entire process. Is your conclusion then that presidents really are fairly ineffectual using the bully pulpit, and that the executive order—?

Reed: No, I'm not saying circumvent it; I'm saying that in politics the most important thing is to win the argument. You can't assume that just because you have a bully pulpit—it is a great advantage. The party that has the White House has one person who is setting the message for that party and the other party has several hundred people in Congress and around the country who are all trying to get on the same talking points and can't do it nearly in as disciplined a fashion. But at the end of the day, you have to win the argument. You have to convince the country that you have the right idea.

It's not as though your pulpit goes unanswered. We faced hundreds of millions of dollars of advertising against our health-care plan, hundreds of millions of dollars of advertising against our tobacco bill.[43] The advantage of the bully pulpit erodes over time. When you're the only one talking about your ideas they sound great, but when the other side starts to bring up some different information, your advantage erodes a little bit. That's why it is very important for the president and the White House team to focus early on on the quality of their product. Every time a White House says, "I think we have a communications problem," that is a red flag that says your product stinks. Or if you hear that they're going to "relaunch an initiative," that means the *Titanic* is coming. It is impossible to relaunch a bad idea.

Eizenstat: I'd suggest again that if you look back at how those presidents who were perceived to be the most successful, who won a second term, Reagan, Clinton, Bush II—they all had a person in the White House who was highly experienced in Washington and who had the capacity to pull together policy and politics, salesmanship and substance, and organize the White House in that way: In Rove's case he wasn't formally chief of staff, but certainly Leon Panetta, John Podesta, Jim Baker for Reagan, who was brought in even though he was the campaign manager for Reagan's opponent, George H. W. Bush. That's what we missed in the first year. Bruce was a very good domestic adviser in every respect, but he was enormously benefited of course by having a president who was world class, and also having an organizational structure that pulled that together. The same again with Reagan, where Jim Baker was a master at that—and with Karl Rove. There's no substitute for that. In the modern presidency, you simply have to have one person who is designated to pull all of that together and to organize the outreach and the policy so that it becomes integrated.

Jacobs: I think that's been a major lesson from the Carter presidency, and we see it in subsequent presidents. You've got to have the coordinator, the Karl Rove type. In the Clinton White House, there were several who took that role.

Mr. Pinkerton, let me come back to this issue about the press as the filter. Marlin Fitzwater famously remarked about the media and the White

House relationship, "It's both our friend and our enemy." I'm paraphrasing. Thinking back on the way the media treated the administration you worked in, was it more enemy or friend?

Pinkerton: To be honest, more of an enemy. We have to go back to the old regime when CBS News and the *New York Times* were dominant. Rush Limbaugh was a minor—he'd come online by then, to use a phrase that wasn't used in 1990, but started. He supported Bush in '92. He was a strong anti-Perot voice, not that it did us any good. He hadn't reached his full potential yet, I guess.

Another word not used then, the "mainstream media" were not for Bush. They liked him well enough. They were personally fond of him. Maureen Dowd wrote a piece, probably for the *New Republic* about 1988 or '89, about the Ralph Laurenization of America and how reporters, the chattering classes in general, all secretly wished that they were Prince Charles and living on an estate somewhere.[44] They identified with Bush 41 on that score a little bit. They admired him but they didn't vote for him and they didn't really agree with him on policy.

Jacobs: Let me just push on that, because there is the left-right issue about the press, but I'm wondering more about the institutional issue. You've talked about the way in which the Bush White House was in some ways encumbered by the president's fumbling of his campaign promise on the—

Pinkerton: Fumbling wasn't quite the word I used, but okay.

Jacobs: I'm being diplomatic. You look at what most economists would say at this point, and I think there were economists at that point who would say, "Hey, the Bush tax bill was an important part of the Clinton success later on in creating budget surpluses." That has not been credited and it really wasn't much part of the press coverage then.[45] Yet the fact is that you've got a president who is not skilled with the media, who doesn't have an accurate sense of the importance of maintaining these campaign promises, and of the political repercussions of ditching them, and the way in which the media is going to have a feeding frenzy on this kind of backtracking.

Pinkerton: Right. Let me just associate myself with something Stu said about the importance of the individual. He mentioned one name in particular,

Jim Baker. If one were to identify the thread of successful policies through the twelve-year period from 1981 to 1993, one would say Reagan's domestic policy was pretty effective. Who was running things back then? Reagan was running things, but who was the prime minister? Jim Baker. Then strangely enough in the Bush 41 era, the domestic policy kind of turned south and the foreign policy was an astounding success, between the reunification of Germany and the coalition that evicted Saddam Hussein from Kuwait. Well, where was Baker then? He was at the State Department.

So one person can make a huge difference. And whether he is available or not—and he did have a canny sense that even if the press doesn't really like you, didn't vote for you, you could still make them your ally and you can still get things done and you can convince them that if they don't support you and write nice editorials about you, the crazies somewhere will take over and that will be bad for the country. You can appeal to sort of their David Broderian institutional sense of, "We've got to keep some stability here, so Jim Baker is our guy and we've got to stop Newt Gingrich," whom I'm a fan of by the way.[46] Nonetheless, in that cosmology, Baker could say, "If you don't support me, Gingrich will run the country and that will be bad."

So you can make use of them on that.

By the way, the Bush 41 White House, when it wanted to, even on more domestic issues, could be effective. There was a Supreme Court confirmation, Clarence Thomas, and that was a case where the Bush 41 White House pulled together pretty well, and we did a pretty good job of getting something through in about the most adverse circumstances you could imagine, in the pre–media breakup age.[47]

Eizenstat: Larry, just one last point that Jim really raises. Presidents will be most effective as salesmen on things in which they really believe. You can have all the organization surrounding them you want, but they have to really believe it. One example that I had on which I actually worked as a private citizen with President Bush I's White House was on selling a reluctant Congress, controlled at that time by Democrats, to give him the authority to send troops into Kuwait to oust Saddam Hussein.[48] I helped get a coalition of Democrats together to work with that. I still have a picture of President Bush thanking me for that, but that's not the point. The point is that this is something he really believed in. He was very effective in selling a reluctant public and Congress on that and in getting a coalition of Democrats and Republicans for what initially had been a very unpopular, but very necessary,

operation. When you believe something, a president can be a much more effective salesman than when he feels it is something that is foisted upon him
and he has to do it for other reasons.

Jacobs: Actually that's a very helpful segue to another set of issues: How effective are presidents at this? You, Mr. Eizenstat, opened by mentioning that
while the president obviously has extraordinary constitutional authority and
powers, particularly in the areas of foreign policy and national security, their
bully pulpit, their ability to mobilize the country, is perhaps their greatest
strength, particularly domestically. I'm curious—we've got administrations
represented here that have had a variety of experiences. The effort to barn-
storm the country on Social Security and introducing partial privatization;
the health-care effort; the effort to reduce the malaise in the country using
the "crisis of confidence" speech—these are all historically notable examples
of presidents investing a lot in this promotional effort, the salesmanship
part, and it not working.[49] Are those exceptions, or is that really a clue that
maybe we're overemphasizing or exaggerating the president's power and the
influence. Ms. Spellings?

Spellings: I was actually going to mention that on top of Stu's comment.
I think if the president is personally very familiar, very committed, very
knowledgeable about an issue, that matters—to the good. It mattered in my
case on education. President Bush, whenever we prepared remarks or talking points, he just knew the stuff. He took off and he felt it in his heart and
people could tell that. That was also true with Social Security. We have an
expression in Texas, "When the horse dies, get off." We didn't get off the
dead horse soon enough, I guess. But the point is, sometimes the president
is the one who is taking the microphone, good or bad, and we're running
the play that has been called.

Jacobs: But does that tell you then that we have an exaggerated sense of the
power of the bully pulpit? You mentioned Social Security—the horse died
and the president didn't get off. Was it because he still liked the horse?

Spellings: He was a true believer. Maybe it's the whole timing of the issue. I
think in hindsight we learned that we should have opened the second term
with immigration, not social security. It was too complicated and wasn't to
be, but he was highly committed to it and that was that.

Pinkerton: If I could just add—the three issues that you raised, the '77 energy plan, the health-care plan in '93 and '94, and Social Security, were all domestic issues. As Stu said, and Richard Neustadt said, presidents don't have that much power. On foreign policy it's different. If you can invoke national crisis—look at Jimmy Carter on the Iran hostage thing. You can go way up [in the polls] and get a lot done if it is foreign policy.[50]

Jacobs: Mr. Reed, do you agree that presidents don't have much power in terms of domestic policy?

Reed: Presidents have a lot of power. I do think that the political system and the coverage of White Houses dramatically overstates the importance of marketing, messaging, and spin, and undervalues the importance of product. The job of a president is not to talk the country into things that it desperately does not want to do; the job of the president is to try to figure out a way to get Washington to take the country where it needs and wants to go. We had enormous political talent in the Clinton White House. We perfected the planned leak; we invented the war room; we had the greatest salesman. But in a country that wants a lot of action to solve its problems but is deeply skeptical about government's ability to run a two-car funeral, as my old boss used to say, that's a very difficult tightrope to walk. It's primarily an intellectual and a policy challenge. It's not a marketing one.

Porter: One of the striking things is that Ronald Reagan's name has not been mentioned yet in the discussion. He is arguably the most successful president we've had in the last fifty years in terms of transforming the country, and he was a remarkable communicator who linked up a set of ideas and a product with the capacity to sell it. One of the ways that he did this was he had someone, Michael Deaver, who introduced something that subsequent presidents have followed, which at the time was called the "line of the day."
    The idea behind this is that people cannot focus on many things simultaneously with success. The president needs to use his powers, to the extent that he has them, to get the people to focus on what he wants them to focus on. Deaver was extraordinarily successful in creating events and photo opportunities, and presidential speeches and travel, so that people had an idea of what Reagan wanted.[51] Let me give you two examples:
    The first thing is that Reagan said he wanted to reverse the rate of growth of federal spending, the rate of growth of federal taxes, the rate of

growth of federal regulation, and to reduce by half the rate of growth of the money supply, in order to bring double-digit inflation down and to generate additional economic growth. He gave this message over and over and over again, very consistently. He produced a set of plans that were—the initial set was optimistic to be sure, but they did create an environment in which he could take a Republican Senate and a Democratic House that was somewhat reluctant and pass the Omnibus Budget Reconciliation Act of 1981 and the Economic Recovery Tax Act of 1981, two striking, landmark pieces of legislation.[52]

Reagan felt deeply about tax reform. He thought that the tax code needed to be changed. Jimmy Carter had tried it and Gerald Ford had tried it without success. We were preparing the '84 state of the union address and Reagan wanted to have in there that he was going to go for fundamental tax reform. Jim Baker and others said, "Look, you mention the word 'taxes' and people are going to think you're trying to raise taxes," because we had gone through the 1982 Tax Equity and Fiscal Responsibility Act, which had been a major tax increase in the wake of the big deficits that had emerged, and the 1984 Rose Garden Compromise, which included another tax element. Reagan ended up raising taxes twelve times while he was in there.[53] But Baker said, "If you mention the word taxes, you're going to get killed."

Reagan said, "Okay, I get to give the speech and tax reform will go in there, but I will modify it to say that I'm instructing the secretary of the treasury to prepare a plan that will be delivered to me on December 1 of 1984. It will be after the election and then we'll do it in the second term." He was relentless in the first two years of his second term in talking about tax reform everywhere he went. I remember he was going to North Carolina and Jesse Helms called and said, "My people down there don't care about tax reform. I want you to come and talk about x."

Reagan said, "I'm coming in and I'm going to talk about tax reform. If you want to be on the stand, fine. If you don't, that's fine as well. I'm going to do this." He pulled the political system, kicking and screaming, to the notion that we are going to have fundamental tax reform. Now, the plan that he advanced was dramatically modified ultimately when it got in the Congress. He had to do an enormous amount of negotiating to get it through. But we did get it. The last time we had a little fundamental change in the tax code was the 1986 act, and that was because Reagan was determined and relentless in pursuing that and had, in fact, a plan whereby he was consistently holding people.[54]

Now let's take the second example, what happened with respect to "Read my lips. No new taxes." Presidents, like all of us, are prisoners of our experi- ence. George Bush's experience as vice president is that he had seen Reagan deal with a deficit problem that had emerged after the 1981–82 recession by bringing together a bipartisan group of Republicans and Democrats, House and Senate, administration, and negotiating a deal. There had been the 1982 "Gang of 17" negotiations that produced the Tax Equity and Fiscal Re- sponsibility Act, and the Budget Reconciliation Act of that year.[55] We'd had another bipartisan negotiation producing what was called the Rose Garden Compromise in 1984. When the stock market crashed in October of 1987, Jim Baker, who was at the treasury, again put together another bipartisan negotiated package.

We now had three examples of where a Republican president would deal with a Democratic Congress in pulling together a bipartisan deficit reduc- tion package. Bush tried in his first year to solve the deficit problem by doing it all on the spending side and he got about 60 percent of what he wanted through. Then as the economy started to slow and the deficit num- bers started to rise, his budget director and others came in and said, "You are going to face a doubling of the deficit if you don't do something."

So he announced that he would deal with this on a bipartisan basis. We'd check with the House and the Senate and we put together a bipartisan group that was going to do it.[56] His initial inclination was to try to do it all on the spending side, but that had never been done before because all of these other compromise packages had included a spending restraint com- ponent and a revenue component. His treasury secretary told him, "Reagan managed to raise taxes by not changing marginal rates. When people think of the income tax, they think of their marginal rates. They can accept some on the gasoline tax increase or closing a loophole here and there. You can agree to have a revenue component in it as long as you hold the line and say you're not going to do it with respect to the top marginal rate."[57] As a result, he said, "The only way that I will do this is if the Democrats will agree to budget caps on the spending side." President Clinton, to his credit, did not throw them overboard, but embraced basically his predecessor's policies and put them in place.

Bush's problem was that he didn't prepare the groundwork. He didn't explain to the country clearly enough why he was doing what he was doing, and as a result the proposal was interpreted, fairly, as a reversal of his pledge without any groundwork being laid as to why you need to do that. As a result he got severely criticized and damaged himself politically.

Jacobs: Stu Eizenstat, let me turn to you to comment on this. You had started off talking about the importance of the policy and the sales being integrated together, not coming up with a policy and then down the road developing a sales strategy. Is the story that we've heard from Roger Porter and Jim Pinkerton about what happened with Bush 41 on the new tax pledge an example of how not to do things?

Eizenstat: Well, yes it is. But we've all tried to be frank about our own failings, and as I've mentioned, popping a major comprehensive energy bill on the country was another example of not having laid the groundwork. We ended up passing three major energy bills. We broke the Gordian knot on pricing of crude oil, which had been controlled by Nixon in wage and price controls, and on natural gas, which had been controlled since Truman's time. We got alternative energy, conservation, syn-fuels, solar. We had the whole package at the end of the day. But it was not until the second and third energy packages that the groundwork had been politically laid with the public that this was really critical to the public. They did not understand. Look, in 1977 there were no huge run-ups in oil prices. That had occurred in '73, '74, but that had diminished. There were no gas lines. We did not perceive, as we should have, our dependence on foreign oil, notwithstanding the boycott in '73.

These are all examples of good policies, the right policies. President Bush was right to do this, to combine the tax increase with spending cuts, and the policies that I'm discussing here as well were the right ones. But that's not what being president is about. We learned that, and the president [Carter] ended up being, in my opinion, the most successful one-term president ever in terms of accomplishments, because we did learn the salesmanship. But we did not understand this during that critical first year, and it is the failures that oftentimes overwhelm the successes.

Jacobs: Bill Galston, Stu Eizenstat and others have been talking about good policy not being enough, that you've got to have this sales element and the promotional part and the political connection to your base as integral to development of policy. Is that the way you see it?

Galston: Well, of course, on one level. But Bruce Reed said something that was so striking that I wrote it down almost verbatim, when he said that the task of government, of the president, is not to pull the people where they desperately don't want to go, but rather to take them where they need to go and want to go. That raises a very important question, which is a classic question of democratic governance. It points to one of the fundamental distempers of democracy. What happens when the people need to go somewhere, but they desperately do not want to go there? Right?

That, it seems to me, is where there is an opportunity for presidential statesmanship of the highest order, but also for presidential failure of the highest order. We can all think of examples. As adults we've all been living through a period where president after president has been unable to persuade the people and take the people towards certain fundamental truths that would deal with certain fundamental underlying problems. We may eventually, or soon, reap the whirlwind from that.

I am really preoccupied with the question of how, in a democracy that is in many respects a populist democracy, which is driven more and more by hyperpartisan media coverage one way or another—Fox and MSNBC are the image of our awful future. I was talking with Bert Carp and he said, "Pretty soon we're not going to have news; we're going to have Democrat news and Republican news." I think we're heading strongly in that direction. How in these circumstances can a president more effectively close the gap between what the country needs and what the people want?

Jacobs: Let me just come over here. Jim Pinkerton is sitting here quietly but I can feel vibrations coming from his chair. Is that the way that you view the challenge?

Pinkerton: I do agree with Bill, as I usually do, that cable news now has conquered American politics—not much legislating and compromising goes on, as opposed to talking points and getting on the air to blast the opponent. All the various gangs—17, 14, I've lost the various numbers—those people tend to get pummeled from the various media corners out there. It is a terrible challenge. Whatever happened, to use an old phrase, to the "vital center"?[58] It's hard to identify who is an establishmentarian any more, because if you could identify him, he or she would get knocked off in the next primary.

I will say this in the spirit of lessons learned—I vehemently disagreed at the time, but now I do see the wisdom of a comprehensive energy policy that takes a look at things like oil imports and that says it's nuts to be sending, exporting, hundreds of millions of dollars to our mortal enemies while shutting down nuclear power. I mean, if there's ever a case where the vital center ought to get together and figure stuff out, it's energy policy, and nobody has dared to do that since Jimmy Carter.

Eizenstat: Three quick points: One, just a gloss on Bruce's very perceptive point about taking the public where it wants to go. A president can often, with the right salesmanship and organization, take the public where it didn't realize it wanted to go but needs to, and to convince the public that that is in fact where it wanted to go. Bill Clinton was a master at doing that, on welfare reform, for example.

Second, Panama Canal was an example of an instance where the public did not want to go. We had 25 percent support when we started to sell the Panama Canal Treaty, and this was an example of the proper integration of good but controversial policy with excellent salesmanship. It was done with enormous public outreach, Margaret, by going into the country, going to swing states, getting Republicans—[Henry] Kissingers and others—to validate this. And ultimately we got to a point where around 65 percent of the public supported it and there was enough political cover. At that point, the public was convinced this was important for peace in Latin America and for our future.

Third point, on the comprehensive energy package: Why did the "malaise" speech happen, and was it the unmitigated disaster that it is perceived to be today? It happened, Jim, because we had broken our pick on the first energy bill, getting a lot done, but with eighteen months of pain. A second energy bill came in '79 and then a third energy bill in 1980. When the president came back from the Tokyo G7 Summit we had an energy speech ready for him to try to get the third energy bill passed.[59] He said, "I've had it. The public has turned me off on energy. They won't listen to me. I've got to step back and talk about what my entire presidency is about or I'll never get anywhere on energy." That led to the Camp David retreat with experts coming up and so forth.[60]

Now there was as violent an argument as I've ever seen in any government in which I've been in, between me and Vice President Mondale on one side and Pat Caddell, Gerry Rafshoon, Jody Powell, and Ham Jordan on the other, about the malaise speech to begin with.[61] I said, "You can't cancel an energy speech and not give an energy speech." "Malaise," by the way, was never used. "People don't want to hear a speech about the American spirit. They think we're the problem with double-digit inflation, not that they're the problem." The compromise ended up with this crisis of spirit speech and then saying that the way to deal with this crisis of spirit is having an organizing principle, which is energy independence—putting that as a second part.

The speech, contrary to my view and Mondale's—we were wrong—was an astounding success. That's not what is perceived now. It was an unbelievable success. Carter's polls shot up 25, 30 percent. We went out with him to Detroit right afterwards to build on this, and it was like the good old days in '76. You'd have thought there was a political resurrection. What killed the crisis of confidence speech was burying the headline just as we were getting momentum, by the cabinet firing, by being perceived to be firing the entire cabinet, and squashing all the momentum that that speech developed.[62] Again, it's a question of prioritizing things and of not trying to mix too many things at once. That was the problem with the crisis of confidence speech, not the speech itself.

Jacobs: I want to come to Bert Carp on an issue. You often hear about presidential salesmanship. It's often described as kind of a bank shot. The president goes out into the country. We see President Obama campaigning for health-care reform as President Bush did on Social Security.

The idea is that the president goes out, whips up, rallies, mobilizes Americans, and then members of Congress hear this and become more supportive of the president's legislation.

Now there's another view about that, which is a little more skeptical: Members already have a view about good policy or concern about their constituents, and thus any number of reasons for not being bowled over by the president going around the country barnstorming. What's your view? Is presidential promotion and salesmanship the way to win over Congress?

Carp: Each one of these things is different. One of the things we have to be careful of—if we identify the person who won the Virginia lottery last week, go and knock on their door and say, "How'd you win the lottery?" they will tell you how they won. "I took my grandchildren's birthdays, divided by the square root of three. . . ." [laughter] You can't just necessarily go back and look at success and then say, "This produced that." These are really complicated and really hard questions.

I believe that members of Congress are the most effective political polling organization there is in this country. They know what people think about the stuff they're trying to peddle. If you as president can have public events that change those kinds of meetings—so, members went to one town meeting last week, and the town meeting they went to this week is different—you should do it. You will see the difference on Capitol Hill immediately. If, on the other hand, you undertake a big public promotional effort and it doesn't move the needle, then these guys—they're different in many ways, but they're all completely focused on this—they will say, "Aha, public education did not move the needle here." Then you can slide backwards quickly, not so much because somebody will say, "Oh, I'll give a speech on the other side," but because they may just say, "Instead of this being number two of the things I might think about or that I might like to do, I'll just move this sucker back to number six." You take your life in your hands when you do these things. If you try it and make it work, you can change the world. But if it doesn't work, you'll lose. You won't stay where you were; you'll slide backwards.

Spellings: I just want to put a finer point on that, and it is this: The culprit for why some of these hard things can't get done is a toxic alliance, for lack of a better word, between the unions and the arch conservatives. They tend to team up for their own reasons on education, on immigration, on trade, on health, on welfare. The town hall meeting happens and the members of Congress are indeed an accurate polling body, because the people that show up at those things are members of the toxic alliance. That just seems to be playing itself out over and over and over.

Jacobs: Mr. Cannon?

Cannon: In light of this recounting of presidential successes, it needs to be said that President Ford had a low record of success, and the reasons are fairly obvious. One, he didn't get elected, so he had no mandate. More important, in the election of '74, something like forty seats in the House changed. So he was confronted with a House that was two-to-one against him and a Senate in which he had thirty-seven Republicans. He had tremendous opposition.[63]

Furthermore, it's candid to say he was not the best of salesmen for his programs around the country. My judgment is that he was a first-rate manager of the White House after the first six or eight weeks. He learned how

192 Stuart Eizenstat et al.

to manage the White House and did a very good job. But he never really succeeded, and what Stu and I have often talked about is the bully pulpit. He was not very good. He didn't come across very well on television. He was a marvelous guy in the office to work with, but put him on television and he looked like exactly what he was, a kind of a dull midwesterner who simply could not project the quality of the guy he was.[64] My opinion is that about half the presidency is managing, and the other half is selling.

Roger has talked about how extraordinarily effective Reagan was, and he was effective for a lot of reasons. He had Jim Baker, who was a master at negotiation. He had Ed Meese, who was anchoring the right and protecting him in whatever he wanted to do. Then he had Mike Deaver, who presented him in these mini-movies that showed Reagan at his absolute best. Reagan was a fascinating man. He would sit there and you would think, He is not going to be able to do this. But get him before that microphone and that camera and he could perform. He could perform brilliantly and sell himself, whatever it was.

There's another reason also that should be mentioned—you touched on it briefly, Roger—he had a Republican Senate. This was a very responsive Republican Senate. Howard Baker was the Senate majority leader and did an extraordinarily effective job through his first votes on the budget.[65] And President Reagan himself was very effective at mobilizing the Republicans in the House and a number of Democrats in the House from the South. He could get it done.

Ford's major success really was in stopping the worst from happening. He had something like sixty-seven vetoes and only seven were overturned.[66] He had been very good on defense as a football player and that's basically what he played.

Porter: We need to remember, with respect to Reagan, that there are really three phases of his presidency. The first is when he came in. He had the wind at his back. He had won a big election, the Republicans had finally gotten control of the Senate, and he had a working majority in the House with the boll weevils. In the midterm 1982 elections, the Republicans lost twenty-six seats in the House of Representatives and suddenly that working coalition in the House was gone. The tone of the negotiations totally changed. It was like a different presidency after the first two years. Then in 1986, the Republicans lost control of the Senate, and now you had both houses that were effectively outside of his control—what legislation comes to the floor at what time, et cetera. It was again a totally different situation.

Presidents *can* be effective spokesmen. Presidents can do a lot, but the context which they face is crucial. Clinton is a classic example of someone who had a very different presidency after the loss of fifty-two or fifty-three seats in 1994.[67]

Reed: It was plenty. I just want to defend the American people here. Reagan was a great communicator. He had the historical good fortune to get out before the consequences of some of his fiscal policies became widely known. Bush paid a price for it. But one of the unfortunate consequences of the Reagan era is that the political world began to think that politics was some kind of magic, that if you could talk to the American people the way Reagan did, that that's all that matters. It isn't the most important thing.

Americans are the most practical people, the most results-driven people on earth. That can either work to a politician's benefit, if he's able to produce good results, or it can be his undoing, if his policies fail. We shouldn't get too enamored of the political pixie dust. It's very important to have a bond with the American people, but as Bill and Stu both said, it's to enable you to be honest with them about where the country needs to go and to figure out how far they can go towards that—because there's no point in trying to take the country to a place that it won't go. They're the boss. They're going to win in the end. The challenge is to show them what the right thing for the country is and to persuade them of that. If you're not doing that, and if your policies don't live up to that promise, then you've never got a chance.

Eizenstat: Let's use a contemporary example: President Carter as part of his early energy package tried to get a very modest gas tax passed as a conservation measure. President Clinton, Bruce, tried to get a BTU tax that made all sorts of sense, and it would have been rebated back so it didn't cost anything and we'd have had it as a conservation measure.[68] Here we are in 2009, and our dependence on foreign oil is twice what it was when Richard Nixon said in 1973 that we were going to be energy-independent in ten years.[69] Here we are, more dependent than ever. Here we are with the whole global warming issue. Most of us at this table, or at least some of us, would say, "Let's go back to that BTU tax. Let's have a fifty-cent gas tax so we can encourage people without the vagaries of oil. Let's do something that taxes the product we don't want to import and gives it back to the American people. . . ." And yet no president is going to take that on at this point, for the reason that Bruce mentions.

There comes some point at which you simply know that the public is not going to listen, and if you try to break your pick on that again and again and again, you prevent yourself from doing the next best thing, which is maybe a cap-and-trade program. It is always a very tough judgment call between what the right policy might be, which had been tried and found to be publicly unsuccessful, and how much the public will get. This is always a tension in the presidency.

Notes

1. Eizenstat's characterization here follows closely that of Richard E. Neustadt, who famously argued that "presidential power is the power to persuade." *Presidential Power and the Modern Presidents: The Politics of Leadership from Roosevelt to Reagan* (New York: Free Press, 1990), 11, 28.

2. The White House public liaison office was set up to help the president organize interest-group activity on behalf of his initiatives. For details on its operation, see Joseph A. Pika, *The White House Transition Project: The White House Office of Public Liaison*, Report 2009-03 (2008), http://whitehousetransitionproject.org/resources/briefing/WHTP-2009-03-Public%20Liaison.pdf (accessed November 1, 2010). The portfolio of the office now also includes intergovernmental relations and has been renamed by President Obama the Office of Public Engagement and Intergovernmental Affairs.

3. The exact nature of Stephen Hess's advice seems to be a bit more ambiguous than Eizenstat suggests here. In Hess's book published in the year of Carter's election, *Organizing the Presidency*, he wrote: "The chief conclusion of this study is that effective presidential leadership in the immediate future is likely to result only from creating more nearly collegial administrations in which Presidents rely on their Cabinet officers as the principal sources of advice." Yet Hess was much more equivocal when writing about the best structure for the White House staff proper, concluding that "there are no immutable designs for organizing the presidency—schemes that usefully transcend a particular administration." Indeed he suggested that any attempt to define such universally "useful structure[s] becomes an attempt to nail currant jelly to the wall." Charles O. Jones holds that by the time Hess's advice was solicited, the decision had already been taken by Carter not to use a chief of staff. Subsequently, consistent with the argument in his book, "Hess proposed a model that permitted 'wide access . . . in a structured setting,' thus allowing more screening than is typical of the spokes of the wheel. It was not altogether clear how the Hess [model of an] 'isosceles trapezoid' [a pyramid with the top cut off] would function in practice. He was merely suggesting a middle ground between the other models." See Hess, *Organizing the Presidency* (Washington, D.C.: Brookings Institution Press, 1976), 154, 174, 177; Jones, *The Presidency in a Separated System* (Washington, D.C.: Brookings Institution Press, 1994), 86.

4. This story is also recounted in Jones, *Presidency in a Separated System*, 86.

5. Carter's first public liaison was Margaret "Midge" Costanze (1932-2010). Every White House office that has responsibility for coordinating efforts with specific external constituencies—such as congressional relations, public liaison, and even the press office—is vulnerable to charges from others that it is more interested in the approval of its external clients than in the president's priorities. See Russell L. Riley, ed., *Bridging the Constitutional Divide: Inside the White House Office of Legislative Affairs* (College Station: Texas A&M University Press, 2010), 10-11.

6. Carter's "Presidential Support Scores" actually seem to run slightly below Kennedy's and Johnson's, but clearly exceed every other president's between Eisenhower and Clinton. George W. Bush's numbers were also higher until his final year in office. Scores compiled and reported in James Thurber, ed., *Rivals for Power: Presidential-Congressional Relations*, 3rd ed. (Lanham, Md.: Rowman & Littlefield, 2006), 5. See also the CQ chart entitled "How Often the President Wins," http://www.cq.com/graphics/weekly/2008/12/15/wr20081215-48partisan-prezsupport-wins.pdf (accessed November 1, 2010).

7. The East Room is the largest space in the White House, a room in the main residence that is often used for ceremonial purposes and for entertaining.

8. Eizenstat misspeaks here, as Carter was succeeded by eight years of Reagan and four more of George H. W. Bush—a point James Pinkerton makes just below.

9. There were more liberal offerings in the 1976 primary season, including Governor Jerry Brown of California and Rep. Morris Udall of Arizona.

10. On whether politicians typically traffic in cynical promise making, see Lawrence R. Jacobs and Robert Y. Shapiro, *Politicians Don't Pander: Political Manipulation and the Loss of Democratic Responsiveness* (Chicago: University of Chicago Press, 2000).

11. Dolph Briscoe, Jr. (1923-2010) was a Texas rancher who served as governor of the state from 1973 to 1979.

12. Eizenstat recounts a slightly more extended version of this story in the Stuart Eizenstat Interview, Miller Center, University of Virginia, Jimmy Carter Presidential Oral History Project, January 29-30, 1982, 26-29.

13. James R. Schlesinger served as secretary of energy for President Carter from 1977 to 1979. He earlier had served as director of central intelligence and secretary of defense in the Nixon and Ford administrations. John D. Dingell, Jr., has served in the U.S. House of Representatives, from Michigan, since 1955, and had established himself by this time as a fierce guardian of his committee's regulatory turf. Henry M. "Scoop" Jackson (1912-1983) was a congressman and then senator from the state of Washington, whose national reputation was forged from vigorous support of American national security interests during the Cold War. Brief biographies of each of these figures, and their role in the Carter years, appear in Burton I. Kaufman, *Presidential Profiles: The Carter Years* (New York: Facts on File, 2006).

14. The reference here is to the red-covered book *Quotations from Chairman Mao Tse-tung* which was the all-purpose handbook for Chinese communists and their sympathizers worldwide.

15. Another account of the natural gas issue in particular, and the development of energy policy in general, is available in the James R. Schlesinger Interview, Miller Center, University of Virginia, Jimmy Carter Presidential Oral History Project, July 19–20, 1984. See also W. Carl Biven, *Jimmy Carter's Economy: Policy in an Age of Limits* (Chapel Hill: University of North Carolina Press, 2002), 155–184.

16. The administration initially sought quick tax cuts to stimulate a stagnant economy, a policy devised in Georgia during the transition period. "The consumer portion of the tax cut consisted of a $50 rebate on 1976 income taxes to be distributed in April, May and June through a reduction in 1977 withholding from pay checks." Biven, *Jimmy Carter's Economy*, 62. Biven elaborates on the tax cut story in ch. 4.

17. Edmund S. Muskie (1914–1996) was a Maine Democrat who served in the U.S. Senate from 1959 to 1980. He chaired the Senate Budget Committee during most of the Carter years. He was nearly designated Carter's vice presidential nominee in 1976 and was named by Carter as secretary of state for the final year of his administration. Carter, *Keeping Faith: Memoirs of a President* (Fayetteville: University of Arkansas Press, 1995), 39.

18. In his Miller Center oral history interview, President Carter recalls, "I almost lost a friend in that episode with Ed Muskie, who was the chairman of the Budget Committee. And although I had consulted with Bob Byrd and with some of the others about it, I didn't consult with Ed Muskie before he got the word. He was very aggravated about it because he was still fighting to line up votes to pass the fifty dollar tax rebate when I decided that it was better for us not to have it at all." Jimmy Carter Interview, Miller Center, University of Virginia, Jimmy Carter Presidential Oral History Project, November 29, 1982, 52. W. Carl Biven asserts that "the abruptness of the decision raised questions about sureness in handling policy issues. There was a loss of credibility." *Jimmy Carter's Economy*, 82.

19. The centrality of discipline to the Bush approach evidently had deep roots, both in Bush's own personal development and in his conception of how politics operates. One analyst, for example, has written of Bush, "Message discipline, both the lack of it and the way the messages had been obscured, was what had killed George W.'s father" politically. Accordingly, message discipline was a hallmark of Bush's first gubernatorial campaign, "the mantra, the four food groups." See Bill Minutaglio, *First Son: George W. Bush and the Bush Family Dynasty* (New York: Three Rivers Press, 1999), 277.

20. Since 1975 George Miller III has been a Democratic member of Congress from the San Francisco Bay area. During the George W. Bush years, he was the ranking Democrat on (and later chair of) the House Education and Workforce Committee. The movie was *Thirteen Days*, starring Kevin Costner.

21. On the role of the state of the union message as a matter of public communication and of internal discipline, see Kathryn Dunn Tenpas, "The State of the Union

Address: Process, Politics, and Promotion," and the transcribed discussion of "Speech-writers on the State of the Union Address," both in *The President's Words: Speeches and Speechwriting in the Modern White House*, eds. Michael Nelson and Russell L. Riley (Lawrence: University Press of Kansas, 2010).

22. The 1995 address was record-setting, but it came in at just under 85 minutes. Clinton delivered a nearly 89-minute state of the union in 2000. Other than Clinton's, annual messages exceeding one hour are rare.

23. Rodney Dangerfield (1921–2004) was an American comedian best known for comic riffs on the theme, "I don't get no respect."

24. The October 19, 1987, cover of *Newsweek* magazine, in anticipation of Bush's run for the presidential nomination, featured a portrait of Bush in his speedboat under the headline, "Fighting the Wimp Factor."

25. Bush joined the navy after the attack on Pearl Harbor and at the age of eighteen became the youngest aviator then commissioned. The Avenger aircraft he was piloting took enemy fire during an assault on Chichijima and subsequently went down in the Pacific Ocean, killing two crew members. He was rescued by the *USS Finback* submarine.

26. *The Conscience of a Conservative* (Bottom of the Hill Publishing) was a book written in 1960 by later Republican presidential nominee Barry Goldwater, an Arizona senator and longtime voice of the conservative wing of the party. It was a touchstone of conservatism at the time. *A Choice Not an Echo* (Pere Marquette Press) was authored by Phyllis M. S. Schlafly in 1964, to promote Goldwater's campaign by fighting any attempts to moderate his message. Later in her career, Schlafly became probably the most prominent public voice among women fighting against feminism and its political influences. Ayn Rand (1905–1982) was a Russian-born novelist whose philosophy and complex works of fiction have been embraced by a range of conservative intellectuals influenced by her libertarianism and advocacy of unfettered market capitalism.

27. Prescott S. Bush (1895–1972) was President George H. W. Bush's father and served in the U.S. Senate from Connecticut from 1952 to 1963. Prescott Bush was a moderate Republican, helping to lead both Planned Parenthood and the United Negro College Fund in the 1940s and 50s.

28. Harris County, Texas, is the county surrounding Houston.

29. Harvey L. "Lee" Atwater (1951–1991) was a Republican political operative from South Carolina renowned for his take-no-prisoners brand of politics. He had a junior-level position in the Reagan administration and then ran the Bush campaign in 1988. Bush rewarded him thereafter by designating him chairman of the Republican National Committee. He died of a brain tumor in March of 1991. Some political analysts believe that President Bush's reelection effort in 1992 suffered materially from Atwater's absence.

30. Grover G. Norquist is a Washington-based anti-tax activist with a broad influence within the Republican Party. One of his core efforts has been to require candidates at all levels of government to sign a pledge not to increase taxes. He reportedly has quipped: "I

don't want to abolish government. I simply want to reduce it to the size where I can drag it into the bathroom and drown it in the bathtub." More on his work can be found at http://www.atr.org/grover-norquist-a3016# (accessed November 2, 2010).

31. The thousand points of light—a phrase coined by speechwriter Peggy Noonan—was a rhetorical device employed by candidate Bush during the 1988 election season to emphasize the importance of multitudes of community organizations in building a better American society. The president's voluntary national service effort grew from that same interest. In his acceptance speech at the Republican National Convention, Bush promised a "kinder, gentler nation"—an effort to distance himself somewhat from the harsher characterizations of the domestic side of the Reagan presidency, a pledge which did not endear Bush to many of the Reagan faithful. YES was an initiative of Bush's national service office to foster voluntary community service among young people.

32. Pinkerton's recollection about the news being posted on the press office bulletin board is confirmed by Richard M. Pious in *Why Presidents Fail: White House Decision Making from Eisenhower to Bush II* (Lanham, Md.: Rowman & Littlefield, 2008), 154–155.

33. Interviews with heads of the White House congressional liaison office verify how important they think it is to be consulted when legislative initiatives are in the process of being crafted. Otherwise, as Bryce Harlow colorfully observed, the presidents' lobbyists are at risk of being handed a lead weight with instructions to "float it across a pond." See Riley, ed., *Bridging the Constitutional Divide*, 60–61.

34. George H. W. Bush was director of central intelligence from January 1976 to January 1977.

35. H. Ross Perot was a Texas businessman who ran for president as an insurgent, independent candidate in 1992. Eizenstat's assertion is that Perot's candidacy benefited Clinton. The evidence on this claim is ambiguous, as Bruce Reed notes below.

36. On Carter's decision to attack the water projects, see Scott A. Frisch and Sean Q. Kelly, *Jimmy Carter and the Water Wars: Presidential Influence and the Politics of Pork* (Amherst, N.Y.: Cambria Press, 2008).

37. Ibid., 40–41.

38. "'I'm mindful of the filter through which some news travels, and somehow you just got to go over the heads of the filter and speak directly to the people,' the President [Bush] told a Baltimore news anchor." Quoted in Charles Zewe, "'Infoganda' in Uniform," Nieman Reports, Nieman Foundation for Journalism at Harvard, Fall 2004, http://www.nieman.harvard.edu/reports/article/100788/Infoganda-in-Uniform.aspx (accessed November 2, 2010).

39. "In 2003, President Bush sprinted out to . . . give five consecutive interviews to regional broadcasters instead of the White House press corps, whom he was snubbing. Nixon pulled the same regional news reporters stunt during his administration because he was feuding with the network anchors." Jack Shafer, "Old Media District Eclipsed by New Bypass," *Slate*, February 9, 2010, http://www.slate.com/id/2244162/ (accessed November 2, 2010).

40. Purple states are swing states, a mixture of red (Republican) and blue (Democratic). Television networks use red and blue to color states on a national map during election-night coverage.

41. Peter B. Wilson was Republican mayor of San Diego (1971–1982), U.S. senator from California (1983–1991), and governor of California (1991–1999). He took a hard-line position against providing state services to illegal immigrants, which alienated Latinos and, some critics assert, gave the Democrats an enduring structural political advantage. When Bush campaigned in California in 2000, he implicitly repudiated Wilson, condemning "the politics of pitting one group against the other." Quoted in Carla Minucci, "Reaching Out to State's Latinos, Bush Distances Himself from Pete Wilson," *San Francisco Chronicle*, April 8, 2000.

42. Limbaugh is a famous conservative radio commentator who routinely used his broadcast microphone to argue against liberalization of immigration laws.

43. Reed's aide, future Supreme Court justice Elena Kagan, had taken "the lead in helping craft the legislation needed to complete a historic $368.5 billion settlement that tobacco companies had agreed to that year to cover state health costs caused by smoking. The legislation needed to define the new authority of the Food and Drug Administration to regulate tobacco, a key settlement provision. It would limit the industry's future liability, a condition of its support, and establish fees and taxes for the industry and limits on advertising." The bill ultimately failed. Alec MacGillis, "Kagan Tested by 1990s Battles over Tobacco Legislation," *Washington Post*, June 4, 2010, available at http://www.washingtonpost.com/wp-dyn/content/article/2010/06/03/AR2010060304921_2.html (accessed November 3, 2010).

44. The editors were unable to identify this source, although the article evidently did not appear in the *New Republic.*

45. One work that considers holistically the roots of the Clinton surplus and the role of the 1990 budget agreement in contributing to it is Allen Schick with Felix LoStracco, *The Federal Budget: Politics, Policy, Process* (Washington, D.C.: Brookings Institution Press, 2000).

46. David S. Broder was a syndicated columnist based at the *Washington Post* until his death in 2011. He was generally considered to be a middle-of-the-road critic who spoke for establishment centrism in Washington.

47. Clarence Thomas is an associate justice of the U.S. Supreme Court, nominated by President George H. W. Bush in July 1991. Although the appointment was successful, the confirmation process was a brutal one, with public airings of sexual misconduct charges against Thomas when he ran the Equal Employment Opportunity Commission in the Reagan and early Bush years. Details of that episode appear in Jane Mayer and Jill Abramson, *Strange Justice: The Selling of Clarence Thomas* (New York: Houghton Mifflin, 1994).

48. The liberation of Kuwait, through Operation Desert Storm, occurred in early 1991. Although there was strong sentiment in the Bush White House that the president's

inherent constitutional authority meant that he could act unilaterally to send American troops into combat, Bush decided to seek congressional consent—and got it. For an inside account of the war effort, including these domestic efforts, see George Bush and Brent Scowcroft, A World Transformed (New York: Vintage Books, 1998), chs. 13–19.

49. Social Security privatization was a George W. Bush initiative. Health care was Clinton's; the "crisis of confidence" was Carter's.

50. Political scientist Aaron Wildavsky wrote (originally in 1966) that "the United States has one President, but it has two presidencies; one presidency is for domestic affairs, and the other is concerned with defense and foreign policy." Although Wildavsky's "two-presidencies" thesis has been the subject of considerable debate among political scientists ever since, the basic assertion of differences in the president's power in these two domains remains almost axiomatic. Wildavsky, "The Two Presidencies," in The Presidency, ed. Aaron Wildavsky (Boston: Little, Brown, 1969), 230–243. For one reassessment, see Scot Schraufnagel and Stephen M. Shellman, "The Two Presidencies, 1984 to 1998: A Replication and Extension," Presidential Studies Quarterly 31, no. 4 (December 2001): 699–707.

51. One very accessible account of the Reagan political team's success in messaging is Martin Schram, The Great American Video Game: Presidential Politics in the Television Age (New York: William Morrow, 1987).

52. On the initial Reagan economic plan, see Hugh Heclo and Rudolph G. Penner, "Fiscal and Political Strategy in the Reagan Administration," in The Reagan Presidency: An Early Assessment, ed. Fred I. Greenstein (Baltimore, Md.: Johns Hopkins, 1983).

53. Former Republican Senator Alan Simpson of Wyoming, addressing members of a presidential commission established to deal with the problems of the federal debt, said, "Let's just disengage ourselves from the myth that Ronald Reagan never raised taxes. He did. And here are four big ones. So I hope this will clear the air for some of the groups today. In 1982, the Tax Equity and Fiscal Responsibility Act, that rolled back about a third of his '81 tax cuts, raised corporate tax rates, and to a lesser extent income tax rates. Raised taxes by almost 1 percent of GDP, which at that time was the largest percentage in peacetime increase ever. [The] 1982 gas tax increase. [The] 1983 Greenspan commission—we know so well; [fellow commission member Alice Rivlin] remembers—we all . . . raised payroll taxes for lower and middle income households to higher than they were before Reagan's '81 tax cuts. Then there was the 1984 deficit reduction tax. Those are the big four. Then there was the Railroad Retirement Revenue Act, Consolidated Omnibus Budget of '85 . . . '86 . . . '87 Continuing Resolution, Omnibus Budget Reconciliation Act of '87, that was $8.6 billion. So there were a lot of them." Quoted in Jon Ponder, "Reagan Raised Taxes at Least 7 Times, Including the Biggest Corporate Tax Hike Ever," July 2, 2010, Pensito Review, available at http://www.pensitoreview.com/2010/07/02/reagan-raised-taxes-7-times/ (accessed November 3, 2010). Reagan's tax increases are also discussed in Joshua Green, "Reagan's Liberal Legacy," Washington Monthly, January/

February 2003, available at http://www.washingtonmonthly.com/features/2003/0301 .green.html (accessed November 3, 2010).

54. A thorough narrative of the enactment of the 1986 tax act appears in Jeffrey H. Birnbaum and Alan S. Murray, *Showdown at Gucci Gulch: Lawmakers, Lobbyists, and the Unlikely Triumph of Tax Reform* (New York: Vintage Books, 1988).

55. On this episode, see Edwin Meese III, *With Reagan: The Inside Story* (Lanham, Md.: Regnery, 1992), 143–147. Meese records there his belief that "the TEFRA compromise— the 'Debacle of 1982'—was the greatest domestic error of the Reagan administration."

56. An account of these negotiations appears in Duane Windsor, "The 1990 Deficit Reduction Deal," in *Principle over Politics? The Domestic Policy of the George H. W. Bush Presidency*, eds. Richard Himmelfarb and Rosanna Perotti (Westport, Conn.: Greenwood Publishing, 2004).

57. Bush's treasury secretary was his longtime personal friend Nicholas Brady. Prior to his service for Bush, Brady had a lengthy career in banking.

58. The term is usually associated with the work of Arthur Schlesinger, Jr., who published a book by that name, originally in 1949. See *The Vital Center: The Politics of Freedom* (New Brunswick, N.J.: Transaction Publishers, 1998).

59. The Tokyo meeting was scheduled in June 1979 for the leaders of the world's major industrialized democracies to discuss the condition of the global economy. According to Daniel Yergin, the Tokyo event turned into "an all-energy summit. It was also a very nasty one. Tempers were badly frayed." Moreover, things were boiling on the home front for Carter. "On the way to the White House one morning, Eizenstat had sat for forty-five minutes in a gas line at his local Amoco station, on Connecticut Avenue, and he had found himself seized by the same almost uncontrollable rage that was afflicting his fellow citizens from one end of the country to the other. . . . So, on the last day of the Tokyo summit, Eizenstat dispatched a grim, depressing memorandum to Carter about the continuing gas shortage: 'Nothing else has so frustrated, confused, angered the American people—or so targeted their distress at you personally.'" Yergin, *The Prize: The Epic Quest for Oil, Money and Power* (New York: Free Press, 1991), 676–677.

60. On this episode, see *"What the Heck Are You Up to Mr. President?": Jimmy Carter, America's "Malaise," and the Speech That Should Have Changed the Country* (New York: Bloomsbury USA, 2009).

61. Patrick Caddell was President Carter's pollster. Gerald Rafshoon was his media adviser and communications director. Jody L. Powell (1943–2009) was his longtime press secretary. Gerald Rafshoon's account of this episode is available in the Rafshoon Interview, Miller Center, University of Virginia, Jimmy Carter Presidential Oral History Project, April 8, 1983, 30–37, http://web1.millercenter.org/poh/transcripts/ ohp_1983_0408_rafshoon.pdf (accessed November 3, 2010).

62. *Time* magazine, in an article headed "Carter's Great Purge," reported of the mass firings: "Across the U.S., a people who had at first been bewildered by the President's

unprecedented ten-day 'summit' at Camp David, then relieved by his forceful speeches on energy, which tried also to set a high national purpose, could only ask: Now what?" July 30, 1979, http://www.time.com/time/magazine/article/0,9171,948464-1,00.html (accessed November 3, 2010).

63. After the 1974 election, the partisan composition of the Senate was 61–38 in favor of the Democrats, and the House was 291–144 in the Democrats' favor. They picked up 49 seats in that midterm.

64. See the discussion of "The Image Problem" in Yanek Mieczkowski, *Gerald Ford and the Challenges of the 1970s* (Lexington: University Press of Kentucky, 2005), 47–55.

65. Howard H. Baker, Jr., was a Republican senator from Tennessee (1967–1985), who later, for a brief time, was Ronald Reagan's White House chief of staff, called on to help repair the damage of the Iran-Contra affair. Baker was a southern moderate with a track record of working across the partisan divide.

66. Ford used the veto sixty-six times; twelve were overridden.

67. The Democrats actually lost fifty-four seats in the 1994 midterms. They also lost control of the Senate that year, with eight seats changing hands.

68. Clinton's BTU tax proposal, offered in his 1993 budget package, was intended to be broad-based, levied on energy itself, rather than confined to one type of fuel. It passed the House but not the Senate, where the administration gave in to pressure to drop it. Many House Democrats who had taken a hard vote on the tax felt betrayed by this turn of events. See Bob Woodward, *The Agenda: Inside the Clinton White House* (New York: Simon & Schuster, 1994), 217–222.

69. President Nixon announced Project Independence in November 1973, in the wake of the Arab oil embargo of that year. The stated intent, reiterated in his January 1974 state of the union message, was to make the United States energy independent by 1980.

Chapter 8

Reality-Based Policymaking: Information, Advice, and Presidential Success *

Paul J. Quirk and Bruce Nesmith

Different presidents take different attitudes toward information and advice about policy decisions. In particular, they show varying recognition that the consequences of their decisions depend on conditions and relationships that exist independently of their hopes, wishes, and ideological beliefs. They thus give different amounts of weight to information that comes from sources generally recognized as credible, or that emerges from serious assessment of conflicting views—as opposed to one-sided, constituency-driven or ideological advocacy. The differences shape their staffs and their advisory and decision processes.

The contrast could hardly be sharper than that between President Barack Obama and his immediate predecessor, George W. Bush. The Bush presidency is easily portrayed, fairly or not, as a morality play about dealing with reality—demonstrating how a president who strays from the straight-and-narrow path of reliable, independent information invites disaster. Using what has become an iconic phrase, a senior Bush aide, in an interview for a magazine article, set the administration apart from what he called, disparagingly, "the reality-based community."[1] The reporter's generally accepted interpretation of the remark—as a proclamation of ideological faith—was in our view inaccurate.[2] But the Bush White House was in fact often criticized as preferring ideology and wishful thinking to objective information—with a steady stream of calamitous consequences in matters ranging from the Iraq War to Hurricane Katrina, climate change, fiscal policy, and regulation of the financial system.[3]

Obama has taken the opposite approach and (notwithstanding a major setback in the 2010 midterm congressional elections) had reasonably

*Kevin Dyrland provided energetic research assistance as well as helpful editorial suggestions. Stella Herriges Quirk read a draft of the chapter and helped make it more reader-friendly.

positive early results, considering the difficulty of the problems he inherited. Top appointees have had academic and career credentials of rare distinction (a Nobel Prize, a Harvard University presidency). They have featured diverse viewpoints, with a centrist tendency. Facing two wars, a financial and economic crisis, and major challenges on health care, climate change, and immigration, among other subjects, Obama has sought advice from a wide range of qualified sources. In fall 2009, he collected advice from multiple credible sources over a period of weeks in reconsidering the administration's strategy in Afghanistan. Despite internal discord on the economic team, Obama's economic strategy largely reflected evidence-based advice. With unemployment remaining high, Obama did not get much credit from the public for his economic management. But the administration's stimulus measures evidently moderated a potentially devastating economic recession and put the economy on a tenuous path toward recovery.[4]

This chapter explores how presidents use information and advice in making policy decisions and what difference it makes for their success or failure. More specifically, it considers whether a president's relying on relatively independent, expert sources and seeking to ensure balanced and thorough deliberations—in other words, conducting what we will call (in homage to the Bush aide) a *reality-based presidency*—enhances his prospects for policy and political success. The George W. Bush morality tale notwithstanding, the answer is not simple. Thoroughly politicized, ill-informed decisions often succeed, at least politically. Decisions made with scrupulous attention to the best available evidence and arguments sometimes fail. And they often have political costs. As a general matter, however, we argue that an evidence-based approach does improve the president's chances for success.

Decisions and Success

Most commentary on presidents assesses their success or failure largely on the basis of their popularity and electoral results—criteria that fit part of any president's goals and can be measured without ambiguity. To assess a president's performance and actual effect on the country's interests, however, requires looking at the quality of his important decisions—that is, considering the merits of those decisions in light of the information reasonably available at the time they were made.

Performance versus Success

The practice of evaluating presidents on the basis of political results is deeply ingrained in commentary on the presidency. Franklin D. Roosevelt, John F. Kennedy, Ronald Reagan, and Bill Clinton were successes by such criteria, and thus are presumed worthy of emulation. In contrast, Gerald R. Ford, Jimmy Carter, and George H. W. Bush were failures—defeated in their bids for reelection—and provide examples to be avoided.

In truth, the president's success or failure in political terms may tell us surprisingly little about his performance. A president can be a resounding political success for reasons that have nothing to do with good decisions or effective management. Such success may reflect good fortune—favorable outcomes resulting from factors beyond the president's control—or bad judgment—distorted perceptions of the relevant outcomes by the public. Indeed, political scientist Larry Bartels presents evidence that distorted perceptions have played a major role in the public's evaluation of presidents' management of the economy.[5] Since 1945, Democratic administrations have produced, or at least witnessed, greater economic growth than Republican ones. Yet Republican presidents have generally received greater electoral boosts for their economic management than Democratic presidents. The apparent reason is that economic growth has been more concentrated in election years during Republican administrations than during Democratic ones—a pattern that may result from the Republicans' emphasis on controlling inflation early in their terms.[6] In any case, Republican presidents have prospered politically from election-year economic gains that were not representative of their overall results.

To avoid being misled by merely political criteria, scholars need to undertake more penetrating investigations of presidential performance. How does a president make decisions? Are his actions apparently appropriate and potentially effective, given the information available and the relevant goals? How do the results stack up against the opportunities that were available?

Assessing Policy Information

To address these questions, scholars need to deal with substantive information about the merits of policies. In most cases, of course, they cannot identify a correct or best policy. Reasonable people disagree, and the differences are often about values or preferences that are not matters for expert judgment. At the same time, policy debates are not simply "up for grabs," such that whatever policy the president chooses is equally satisfactory from the standpoint of performance. On most issues, there is a roughly identifiable, limited range of positions that can be cogently defended—reflecting the combined effect of differences among widely shared goals and values and as yet unresolved uncertainties about empirical issues.[7] For example, evidence on the role of human activity in climate change, by nearly all competent accounts, warrants serious measures to reduce emissions of greenhouse gases; but the magnitude of the potential harm and the appropriate severity of remedial action remain uncertain.[8] Similarly, most economists endorse fiscal stimulation during a serious recession; they disagree, however, about the amount of stimulation and the proper mix of spending and tax cuts, and these disagreements are partly a matter of their differing priorities. Responsible liberal and conservative experts and policymakers will often have predictably different views, within the defensible range.

We argue that the country's interests are best served when the president pays close attention to evidence-based advisers and the relatively objective information that they bring to bear. Doing so does not ensure desired outcomes. Among other reasons, the experts are sometimes wrong. As psychologist Philip Tetlock has shown, they are also overconfident in the reliability of their judgments.[9] Nevertheless, decisions that take into account information from academic researchers, leading think tanks, career specialists and analytic staff in the government, and other reputable sources of policy expertise, will generally have superior prospects for success. To doubt that advantage is essentially to reject systematic inquiry as such.[10] In particular, we suggest that a president should not bet the country's interests on claims or arguments—advanced by ideologues, interested parties, or fringe academics, among others—that do not have substantial credibility among recognized experts.

Policy Information in the White House

To make appropriate decisions, presidents need advisory processes that enable them to weigh and integrate three categories of considerations.

1. *Political strategy.* A president may prefer a policy because it has support from the party's ideological or interest-group base, will appeal to swing voters, or will receive favorable coverage in the news media.[11] He may also choose policies on the basis of potential congressional support. Some

of the president's top staff will have experience and specialized skills in making the relevant political judgments.

2. *Ideology and values.* Ideologies—whether liberal, conservative, or some variation—incorporate policy prescriptions in the form of very general beliefs and attitudes. Presidents, like other politicians, will recognize the prominent ideological positions; know the general arguments about them; and hold some ideological beliefs of their own. Ideological positions also motivate a president's political base and may define a real or perceived electoral mandate. Some advisers serve as keepers of the ideological flame—promoting policy goals, rather than merely political ones, but defining those goals ideologically.

3. *Evidence-based policy information.* Presidents have access to a large amount of relatively objective, nonpartisan information about policy. It originates from sources both within government (the Central Intelligence Agency, the Treasury Department, and analytic units in many agencies) and outside government (think tanks, scientific organizations, universities). It is also institutionalized in certain parts of the Executive Office of the President, such as the Council of Economic Advisers (CEA) and the permanent staff of the Office of Management and Budget (OMB). But using this information is generally, from a political standpoint, optional. A president can make decisions on the basis of ideology and constituency support with little or no political penalty—provided only that any losses in the substantive quality of decisions do not have apparent short-term adverse effects.[12]

These three types of advice account for three principal categories of presidential advisers—which we will call, respectively, *political strategists, ideologues,* and *evidence-based advisers.*[13] The different types are not always easily identified. Some senior aides play combinations of these roles, and their orientations may not be apparent from their resumes. Reagan's first White House chief of staff, James Baker, had managed a presidential campaign—the quintessential role for a political strategist—but also had a strong orientation toward evidence-based advising. Even some elected politicians are evidence-oriented. Clinton, for example, could keep up with economists and business leaders in detailed discussion of economic issues.

The different categories of advisers are often in conflict. Clinton's evidence-based adviser Bruce Reed, a founder of the centrist and cerebral Democratic Policy Council, observes, "There's always a tension between the political advisers and the facts."[14] In her survey of staffing arrangements from the Nixon to the Clinton presidencies, Karen Hult finds that presidents have increasingly strengthened political advisers and weakened policy experts. She argues that the decline of substantive expertise in the White House has made it more difficult for presidents to construct workable policy compromises or impose losses on powerful constituencies.[15]

In addition, every president will behave differently at different times. They begin their terms full of confidence, ambition, and idealism, and thus focused on substantive achievement. As setbacks occur, they may focus more on popularity and elections. Barack Obama began his presidency with major substantive initiatives dealing with the economic recession and health care. In March 2010, however, with his poll numbers dropping and continued Democratic control of Congress in doubt, he announced a surprisingly broad proposal to expand offshore oil drilling, only to suspend it less than a month later when a massive oil spill in the Gulf of Mexico made the initiative less popular.[16]

Some evidence indicates that presidents pay more attention to evidence-based advising on issues that they care about more deeply. For example, Richard Nixon was personally interested almost exclusively in foreign policy. He was generally willing to shape economic and social policies for political purposes.[17] George W. Bush's education secretary, Margaret Spellings, suggests that the president's personal commitment to an ultimately unsuccessful Social Security reform proposal in 2005 made him oblivious to political calculation: "We have an expression in Texas, 'When the horse dies, get off.' We didn't get off the dead horse soon enough, I guess. . . . [Social Security reform] was too complicated and wasn't to be, but he was highly committed to it and that was that."

In the remainder of this chapter, we explore the incidence of evidence-based presidential decision making and consider its consequences for presidential success, both substantive and political.

Case Studies

We consider the experiences of three presidents: Ronald Reagan (1981–1989), George H. W. Bush (1989–1993), and Bill Clinton (1993–2001). Besides including representatives of both political parties, our set of cases presents variation in the presidents' reputed orientations toward the various kinds of advice as well as in their perceived success. Reagan notoriously ignored mainstream advice, at least on economic issues. Bush and Clinton were more orthodox, with Clinton the most attentive of the three to expert analysis. Reagan and Clinton were both reelected and left office with high approval ratings, while Bush had the opposite experience. Taken together, this set of presidents should provide opportunity to challenge, and possibly reassess, the morality-play account of evidence-based decision making. We look at these presidents' personal orientations and dispositions toward information; the structures and personnel they relied upon for policy advice; and the influences of their decisions, along with the policy and political outcomes, on the most important domestic initiatives of their presidencies. Simply put, we ask: what was the role of evidence-based advice, and with what policy and political consequences?

Ronald Reagan

Ronald Reagan entered the presidency amid the wreckage of the Carter administration, having run his 1980 campaign on three central promises: major tax cuts, reduced spending on domestic programs, and increased spending on defense. In making appointments, Reagan sought individuals who supported these objectives with missionary zeal. For the most part, he sought advice that echoed his own simple and confident beliefs. At times, however, he proved open to evidence-based advice, with results that included some of his principal achievements.

Advising structures. Reagan was personally inclined to overlook evidence-based advice because of a combination of firmly held beliefs and limited patience for substantive issues. He treated as articles of faith that government efforts to manage the economy are ineffective; that tax cuts have great benefits, essentially regardless of circumstances; and that welfare programs harm their recipients instead of helping them.[18] His rejection of complexity arguably had some advantages. Along with his appointment of like-minded individuals to run executive branch agencies, it gave a clear direction to his administration in most areas of policy.[19] But it also made it difficult for the administration to recognize important complications and difficulties—such as the actual existence of environmental problems.[20]

Although some advisers claimed that Reagan was highly engaged in policymaking,[21] he in fact took a casual approach to substantive issues. He knew what policies he wanted, which made details and complicating factors irrelevant. He was reportedly "perplexed" by a crucial July 1981 staff session on his historic tax cut, failing to understand important elements of the most ambitious policy initiative of his presidency. His concern was to make sure the administration didn't budge on the objective of a 25 percent rate cut, not to learn the relevant economics. But the economics were not trivial: after the meeting, OMB director David Stockman reports White House staff member Richard Darman wondering, "I don't know which is worse . . . winning now and fixing up the budget mess later, or losing now and facing a political mess immediately."[22] If anything, Reagan's detachment increased during his second term, perhaps because of aging or even the early stages of Alzheimer's disease.[23]

At the outset of his presidency, Reagan had three top White House aides, who provided a mix of the three types of policy advice, with a strong conservative ideological tilt. Baker, his chief of staff, combined political advice with concern for the evidence-based perspectives of economists and other experts; Michael Deaver, assistant to the president and deputy chief of staff, was strictly political; and Edwin Meese III, counselor to the president, was the voice of conservative ideology.[24] Each of them had a roughly defined area of jurisdiction—Meese overseeing the Cabinet and advisory staff, Baker the implementing agencies, and Deaver the personal aspects of the presidency— but they met constantly to coordinate with each other and with Reagan.[25] Baker and Meese generally worked out their substantive disagreements without taking them to the president, a practice that reduced the demands on Reagan (and his influence).[26] Other high-level advisers provided mostly ideological advice. Economist Martin Anderson of the Hoover Institution, named as assistant to the president for policy development after advising on domestic policy during the campaign, emerged as the champion of Reagan's ideological agenda against initiatives from the departments and agencies.[27] After Anderson left the administration in 1982, the role of conservative enforcer was eventually taken over by Christian conservative activist Gary Bauer.[28]

The triumvirate arrangement ended at the beginning of Reagan's second term in 1985 when chief of staff Baker and Treasury Secretary Donald Regan, in an ill-advised move approved by Reagan, switched jobs; Deaver left the administration; and Meese became attorney general. Regan ran a more hierarchical and even authoritarian White House, and Reagan became more isolated from policy information.[29] After Regan resigned in 1987 amid the Iran-Contra scandal, his successors as chief of staff, Howard Baker and Kenneth Duberstein, focused on restoring the president's public image and achieving diplomatic breakthroughs with the Soviet Union, rather than on domestic policy.[30]

Policy issues. The economy was central to Reagan's election campaign and first year in office, with a major 1981 tax cut the centerpiece of his administration. He spent the rest of his presidency dealing with the resulting budget deficits. Other major domestic issues of the Reagan years included Social Security financing, tax reform, and welfare.

The Economy. Reagan came to office with the economy in disarray. For much of the preceding decade, there had been high levels of both inflation and unemployment, a painful combination that conventional economic theory did not contemplate as a possibility. Government spending and average tax burdens had also risen, exacerbating the public discontent.[31] Dealing with these problems was complicated by the collapse of the Keynesian consensus that had guided economic thought for decades (and that would reemerge to a great extent during the economic crisis of 2008–2009). The lack of consensus among mainstream economists made it easier for the Reagan administration to seize upon unorthodox economic advice.[32] The results were mixed, but economic growth proved more healthy than evidence-based economic advice would have predicted.

Many economists in the late 1970s turned to a "new" classical economics, which rejected government stabilization policies as futile, and monetarism, which argued that government's only useful economic policy was to avoid inflation by ensuring steady growth of the money supply.[33] In 1979, as inflation approached 20 percent, the Federal Reserve Board under chair Paul Volcker sought to bring it under control by restricting the money supply, resulting in a deep, though brief, recession in 1981–1982.[34]

From Reagan's major campaign address on economic policy in September 1980 through the end of his first year as president, administration policy was instead driven by a fringe doctrine called "supply-side economics." Promoted in the late 1970s by an obscure economist, Arthur Laffer, and Rep. Jack Kemp (R-NY), the supply-siders claimed, without credible evidence or theoretical support, that large cuts in tax rates would induce so much additional investment and work effort that tax revenues would actually increase. Mainstream economists dismissed the claims as fantasy. (Tax cuts can bring about increased revenue under special circumstances—by stimulating demand and increasing economic activity during a period of excess capacity and unemployment. Under most circumstances, tax cuts reduce government's share of national income, and revenue declines.) But Reagan learned about the supply-side claims, bought into them thoroughly, and proposed a huge tax cut as the centerpiece of his presidential campaign.[35]

Most of Reagan's campaign advisers on economic issues were not supply-siders. They included monetarists (Alan Greenspan, Beryl Sprinkel), regulatory reformers (Murray Weidenbaum), and deficit hawks (Stockman).[36] But Reagan's faith-based commitment to the supply-side doctrine led him to dismiss their criticisms. "I don't care," Reagan responded in 1980 when Greenspan and Charls Walker attempted to counsel him about the dangers of deficits. He appointed several supply-side advisers to high-level positions in the administration.[37] In the shaping of the first-year economic program, Treasury Secretary Regan, a tax-cut proponent, beat back evidence-based objections to supply-side claims from OMB and the CEA by appealing to Reagan's political values.[38]

Political considerations supported dramatic tax cuts as well. Even Reagan's non-supply-side advisers were anxious to take advantage of the economic stress to get conservative policies enacted. Stockman and Kemp wrote a memo to the president-elect in November 1980, called "Avoiding a GOP Economic Dunkirk," advising quick action on spending and tax cuts to prevent economic catastrophe. Ideological conservatives also saw the opportunity, if they cooperated with the supply-siders on quick action, to achieve policy goals including cuts in social program budgets and business regulation.[39] Reagan's political advisers, such as Richard Wirthlin, anticipated political benefits from the decisive action as well as the benefits individuals would feel from lower taxes. Hence Stockman, as budget director, was pressed to work as quickly as possible, with little opportunity to clarify the consequences of major tax cuts for the budget deficit.[40]

Reagan's policy for economic recovery was announced in a televised address to Congress on February 18, 1981. Optimistic forecasts, well out of the economic mainstream and privately dubbed "Rosy Scenario" by Stockman, provided the appearance of long-term fiscal health, predicting a balanced budget in two years because of economic growth stimulated by the tax cuts as well as substantial nondefense budget cuts.[41] Reagan ignored the concerns of CEA chair Weidenbaum that the administration's economic growth forecasts were unrealistic.[42]

The Rosy Scenario proved spectacularly inaccurate, and the evidence-based advice correct. Congress passed the tax cuts in August 1981, and while the economy began to grow in 1983, it did not come close to making up for the revenue lost by the tax cut. Few spending cuts—many of them left unspecified by a "magic asterisk" in Reagan's proposal—ever materialized. The budget deficit nearly doubled by 1984 to 5.0 percent of gross national product.[43]

An accumulation of data from OMB and the CEA eventually forced the administration to rethink its approach, and advisers concerned about the deficit began to get a hearing in staff discussions.[44] The more evidence-centered James Baker gained additional control over policy advising at the senior staff level, and supply-side economic advisers Paul Craig Roberts and Norman Ture left the administration.[45] Reagan cooperated with Congress on measures to raise revenue in 1982 and 1984.[46] The Tax Equity and Fiscal Responsibility Act (TEFRA) of 1982 originated in the Republican-controlled Senate Finance Committee, chaired by Republican deficit hawk Robert Dole. It undid a small portion of the 1981 tax cut. Reagan was not involved in negotiations over the bill, but demonstrated flexibility by advocating it to Congress prior to the August 1982 floor votes.[47]

Whether the 1981–82 experience significantly changed the president's prior, highly ideological approach to economic policy is not clear. Immediately after signing the tax increase he returned to his anti-tax rhetoric in a series of public speeches.[48] Reagan and Regan opposed a 1983 proposal by Baker, Stockman, and others to establish a commission to oversee efforts to reduce the deficit.[49] Martin Feldstein, a conservative Harvard economist, who had replaced Weidenbaum as chair of the CEA, resigned in 1984 over his inability to influence budget and tax policy, at which point Reagan allowed the post—normally occupied by a distinguished economist, and intended to provide independent advice—to remain vacant for nearly a year.[50] Baker and Richard Darman, who moved to the White House from the Treasury Department in 1985, continued to pursue deficit reduction through tax increases in Reagan's second term, but were unable to persuade the president to support them.[51] Still, political scientist John Sloan credits TEFRA and its successor, the Deficit Reduction Act of 1984, with encouraging the Federal Reserve Board to loosen monetary policy and facilitate the extended period of economic growth that followed.[52]

Reagan's economic policymaking was largely a product of ideology, with occasional nervous peeks at real-world considerations. Congress mostly went along with his 1981 proposals. Despite the ideological policymaking, some indicators of the results were highly favorable: consistent economic growth from 1982 to 1990, inflation under control, and rising stock prices. On the other hand, even beginning from a deep recession, economic growth was no higher than the long-term average. The economy featured stagnating productivity, ballooning budget and trade deficits, and increasingly severe income inequality.[53] Politically, however, the supply-side fantasy worked out well. Despite the economy's weaknesses, Reagan campaigned on the sustained growth and cruised to reelection in 1984.

Social Security Reform. In dealing with Social Security, Reagan confronted a program that had long been disliked by conservatives, was financially unsound—with declining revenues and increasing costs—and yet was extremely popular with the general public. In addition, he was politically vulnerable on the subject because of critical statements he had made about Social Security earlier in his career. In his first year, Reagan nevertheless proposed drastic cuts in the program, motivated by conservative ideology and the need for large spending reductions to go along with his tax cuts. But the effort was massively deficient in political strategy. Eventually, Reagan took a very different, evidence-based approach, designed not to bury Social Security, but rather to ensure its long-term solvency.

Reagan's Health and Human Services (HHS) Department proposed substantial cuts to Social Security in the spring of 1981. His advisers, however, were divided. HHS secretary Richard Schweiker wanted to increase Social Security revenue by expanding the program to include federal workers; Roberts and economic adviser William Niskanen opposed the program for ideological reasons and sought to eliminate or reduce it; and Stockman saw Social Security as the largest available target for budget cuts. Shortly after Stockman and Anderson out-argued Schweiker at an April 1981 policy meeting, Stockman brought forward a set of substantial program cuts, telling the president, improbably, they were merely technical and yet would yield substantial savings. Reagan did not question Stockman's claims, which proved far off the mark.[54]

Reagan's political advisers were not involved in formulating the program. With more recognition of its political hazards than Reagan had shown, they commenced efforts to minimize the damage. Chief of staff Baker ordered that the plan be released by HHS, not the White House, and refused to have Reagan make a televised address on its behalf. Even so, the result was a political rout. The Senate emphatically rejected the plan, amid devastating criticism of a provision that eliminated benefits for early retirees, effective immediately. The proposal provided the basis for some of the Democrats' most potent attacks on the administration in the 1982 congressional election campaign.[55]

The ideological approach having failed, with no solution in sight for So-cial Security's long-term problems, Republican congressional leaders, partic-ularly Sen. Howard Baker of Tennessee and Rep. Robert Michel of Illinois, persuaded Reagan to create a bipartisan National Commission on Social Security Reform in 1982. The commission facilitated an effective integra-tion of evidence-based analysis and political strategy.[56]

The commission's proposal emerged in early 1983, after intensive eleventh-hour negotiations that included top Reagan staff members Stockman, Dar-man, and legislative liaison Kenneth Duberstein.[57] The package of benefit cuts, payroll tax increases, and taxes on benefits for high-income retirees was expected to ensure seventy-five years of sound financial footing for Social Security. The plan was accepted by President Reagan and Democratic and Republican congressional leaders, and then was passed by Congress, despite persistent public ambivalence and opposition from labor unions and groups representing the elderly.[58]

Tax Reform. In his second term, Reagan collaborated with efforts to ad-vance evidence-based congressional tax reform that originated in separate proposals by Sen. Bill Bradley (D-NJ) and Rep. Jack Kemp (R-NY). In con-trast with his 1981 tax cut, Reagan's promotion of tax reform championed standard economic doctrine about the structure of the tax code and repre-sented a high point of evidence-based policymaking in his presidency. The administration's bill was developed by mainstream tax experts in the Trea-sury Department, beginning under Donald Regan and concluding under James Baker. The secretaries gave Treasury specialists autonomy throughout the bill's formulation, shielding them from congressional pressure, and even from other parts of the administration, such as the CEA.[59]

Reagan himself had required some persuasion on tax reform, initially viewing it as a cover for tax increases.[60] But Secretary of State George Shultz convinced him during a 1982 golf game that a broader tax base would al-low lower overall rates. Regan, too, came to see tax reform as a way to avoid increases in tax rates. After he became chief of staff in 1985 he kept the issue in front of the president.[61] Reagan agreed to take on the initiative in principle in January 1985, presented the administration's proposal in the spring, and helped to promote tax reform to the public.[62] His grasp of the subject remained sketchy: he was surprised to learn from a reporter that the bill would raise corporate taxes. In response to a question at a public ap-pearance about simplifying the tax code, he just said "Wow" and turned to Regan.[63]

Nevertheless, once convinced, Reagan was committed to the effort. Strenuous lobbying by the president and other members of the administration, along with a cut in top rates devised by Senate Finance Committee chair Robert Packwood (R-OR) in exchange for closing loopholes, carried the bill through to passage.[64]

The Tax Reform Act emerged from interbranch negotiations that were even longer and more perilous than those over Social Security reform, and with as little anticipated payoff in public support. As with Social Security, Reagan's deference to real-world expertise helped enable passage of the act. As a result, the tax code was substantially simplified and top rates lowered—reducing substantially, for a period of time, the economic inefficiency of the tax code.[65]

Welfare Reform. Reagan's welfare policy was driven mainly by his pristinely uncomplicated conservative ideology. Belief in the corrosive effects of welfare dependency was central to the ideological perspective that Reagan shared with most of his senior aides.[66] Martin Anderson wanted to abolish all anti-poverty programs, saying that their disincentives to work created a "wall" that kept people in poverty.[67] Late in his presidency, however, Reagan deferred to evidence-based advice from then chief of staff Howard Baker and signed a major bill that comported with policy analytic findings in expanding both work requirements and social services for welfare recipients.

Poverty analysts generally recommended three approaches to changing the incentives of the large group of long-term welfare recipients that had appeared by 1980: social services, such as job training and child care, to enable recipients to hold a job; a negative income tax, such as the Earned Income Tax Credit, which would allow recipients to keep earnings from work without losing benefits; and workfare, which would require work as a condition of benefits.[68] None of these approaches entailed benefit cuts, particularly for those already working. Such cuts would take away much of the benefit of their work effort.[69]

Reagan's first move on welfare was nevertheless simply to cut benefits, overlooking the concerns with recipients' incentives, among other adverse consequences for the low-income population. Welfare cuts included in the Omnibus Budget and Reconciliation Act of 1981 were designed by three conservative advisers who had worked for Reagan in California: White House aide Robert Carleson, Health and Human Services undersecretary David B. Swoap, and Social Security Administration commissioner John A. Svahn.[70] Perversely, from the standpoint of reducing dependency, the majority of the cuts fell on recipients with jobs: benefits for the working poor were capped, benefit cuts were imposed for each dollar they earned, and they were made ineligible for Medicaid.[71]

The 1981 welfare changes were controversial, with moderate senators of both parties criticizing their severity. Reagan attempted no further benefit cuts. A stalemate on welfare ensued, with liberals and conservatives seeking change in opposite directions. It was broken only by passage of the 1988 Family Support Act, an incremental reform that improved incentives to work and discouraged dependency in modest ways while largely avoiding divisive issues.[72] In signing the congressionally initiated measure, Reagan followed the advice of former senator Howard Baker, who was close to the bill's sponsor, Sen. Daniel Patrick Moynihan (D-NY). Reagan rejected ideologically motivated advice from more conservative aides, such as Charles Hobbs and William Bell, who criticized the measure's mandates on states governments and work requirements for individuals as too weak.[73]

In 1981, Reagan's approach to welfare was proactive and ideological. In 1988 he went along with a much-compromised, evidence-based measure produced by Congress. Substantively, the measures made little dent in the problem of dependency, which remained prominent on the policy agenda. Politically, Reagan may have paid a modest price for his early ideological severity. In the 1988 election campaign, GOP nominee George H. W. Bush felt compelled to promise "a kinder, gentler nation" under his administration.

Reagan assumed the presidency possessed of billboard-simple conservative convictions about domestic policy. In the early stages, he also relied heavily on ideologically oriented advisers. As a result, his major early proposals—the tax cut, the cuts in welfare benefits, and the ill-fated Social Security measure—often failed to take into account the realities of policy or, in the case of Social Security, those of politics. He experienced some corresponding negative results—a ballooning budget deficit, increased welfare dependency, and major Republican losses in the 1982 midterm elections. Contrary to the public image of his presidency, much of Reagan's success stemmed from his ability on occasion to set ideological belief aside. When he relied on evidence-based advisers, he achieved major policy change in the areas of Social Security and tax reform, as well as some moderation of the budget deficit. Reagan concluded his presidency under favorable economic conditions and with generally high public approval and was succeeded by a president of his own party.

George H. W. Bush

After campaigning for president on broad themes with minimal policy content—such as being for patriotism and against liberalism—George H. W. Bush succeeded Reagan in January 1989 with few domestic policy goals.[74] He stressed experience and competence in his appointments. With important exceptions, he was mostly responsive to orthodox, evidence-based advice on major domestic issues.[75]

Advising structures. In contrast to the true-believer Reagan, Bush was by disposition moderate and pragmatic. A former director of the Central Intelligence Agency, he was prone to recognize specialized knowledge. Prone also to indulge his personal interests, he chose from the start of his presidency to focus almost exclusively on foreign policy, providing little direction on domestic policy. He delegated responsibility for domestic policy to two evidence-based advisers: OMB director Richard Darman, a deficit hawk, and chief of staff John Sununu, who had ties to the business and conservative communities. Other evidence-based advisers—secretary of the Treasury and longtime Bush friend Nicholas Brady, and Assistant to the President for Domestic and Economic Affairs Roger Porter—were occasionally influential.[76] Ideological conservatives in the administration, including Charles Kolb and James Pinkerton of the Domestic Policy Council, had less influence and came to see the Bush years as a "lost opportunity."[77] Staff units, such as the CEA and the Domestic Policy Council, were marginalized regardless of their advising orientation.[78]

Bush began to focus on domestic policy—by his own admission, belatedly—in the last year of his term. The abrasive Sununu was succeeded as chief of staff by two more evidence-based advisers, Samuel Skinner and then James Baker. But with the 1992 election imminent they had little influence either on policy or on Bush's political fortunes.[79]

Policy issues. Despite his lack of activist impulses, Bush was forced to become engaged in domestic policy by the budget deficit he inherited from Reagan and a recession that began during his second year in office. In addition, Porter, a veteran of two previous Republican administrations, pushed the departments to develop initiatives that addressed Bush's campaign themes—spending cuts, drug control, and environmental protection—without further guidance from the president.[80] The administration's generally competent approach was overshadowed at the time by the recession's effects, which persisted past the 1992 election, and by Bush's decision to reverse an incautious, absolute pledge not to raise taxes that he made during the 1988 campaign.

The Economy. At the outset, Bush faced nearly unprecedented peacetime federal budget deficits. The deficit for fiscal year 1989 was projected to be $155 billion, down from Reagan's peak years, but still double the level of 1981.[81] The deficit presented Bush with a severe conflict between his policy goals and political considerations. Bush and his advisers chose an evidence-based attack on the deficit—an effort that was expected to yield long-term economic benefits, but which they mishandled politically at great cost to the president.

Bush had handicapped his own policy response through a reckless, pact-with-the-devil promise in the 1988 presidential campaign never to raise taxes. His memorable use of the Clint Eastwood line "Read my lips!" to punctuate the promise removed any possibility of backing away from it at a low-to-moderate political cost. Even before the inauguration, his advisers were speculating about how long he could keep the pledge. They decided that the 1990 budget could be finessed, postponing the hard decisions and political reckoning. The Democratic-controlled Congress accommodated the tactic, with some grumbling: "He picks the [spending] increases and lets us make the cuts," complained Rep. Charles Schumer (D-NY).[82]

But by 1990 the stage was set for real choices—and political disaster for Bush. His evidence-based substantive advisers, especially Darman and Sununu, believed the deficit had to be addressed to avoid clumsy, automatic, across-the-board spending cuts under the Gramm-Rudman-Hollings Act of 1986. With the Democrats in control of Congress, they concluded that Bush would need to accept some increases in tax revenue.[83] Bush's political advisers were not involved in the decision to raise taxes. Preoccupied with the crisis leading to the Persian Gulf War, neither was Bush, who delegated the extraordinarily difficult budget issue almost entirely to Darman.[84]

Darman and Sununu negotiated with Democratic congressional leaders to produce a balanced package of tax increases and spending reductions. In May 1990, with Democrats insisting as a condition for beginning negotiations that tax increases be on the table, Bush and his advisers conceded the point, believing at the time that the economic and political fallout of further stalemate would be worse than that of breaking the tax pledge. In a comically inept ploy to minimize the short-term negative publicity, the White House announced the decision by posting a memo on the bulletin board in the press office.[85] An initial agreement fell apart in September in a rebellion by congressional Republicans, a devastating embarrassment for the president. But in October the administration finally achieved a deal that reduced the budget deficit by about $500 billion over five years. About a third of that amount came from tax increases, mainly raising the top rates on individual incomes, and about two-thirds from spending cuts.[86] The deal also established a "pay-as-you-go" system for future spending programs, which helped both to restrain spending for the next decade and to establish the foundation for economic growth and balanced budgets in the mid-to-late 1990s.[87]

Despite its merits as policy, Bush and his advisers failed to prepare the public for their policy shift, leading to political catastrophe. Besides having the first agreement rejected by his own party, the broken promise haunted him through his unsuccessful 1992 reelection campaign.[88] Adviser James Pinkerton recalls, "If there's one phrase that people remember, it's 'Read my lips.' If there's one thing that we just beat in the political sense over and over again in 1988, it was 'We're not going to raise taxes.' . . . Then there we were. Talk about no sales job!"

By the time of the 1990 budget agreement, the economy was already posing an additional challenge for the Bush administration: it had sunk into a recession. And although a recovery began fairly quickly, by mid-1991, it was slow and uneven, such that the misery was felt throughout the reelection campaign. As with the budget deal, Bush sided primarily with evidence-based advisers, and again paid a political price.

At the outset of the recession, Darman, Brady, and CEA chair Michael Boskin believed that it would last less than a year, typical of recessions in the post–World War II era, and that job growth would resume in plenty of time to prevent electoral damage.[89] They argued that any attempt at economic stimulus would come too late to do any good and would risk overheating the economy as well as adding to the federal deficit.[90] Their stand-pat advice reflected what most economists were saying at the time.[91] Bush largely followed the advice and resisted congressional attempts to stimulate the economy through public works spending.[92] As late as October 1991, he told audiences such as the American Gas Association that he didn't want to do anything that would "make the situation worse."[93]

The advice proved only partly correct. The performance of the economy vindicated the administration's major decisions, as a strong recovery was under way by late 1992 and led to an economic boom for the rest of the 1990s. But the improvement did not come quickly enough to protect Bush from electoral harm. The Clinton campaign focused heavily on Bush's lack of action, accusing him of indifference to the country's hardship. The combination of his breaking the no-new-taxes promise and presiding, seemingly passively, over the slow recovery largely sank Bush's chances for reelection.[94]

The National Drug Control Policy. In dealing with an epidemic of cocaine use that created one of the most inflammatory issues of his presidency, Bush reversed course sharply, first embracing and then abandoning evidence-based advice in a highly politicized policy debate. Many of his resulting recommendations were passed by Congress and undoubtedly helped Bush politically. But their substantive consequences were unfortunate.

Initially, Bush sought to heed the advice of a broad range of policy experts, as well as of Treasury Secretary Nicholas Brady, to shift resources from law enforcement and interdiction of smuggling—which had predictably failed to reduce the availability of illegal drugs—to efforts at anti-drug education and treatment of addiction.[95] In a remark that could have been made by a policy analyst, Bush told reporters during his first week in office, "The answer to the problem of drugs lies more on solving the demand side of the equation than it does on the supply side—than it does on interdiction or sealing the borders."[96]

Within a few months, however, Bush had abandoned the evidence-based approach. The National Drug Control Policy he announced in a September 1989 nationally televised address called for few changes from existing policy, and those few mainly expanded law enforcement and resources for interdiction.[97] John Greene attributes this switch to ideological advice from William Bennett, the head of the Office of National Drug Control Policy, whom Bush had appointed to appeal to conservatives.[98] Journalists Michael Duffy and Dan Goodgame attribute it to political advice from Sununu, who noted that the tougher approach polled better.[99] Policy experts panned the measure.[100] Nevertheless, Congress enacted some of Bush's recommendations in 1990.

Governmental policy on illegal drugs did not become more evidence-based, or focused on reducing demand, during the Bush administration. Despite the president's awareness of the evidence-based policy advice, political considerations outweighed it. Fifteen years later, the prison population had grown enormously, and federal officials proudly displayed (as if they were evidence of success) ever larger intercepted shipments of illegal drugs. But the supply of cocaine had only increased, as had the number of teenagers who reported using illicit drugs.[101]

Clean Air. In a signal episode of evidence-based policymaking, Bush broke a nine-year stalemate between business and environmentalists over reauthorization of the 1970 Clean Air Act.[102] His measure incorporated policy analysis that showed positive effects of environmental protection on public health and major efficiency advantages (beneficial for both health and the economy) from replacing traditional command-and-control regulatory methods with market-oriented measures that essentially put a price on pollution.[103]

Economists as well as business leaders had complained that environmental regulations often required large outlays by businesses for relatively small gains in environmental quality.[104] The administration's evidence-based response included a market-oriented strategy to reduce pollutants that contributed to acid rain. Bush performed a political balancing act, seeking to distance himself from Reagan's pro-producer approach without alienating the Republicans' business constituency, and there was no significant push from anywhere within the administration to pursue a different course for ideological or political reasons.

Originating in the Environmental Protection Agency (EPA), the strategy Bush adopted was endorsed by a broad coalition called "Project 88." The coalition included both environmentalists and business leaders, each of whom saw the potential for gains from the measure.[105] The working group that formulated the administration's clean air proposal included advocates for businesses concerned about the negative consequences of excessive regulation—such as Robert Grady of OMB—and environmentalists concerned about the negative effects of pollution—particularly William Rosenberg of the EPA—as well as Porter and presidential counsel C. Boyden Gray.[106] Porter was instrumental in bringing agencies together and facilitating consensus.[107]

Bush's Clean Air proposal was announced in June 1989. Under an emissions trading provision, industries would be issued permits to emit a certain amount of sulfur dioxide and nitrous oxides, which they could sell to other polluters to the extent they were able to reduce their own emissions below their permitted levels. During negotiations in Congress, Bush successfully played the business and environmentalist coalitions against each other, splitting the differences between them on most provisions.[108] He used veto threats to keep the Democratic Congress from imposing overly severe regulations, while relying on Sununu to keep conservatives on board.[109] Each side doubtless was aware that momentum for clean air legislation had increased after the long stalemate and that rejecting Bush's proposal might well result in a worse outcome.

Bush's efforts not only broke a long stalemate over reauthorization of the Clean Air Act, but also achieved important evidence-based improvements over existing law: new programs for acid rain, airborne toxics, and urban air quality, as well as gradual elimination of ozone-depleting chemicals.[110] Despite the advice of EPA director William Reilly and science adviser D. Allen Bromley, the new law did not address the growing threat of climate change, because Sununu vetoed the notion.[111]

Assessments of the emissions trading program for sulfur dioxide initiated under the 1990 Clean Air Act have been positive. A number of studies found emissions significantly reduced, at a savings of several billion dollars a year. Air quality has improved, although with less reduction of toxic air pollutants than of some others.[112] At the same time, there is no evidence that the measure had any effect on Bush's public standing. Neither Bush nor Clinton used clean air as an electoral issue in 1992.

While devoting most of his attention to foreign policy, Bush used centralized, evidence-based advisory arrangements to obtain relatively nonideological substantive advice on domestic policy and was generally inclined to heed it. On the budget deficit, the recession, and the environment, the administration produced realistic, analytically defensible measures and had significant policy achievements. Perhaps because of his lack of personal investment in domestic policy, however, Bush occasionally made notably radical departures from evidence-based policymaking in pursuit of popular support—including his untenable absolute promise not to raise taxes and his rapid restoration of the enforcement-and-interdiction strategy for controlling illicit drugs. Ultimately, Bush was not successful politically. He lost popular support and failed to win reelection partly because his inconsistent attitude toward evidence-based policymaking resulted in a grossly apparent broken promise, and above all because he had bad luck with the timing of an economic recession and recovery. He exacerbated his political troubles through frequently inept communication with the public.

Bill Clinton

Launching his presidency in 1993 with a centrist, yet ambitious agenda, Bill Clinton had high aspirations for policy accomplishment. Democratic majorities in both houses of Congress, eager for change after twelve years of Republican control of the White House, shared many of his objectives for reforming the economy, health care, welfare, and government operations.

He chose policy advisers with policy expertise, while also giving high priority to gender and racial diversity. The Clinton White House was highly open to evidence-based policy information. It had serious weaknesses, however, in policy formulation and political strategy.

Advising structures. Clinton, easily the most knowledgeable about domestic issues of modern presidents, approached the office as a policy virtuoso. Inquisitive about a broad range of domestic policy, capable of mastering large volumes of complex information, and inclined to lengthy, wide-ranging policy conversations, Clinton anticipated acting as his own policy director. He made his staff appointments late in the transition period, indicating that advising structure "would be a system operating around the president as the main star."[113] He was more pragmatic than ideological, with ties to the middle-of-the-road Democratic Leadership Council as well as to liberal civil rights and gay rights groups.

In his first year, Clinton was in effect his own chief of staff—meeting directly with numerous individuals, inside and outside the administration, about policy matters. The practice exposed him to an abundance of evidence-based advice and enabled him to play a central role in policy formulation. Adviser Bruce Reed says that Clinton relished a hands-on approach to policymaking, modifying and synthesizing the options presented to him. But the arrangement also led to difficulty establishing priorities among agenda items.[114] In addition, it allowed too much policy detail to float up to Clinton himself, who despite his mastery of issues, had difficulty making decisions.[115] The result was a massively informed but often chaotic policymaking process.[116]

Little attention was given to White House staffing during the transition.[117] The nominal chief of staff, Arkansas business executive Mack McLarty, had no Washington experience and was given little authority. "Bill Clinton is obviously a very engaged person," McLarty told the *New York Times*. "He is going to be deciding what gets to his desk." McLarty described his own position as "not . . . a terribly aggressive gatekeeper."[118] Clinton's stated intention to provide McLarty with experienced deputies was not carried out.

Besides the haphazard advisory structures, Clinton, more like Bush than Reagan, provided his staff little in the way of policy direction. For health-care and welfare policy, Clinton relied on large task forces, which were well designed for accumulating information from a variety of perspectives but not for framing or making decisions. Other structures, like the CEA and the Domestic Policy Council (DPC), received less attention from the president.

DPC head Carol Rasco, from Clinton's gubernatorial staff in Arkansas, was inexperienced. The DPC rarely met and did not figure in the formulation of major policy initiatives.[119]

Clinton did employ a more centralized advising structure for economic policy. He relied heavily on a few key advisers: National Economic Council chair Robert Rubin (a former executive with the investment banking firm of Goldman-Sachs), OMB director Leon Panetta (former chair of the House Budget Committee), Treasury Secretary Lloyd Bentsen, and Deputy Treasury Secretary Robert Altman, as well as Federal Reserve Board chair Alan Greenspan.[120]

In his second year, Clinton replaced McLarty as chief of staff with Panetta, who was succeeded in 1996 by Erskine Bowles. Panetta and Bowles brought order to the policymaking process. But by that time, the administration's shortcomings had helped enable the Republicans to capture control of Congress in the 1994 midterm elections, and Clinton was reduced to fending off Republican initiatives.[121] In doing so, Clinton relied heavily on Republican political consultant Dick Morris for political strategy, often finding ways to win the battle for public opinion by staking out moderate positions and portraying Republican initiatives as extreme.[122]

Policy issues. Clinton entered the White House with a long wish list of policy initiatives. Chief among his campaign promises were economic stimulus and investment, health-care reform, and welfare reform. Circumstances soon added items to the agenda. Deficit reduction rose in prominence as an objective. In foreign policy, free-trade agreements and military interventions in Somalia and the Balkans exacerbated the frenetic activity of Clinton's first year.

After the first two years, several factors—Republican control of Congress, amid intense partisan polarization; a booming economy that diminished the urgency of policy changes; and the Monica Lewinsky scandal and impeachment—severely constrained the administration's scope for policy activity.

The Economy. Between the 1992 campaign and his inauguration, Clinton shifted the emphasis of his economic policy to deficit reduction after a pitched battle within the administration. This new posture followed orthodox economic advice and contributed to the achievement of a balanced budget in 1998.

A large group of Clinton's economic advisers, along with Greenspan, urged the president-elect to deal with the budget deficit.[123] Economists warned that excessive deficits would "crowd out" private investors from credit markets or even lead to collapse of the financial sector.[124] The deficit hawks' argument was buttressed by budget data released by the outgoing Bush administration in late 1992, showing that the projected deficit for fiscal year 1993 had risen to $290 billion, with comparably large deficits for the remainder of the decade. They argued that economic stimulus was no longer appropriate because recovery was already under way.

Other advisers, particularly Labor Secretary Robert Reich, CEA chair Laura Tyson, and communications director George Stephanopoulos, urged Clinton to continue with stimulus—pointing to the unemployment rate, which remained above 7 percent, and arguing that the government needed to support public investments to make the country internationally competitive.[125] As Clinton aide William Galston observes, each side in the debate "represented a different set of genuinely important promises that Bill Clinton had made." In the end the deficit hawks, reflecting the majority of mainstream economic advice, proved to have Clinton's ear.

In February 1993 Clinton and his advisers, working quickly, presented an economic plan that followed in broad outline what most economists were advising. It consisted of a sizeable deficit reduction package about evenly split between spending cuts and tax increases, along with a diminished public investments program.[126] The investments program was defeated by a Senate filibuster led by Republican leader Robert Dole. The deficit reduction package, with additional spending cuts, passed both houses despite several Democratic defections and Republican opposition to the tax increases.

After the Republicans took control of Congress in 1994, Clinton largely acceded to their aggressive approach to spending cuts—based on a political strategy of "triangulation," recommended by Morris and designed to distinguish Clinton from more liberal congressional Democrats.[127] Clinton successfully drew the line at GOP calls for large cuts in income taxes and entitlement spending.[128] By 1998 the economy was growing so fast that it obviated difficult choices on the budget. Clinton vetoed a Republican tax cut in 1999 on the grounds that it would eventually bring about either a return to large deficits or deep cuts in entitlement spending.[129]

Clinton's orthodox economic policies were followed by an extended economic boom, making the Clinton presidency an apparent dramatic success on the economic front. Sixteen million jobs were created in eight years, driving the unemployment rate below 4 percent by 2000. Inflation remained low and the budget deficit was eliminated. To what extent Clinton's evidence-based policies caused the boom, however, is a matter for debate. Analysts give varying degrees of credit to several factors outside of Clinton's control: business restructuring; technological innovation, featuring computers and the Internet; looser monetary policy by the Federal Reserve Board; an expansion of global trade; and low oil prices and a strong dollar, among others.[130] Politically, the strong economy was not enough to overcome the series of gaffes, scandals, and policy failures that beset the Clinton White House in 1993 and 1994, when the Democrats lost control of Congress in the midterm elections.[131] But it did help Clinton skate to an easy reelection in 1996 and to weather the Monica Lewinsky scandal and Republican impeachment effort in 1998 and 1999.[132]

Health-Care Reform. The Clinton White House was more than adequately attuned to evidence-based expertise on health care, amassing a huge amount of information. It performed far less well in designing a workable policy and devising an effective strategy to promote it.

American health care in the early 1990s suffered from runaway cost increases and rising numbers of uninsured citizens.[133] In the 1992 campaign, Clinton promised to solve both problems through broad reform of the health-care industry. To be successful, however, a health-care initiative would have to resolve conflicts among a daunting array of interests.[134]

Clinton announced his support for an approach based on managed competition in September 1991, more than a year before the election. An archetypical evidence-based reform, managed competition had been developed in the 1970s by economists and health policy analysts as a strategy for correcting several defects of the health-care marketplace. It would ensure universal coverage. But unlike a government-run system, it would allow consumers to choose among competing private plans in a regulated market—with coverage subsidized by employers and the government.[135] The choice of this strategy had both policy and political motives. Clinton and his advisers for health policy—Atul Gawande and Ira Magaziner—defined themselves as New Democrats, who sought to preserve the advantages of private markets. They also believed that managed competition had broad enough appeal to get passed.[136]

After the inauguration, Clinton quickly attempted to fulfill his campaign promises on health care. To develop a specific legislative proposal, he appointed a twelve-member task force, representing the relevant executive agencies and led by his wife, Hillary Rodham Clinton. The task force in turn was served by an advisory group led by Magaziner.[137]

The task force was useful for gathering information spanning a variety of perspectives, but not for weighing alternatives or making decisions. Partly in the hope of co-opting a substantial group of experts, it was allowed to proliferate advisory subgroups, which eventually numbered more than 30, and individual members, topping out at the ludicrous figure of 630.[138] The task force consulted widely with affected interests and assembled a vast body of evidence-based analysis.

There are diverse diagnoses of the causes of the Clinton health-care plan's political failure. Jacob Hacker argues that, in trying to come up with a policy design that would elicit broad support, Clinton and his advisers overlooked the importance of actually negotiating with the other major players in Washington, especially the relevant congressional committee chairs, and that in promoting his measure to the public, he failed to explain how it would work.[139] Richard Pious, by contrast, argues that Clinton was attempting a comprehensive policy solution when nonincremental policy change was politically impossible.[140] Substantively, the plan was extraordinarily complex and, at least in appearances, highly bureaucratic. Clinton ignored economic advisers who sought a less extravagant program, with more cost-sharing and fewer benefits.[141] Congressional Republicans chose a strategy of implacable opposition, and some business interests took advantage of public confusion to mount highly effective television advertisements attacking the proposal, often misleadingly.[142] Public support, initially high, sank precipitously over the course of the public debate.

By the late summer of 1994, the Clinton plan's political and substantive flaws combined to scuttle the bill in the Senate, where it never came to a vote. Even though no alternative strategy suggested itself as obviously more promising, the defeat contributed to an image of chaos and incompetence that hung over the administration during Clinton's first two years, an image heavily penalized by the voters in the 1994 midterm elections.[143]

Welfare Reform. Initially, much as with health care, Clinton relied on a large task force of policy experts and affected interests to develop an evidence-based proposal for welfare reform. But the administration took so long to act that the bill's introduction shortly before the 1994 midterm elections was little more than a symbolic gesture. In the next Congress, considerations of saving his own electoral skin led Clinton to sign a Republican version of welfare reform that ignored mainstream analysis and appealed to public disapproval of welfare recipients.

Clinton had compelling grounds for making welfare reform a top priority. As William Galston observes, Clinton had given welfare reform "the highest level of emphasis" during the election campaign: "In the key swing states in the ten days before the November election, the only ads that were up were welfare reform ads."

The Clinton welfare reform task force numbered thirty-two people. The three co-chairs were ideologically diverse, leading members of the evidence-based community: Health and Human Services assistant secretaries David T. Ellwood and Mary Jo Bane, academic specialists on poverty and welfare, who sought to reduce dependence through services rather than sanctions; and deputy domestic policy adviser Bruce Reed, the Democratic Leadership Council cofounder, who pushed for work requirements and time limits on benefits. As with health care, the task force proved complex to the point of unwieldiness, with unclear decision processes. It referred too many decisions to the president, who often responded in vague terms that opposing factions interpreted in opposite ways.[144]

The administration's proposed Work and Responsibility Act provided work requirements for welfare recipients that would be phased in slowly and with flexibility, along with a modest package of social services.[145] The bill was an embodiment of centrist, evidence-based welfare policymaking. But it was introduced too late in the session—four months before the 1994 midterm elections—to be considered by a Congress that already was dealing with major issues of health care, crime, and trade, and thus was set aside for the succeeding Congress.[146]

After the Republican takeover, however, Congress had very different ideas. The new Republican majority presented a hard-line, conservative measure that cut welfare benefits, limited eligibility, increased work requirements, and imposed strict time limits on eligibility for benefits. The ideological measure overlooked extensive research indicating very limited employment gains for welfare mothers under existing workfare programs.[147] Senator Moynihan—a distinguished academic and cosponsor of the 1988 welfare bill signed by Reagan—warned that the bill would put millions of children at risk of hunger and homelessness. Clinton vetoed versions of the Republican welfare bill in December 1995 and January 1996, citing its cuts in food stamps, school lunches, and benefits to immigrants.[148] In July 1996, Rubin, Panetta, and Health and Human Services secretary Donna Shalala (in addition to Ellwood and Bane) recommended that he veto a slightly amended third Republican bill. In the heat of his reelection campaign, however, Clinton accepted the political advice of Morris and Vice President Al Gore that he needed to sign it.[149]

For purposes of the campaign, Clinton was able to claim a major policy achievement: "ending welfare as we know it." But contrary to his centrist, evidence-based approach, the law was largely an expression of populist conservative ideology: families receiving welfare would be dropped from the rolls after two years, work requirements passed in 1988 would be accelerated, mothers under the age of twenty-one would be ineligible for benefits, and mothers who bore children while receiving welfare would receive no additional benefits to support them, among other provisions. Bane and Ellwood resigned in protest of the president's signing it.

Despite the triumph of ideological and political considerations over evidence-based policy advice, early assessments of the 1996 welfare reform were quite favorable. By 2001, welfare caseloads had fallen by 50 percent, along with rising rates of employment for single mothers, declining child poverty rates, and a higher percentage of children living with married parents. Analysts interpreted the data cautiously, however. The encouraging results had coincided with a sustained economic expansion that touched the entire income distribution. When the economy went into recession in 2001, the condition of the poor deteriorated. Many former welfare recipients who took jobs found themselves worse off because of the loss of health and food stamp benefits.[150] Even so, however, the bleakest scenarios envisioned by researchers and liberals had not materialized.[151]

Clinton sought and received a steady diet of competent, objective advice about public policy. But ill-managed decision processes in his first two years—enabling, rather than compensating for, his personal difficulty in making decisions—undercut his efforts. He was well served by his economic advisers, who helped him respond to changing economic conditions, reduce budget deficits, and lay the groundwork for a long period of sustained economic growth. Yet, partly as a result of his political and managerial failures, Clinton spent most of his presidency merely defending the status quo against an aggressive Republican congressional majority.

Conclusion

Our review of the leading issues in domestic policy in the Reagan, George H. W. Bush, and Clinton presidencies suggests three conclusions about the role of evidence-based advice in presidential decision making and success, or, more simply, about the reality-based presidency. First, presidents differ, sometimes dramatically, in their orientations toward information and expertise. Among the three presidents in our study, Bush and Clinton were both far more attentive to information and advice from reputable sources than Reagan was—in much the same way that Barack Obama has been more attentive than George W. Bush. The differences reflect personality—including basic cognitive traits—as well as prior experiences.[152] But whatever the causes, we can expect similar sharp differences to occur among future presidents, if only because the process of electing presidents readily permits such differences.

Although the White House staff and other senior administration officials often influence the president's responses to evidence-based advice, their effects are secondary to the president's own dispositions. As Roger Porter says, "Ultimately, presidents make the decisions." Porter, who served on the White House staffs of three presidents and has written and taught about presidential advisory processes, cautioned against assigning the staff too much credit or blame for the president's performance.[153]

Fundamentally, as William Galston says, "every president gets the White House he deserves." The president selects senior aides, with one orientation or the other, on the basis of his preferred style of advice. He then depends on that advice. The accounts of all our cases turn crucially on who had the president's ear or was assigned to coordinate a policymaking process. But these accounts never suggest that a president got a much different kind of advice than what he wanted. No president who wanted to know about research and hard data was instead treated to professions of ideological faith, or vice versa.

In addition, an individual president will vary in his or her approach to policymaking over time, and from one issue to another. Some presidents, such as Clinton—who studied politics and economics as a Rhodes Scholar—are so to speak born reality-based. Others, such as Reagan—when he confronted the enormous budget deficits that resulted from his evidence-defying 1981 tax cut—have reality thrust upon them. Yet even such extreme cases will exhibit a good deal of variation. Under electoral pressure, Clinton the policy-wonk president signed and claimed credit for a welfare reform bill that was driven mainly by populist conservative ideology. After the deficit experience, Reagan adopted analytically based policies on Social Security, tax reform, and welfare reform.

Second, evidence-based decision making often will not serve the president's purely political interests, particularly when responsible economic management calls for increasing taxes or cutting benefits. Both Bush and

Clinton pursued mainstream economic policies and initially paid a high political price. Clinton eventually benefited from economic gains to which his policies had contributed, but Bush received no such compensation. Of course, there is nothing to be gained from ignoring evidence-based advice out of sheer perversity. Presidents discount such advice primarily when tempted to do so by some ideological or constituency consideration. From a political standpoint, succumbing to such temptation may be the path to success. President Bush's pandering to an uninformed public on policies to fight drug abuse undoubtedly bolstered his popular support. His economically scrupulous acceptance of a tax increase to reduce the deficit was an important element of his political undoing.

Third, in a general and not very reliable way, evidence-based policymaking is likely to serve the nation's interests. To be sure, acting on evidence-based advice is not a certain means to policy success. Experts are generally overconfident about the accuracy of their judgments.[154] Evidence-based analysis provided strong grounds for criticism of both the 1981 tax cuts and the 1996 welfare reform, but the results of these policies appear better than that evidence predicted. Reagan's supply-side fantasy led to unprecedented peacetime deficits that lasted into the 1990s, but the economy also experienced two extended booms during and shortly after his presidency.

Nevertheless, from the standpoint of policy success and the nation's interests, a reality-based presidency is a better gamble than the alternative. Our cases include numerous instances of relevant experts in effect predicting the results of policies, and those results actually occurring. Both Clinton's and Bush's mainstream economic policies were economically successful. The long-term success of Reagan's economic policies probably depended on the subsequent deficit reduction undertaken by Reagan himself, Bush, and Clinton. And the nation still suffers the consequences of decisions by Bush and other leaders to ignore reputable advice on effective methods of combating illegal drugs in the 1980s and 1990s. The "reality-based community" is in the end the most competent source of guidance.

In short, rather than leading the cheers for almost any president who manages to get reelected and remain popular, through whatever good fortune or other means, scholars should give closer scrutiny to a president's decision making. They should examine each president's orientation toward real-world evidence about problems and policies and attempt to weigh the actual effects of their decisions. From the standpoint of citizens casting their votes in a presidential election, these concerns will not (and arguably should not) trump the primary considerations of party and ideology. But, other things roughly equal, the voters should strongly prefer a reality-based presidency.

Notes

1. Ron Suskind, "Without a Doubt: Faith, Certainty and the Presidency of George W. Bush," *New York Times Magazine*, October 17, 2004.

2. The aide went on to explain, evidently in reference to foreign policy, that "we're an empire"—able to change the world, rather than merely deal with a given reality. Thus he was not attesting to ideological or religious faith, but rather was offering an exalted view of American power.

3. George Packer, *The Assassin's Gate: America in Iraq* (New York: Farrar, Straus and Giroux, 2005); Daniel Benjamin and Steven Simon, *The Next Attack: The Failure of the War on Terror and a Strategy for Getting It Right* (New York: Times Books, 2005); Larry Jay Diamond, *Squandered Victory: The American Occupation and the Bungled Effort to Bring Democracy to Iraq* (New York: Times Books, 2005); Richard A. Clarke, *Against All Enemies: Inside America's War on Terror* (New York: Free Press, 2004); James Risen, *State of War: The Secret History of the C.I.A. and the Bush Administration* (New York: Free Press, 2006); Seymour M. Hersh, *Chain of Command: The Road from 9/11 to Abu Ghraib* (New York: HarperCollins, 2004); Bruce R. Bartlett, *Impostor: How George W. Bush Bankrupted America and Betrayed the Reagan Legacy* (New York: Doubleday, 2006); Ron Suskind, *The Price of Loyalty: George W. Bush, the White House, and the Education of Paul O'Neill* (New York: Simon & Schuster, 2004); Douglas Brinkley, *The Great Deluge: Hurricane Katrina, New Orleans, and the Mississippi Gulf Coast* (New York: Morrow, 2006); Joseph Romm, "Ignoring the Climate Change Alarm," *Guardian*, July 9, 2008, http://www.guardian.co.uk/commentisfree/2008/jul/09/georgebush.climatechange (accessed July 16, 2009); Peter N. Spotts, "Has the White House Interfered on Global Warming Reports?," *Christian Science Monitor*, January 31, 2007, http://www.csmonitor.com/2007/0131/p01s04-uspo.html (accessed July 16, 2009).

4. "Off to Work They Go," *Economist* 389, no. 8608 (November 29, 2008), 31–32; Peter Baker, "The White House Looks for Work," *New York Times Magazine* (January 23, 2011), http://www.nytimes.com/2011/01/23/magazine/23Economy-t.html?_r=1 (accessed February 14, 2011). John Cassidy, "Timothy Geithner's Financial Plan Is Working—And Making Him Very Unpopular," *New Yorker* 86, no. 4 (March 15, 2010), 26.

5. Larry M. Bartels, *Unequal Democracy: The Political Economy of the New Gilded Age* (Princeton, N.J.: Princeton University Press, 2008), esp. ch. 4.

6. Bartels, *Unequal Democracy*, p. 99.

7. The latitude for disagreement reflects the range of uncertainty about empirical issues among those qualified to judge, along with the degree of conflict or disagreement about the affected values or interests among sizable groups of citizens.

8. The Intergovernmental Panel on Climate Change estimates of the long-term effects range from devastating to relatively modest; cf. "The Clouds of Unknowing: The Science of Climate Change," *Economist*, March 20, 2010, www.economist.com/printedition/index.cfm?d=20100320 (accessed May 18, 2010).

9. Philip E. Tetlock, *Expert Political Judgment: How Good Is It? How Can We Know?* (Princeton, N.J.: Princeton University Press, 2006). See also Richard M. Pious, *Why Presidents Fail: White House Decision Making from Eisenhower to Bush II* (Lanham, Md.: Rowman and Littlefield, 2008), 247–251; David H. Freeman, *Wrong: Why Experts Keep Failing Us—And How to Know When Not to Trust Them* (Boston: Little, Brown, 2010).

10. For an insightful, often skeptical discussion of the relative value of professional policy analysis, compared with the "ordinary knowledge" of other participants in policymaking, see Charles E. Lindblom and David K. Cohen, *Usable Knowledge: Social Science and Social Problem Solving* (New Haven, Conn.: Yale University Press, 1979). Rather than explore this large subject, we will make two observations. First, the comparative advantage of systematic research varies enormously from one issue to another. Second, an effective evidence-based adviser will integrate whatever insights systematic, professional analysis has to offer with a large amount of ordinary knowledge, reflecting a variety of perspectives. There should be no instances in which access to systematic evidence will make an adviser less reliable, rather than more.

11. Paul Light, *The President's Agenda: Domestic Policy Choice from Kennedy to Clinton*, 3rd ed., (Baltimore, Md.: Johns Hopkins University Press, 1998); Daniel J. Tichenor, "The President and Interest Groups: Allies, Adversaries, and Policy Leadership," in *The Presidency and the Political System*, 9th ed., ed. Michael Nelson (Washington, D.C.: CQ Press 2010), 264–294; B. Dan Wood and Jeffrey S. Peake, "The Dynamics of Foreign Policy Agenda Setting," *American Political Science Review* 92, no. 1 (March 1998): 173–184.

12. On the role of near-term, visible consequences in motivating a president to refrain from "pandering"—that is, making substantively inferior policy decisions for the sake of popular support—see Brandice Canes-Wrone, *Who Leads Whom? Presidents, Policy, and the Public* (Chicago: University of Chicago Press, 2005). Canes-Wrone suggests that concern about such consequences deters most presidential pandering. We suspect that opportunities for politically successful pandering are quite abundant.

13. We also use the term *reality-based* in certain contexts to evoke the Bush aide's notion of a "reality-based community." There is such a community in the sense of an unorganized, large population of policymakers, experts, and others who share certain general principles of investigation and inference and criteria for recognizing expertise. The term is misleading, however, if it is taken to imply that members of this community always or necessarily grasp the *reality*, in the sense of objective truth, in any area. The most we would claim is that they use grounds for inference and judgment that, as a general matter, are superior to those used by others.

14. Unless otherwise noted, all quotations from domestic policy advisers are from the transcripts of the Miller Center symposium reported in chapters 3, 5, 7, and 9.

15. Karen M. Hult, "Strengthening Presidential Decision-Making Capacity," *Presidential Studies Quarterly* 30, no. 1 (March 2000): 27–46.

16. John Broder, "Obama to Open Offshore Areas to Oil Drilling for First Time," *New York Times*, March 31, 2010, http://www.nytimes.com/2010/03/31/science/earth/31energy.html (accessed May 11, 2010); Sheryl Gay Stolberg and John Broder, "Obama Seeks to Split Agency That Monitors Oil Drilling," *New York Times*, May 11, 2010, http://www.nytimes.com/2010/05/12/us/12interior.html?ref=politics (accessed May 11, 2010).

17. M. Stephen Weatherford, "Comparing Presidents' Economic Policy Leadership," *Perspectives on Politics* 7, no. 3 (September 2009): 546; Edward R. Tufte, *Political Control of the Economy* (Princeton, N.J.: Princeton University Press, 1978), 45–55.

18. Bert A. Rockman, "The Style and Organization of the Reagan Presidency," in *The Reagan Legacy: Promise and Performance*, ed. Charles O. Jones (Chatham, N.J.: Chatham House, 1988), 7–10; Dana Rohrabacher, "The Goals and Ideals of the Reagan Revolution," in *The Reagan Revolution?*, eds. B. B. Kymlicka and Jean V. Matthews (Chicago: Dorsey, 1988), 25–41.

19. John H. Kessel, "The Structures of the Reagan White House," *American Journal of Political Science* 28:2 (May 1984): 233–238, argues that the Reagan senior staff was unusual in the degree to which they shared a common ideological predisposition; see also Colin Campbell, *Managing the Presidency: Carter, Reagan, and the Search for Executive Harmony* (Pittsburgh: University of Pittsburgh Press, 1986), 80; Richard P. Nathan, "The Reagan Presidency in Domestic Affairs," in *The Reagan Presidency: An Early Assessment*, ed. Fred I. Greenstein (Baltimore: Johns Hopkins University Press, 1983), 71–73.

20. Paul J. Quirk, "Presidential Competence," in *Presidency and the Political System*, ed. Nelson, 112–113; Campbell, *Managing the Presidency*, 70–71.

21. Kessel, "Structures of the Reagan White House," 254; Hugh Heclo and Rudolph G. Penner, "Fiscal and Political Strategy in the Reagan Administration," in *Reagan Presidency: An Early Assessment*, ed. Greenstein, 40–41.

22. John Sloan, *The Reagan Effect: Economics and Presidential Leadership* (Lawrence: University Press of Kansas, 1999), 144; the quotation is from David Stockman, *The Triumph of Politics: Why the Reagan Revolution Failed* (New York: Harper and Row, 1986), 263.

23. Campbell, *Managing the Presidency*, 110–111. Reagan was diagnosed with Alzheimer's Disease (AD) in 1994, less than five years after leaving office. Mild cognitive difficulties, including apathy, can occur as much as eight years before the criteria for clinical diagnosis of AD are met (L. Bäckman, S. Jones, A. K. Berger, E. J. Laukka, and B. J. Small, "Multiple Cognitive Deficits during the Transition to Alzheimer's Disease," *Journal of Internal Medicine* 256, no. 3 [September 2004]: 195–204). On the other hand, Reagan was already criticized as uninformed and inattentive during the 1980 campaign.

24. Rockman, "Style and Organization," 11, 18; Campbell, *Managing the Presidency*, 94–95; Marcia Lynn Whicker, "Managing and Organizing the Reagan White House," in

The Reagan Presidency: An Incomplete Revolution?, eds. Dilys M. Hill, Raymond A. Moore, and Phil Williams (New York: St. Martin's, 1990), 50–52.

25. Campbell, *Managing the Presidency*, 94, 101–105; Kessel, "Structures of the Reagan White House," 251–254.

26. Kessel, "Structures of the Reagan White House," 254.

27. Shirley Anne Warshaw, *The Domestic Presidency: Policy Making in the White House* (Boston: Allyn and Bacon, 1997), 121–125.

28. Warshaw, *Domestic Presidency*, 137–140.

29. Campbell, *Managing the Presidency*, 108–111; Whicker, "Managing and Organizing," 57–59.

30. Warshaw, *Domestic Presidency*, 141–143.

31. Heclo and Penner, "Fiscal and Political Strategy," 22–24.

32. Herbert Stein, *Presidential Economics: The Making of Economic Policy from Roosevelt to Reagan and Beyond*, 2nd ed. (New York: American Enterprise Institute, 1988), 322; Alan Blinder (*Hard Heads, Soft Hearts: Tough-Minded Economics for a Just Society* [Reading, Mass.: Addison-Wesley, 1987], 67) agrees, "Macroeconomics has been in utter disarray since the Keynesian consensus broke down in the 1970s."

33. William R. Keech, *Economic Politics: The Costs of Democracy* (Cambridge: Cambridge University Press, 1995), 33–41.

34. Stein, *Presidential Economics*, 229.

35. Ibid., ch. 7; Heclo and Penner, "Fiscal and Political Strategy," 25–26; Anthony S. Campagna, *U.S. National Economic Policy, 1917–1985* (New York: Praeger, 1987), 487–491; G. Calvin MacKenzie and Saranna Thornton, *Bucking the Deficit: Economic Policymaking in America* (Boulder, Colo.: Westview, 1996), 126–127.

36. Sloan, *Reagan Effect*, 108; Joseph J. Hogan, "Reaganomics and Economic Policy," in *Reagan Presidency: An Incomplete Revolution?*, eds. Hill, Moore, and Williams, 141–142.

37. W. Elliot Brownlee and C. Eugene Steurle, "Taxation," in *The Reagan Presidency: Pragmatic Conservatism and Its Legacies*, eds. W. Elliot Brownlee and Hugh Davis Graham (Lawrence: University Press of Kansas, 2003), 159–160; Sloan, *Reagan Effect*, 108.

38. Rockman, "Style and Organization," 20.

39. Heclo and Penner, "Fiscal and Political Strategy," 27–28.

40. Sloan, *Reagan Effect*, 105–110; Hogan, "Reaganomics," 139–144.

41. Sloan, *Reagan Effect*, 114–115.

42. Hogan, "Reaganomics," 142.

43. Brownlee and Steurle, "Taxation," 161.

44. Heclo and Penner, "Fiscal and Political Strategy," 37–38, argue that budget director Stockman's apparent confessions in an interview published in the November 1981 *Atlantic Monthly* weren't as sudden as they appeared to the public. They reflected a "continuous series of conversations and arguments spread over many months" at the senior staff level.

45. Brownlee and Steurle, "Taxation," 162.

46. John B. Gilmour, *Reconcilable Differences?: Congress, the Budget Process and the Deficit* (Berkeley: University of California Press, 1990), 123-124; Dennis S. Ippolito, *Uncertain Legacies: Federal Budget Policy from Roosevelt through Reagan* (Charlottesville: University of Virginia Press, 1990), 71-73.

47. Heclo and Penner, "Fiscal and Political Strategy," 34-36; Brownlee and Steurle, "Taxation," 163.

48. Heclo and Penner, "Fiscal and Political Strategy," 39.

49. Brownlee and Steurle, "Taxation," 166.

50. Rockman, "Style and Organization," 21-22. At one point, Chief of Staff Regan scoffed that the part of that year's *Economic Report of the President* written by Feldstein could be thrown away (Hugh S. Norton, *The Quest for Economic Stability: Roosevelt to Reagan* [Columbia: University of South Carolina Press, 1985], 234).

51. Brownlee and Steurle, "Taxation," 167-168.

52. Sloan, *Reagan Effect*, 228-229.

53. Sloan, *Reagan Effect*, esp. 228-231; cf. also Hogan, "Reaganomics," 150-156, on the budget and trade deficits.

54. Sloan, *Reagan Effect*, 133-134; Martha Derthick and Steven M. Teles, "Riding the Third Rail: Social Security Reform," in *Reagan Presidency: Pragmatic Conservatism*, eds. Brownlee and Graham, 185-193.

55. Derthick and Teles, "Riding the Third Rail," 193-194; Sloan, *Reagan Effect*, 134-135; Nathan, "Reagan Presidency," 56-57.

56. Derthick and Teles, "Riding the Third Rail," 202-203.

57. Ibid., 198-199.

58. Paul Light, *Still Artful Work: The Continuing Politics of Social Security Reform* (New York: McGraw-Hill, 1995), chs. 16-17; Edward D. Berkowitz, *Robert Ball and the Politics of Social Security* (Madison: University of Wisconsin Press, 2003), 318-321.

59. Brownlee and Steurle, "Taxation," 166-167; Campbell, *Managing the Presidency*, 77.

60. Brownlee and Steurle, "Taxation," 158.

61. Ibid., 164-171.

62. Ibid., 172.

63. Jeffrey H. Birnbaum and Alan S. Murray, *Showdown at Gucci Gulch: Lawmakers, Lobbyists, and the Unlikely Triumph of Tax Reform* (New York: Random House, 1987), 73; David Hoffman, "President Postpones Tax Blitz," *Washington Post*, July 4, 1985.

64. Birnbaum and Murray, *Showdown at Gucci Gulch*.

65. Sheldon David Pollack, *The Failure of U.S. Tax Policy: Revenue and Politics* (New York: Penguin, 1996).

66. Gillian Peele, "The Agenda of the New Right," in *Reagan Presidency: An Incomplete Revolution?*, eds. Hill, Moore, and Williams, 38.

67. Nathan, "Reagan Presidency," 58.

68. Mildred Rein, *Dilemmas of Welfare Policy: Why Work Strategies Haven't Worked* (New York: Praeger, 1982), chs. 2-4.

69. Rein, *Dilemmas*, 154–155.

70. Nathan, "Reagan Presidency," 76–77.

71. Ibid., 60.

72. R. Kent Weaver, *Ending Welfare as We Know It* (Washington, D.C.: Brookings Institution Press, 2000), 92; Theodore R. Marmor, Jerry L. Mashaw, and Philip L. Harvey, *America's Misunderstood Welfare State: Persistent Myths, Enduring Realities* (New York: Basic Books, 1990), 231–236.

73. Gareth Davies, "The Welfare State," in *Reagan Presidency: Pragmatic Conservatism*, eds. Brownlee and Graham, 222–225.

74. John Robert Greene, *The Presidency of George Bush* (Lawrence: University Press of Kansas, 2000), ch. 5; David Mervin, *George Bush and the Guardianship Presidency* (New York: St. Martin's, 1996), 87–90; Thomas Weko and John H. Aldrich, "The Presidency and the Election Campaign: Framing the Choice in 1988," in *Presidency and the Political System*, ed. Nelson, 263–286; Jack W. Germond and Jules Witcover, *Whose Broad Stripes and Bright Stars?: The Trivial Pursuit of the Presidency, 1988* (New York: Warner, 1989).

75. Ryan J. Barilleaux and Mark J. Rozell, *Power and Prudence: The Presidency of George H. W. Bush* (College Station: Texas A&M Press), 20–21; Joel D. Aberbach, "The President and the Executive Branch," in *The Bush Presidency: First Appraisals*, eds. Colin Campbell and Bert A. Rockman (Chatham, N.J.: Chatham House, 1991), 238–240.

76. Warshaw, *Domestic Presidency*, ch. 6.

77. Barilleaux and Rozell, *Power and Prudence*, 134. Their complaints are documented in Charles Kolb, *White House Daze: The Unmaking of Domestic Policy in the Bush Years* (New York: The Free Press, 1994); James Pinkerton, "Life in Bush Hell," *New Republic* (December 14, 1992), 22.

78. Colin Campbell, "The White House and Presidency under the 'Let's Deal' President," in *Bush Presidency*, eds. Campbell and Rockman, 211–212; David B. Cohen, "George Bush's Vicar of the West Wing: John Sununu as White House Chief of Staff," *Congress and the Presidency* 24, no. 1 (Spring 1997): 44–45; Greene, *Presidency of George Bush*, 49–50; Mervin, *George Bush*, 60–63.

79. Warshaw, *Domestic Presidency*, 173–178.

80. Ibid., 163–171.

81. Barilleaux and Rozell, *Power and Prudence*, 135.

82. *Congressional Quarterly Weekly Report*, February 11, 1989, 280.

83. Barilleaux and Rozell, *Power and Prudence*, 35; Greene, *Presidency of George Bush*, 80; Mervin, *George Bush*, 129.

84. Mervin, *George Bush*, 138–139.

85. Daniel P. Franklin, *Making Ends Meet: Congressional Budgeting in the Age of Deficits* (Washington: CQ Press, 1993), 60–62; Mervin, *George Bush*, 131–132.

86. Greene, *Presidency of George Bush*, 86.

87. Franklin, *Making Ends Meet*, 98–99; Alan S. Blinder and Janet L. Yellen, *The Fabulous Decade: Macroeconomic Lessons from the 1990s* (New York: Century Foundation, 2001), 5–6.

88. Mervin (*George Bush*, 151–153) raises the question of whether the policy could have been communicated better, thus mitigating some of its disastrous political effects for Bush. He notes that Bush declined to undertake a sustained public appeal beyond "a brief, insipid television address" and cites a number of Bush advisers to the effect that, in the words of Cabinet Secretary Edie Holiday, "[We could] have managed the policy change had [communications] been conducted properly." Cf. also Stuart Eizenstat, "What Bush Should Do about Taxes," *Washington Post National Weekly Edition*, June 25–July 1, 1990, 29; Pious, *Why Presidents Fail*, ch. 7.

89. Barilleaux and Rozell, *Power and Prudence*, 42.

90. Michael Duffy and Dan Goodgame, *Marching in Place: The Status Quo Presidency of George Bush* (New York: Simon and Schuster, 1992), 245–246.

91. Peter Passell, "Spurning Fine-Tuning," *New York Times*, December 11, 1991, A1, C4; John R. Cranford, "Hill's Response to Recession Defies Economists' Advice," *Congressional Quarterly Weekly Report*, January 25, 1992, 160–163.

92. Greene, *Presidency of George Bush*, 161; Barilleaux and Rozell, *Power and Prudence*, 35.

93. Duffy and Goodgame, *Marching in Place*, 71.

94. Paul Brace and Barbara Hinckley, "George Bush and the Costs of High Popularity: A General Model with a Current Application," *PS* 26, no. 3 (September 1993): 501–506.

95. The fatal flaw of the enforcement and interdiction strategy is that there is an effectively endless supply of individuals willing to work in the drug trade. Duffy and Goodgame, *Marching in Place*, 104.

96. Ibid.

97. Barilleaux and Rozell, *Power and Prudence*, 25; Steven R. Belenko, *Crack and the Evolution of Anti-Drug Policy* (Westport, Conn.: Greenwood, 1993), 166; Greene, *Presidency of George Bush*, 72.

98. Greene, *Presidency of George Bush*, 71–74.

99. Duffy and Goodgame, *Marching in Place*, 104.

100. John J. DiIulio, Jr., "Crime," in *Setting Domestic Priorities: What Can Government Do?*, eds. Henry J. Aaron and Charles L. Schultze (Washington, D.C.: Brookings Institution Press, 1992), 112; Burt Solomon, "Vulnerable to Events," *National Journal*, January 6, 1990, 9.

101. Gary L. Fisher, *Rethinking Our War on Drugs: Candid Talk about Controversial Issues* (Westport, Conn.: Praeger, 2006), 1.

102. Barilleaux and Rozell, *Power and Prudence*, 25; Mervin, *George Bush*, 94.

103. Kevin M. Esterling, *The Political Economy of Expertise: Information and Efficiency in American National Politics* (Ann Arbor: University of Michigan Press, 2004), ch. 6.

104. Gary C. Bryner, *Blue Skies, Green Politics: The Clean Air Act of 1990 and Its Implementation*, 2nd ed. (Washington, D.C.: CQ Press, 1995), 32–40; cf. also Marc K. Landy, Marc J. Roberts, and Stephen R. Thomas, *The Environmental Protection Agency: Asking the Wrong Questions, from Nixon to Clinton*, expanded ed. (New York: Oxford University Press, 1994).

105. Bryner, *Blue Skies*, 114–116 and 137–138n46.

106. Greene, *Presidency of George Bush*, 77–78; Bryner, *Blue Skies*, 114–117.

107. Warshaw, *Domestic Presidency*, 170–171.

108. Duffy and Goodgame, *Marching in Place*, 87, 99–100.

109. Bryner, *Blue Skies*, ch. 3; Duffy and Goodgame, *Marching in Place*, 118.

110. Bryner, *Blue Skies*, ch. 4; Greene, *Presidency of George Bush*, 77–78.

111. Campbell, "White House and Presidency," 212.

112. Judith A. Layzar, *The Environmental Case: Turning Values into Policy*, 2nd ed. (Washington, D.C.: CQ Press, 2006), 292–297; A. Myrick Freeman, "Economics, Incentives, and Environmental Policy," in *Environmental Policy: New Directions for the Twenty-First Century*, eds. Norman J. Vig and Michael E. Kraft (Washington, D.C.: CQ Press, 2006), 206; Richard N. L. Andrews, "Risk-Based Decision Making: Policy, Science, and Politics," in *Environmental Policy*, eds. Vig and Kraft, 226.

113. Charles O. Jones, "Campaigning to Govern: The Clinton Style," in *The Clinton Presidency: First Appraisals*, eds. Colin Campbell and Bert A. Rockman (Chatham, N.J.: Chatham House, 1996), 21–27.

114. Colin Campbell, "Management in a Sandbox: Why the Clinton White House Failed to Cope with Gridlock," *Clinton Presidency*, eds. Campbell and Rockman, 64–65; Peri E. Arnold, "Clinton and the Institutionalized Presidency," in *The Postmodern Presidency: Bill Clinton's Legacy in U.S. Politics*, ed. Steven E. Schier (Pittsburgh: University of Pittsburgh Press, 2000), 23.

115. Campbell, "Management in a Sandbox," 69; Richard E. Cohen, *Changing Course in Washington: Clinton and the New Congress* (New York: Macmillan, 1994), 46.

116. Jeffrey H. Birnbaum, *Madhouse: The Private Turmoil of Working for the President* (New York: Times Books, 1996).

117. Jeffrey H. Birnbaum and Michael K. Frisby, "Clinton's Slow Start Picking a Team and Policies Dooms His Hope of Hitting the Ground Running," *Wall Street Journal*, January 13, 1993, A16.

118. Michael Kelly, "Clinton's Chief of Staff Ponders Undefined Post," *New York Times*, December 14, 1992, B6.

119. Campbell, "Management in a Sandbox," 78. Warshaw (*Domestic Presidency*, 186) suggests Rasco's appointment was driven by Clinton's goal of gender diversity at all staffing levels.

120. Campbell, "Management in a Sandbox," 77–78; Cohen, *Changing Course*, 13; Raymond Tatalovich and John Frendreis, "Clinton, Class and Economic Policy," in *Postmodern Presidency*, ed. Schier, 45–46.

121. Campbell, "Management in a Sandbox," 79–80; Charles E. Walcott and Karen M. Hult, "White House Structure and Decision Making: Elaborating the Standard Model," *Presidential Studies Quarterly* 35, no. 2 (June 2005): 310.

122. William C. Berman, *From the Center to the Edge: The Politics and Policies of the Clinton Presidency* (Lanham, Md.: Rowman and Littlefield, 2001), 47–50.

123. Christopher J. Bailey, "Clintonomics," in *The Clinton Presidency: The First Term, 1992-1996*, eds. Paul S. Herrnson and Dilys M. Hill (New York: St. Martin's, 1999), 86-88; Berman, *From the Center*, 20-21; Tatalovich and Frendreis, "Clinton, Class and Economic Policy," 47-48.

124. Blinder and Yellen, *Fabulous Decade*, 15-16.

125. Berman, *From the Center*, 21; Tatalovich and Frendreis, "Clinton, Class and Economic Policy," 47-48.

126. Berman, *From the Center*, 23-24; Cohen, *Changing Course*, 75-80.

127. Berman, *From the Center*, 49-50; Arnold, "Clinton and the Institutionalized Presidency," 29-30; Tatalovich and Frendreis, "Clinton, Class and Economic Policy," 51.

128. Berman, *From the Center*, 54-56.

129. Tatalovich and Frendreis, "Clinton, Class and Economic Policy," 57.

130. William D. Nordhaus, "The Story of a Bubble," *New York Review of Books* 51, no. 1 (January 15, 2004), http://www.nybooks.com/articles/16878 (accessed July 20, 2009); Joseph E. Stiglitz, *The Roaring Nineties: A New History of the World's Most Prosperous Decade* (New York: W.W. Norton, 2003), esp. ch. 2; Jeffrey Frankel and Peter Orszag, "Introduction," in *American Economic Policy in the 1990s*, eds. Jeffrey Frankel and Peter Orszag (Cambridge, Mass.: MIT Press, 2002), 8-15; Blinder and Yellen, *Fabulous Decade*, 6-14; Dean Baker, "Something New in the 1990s?: Looking for Evidence of an Economic Transformation," in *Unconventional Wisdom: Alternative Perspectives on the New Economy*, ed. Jeff Madrick (New York: Century Foundation, 2000), 219-223; Tatalovich and Frendreis, "Clinton, Class, and Economic Policy," 53-56.

131. M. Stephen Weatherford and Lorraine M. McDonnell, "Clinton and the Economy: The Paradox of Policy Success and Political Mishap," *Political Science Quarterly* 111, no. 3 (Autumn 1996): 403-436.

132. Brian Newman, "Bill Clinton's Approval Ratings: The More Things Change, the More They Stay the Same," *Political Research Quarterly* 55, no. 4 (December 2002): 781-804; Jeffrey E. Cohen, "The Polls: Change and Stability in Public Assessments of Personal Traits, Bill Clinton, 1993-99," *Presidential Studies Quarterly* 31, no. 4 (December 2001): 733-741.

133. Henry J. Aaron, *Serious and Unstable Condition: Financing America's Health Care* (Washington, D.C.: Brookings Institution Press, 1991).

134. Aaron, *Serious and Unstable Condition*, ch. 1; Linda A. Bergthold, *Purchasing Power in Health: Business, the State, and Health Care Politics* (New Brunswick, N.J.: Rutgers University Press, 1990); Dennis Hevesi, "Polls Show Discontent with Health Care," *New York Times*, February 15, 1989, A16.

135. Jacob S. Hacker, *The Road to Nowhere: The Genesis of President Clinton's Plan for Health Security* (Princeton, N.J.: Princeton University Press, 1997), chs. 2-3.

136. Hacker, *Road to Nowhere*, ch. 4; Haynes Johnson and David S. Broder, *The System: The American Way of Politics at the Breaking Point* (Boston: Little, Brown, 1996), ch. 5.

137. Johnson and Broder, *System*, 104.

138. Hacker, *Road to Nowhere*, 122–124; Berman, *From the Center*, 27; Johnson and Broder, *System*, ch. 6.

139. Hacker, *Road to Nowhere*, 170–180.

140. Pious, *Why Presidents Fail*, ch. 8.

141. Hacker, *Road to Nowhere*, 126–128.

142. Berman, *From the Center*, 28; Hacker, *Road to Nowhere*, 168–170; David W. Brady and Kara M. Buckley, "Health Care Reform in the 103rd Congress: A Predictable Failure," *Journal of Health Politics, Policy, and Law* 20 (Summer 1995): 447–454; Theda Skocpol, "The Rise and Resounding Demise of the Clinton Health Security Plan," in *The Problem That Won't Go Away: Reforming U.S. Health Care Financing*, ed. Henry J. Aaron (Washington, D.C.: Brookings Institution Press, 1996), 51–52.

143. Cf. Weatherford and McDonnell, "Clinton and the Economy"; Cohen, "Polls."

144. Weaver, *Ending Welfare*, 233–235.

145. Weaver, *Ending Welfare*, 242–245; Alice O'Connor, *Poverty Knowledge: Social Science, Social Policy, and the Poor in Twentieth-Century U.S. History* (Princeton, N.J.: Princeton University Press, 2001), 288–290.

146. Jason DeParle and Steven A. Holmes, "A War on Poverty Subtly Linked to Race," *New York Times*, December 26, 2000, A16.

147. Gary Mucciaroni and Paul J. Quirk, *Deliberative Choices: Debating Public Policy in Congress* (Chicago: University of Chicago Press, 2006), ch. 3.

148. Weaver, *Ending Welfare*, 320.

149. Weaver, *Ending Welfare*, 327–328; Berman, *From the Center*, 65.

150. Kasia O'Neill Murray and Wendell E. Primus, "Recent Data Trends Show Welfare Reform to Be a Mixed Success: Significant Policy Changes Should Accompany Reauthorization," *Review of Policy Research* 22, no. 3 (May 2005): 301–324; Sarah Glazer, "Welfare Reform: The Issues," *CQ Researcher* 11, no. 27 (August 3, 2001), 603–614; Harrell Rodgers, "Evaluating the Devolution Revolution," *Review of Policy Research* 22, no. 3 (May 2005): 275–299.

151. Lawrence M. Mead, "Research and Welfare Reform," *Review of Policy Research* 22, no. 3 (May 2005): 401–421.

152. Fred Greenstein, *The Presidential Difference: Leadership Style from FDR to George W. Bush* (Princeton, N.J.: Princeton University Press, 2004).

153. Roger B. Porter, *Presidential Decision Making: The Economic Policy Board* (New York: Cambridge University Press, 1982).

154. Tetlock, *Expert Political Judgment*.

Chapter 9

Lessons from Domestic Policy Successes and Failures

Featured participants at this session were Stuart Eizenstat
(on Jimmy Carter); William Galston (on Bill Clinton); Egil "Bud" Krogh
(on Richard M. Nixon); James Pinkerton (on George H. W. Bush); and
Roger Porter (on Gerald Ford, Ronald Reagan, and George H. W. Bush).
This panel was moderated by Professors Paul Quirk (University of
British Columbia) and Bruce Nesmith (Coe College).

Quirk: The earlier sessions we've been having here have talked about various aspects of the domestic policymaking operations of the White House. We talked about campaigns and the relationship between campaigns and governing, especially the transition. We talked specifically about policy formulation processes and then about the process of getting out the message. This is a session to step back and think about what overall is really critical. What we would like you to do is to reflect on what were the really significant successes and failures in domestic policy of the presidencies that you're associated with, and what staff had to do with that. We'll go in something like chronological order, starting with Bud Krogh.

Krogh: I'm going to start with a topic that I did not have much to do with and maybe that's why it was such a great success: the environment. This was hardly an issue in the 1968 campaign. I don't think that either candidate [Hubert] Humphrey or candidate Nixon talked about it more than once or twice. We came into office January 1969, and all of a sudden this issue started becoming important. I'm not sure the president was terribly interested in it, but he gave a lot of responsibility to staff to develop some initiatives.[1]

During that first year, John Ehrlichman had transited from being counsel to the president to assistant to the president for domestic affairs. I went with him in that transition. John Whitaker on the White House staff became the point person on environmental policy.[2] And that first year, 1969, we began to look at what's going on in the Congress on the environment.

243

They'd passed the National Environmental Policy Act in 1968, so we felt, well, there is some congressional support for this.[3] We were not immune to what was going on in the Congress. Senators Scoop Jackson, Gaylord Nelson, and others were really championing this idea of some environmental legislation.

Nineteen sixty-nine was a learning year about what was really at stake. Then, toward the end of 1969, 1970, 1971, one of the most major explosions in domestic policy legislation occurred. Reorganization Plan No. 2 was adopted in 1970, which set up the Environmental Protection Agency.[4] A gentleman in the Department of Justice, William Ruckelshaus, was asked to head that agency.[5] Russell Train from the Department of the Interior came over to run the Council on Environmental Quality.[6] John Whitaker had that assignment on the White House staff, natural resources and the environment, and John Ehrlichman was very successful in being able to persuade the president that this was an important subject.

You asked, Paul, about the role of staff in this. I would say that the environmental program moved forward because there were exceptionally talented people on the staff in CEQ, Council for Environmental Quality, in the Environmental Protection Agency, who were committed and were very effective. What was the result of their working together? The reorganization plan that set up the Environmental Protection Agency. We submitted seven [reorganization] initiatives, and all seven of them were adopted by Congress; rather, they were not voted down. They had sixty days to vote down an initiative.

Clean water, clean air, endangered species—endangered species came at the end of that period, in 1973. The major legislative pillars of the environmental movement were established at that time. There were public figures—Denis Hayes started Earth Day in 1970, and I remember wondering if it really was my job on the White House staff to assemble on the banks of the Potomac River to start pulling out logs and a lot of junk from the river. But we said, "We have to be part of this major national movement." There was a lot of support within the White House staff for what we were doing. That four-year period from 1969 to 1973 was a halcyon period in legislative work, in executive orders that were adopted, and I attribute a lot of it to the four gentlemen that I have mentioned: John Ehrlichman, Russell Train, Bill Ruckelshaus, and John Whitaker.[7]

We also had tremendous support on the Hill. The environment had been primarily a Democratic issue, but I think we borrowed it for that four-year period. There might be another term that's stronger [*laughter*] but basically I don't want to go there, because we did get in trouble in other areas, too. That was a success.

I'm not sure the president was ever terribly comfortable with what we were doing on environmental policy, but he signed all the bills. When you read some of his histories afterward, you look back and say, "Well, maybe we overdid it on the environmental side." When you look today at global warming being the critical issue that we're trying to address in domestic policy, you can look all the way back and say, "Where did this interest start? What was done?" That was a success. And [*smiling*] we didn't have any failures.

Quirk: Now the fair thing is for you to talk about a failure.

Krogh: Well, we did a lot of reorganization plans that were adopted. Our major failure was trying to reorganize everything.

We had a proposal that we sent to the Hill in 1971 where we were going to consolidate seven departments and agencies into four. They were: community development, natural resources, human resources, and economic affairs.[8] That act itself would probably have alienated every special-interest group, every major congressional committee and staff, and the bureaucracy. There were no allies for this, except a few people thought we ought to organize around function rather than around just one of these simple functional aspects—transportation, energy, what have you. That failed. It was a stillbirth when it got up to Congress. I think the idea is still good but that was a failure, because there was really no effort to try to lay the foundation for what we needed to do. It's still a good idea, but unlikely to occur anytime in our lifetime.

Quirk: And will you connect that to the staff in some way?

Krogh: Yes. I would say staff was being motivated in part by some very good ideas that came out of the Ash Council on Organization. We thought that basically organizing around functions and being able to put people in charge that could resolve a lot of the tradeoffs was a good idea. But then to put it all in one package and send the entire thing up to Congress and say, "Pass that," was really an overwhelmingly difficult, maybe impossible, task.[9]

Quirk: Was there a lack of integration of congressional people into the process of developing the proposal?

Krogh: Yes. I don't think there was really close interaction between the Congress and the presidential staff when we sent that bill up. I sometimes look back on it and wonder how serious it was, because when they really wanted to pass something it was very close interaction. In the drug area, we had very close interaction between Congress and the White House staff, the Office of Management and Budget, in developing legislation. We were able to get things through without a dissenting vote.

Quirk: Stu, can I turn to you?

Eizenstat: Let me start with the successes, which I believe merit saying that President Carter had as many legislative successes as any first-term president and would equal those of most two-term presidents.[10]

Three major energy bills were passed, which laid the groundwork for our energy policy today: breaking the Gordian knot on pricing for oil and natural gas and therefore encouraging their domestic production; major conservation initiatives and major initiatives from solar to syn-fuels for alternative energy; and the first major CAFE [Corporate Average Fuel Economy] standards, fuel-efficiency standards, which set in 1977 fuel-efficiency standards through 1985. Today we're twice as dependent on foreign oil as we were then. The average fuel efficiency standard for our automobiles is less than it was in 1985.[11]

He was a major conservation president, I think the greatest since Theodore Roosevelt, setting aside massive public land with the Alaska Lands bill, wetlands—building, Bud, on many of the things that President Nixon did.[12] He deregulated all forms of transportation—airlines, trucking, bus, rail—and brought airline travel to the great middle class who couldn't afford it before.[13] He created two major departments, Energy and Education, made Margaret Spellings's job possible, but brought those two issues up to the cabinet level and therefore up to a higher level of public attention. Got the Tokyo Trade Round passed with only two dissenting votes.[14] Passed the Panama Canal Treaty legislation in both the Senate and House, and of course [Strategic Arms Limitations Treaty] SALT II and the Camp David accords.[15]

Having said all of that, it reminds me of my father's story about the boxer who comes back bloodied after the third round, sits on the stool, and the manager says, "You're doing great. The guy didn't lay a glove on you." And the boxer says to the manager, "You better watch the referee. Somebody is beating the hell out of me." [*laughter*] So the question was, why did we get the hell beat out of us in 1980?

I want to suggest that there are two major reasons: The first, which hope-fully we will get into more detail later, is external events that impact on a presidency, in this case, the great inflation of the 1970s, which bedeviled President Nixon and President Ford and President Carter; and the Iranian Revolution, which not only led to the hostage crisis but also to a spike in gas prices and to gas lines.[16]

But there were also self-inflicted wounds, and this gets back to your ques-tion about staff and organization. The president under the Constitution has actually limited authorities, except being commander-in-chief. In the domestic area his primary capacity is to initiate legislation and then be the salesman-in-chief for it. In order to do that, you have to have a very clear message, you have to set your priorities, and you have to have a communica-tions strategy that is integrated into that. And that depends, to begin with, on having a highly organized White House staff.

We made the mistake of not having a chief of staff for the first year of our administration, adopting a so-called "spokes-of-the-wheel" concept, in which senior aides each had equal access.[17] That meant there was no single person who could create these priorities, limit them, focus the president's attention, develop a communications strategy around them. Closely aligned to that was not having an experienced White House staff. I was, in a sense, the veteran, having served one year in the Johnson White House and in the Humphrey campaign. But all the senior people were largely inexperienced, with an inexperienced president who had spent four years as governor.[18]

Others learned the lesson from that by bringing in people like Jim Baker for Ronald Reagan, people like Leon Panetta or John Podesta for President Clinton, Rahm Emanuel for Obama—people who knew Washington, par-ticularly for those who came from outside of Washington. Not knowing Washington is a terrific problem because it's a complicated place with many power centers. You've got to have not only a chief of staff, but you've got to have a staff that has some experience with Washington.

Another self-inflicted wound was priorities. We learned after the first year how to set them and they were set very effectively through the vice presi-dent's office, focusing only on two or three a year. But that first year we tried to do everything—a major energy bill, a major hospital cost-containment bill, airline deregulation, welfare reform, a stimulus package—and therefore we confused the message. There wasn't a clear, focused message around which the public could organize, and about which the president could mobilize public opinion and get Congress to pass it. So inevitably, although a lot got done, it always paled in comparison to the number of things that weren't done, particularly since they were done in a comprehensive way, which again teaches me the lesson that Congress is an incremental institution. It can take things in bits and pieces. If you load too many big, comprehensive measures before it, then what will come back will inevitably pale in comparison.

The last self-inflicted wound, I would put under the title "No Surprises." Congress hates surprises. You have to prepare the Congress for what you're proposing. The hit-list for water projects was a surprise that hit congressmen right in the solar plexus, right in their own home districts, where they like to cut ribbons for new projects. It was not prepared. There was no warning for it. The first energy bill—which was prophetic, courageous and did lay a sound future—had not been a major issue in the campaign. The president put in Jim Schlesinger, who organized it under a ninety-day deadline, to do it with no consultation on the Hill, no interagency review. The secretary of the treasury, Mike Blumenthal, and Charlie Schultze, the president's economic adviser, came in with a memo just before the ninety-day deadline saying, "We haven't seen this. We need to know what the cost implications are."[19]

Those to me are the successes and failures. We learned from our failures; that's why we had so many successes. But that very first year was a very difficult year, and that set the pattern of people's thinking about the administration and their capacity to work with Congress.

Quirk: There's one puzzle about this. It strikes me that the core of what you said comes back to this point about inexperience, people who didn't have the background to know how to operate in Washington. Some of these other things look like consequences of that. Let me get to what I think is the really interesting thing here: Did anybody make the point to President-elect Carter, prior to his taking office, that, "You're putting together a lot of people who haven't been there"? What was the ultimate source of this? Was it because of the president's kind of lack of understanding or something else?

Eizenstat: Every president wants to bring with him the people who made his election possible. You had the California gang who came with Reagan. You had the Georgia gang that came with us. Nixon had his group.[20] Every president wants people he can trust. There is always a risk of bringing somebody in from the outside. But President Reagan made a very fundamental decision, learning from our lesson. He took the campaign manager of his principal opponent in the campaign to be his chief of staff, to sort of mellow the people around him and to bring that experience—namely Jim Baker.[21] And that was something we were not advised to do.

President-elects are at the peak of their power. The transition into office is not a time when people like to go up to him and say, "Mr. President, you're not doing the right thing." So at the end of the first year, we did bring people like Anne Wexler in, who were experts, to run public liaison. Later we were to bring Lloyd Cutler in as counsel, but that wasn't done at the beginning. And we paid a frightful price for it.

Quirk: Roger, you have three presidents, but to simplify things, why don't you maybe focus on President Reagan. We have Jim Pinkerton here to talk about President Bush.

Porter: Okay. Let me just mention a word about President Ford first, because omitting him in this context would be unfortunate.

During the three months before Gerald Ford took office, the wholesale price index—we now call it the producer price index—was increasing at an annual rate of 37 percent. This is the most explosive outburst of inflation in United States history. At the same time that inflation was increasing at high double-digit levels, the unemployment rate was increasing, something economists had told us was not possible because of this wonderful thing we call the Phillips Curve, which postulates an inverse relationship between inflation and unemployment. And now we had the worst of both worlds, rising inflation and rising unemployment.[22]

Four days after taking office, Gerald Ford decided to convene a summit conference on inflation, at the urging of congressional leaders, to decide what to do.[23] And in one of those meetings he convened a group of thirty leading economists; fifteen of them were Democrat and fifteen of them were Republican. They included names that would be familiar to all of you.[24] After meeting for three hours, he asked Arthur Okun, who had been President Johnson's chairman of the Council of Economic Advisers, to summarize.[25] Arthur Okun said, "The one thing on which we all agree is that inflation is bad and must be brought under control. One thing on which we can all agree is that we have an excessive amount of regulation and that we need to begin to deregulate transportation, energy, telecommunications, financial services, et cetera.

And that began very early in President Ford's term and was followed by President Carter and followed by President Reagan and followed by President Bush and followed by President Clinton and followed by the second President Bush, in a series of measures which have, in fact, done an enormous amount of good with respect to the overall performance of our economy.

President Ford made a very difficult decision in his first state of the union address—Jim Cannon, who is with us, will remember it, too. He came in on August 9th and he delivered his first state of the union address on January 21st—that he would propose no new spending programs until he had brought inflation under control.[26] He worked relentlessly, and the great forgotten fact of the 1976 election is that he had brought inflation down to 4.8 percent for 1976, which I think is one of the underappreciated accomplishments of a president who was willing to take decision after decision to do this. He did this because he had a staff that was organized through what was called the Economic Policy Board, which took all issues to him and were relentless in basically saying, "The prism through which you need to view this is, how can we effectively bring inflation under control?"

Now when President Reagan came in, he again had an enormously challenging task as to what he should do with respect to the economy because, as Stuart pointed out, we had gotten back on the inflationary binge and we had two years of back-to-back double-digit inflation, 21.5 percent prime interest rate, and virtually no growth in the previous two years. He proposed a plan that was put together and implemented by his staff, but that he was integrally involved in. It would restrain the rate of growth of federal spending, the rate of growth of taxation, the rate of growth of regulation, et cetera. That again was something that he was relentless in introducing, the notion that market-oriented arrangements would be the preferable way with which to address these. For the most part that was followed for the next twenty-five years.

When we're assessing presidents' successes and failures, we need to not simply look at the moment it is enacted. We need to see the longer sweep of history. Now, this sounds like a great success story, but there was a problem. President Reagan knew when he came in that we were facing a difficulty with respect to entitlement spending.[27] We'd had an increase in entitlement spending in real terms for the previous fifteen years, of 9 percent a year compounded for fifteen years. One of the problems was in Social Security, so he tackled that right at the beginning of his first term. He made a proposal that was not adequately—it was actually leaked to the press two days before it was announced. The Republican-controlled Senate voted 98–0 on a sense of the Senate resolution two days later disparaging the president's plan. It was effectively killed.[28]

[House Speaker] Tip O'Neill beat him around the head and shoulders for the next eighteen months, trying to convince Americans that civilization as we know it was going to end, and Reagan lost twenty-six seats in the mid-term elections. He came back to try to address Social Security again at the beginning of his second term. He got it through by one vote in the Senate, one of these perilous dramas, but could not get the restraint on the COLAs [cost of living adjustments] that had been put in, in 1972.[29] That was, in retrospect, one of the great mistakes that we've made, because it put us on a path that has created huge problems for every president since then with respect to how we deal with entitlements.

Quirk: What about staff on this, then? You told the story of enormous successes and a seemingly gross mistake, or at least failure. Is there a staff story underlying this?

Porter: Ultimately, presidents make the decisions. I don't think it's fair for presidents to blame or give credit unnecessarily to staff. What staff exists to do is to make sure that the president understands what his real choices are, and what are likely to be the pattern of costs and benefits associated with various courses of action, and to make sure that the numbers that are being presented to him are accurate and that they are not inflated or based on hope rather than reality. And to help him understand what in fact his real choices are. For the most part, in Ford and Reagan and in the first Bush's term, staff did a reasonably good job of making sure that the president understood what those real choices were.

Krogh: Roger is being very kind and gracious here because he mentioned 1972 as when they did index social security payments to the COLAs, to the cost of living adjustment. That was under Richard Nixon. It seemed like a good idea at the time, [*laughter*] let me just put it that way.[30]

Quirk: Let's move on to Jim.

Pinkerton: One important point to bear in mind about the Bush 41 administration was that he was the first president to represent the third consecutive term for his party since Truman. If you just think about the cycle of congressional strength that a president has, it pretty much goes straight down from the moment he's sworn in to when he leaves office. And so, by the time that we came in in 1989, Republicans were in a severe minority with no prospects of getting it back. The country had rejected Michael Dukakis, but it wasn't as if they were in love with the Republican regime after eight or nine years of just being in charge.[31]

And we shouldn't forget things like Iran-Contra, which had been a major consuming thing in '87 and '88, when President Bush came in. Therefore, much of his agenda was pretty much set by a combination of the Democrats in Congress and the media. And when your job is to negotiate things like the Clean Air Act and the assault weapons ban and the Americans with Disabilities Act, I can't think of anybody I would rather have doing my negotiating for me than Roger Porter, who had an infinite technical understanding of those issues and a degree of patience—I guess that's a virtue, suffering fools gladly—not to say anything bad about the Congress, or the cabinet. [*laughter*] Anyway, that was an incredibly difficult task that Roger performed brilliantly.

The cap-and-trade legislation, which he merged in the Clean Air Act, was a major new idea.[32] It is very hard to both enunciate a new idea and then actually get it implemented. It's one thing to be a bright young thing thinking of something, but then, to actually get it done—and in the same breath, Roger and Bill Reilly and [John] Sununu managed to get the country, with lots of Democrats, thinking that, yes, we have this profound new idea on market forces for emissions controls. Anyway, it didn't do Bush 41 much good politically, because the Democrats, frankly, got most of the credit and the Republican base hated most of those things. But sometimes you just get dealt that set of cards by virtue of where you come in in the cycle.

I do want to associate myself with what Stu said about extraneous events and what Roger said about the grand sweep of history, and that is, it is important. Not that Bush is unique in this score, but big things were happening in the world. You know, the fall of the Berlin Wall, Tiananmen Square—these are both things that happened in the first year of the Bush presidency. A third incident that really had a huge effect on me was the Central Park jogger case, which was late '89.[33] That's when it really hit me that we've had this consensus about big government and the welfare state and stuff like that, and boy, is it lousy in its functioning. As we can see in this case, you have this horrible crime right in New York City in this horrible situation, and this emergence of an underclass, and that's obviously a severe indictment of something that we're doing.

And then of course in addition you had technology. The computer came along in a big way. Here's where the Bush 41 White House was struggling, and I mean that in a good way, to deal with these things. What does it mean when your old systems of government just aren't working very well, when old bureaucracies are collapsing—[Leonid] Brezhnev had passed away by then[34]—when there just isn't motion, the public housing authorities are corrupt, the schools aren't any good, when we are a nation at risk? What I tried to struggle with in the Bush 41 era, with Roger's indulgence, was to say, "Look, are we learning new things about empowerment and market forces and flattening pyramids and things like that? Are we seeing it in business? Are we seeing it in effective governments?"

We were lucky enough to have the author of *Reinventing Government*, David Osborne, come to visit us several times and we had discussions with him.[35] I guess this is a case where a lot of the intellectual capital that was generated from people like Bruce Babbitt and Hernando de Soto and people like that actually didn't do Bush 41 any good, because, frankly, he wasn't that interested.[36] But the Clinton administration was able, with the help of people like Bill Galston and Elaine Kamarck, to bring in the reinventing government effort and to start applying these lessons of management and restructuring and reorganization to great positive effect, not only for the Clinton administration but also for America.[37]

Nesmith: Is it possible for a president to structure advising in such a way that he can get wind of earth-shaking trends like that, or is it pretty much always focused on narrow issue management?

Pinkerton: It's possible, I suppose. But I sort of associate myself with what Henry Kissinger said: You bring in all the intellectual capital you have when you come to the job. You're just too busy during the course of things to make that kind of pivot. But I'm sure others would have examples, too, of presidents who were more alert to trends in the culture and the larger climate.

Quirk: We'll move on to Bill, please, for the Clinton administration.

Galston: Coming last reminds me of one of my favorite, favorite stories. It involves one of my favorite people, Morris Udall, who'd taken a freshman member of Congress in tow. They were actually seated next to each other when this very long debate just went on and on and on. Finally the freshman couldn't take it any longer and he tapped Udall on the shoulder and said, "Why are they still talking? Everything has been said." And Udall smiled at him and said, "Yes, son, but not everybody has yet said it." [*laughter*]

So that's my role, to repeat with emphasis. But let me just give you a few things on the staffing issue that I've learned, not only from my experience in the White House, but from the observation and study of other people's experience in the White House. I hope that future presidents will all put this in the bank, as will their staffs.

Number one: Under modern circumstances a strong chief of staff is a necessity. We've tested all the alternatives, and yes, there are downsides to a strong chief of staff, but a president has to be smart enough to manage the downsides because the downside of not having one is prohibitive.[38]

Number two: You do need keepers of the flame, loyalists who are prepared to remind the president and the people around the president that there was a campaign and that the president stood for something during the campaign and needs to keep that in mind during governance.

Third, and pulling to some extent in the other direction: Experience matters, and very frequently, loyalists are inexperienced and the experienced are not too loyal. A president has to be able to manage that, but frankly, it was self-defeating for the Clinton White House on day one to take the position, basically, that nobody who had served in a previous Democratic administration could serve in the Clinton White House. I'm seated next to someone [Eizenstat] who could have done us a great deal of good if he'd been in the White House from day one, I believe, and there are reasons, rooted in inexperience and hubris, why he wasn't. [*laughter*]

Fourth: The fourth thing I've learned is that you cannot outsource the president's agenda, either to the departments or agencies or to the Congress. Cabinet government won't work for the president under modern circumstances, although the cabinet is very important for other purposes. But congressional government won't work, either.

Finally, and this is something I learned from personal experience: Draw on the permanent staff that is available to you, particularly in the Office of Management and Budget. When I got into the White House, I didn't understand what the Office of Management and Budget was, what an enormous repository of institutional policy memory it was and how much your own thoughts could be leveraged by the wisdom and experience of people who'd been working on particular policy areas for so long. If I could pass on one piece of advice to young people coming into the White House as part of a president's team: Find out who your counterparts are, not only in the departments and agencies, but also in the Office of Management and Budget. Don't take everything they say as gospel, but listen very carefully.[39]

And now, if I may, I want to segue into a somewhat broader set of reflections about success and failure in the policy realm. These are some rules of thumb I've taken away:

First of all, begin strong. As the old saying goes, you never get a second chance to make a first impression. Every president, every new administration, has to think very hard about how to lead from strength. If you stumble into something like the "don't ask, don't tell" controversy, you're going to pay a price because what comes first helps to frame the public understanding of everything that comes next. Stu Eizenstat has talked eloquently about the successes of years two through four of the Carter administration, but also the extent to which the difficulties of year one framed that in the public understanding. That's paradigmatic of a larger truth.

Secondly, in all sorts of ways, consistency with your campaign is important. If you say you're going to focus like a laser beam on the economy, as Bill Clinton did, don't stumble into "don't ask, don't tell." If you say you're going to be a new kind of Democrat, then when members of Congress tell you, "Don't do welfare, do health care first," maybe you ought to push back and say, "I'm not sure that's why I was elected."

Third, you really have to focus and select. Campaigning is about addition, but governing is about selection. Nineteen thirty-three to thirty-four, the Hundred Days, and Lyndon Johnson's 1965-66 Great Society period are historical anomalies that no president is wise to rely on. Generally speaking, you cannot do that much. You cannot flood the zone and hope to complete very many passes. When you need to choose among elements of your agenda, make clean choices, as Bill Clinton did early in 1993, when he had to figure out whether to give the emphasis to public investment or to fiscal prudence. During the campaign he didn't think he was going to be faced with that choice, but circumstances changed. He had to adjust. He had to adjust by making a choice. Large and sustainable changes are rarely built on slender, partisan majorities.[40]

Welfare reform, one of the great victories of the Clinton administration, proved to be important and sustainable precisely because, when it happened, it was a bipartisan effort. Take what you can get and declare victory. If you hold up your veto pen and say, "If I don't get a hundred percent of what I want, I'm not going to take anything," you're likely to get nothing, and you're likely to pay a huge political price for getting nothing.

Finally, we've been asked to talk about success. Well, success is an ambiguous or perhaps Janus-faced concept, because there is policy success and political success. What succeeds politically doesn't necessarily succeed in policy terms and vice-versa. What do you do when there's a tension between those two things? I mean, no president can be indifferent to sustained political support, but at the same time achieving sustained political support at the cost of doing what needs to be done is a hollow victory. Staff people around the president have to be worried about feeding a president's desire for sustained high poll ratings. At some point, you have to say, "Mr. President, you're right. You're going to pay a price. We're all going to pay a price. But if we don't do this, we'll never get another chance and the country will be the worse for it."

Nesmith: To bring it down to cases, are there, for lack of a better word, failures, in the early stages of the Clinton administration that an experienced hand like Stu Eizenstat could have helped to prevent?

Galston: Well, let's take what I view as one of the defining decisions of the early Clinton administration. We were getting lots of different advice about welfare and health care—which one to lead with. It is a matter of record that Bill Clinton moved to the highest level of emphasis during the campaign the idea of ending welfare as we know it. Indeed, in the key swing states in the ten days before the November election, the only ads that were up were welfare reform ads. That represented a pretty solemn undertaking with the American people, and I suspect very strongly that if there had been a Stuart Eizenstat as deputy chief of staff for policy—he can speak for himself, but I think he would have put his thumb down on the scale and said, "Mr. President"—and to the people around him—"this is one of the things you were elected to do, not eventually, but immediately. And yes, Congress is going to tell you don't do it, but I think you have to insist."

That might have made for some very tense conversations, not only with the president but with others very close to the president. That is one of those areas where a combination of experience plus distance might have served the Clinton White House very well.

Nesmith: Let's bring some more people into the conversation now. We'd like to talk about how the politics of an issue and the political advice mixes with more substantive advice—what Bruce Reed has soon-to-be famously called the "wonks and hacks" tradeoff. To break it out further, we can differentiate among the policy wonks: those who have ideological commitments or maybe traditional partisan views, and those who have relatively objective information. How are all these varying types of information integrated, in your experience?

Reed: Well, the definition of success is not what most of the political world thinks. It's not just winning elections, though you can't do anything, in fact, unless you do. It's not just legislative victories, although they certainly beat legislative failures. Even when you pass a law, the work has just begun. The real definition of both policy and political progress is actual results, actual progress for the country.

And that is the hardest thing for a White House, young or experienced, to recognize, that over time the best politics is policies that actually work. We had plenty of successes that were political successes. Welfare reform was an enormous political success that helped us get reelected, but the only reason that it stands as a real success is that it helped move a bunch of people out of poverty and ended welfare as a way of life.[41] The challenge for all of us wonks is that the rest of the White House is generally looking for short-term political victories in order to keep the bicycle moving. That tension between the two tribes of hacks and wonks is always great.

I can remember a few times where the hacks were so worried about short-term political interests. We had a bill that had passed Congress and they'd sent it down to the White House and the political and communications advisers said, "Well, the president's busy right now. We're on a different message and we need to put that off for a couple of weeks." It took one of the wonks to point out, "Actually, if we wait two weeks that will be a pocket veto." You know, the hacks are just doing their job.

We had one of the most breathtakingly cynical hacks in modern American history, Dick Morris.[42] The definition of success for his job was to get the president reelected. That's not the definition of success for a lot of the rest of us. We used that to our advantage. We had what we referred to as the madman theory. Our madman was our crazy political adviser, who was full of a bunch of ideas, and three out of ten of them would have had some merit, and the others would have led to our immediate undoing. But we used it to force the bureaucracy to do ideas that might make sense. The fact that wonks are always fighting an uphill battle in that regard is one of the greatest challenges of the job.

When I became domestic policy adviser, Stu Eizenstat came in and told me about a great tradition that—I'd love to hear from others whether they had it as well. He told me that when he became domestic policy adviser, his Republican predecessor had left a bottle of malt whiskey in the office safe, which he said was a tradition that dated from John Ehrlichman. When Margaret came in I left behind a bottle of whiskey as well. I think there is a reason that domestic policy advisers need to keep a bottle handy. [*laughter*]

Eizenstat: Just for public record, after being nominated by President Clinton to go to Brussels and be Ambassador to the EU [European Union], with my name sent to the Senate and the EU having given what's called *agrément*, Mack McLarty called me over in May of the first year of the administration and said, "Stu, we've decided we need more experience in the White House. Would you be deputy chief of staff?" I said, "But I'm going to Brussels." He said, "The president wants you to stay here." I went back home to talk to my wife and she said, "Well, if that's what the president wants—I guess I won't have any Belgian lace, but you'll be doing something that the president wants." So I called Mack back and said, "If this is what the president wants, fine." Three days later, I was told I was going to Brussels. It ended up being good for me because it gave me an international profile for eight years as undersecretary of state and other things, but I'll leave the rest to history.

I want to talk about supervening events that occur that disturb this well-planned campaign promise thing, that disturb the organizational capacity. Certainly, Jim Pinkerton had it with the Saddam Hussein invasion of Kuwait.[43] I want to talk about two aspects of it: one that might have been better anticipated by good staff work, and one that couldn't. But then the test is, how does the staff react?

The Iranian Revolution occurred in 1979 when the Ayatollah Khomeini came out of exile, came back to Tehran, and we've borne the consequences of it, not only in Iran but worldwide ever since. It would have taken a creative genius to understand the forces leading to that. Now, obviously we saw that the Shah was on very shaky ground.[44] The question is how do you react? And I don't want to talk about the hostage crisis now. We're dealing with domestic issues. I want to talk about the domestic impact, which was a rise in gas prices and gas lines, because five million barrels of oil were taken out of production during the revolution, because of the chaos in Iran.

Now here's where the policy mistake was made. We had had the courage to deregulate natural gas, regulated since Truman's day. We had had the courage to deregulate crude oil, regulated since wage and price controls under Nixon, combined with a creative windfall profits tax to get the Democrats to go along. This was one of the worst mistakes I made: If we had recommended to the president deregulating the price of gasoline, there would have been—and yes, we were all concerned about it during a time of high inflation—an initial spike in prices, but that was going to happen anyway. There would have been a market setting price, but there would have been no gas lines. The market would have sorted that out. It was an unexpected situation. We didn't react to it in this respect in ways—Bert Carp and I had a disagreement about that. He was very strongly against it. But in any event, that was one thing.

The second, however, is the great inflation of the 1970s. The great inflation started with LBJ's guns-and-butter policy. It continued because of two oil shocks, one under President Nixon, '73–'74, the second under President Carter, '79–'80, which doubled the price of crude oil in a twelve-month period. Doubled the price of crude oil and increased inflation from 7.5 percent to about 11 percent and sent interest rates up.

Now the question is: Could this have been anticipated, and could we have dealt with it in a better way? It bedeviled President Nixon, who put wage-and-price controls on as a conservative president. It bedeviled President Ford, who did the much-vaunted "Whip Inflation Now" program with the WIN buttons. And it bedeviled us. We did everything from budget cuts to credit controls to wage-based incentives to wage-and-price guidelines to inflation czars. The forces of inflation were so ferocious, and we could have perhaps seen that better because inflation did go down, as Roger said, during the Ford period. We thought it was going to be extinguished.

We fought the election in '76—and this is where campaign promises come in—against the "Ford recession." We were going to stimulate the economy. We were going to create more public jobs. We took our eye off the fact that that inflation was a smoldering ember; it had not been extinguished. Once it dawned on us that, in fact, this was getting into the wage-price spiral, all of these efforts made us look ineffectual because we were dealing with a fero-cious external circumstance.

To his great credit, at the very end of his presidency, the last year, before the election, and over the objection of his economic and political advisers, President Carter finally said, "We've got a Fed chairmanship to fill. I'm go-ing to bring Paul Volcker in." Volcker told him point blank, "If you ap-point me, I'm going to choke this economy. I'm going to raise interest rates. That's the only way to drain inflation out." We said, "This is going to lose your election for you."[45] He said, "I've tried everything else. I'm not going to hand my legacy over to my successor, if I don't have a second term. I'm not going to leave him inflation. I'm going to take those risks." He was very courageous in doing so. But this was a question of an external circumstance that perhaps might have been better anticipated. But even if it were, I would suggest that with that second oil shock, because of the revolution, it would have been very difficult to avoid the consequences.

It was also the end of an economic era. It was the end of Keynesian economics. It was the rise of the Milton Friedman monetary supply. And I would suggest, Bert, that one of the things, as I look back—our fiscal policy was not stimulative. We had a very low budget deficit, even with the first and second stimulus packages, but we had a very expansionary monetary policy. The change in Keynesian economics was basically the end of this era and the focus on tight monetary policy. It ended up benefiting President Reagan. It ended up helping lose our election, but President Carter did ultimately put in place a policy that dealt with the great inflation of the '70s that bedeviled three presidents.

Nesmith: What were his economic advisers suggesting?

Eizenstat: Going back to the beginning of the first stimulus—Mike Blumen-thal, who had been accused as secretary of the treasury of "talking down the dollar," that is, having a low dollar to stimulate exports as part of our stimulus package, turned 180 degrees and became the inflation hawk. He recommended that we drop the $50 tax rebate from the package, which had been designed to have no long-term budget impact and was just to stimu-late the economy. And the president made the decision—after it had passed the House, and after Senator [Edmund] Muskie, the chairman of the Sen-ate budget committee, had put it into a third budget resolution—to pull it off the table because of Blumenthal's recommendation, and Bert Lance's at OMB [Office of Management and Budget]. We paid a frightful political price for that. It perhaps in macroeconomic terms was the right thing. I think that Charlie Schultze, who was his chief economic adviser, feels that the '77 stimulus package was the right thing to do to get the economy back on track, that the '78 stimulus package was a mistake, and by that time we should have seen the underlying inflation and not over-stimulated the economy the second time.

Quirk: Are there models for integrating the political and substantive considerations that work better, or that lead to failure? It seems like quite a few of the cases that we've talked about were ones where either very important political considerations were overlooked, or where political considerations were allowed to dominate despite important negative substantive consequences. Maybe all of those presidents would have avoided those decisions if they had been aware of both sides.

Pinkerton: One model is whether or not you're running for reelection and whether you have to worry about that. I can remember being in the Old Executive Office Building with Lee Atwater in the summer of 1983—I worked as an ant in the Reagan administration as well—and the TV came on and the Soviets had shot down KAL-007, this airliner with hundreds of people on it.[46] President Reagan was in Santa Barbara. It was a weekend, as I recall. Atwater got on the phone with Ed Meese—they rotated who was sort of minding the president out there—and said, "Look, you've got to do something." And he said, "Oh, well, the Pentagon's handling it." I can't remember exactly what Reagan did, but we got something done, and Atwater wasn't by any means the only one doing it but he was sort of the one on watch at that point.

  That was 1983. Compare that to Bitburg, which was 1985. Bitburg was a public relations fiasco, when President Reagan visited this German SS cemetery.[47] It's inconceivable to me that this would have happened if they'd had a reelection campaign ahead of them. Because they didn't, the wonks could defeat the hacks, to use Bruce's formulation, and say, "Well, Chancellor [Helmut] Kohl blah, blah, blah, tells us we have to do this."

Galston: The reason that I, to some extent, pushed back against the staff-centric formulation of the initial question is that I deeply believe that, in the end, every president gets the White House he deserves. That is to say, it is not the case that presidents are betrayed by their staffs, because the staff that the president has around him and the way that staff is organized reflects the president's character, personality, and predilections. And what that tells me is that, at the end of the day, this integration of the policy considerations and the political considerations is one of the president's highest responsibilities, and at the end of the day, that is a judgment that the president can't delegate, when it really matters.

Presidents who are really good at keeping those two things in balance are the ones who will succeed. The ones who give too much weight to politics will win hollow victories at best. And the ones who say, "Damn the torpedoes, full speed ahead. We'll do the right thing," will be noble failures. We can try to organize institutions to the best that human ingenuity will allow, but at the end of the day, institutions can perhaps mute the amplitude of variation in decision making, but they cannot substitute for wisdom and judgment in the person at the top.

Eizenstat: Just one anecdote on what Bill said: Ham Jordan, who later became chief of staff, unfortunately not in the first year, once joked that the worst thing you could say to President Carter was, "This will help you politically," because there was the sense that his ultimate political reward would come with reelection if he did the right thing.[48] That led him to take on every kind of difficult issue—energy and so forth, Panama Canal, the Israelis and the Palestinians—with many successes, but with much broken crockery.

And I think at the end of the day, Bill, it might have succeeded. He might have ultimately been rewarded, notwithstanding not merging the politics and policy, if these external events of the great inflation and the hostage crisis hadn't occurred. But that's a mighty big "if."

Carp: I just want to say that the White House really does three things, and those three things are things that in the end only the president can do, for better or for worse. You have to lead and inspire this enormous executive branch, which is outside the White House but very real and very important. If they're not picking up on your attitudes—they're the people Americans deal with every day. You have to persuade members of Congress to do things that they don't want to do, which often means things against their political interests, things like voting for the Panama Canal Treaty and saying good-bye to a Senate seat. And that's something, in the end, only the president can do, however he does it. Then you have this role that we maybe have spent too much time on, speaking to the American public. Really only the president can do that.

People who get elected to the presidency have great strengths in these things; otherwise, they don't get elected president. You can easily be elected president and not know very much about managing anything, even if you've been a governor. You have to be able to give a speech, you have to be able to get people, including politicians, to follow you. You've got some talent in these areas. But you don't necessarily have to know anything about managing.

A lot of politicians live in a stream of information. There's enormous information that comes to people who hold most elected offices. And yet when you get to the White House, that stream of information is cut off. Before, they've always talked to reporters and they've talked to state legislators, and they have town meetings where people ask them real questions and people call them up on the phone and yell at 'em. And then this stuff all stops.

While I agree with you that presidents get the White House staffs they deserve, the ones who get that staff too late are at a tremendous disadvantage.

Cannon: President Ford, not having been elected of course, was initially not at all interested in being elected. In fact, his first days in office he told Kissinger, "I'm going to make an announcement that I'm not going to run for election." And Kissinger, for self-serving reasons and the public interest as well, probably, said, "You can't do that, Mr. President. You reduce yourself to—you neutralize yourself if you make that announcement this day." So President Ford said, "Okay, all right. I guess you've got a good point, Henry."

I guess he'd probably been in office six months before he decided, "Well, I like this job. I can't see anybody else around who's likely to be better than I am at this so maybe I will run for office." But he still hadn't done anything. In fact, I think it was in May of '75 that I talked to [Donald] Rumsfeld one day and said, "You know, we're not doing anything to get elected." And Rumsfeld said, "Well, that's right." So I said, "Well, if I may, I'd like to go in and tell him this." And he said, "You go right ahead."[49] [*laughter*]

So I went in to see the president and I said, "Mr. President, we're not doing enough to get elected." And he said, "Well, I figure this, Jim. If the party thinks I should be nominated, they'll nominate me, and if the country thinks I should be elected, they'll elect me. That's the way I've always done it in my congressional district, and so that's my plan." I tried to say, "Mr. President, it doesn't work that way. You've got to go out and get these delegates," but still we didn't do anything until Stu Spencer came in and said, "Mr. President, he's not talking about running; Reagan *is* running, and so we've got to get going."[50] Only then did President Ford activate, if that's the right word, his campaign.

Stu Eizenstat's mentioned that the worst thing you could do was to tell Carter, "This is going to help you politically," because he'd almost always do the other thing. This was true of Ford as well. All through the campaign— we needed Texas badly. It was the Texas primary and President Ford sent Kissinger to South Africa, I believe, and the political people said that was a disaster.[51] And the president said, "That's the right thing to do. We're going to do that."

So we never really got started until too late. We virtually invited Reagan into the campaign, and it was touch-and-go all the way and we barely made it. We wouldn't have made it, in my opinion, except [Nelson] Rockefeller took himself off the ticket.[52] But if he'd been on the ticket we would not have won some of the southern delegations, particularly Mississippi, which was instrumental in making the difference. Ford is an anomaly in the sense that he didn't really want to run for president. He didn't want to do what you had to do but he was forced into it by Reagan's entry into the campaign. Once he got into it, well, he was enough of a competitor that he said, "I'm going to win this." He went to the maximum to do it, and of course barely won the nomination, and then in the general election made some mistakes that—particularly in freeing Poland in the third debate.[53] [*laughter*]

Eizenstat: Jim's point is so important, and I'd like to focus in on this—that is, keeping your party united as you govern and then going into your reelection. With respect to the 1976 campaign, your party was split by a more conservative candidate, Reagan, running against a more moderate. In 1980, we had exactly the flip side. Our party was divided between a more liberal candidate, who was Senator [Edward] Kennedy, and a more conservative one.[54]

Senator Kennedy spoke to the hearts of many of the delegates at that convention in New York.[55] I've never seen such anger against the budget cuts we were required to do because of the inflation problem. So, if you can't politically keep your own party together, it's very difficult to govern and very difficult to get reelected.

Porter: You not only need to keep your own party together, you need to keep your own White House together. People in the White House work on particular staffs. They work on the domestic policy staff or the Office of Public Liaison or the Office of Legislative Affairs. That's where the bulk of your day is spent, working on that slice of the action.

But what presidents need is to have presented for them an accurate and as detailed a map as possible of what I like to call substantive and political reality. They have to understand the substance from the people who are in their policy operation, producing what Bruce keeps referring to as "the product." And they also have to understand what political realities are, with respect to how they're going to deal with the Congress and organized interest groups and the press and the public. In that respect, it is important for them to have someone in the place—and this has now gravitated to the chief of staff's office—to bring those elements together. Because the kinds of people that are attracted to positions in the policy operations are not necessarily people that have the same skill set as the people who deal with all of these outside constituencies. There are some rare individuals, and I'd say Stu is an example of one of them, who can work well in both of those arenas, but the norm is you really need a place that is providing that coordination.

Presidents do have the staff that they select. They're the ones who are in charge. But I think it was a real asset to President Clinton to have someone like Bruce there, willing to do what President Clinton knew needed to be done, which was basically to pull his party to a different part of the political spectrum on welfare reform. We had tried to get the essence of what welfare reform is, that there are limits on the amount of time you can get it, and that there is going to be a work requirement, and we weren't able to do it in the Reagan and Bush administrations.

President Clinton, to his credit, with the support of some excellent staff work, took it on. He vetoed it twice. When he finally signed it, the third time, he had two or three resignations of people who were in his administration who just thought he had capitulated.[56] I think it was a very challenging, difficult thing for him to do. Bruce would know a lot more about all of the internal calculations that were going on in his mind about why he vetoed it the first time, why he vetoed it the second time, why he was willing to sign it the third time. But in that sense, good staff work on the part of people who are trying to teach him and help him to understand substantive reality and political reality ultimately made the difference. That doesn't happen automatically in White Houses. You need to have a place that brings those people together and keeps them talking well with one another.

Galston: The difficulty is that if you put too much weight on the highly desirable outcome of keeping your party together, then if you're an insurgent candidate who's challenged your party's orthodoxy, that almost by definition means that you have to set aside or defer your most distinctive attributes. Right? So Bill Clinton, not only on welfare but especially on trade, in 1993, as you know very well, Stu, had to choose between his conception of the long-term economic welfare of the country—including trade treaties, NAFTA [North American Free Trade Agreement] and the GATT [General Agreement on Tariffs and Trade], now known as the World Trade Organization—and the party's conventional approach. This after he campaigned on and spilled some blood over these issues during the campaign. If he'd adopted as his criterion, "Don't split the party," those trade measures would never have gone forward to the Congress.[57]

This is one of the perennial challenges of governing, to the extent that you're not just a custodian of the status quo inside your own party. Given the condition of the political parties, the last thing we need right now is custodians of the status quo.

Krogh: I want to associate myself with what Bill Galston has said about how presidents are responsible for the staff that they select. One thing you don't do is set up an operational unit inside the White House to investigate something, because they're not very good at it. They might be picked because they're loyal, but they don't have the background or the experience.

Stu was talking about extraneous events that happen, and ours was the release of the Pentagon Papers to the *New York Times*. It just hit that White House like a hammer. A unit was set up to investigate it. Very unfortunately for the country and for me, I was selected to be the co-director of that unit and picked G. Gordon Liddy and E. Howard Hunt, and I think the three of us were not the varsity squad to do that kind of work.[58] [*laughter*]

And I want to say the rest is history, but when you do look at domestic policy achievements in the Nixon White House, things were going very well in 1969, '70, '71. Then there was this little glitch with the Papers, and the investigation led to Watergate in 1972. Two of those folks involved had worked for me, and the rest of our time there was spent trying to figure out how we handle that. We lost the momentum. When you think about what could have been accomplished in that second term, but for that—"extraneous" is maybe a gentle way of describing what that event was, but it really deflected people's attention. It sapped their energy. It was hard to be aggressive in 1973 and in 1974 when so much attention was on, how do we survive?

When you talk about loyalty and experience, Bill, that's really important, to select people to come onto the staff who have experience, who have background. Stu had it before he joined that staff initially. Roger, you've had the experience built up over time. Dave Gergen, your colleague, has helped a lot of presidents and they selected him not because he might have served a Republican, first of all, but because he knew what needed to be done on the White House staff.[59] There is great value in having that.

Unfortunately, while we had a strong chief of staff, the experience level [among Republicans] in Washington, D.C., was not high. But we had some there—Bryce Harlow, Clark McGregor—who really did know how to work in Washington, but they were not necessarily listened to, because the president would often respond to those who hadn't had that experience.[60] I just want to align myself with that.

And the other point that you made is very important. When you come into the White House staff you have this wonderful entity, the Office of Management and Budget, and there are people there whose careers have been in these substantive areas. You need to find out who they are, to work closely with them. We had, fortunately, guys like Sam Hughes and Dwight Ink, who knew how to organize the government.[61] We listened to them . . . after awhile. [laughter] We should have started right at the beginning.

Pinkerton: The notion that the president gets the staff he deserves is certainly, in the scheme of things, well taken. But there are exceptions to every rule. The exception I think of a lot is the Iran-Contra situation. It's not to say that Reagan didn't ultimately bear responsibility for all the people involved, but there are some wrinkles that are worth noting.

For example, in 1981—in the Reagan White House there's a beautiful conference room, Room 208, that was the office of the secretary of the state, historically, back when the Department of State was in the EOB [Executive Office Building]. There was a fellow named Richard Beal, who long ago passed away, who had a long-range planning job inside the Reagan White House, and he said, "You know, what we need to do is create another Situation Room."[62] There's a Situation Room in the West Wing. That's the one where President Kennedy handled the Cuban Missile Crisis. "We ought to have another one. Why don't we take this conference room, this under-utilized"–I didn't think it was under-utilized but nobody asked me–"Room 208 and turn that into another Sit Room?"

And so they did. It had all the trappings. And if you're a colonel in the Pentagon and you get a call from the Sit Room, you don't really know whether it's the one underneath the Oval Office or the one in the EOB. All sorts of people who I guarantee Ronald Reagan didn't know, like Oliver North, could get access to the Room 208 Sit Room. They could sit there and call up the ayatollah and the contras and arms dealers and make things happen in a way that just completely got out from under control of Don Regan and all the rest of them.

So, little things in the organization of the White House matter a lot. Creating the equivalent of a mace and a scepter in the Sit Room and handing that out to people with red passes proved to be a huge mistake, but not intentional.

Quirk: It sounds like presidents get the White House staff that they deserve unless they get one that's worse. [*laughter*] So the question is, is there a way to ensure that they get at least what they deserve, because this was, I think, a matter of inattention.

Pinkerton: Combined with runaway entrepreneurship at a low staff level.[63]

Galston: Of course, Hamlet famously said, "If we were all treated according to deserts, none of us would escape whipping."[64] A little bit of humility goes a long way here.

Eizenstat: One of the things one has to recognize in terms of organizing the White House staff is the powerful impact the campaign staff around the president has had. All of us have gone through this, but to the public that hasn't, as difficult as governing is, as excruciating the number of hours that you have to work in the White House, nothing compares to working in a presidential campaign, because it's all or nothing. If you make a mistake in the White House, you've got another day. If you make a mistake on the campaign trail, you don't.

The people who start with the president during the time he's first running, the loyalists, when he's barely known, and go through the snows of Iowa and into New Hampshire–you build a bond with the president, a bond of loyalty and trust that can't be substituted for by others. That's why it's so difficult to take that group, which having worked so hard can already see their seats in the White House, and tell them, "We're sorry, it's great that you did all this but we've got to bring some experience into this." That's a very difficult thing to do and it's a very difficult thing to convince the president to do. The presidents that can do it and say to that staff, "You're going to have a position, but I've got to bring some other people in," are the ones who, at the end, can mix the loyalty and the experience. You need both. They will be the most successful presidents.

But let me tell you, it is not easy for the president-elect to say that to someone who has been with him for two years, when no one thought he had a chance. And it's even more difficult for the people who made that unbelievable human sacrifice and family sacrifice, to be told that they are not going to get their preferred position.

Notes

1. See generally J. Brooks Flippen, *Nixon and the Environment* (Albuquerque: University of New Mexico Press, 2000). See also, Sara Dant Ewart, "Environmental Politics in the Nixon Era," *Journal of Policy History* 15, no. 3 (2003): 345–348; Joan Hoff, *Nixon Reconsidered* (New York: Basic Books, 1994), 21–27.

2. See John C. Whitaker, *Striking a Balance: Environment and Natural Resources Policy in the Nixon-Ford Years* (Washington, D.C.: American Enterprise Institute, 1976).

3. Although Krogh misstates by a year the date of the National Environmental Policy Act (NEPA, 1969), there were indeed growing signs of environmental awareness in Washington before Nixon's inauguration. These included the Clean Air Act in 1967 and a series of important parks and conservation measures.

4. Reorganization Plan No. 2, sent to Congress on March 12, 1970, actually established the Domestic Policy Council and the Office of Management and Budget. Reorganization Plan No. 3 followed quickly on July 9, and it, in fact, established the Environmental Protection Agency and the National Oceanic and Atmospheric Administration.

5. William D. Ruckelshaus was an Indiana Republican who had been active in state politics but failed in two attempts to go to Washington as an elected legislator. In 1969 and 1970 he headed the civil division in the U.S. Department of Justice and then was placed by Nixon at the EPA in 1970. From there he spent a short period as acting head of the Federal Bureau of Investigation, and then returned to the Justice Department in 1973. He resigned his post, along with Attorney General Elliott Richardson, rather than follow Nixon's instructions to fire the Watergate prosecutor looking into White House misdeeds. This was the so-called "Saturday Night Massacre." He returned to head the

EPA under President Reagan in 1983, when the agency was suffering serious problems of regulatory malfeasance.

6. Russell E. Train was a pioneer in the environmental movement in the 1950s and 1960s and was one of the leading figures in the creation of the World Wildlife Fund. He was an undersecretary in the Interior Department in 1969 and 1970; chaired the Council on Environmental Quality from 1970 to 1973; and served as EPA's administrator from 1973 to 1977. The CEQ was established by NEPA in 1969 to provide advice and guidance to the president in developing national environmental policy and to help to coordinate the work of the relevant line agencies in dealing with environmental issues.

7. In a June 29, 1971, memorandum for the president, Whitaker directly took on Nixon's questions about the political potency of the environmental issue: "I presume your basic reaction to the environment issue is that it is media created and may soon peak out, and appeals only to the liberals you can't reach anyway in '72. Therefore, you have formed a basic conclusion that pushing too hard on the environment is a bad tradeoff in terms of alienating your 'natural constituencies,' the rural heartland people and the businessman. Also pollution laws could slow down the economy and you are, of course, wary of this." Whitaker then records his own assessment that the environment is a major and growing issue, and cites polling data to confirm that Nixon's "natural constituencies" share these concerns. In a dismissive longhand note on the original, Nixon grumps that "I am not at all impressed with this memo," in part because the pollster used "did not have the brains to put the real question—what if you have to choose between jobs and a nice park." The memo, with marginalia, is available through the Nixon Library website, at http://www.nixonlibrary.gov/virtuallibrary/documents/jan10/034.pdf (accessed November 3, 2010).

8. In his 1971 state of the union message, Nixon said: "I propose, therefore, that we reduce the present 12 Cabinet Departments to eight. I propose that the Departments of State, Treasury, Defense, and Justice remain, but that all the other departments be consolidated into four: Human Resources, Community Development, Natural Resources, and Economic Development. Let us look at what these would be:

—First, a department dealing with the concerns of people—as individuals, as members of a family—a department focused on human needs.

—Second, a department concerned with the community—rural communities and urban communities—and with all that it takes to make a community function as a community.

—Third, a department concerned with our physical environment, with the preservation and balanced use of those great natural resources on which our Nation depends.

—And fourth, a department concerned with our prosperity—with our jobs, our businesses, and those many activities that keep our economy running smoothly and well.

Under this plan, rather than dividing up our departments by narrow subjects, we would organize them around the great purposes of government. Rather than scattering responsibility by adding new levels of bureaucracy, we would focus and concentrate the responsibility for getting problems solved."

9. Having failed legislatively, however, Nixon attempted to win the battle in another way, using "executive orders effectively to implement his rejected reorganization plan by naming four cabinet members as counselors to the president and instructing them to coordinate the seven departments as if they had been formally combined into four." Graham G. Dodds, "Executive Orders from Nixon to Now," in *Executing the Constitution: Putting the Presidency Back in the Constitution*, ed. Christopher S. Kelley (Albany: State University of New York, 2006), 67.

10. Carter's legislative record is the subject of Charles O. Jones, *Jimmy Carter and the United States Congress* (Baton Rouge: Louisiana State University Press, 1988).

11. These and other matters are extensively explored, by scholars and active participants in the Carter presidency alike, in Herbert D. Rosenbaum and Alexej Ugrinsky, *The Presidency and Domestic Policies of Jimmy Carter* (Westport, Conn.: Greenwood Press, 1994).

12. Upon Senate passage of the Alaska Lands bill, which set aside over 100 million acres of parkland and wildlife refuges, Carter announced, "The resolution of the Alaska lands question is the most important conservation measure to come before any Congress or any President in this century." *Public Papers of the Presidents of the United States: Jimmy Carter, May 24–September 26, 1980* (Washington, D.C.: Government Printing Office, 1982), 1548.

13. On Carter and deregulation, see Alfred Kahn Interview, Miller Center, University of Virginia, Jimmy Carter Presidential Oral History Project, December 10-11, 1981, http://web1.millercenter.org/poh/transcripts/ohp_1981_1210_kahn.pdf (accessed November 8, 2010).

14. See Gilbert Winham, *International Trade and the Tokyo Round Negotiations* (Princeton, N.J.: Princeton University Press, 1987).

15. For a survey of Carter's efforts in all these areas, see Robert A. Strong, *Working in the World: Jimmy Carter and the Making of American Foreign Policy* (Baton Rouge: Louisiana State University Press, 2000).

16. On inflation, see J. Bradford De Long, "America's Peacetime Inflation: The 1970s," in *Reducing Inflation: Motivation and Strategy*, eds. Christina Romer and David Romer (Chicago: University of Chicago Press, 1997), 247-276. On the Iranian Revolution, see Carter's own account in *Keeping Faith: Memoirs of a President* (Little Rock: University of Arkansas Press, 1995), 5-16, 441-580.

17. See the discussion on this topic in Chapter 7, especially the early comments by Stuart Eizenstat.

18. President Carter has said that he believed the initial staff deficiencies in Washington politics were compensated for in two ways: the close integration of Mondale's vice presidential staff into the main White House, and the presence of major Washington

experience in the cabinet. See Jimmy Carter Interview, Miller Center, University of Virginia, Jimmy Carter Presidential Oral History Project, November 29, 1982, 9.

19. W. Michael Blumenthal, a German-born economist, diplomat, and businessman, served as secretary of the treasury for Carter from 1977 to 1979. Charles L. Schultze, also an economist, directed the Bureau of the Budget for most of Lyndon Johnson's full term as president and then chaired the Council of Economic Advisers from 1977 to 1981.

20. Although some who came with Nixon to Washington did have shared California roots—including chief of staff H. R. Haldeman and press secretary Ronald L. Ziegler—Nixon actually had moved to New York City in the early 1960s. Some followed Nixon from New York, most notably attorney general John N. Mitchell. Carter's Georgians included top political adviser (and later chief of staff) Hamilton Jordan, press secretary Jody Powell, and congressional liaison Frank Moore. The Californians who came to Washington with Reagan included counselor (later attorney general) Edwin Meese, media aide Michael Deaver, and Judge William Clark, whom Reagan deployed in a number of positions, including national security adviser.

21. James A. Baker III had, during the primary season, worked for his old friend from Texas, George H. W. Bush.

22. The extraordinary rise in both those figures simultaneously led Jimmy Carter to attack Ford in the 1976 campaign for what was effectively the sum of the two, combined into the "misery index."

23. On August 12, 1974, four days after Nixon's resignation, President Ford announced: "A month ago, the distinguished majority leader of the United States Senate [Mike Mansfield (D-MT)] asked the White House to convene an economic conference of Members of Congress, the President's economic consultants, and some of the best economic brains from labor, industry, and agriculture. Later, this was perfected by resolution [S. Res. 363] to assemble a domestic summit meeting to devise a bipartisan action for stability and growth in the American economy. Neither I nor my staff have much time right now for letter writing. So, I will respond. I accept the suggestion, and I will personally preside. Furthermore, I propose that this summit meeting be held at an early date, in full view of the American public. They are as anxious as we are to get the right answers. My first priority is to work with you to bring inflation under control. Inflation is domestic enemy number one." Available at http://www.presidency.ucsb.edu/ws/index.php?pid=4694 (accessed November 15, 2010).

24. This meeting was held in the East Room of the White House on September 5, 1974, and included some 180 people, including economists and members of Congress. A roster of participants can be found in the President's Daily Diary for this date at http://www.ford.utexas.edu/library/document/diary/pdd740905.pdf (accessed November 15, 2010).

25. Arthur M. Okun (1928–1980) served on the economics faculty at Yale and chaired the Council of Economic Advisers in 1968 and 1969.

26. Ford's actual pledge was mildly different: "I have just concluded the process of preparing the budget submissions for fiscal year 1976. In that budget, I will propose

legislation to restrain the growth of a number of existing programs. I have also concluded that no new spending programs can be initiated this year, except for energy." The text of that speech can be seen at http://www.ford.utexas.edu/library/speeches/750028.htm (accessed November 15, 2010).

27. On this subject, see Paul Pierson, *Dismantling the Welfare State?: Reagan, Thatcher, and the Politics of Retrenchment* (Cambridge: Cambridge University Press, 1994).

28. See Steven F. Hayward, *The Age of Reagan: The Conservative Counterrevolution, 1980–1989* (New York: Crown Forum, 2009), 155–157.

29. Ibid., 469–470.

30. Nixon approved a number of liberal entitlement and welfare reforms in 1972, but later expressed regret at having signed off on automatic cost-of-living adjustments. See Hoff, *Nixon Reconsidered*, 135.

31. Dukakis lost the electoral vote to George H. W. Bush by 426 to 111.

32. See Jeanne M. Denis, "Smoke for Sale: Paradoxes and Problems of the Emissions Trading Program of the Clean Air Act Amendments of 1990," 40 *UCLA Law Review* (1992–1993): 1101.

33. Pinkerton's reference is to a widely reported incident in Central Park that occurred on the night of April 19, 1989, in which a female jogger was attacked, reportedly by a group of black teenagers "wilding" in the park. She was raped and severely beaten, nearly to death. The brutality of the incident, and the youthfulness of the assaulters, was taken by many observers as an index of the decline of American society. Five young suspects (including four juveniles) were convicted, partly on the strength of confessions, but a later confession by a different person, positively linked to the case by DNA evidence, led to those earlier convictions being vacated—and charges by some activists of police and prosecutorial misconduct. One detailed account, written before the final resolution of the case, is Chris Smith, "Central Park Revisited," *New York*, October 21, 2002, available at http://nymag.com/nymetro/news/crimelaw/features/n_7836/ (accessed November 16, 2010).

34. Leonid I. Brezhnev (1906–1982) was a longtime leader of the Soviet Union, from 1964 to 1982, whose physical infirmities, brought on by advanced age and ill health, came to represent for many critics sclerosis in the USSR's policy and thinking.

35. See David Osborne and Ted Gabler, *Reinventing Government: How the Entrepreneurial Spirit is Transforming the Public Sector* (New York: Penguin, 1993). This book was influential in bringing greater flexibility and private-sector approaches into the public sector.

36. Bruce E. Babbitt is former Democratic governor of Arizona (1978–1987) and secretary of the interior in the Clinton administration (1993–2001). He was known as an innovative governor. Hernando de Soto is a Peruvian economist who helped bring free-market practices to South America in the 1980s and '90s.

37. Elaine C. Kamarck is a member of the faculty of the Kennedy School of Government at Harvard. She worked in the Clinton White House helping to direct its Reinventing Government initiative.

38. More extended discussions on this topic appear in Terry Sullivan, ed., *Nerve Center: Lessons in Governing from the White House Chiefs of Staff* (College Station: Texas A&M Press, 2004).

39. See Shelley Lynne Tomkin, *Inside OMB: Politics and Process in the President's Budget Office* (Armonk, N.Y.: M.E. Sharpe, 1998).

40. Galston is indirectly quoting Thomas Jefferson here: "Great innovations should not be forced on a slender majority," Jefferson wrote to Thaddeus Kosciusko in 1808.

41. On this subject, see Jeff Grogger and Lynn A. Karoly, *Welfare Reform: Effects of a Decade of Change* (Santa Monica, Calif.: RAND Corporation, 2005).

42. Dick Morris was a political adviser with a clients in both parties, who shared deep roots with Clinton. He was not, however, a member of the team that elected Clinton president in 1992. After the Democrats lost control of both houses of Congress in the 1994 midterm elections, Clinton secretly brought Morris back into the fold. He was an important force in the White House in 1995 and 1996, until his own scandal, with a prostitute, ended his relationship with Clinton. Morris's account of these times is related in *Behind the Oval Office: Winning the Presidency in the Nineties* (New York: Random House, 1997).

43. Iraq's Hussein unexpectedly ordered the invasion of neighboring Kuwait in August 1990. That had a profoundly disruptive effect on President George H. W. Bush's agenda, but his response to the emergency actually had the effect of elevating his popular standing, enormously but temporarily.

44. Grand Ayatollah Ruhollah Khomeini (1902–1989) was an exiled Iranian religious leader who left Paris in 1979 to help complete the Iranian Revolution of that year. The religious-based uprising was directed against the secular leader of Iran, the U.S.-backed Shah Mohammad Reza Pahlavi (1919–1980).

45. Longtime Carter adviser Bert Lance reportedly phoned Carter, when news of the potential Volcker appointment became known, in opposition to the idea. "If he appoints Volcker, he will be mortgaging his reelection to the Federal Reserve." Quoted in Joseph B. Treaster, *Paul Volcker: The Making of a Financial Legend* (New York: John Wiley & Sons, 2004), 62. See also W. Carl Biven, *Jimmy Carter's Economy: Policy in an Age of Limits* (Chapel Hill: University of North Carolina Press), ch. 11.

46. Korean Airlines Flight 007 was shot down by Soviet military aircraft on September 1, 1983, killing all 269 people aboard the flight. Although the Soviets accused the United States of deliberately provoking the incident, the available evidence suggests that the flight wandered accidentally into restricted airspace en route from Alaska to Seoul.

47. Reagan accepted an invitation from Chancellor Helmut Kohl in May of 1985 to commemorate German casualties from World War II by laying a wreath in a cemetery in Bitburg. Overlooked at the moment the invitation was accepted was the fact that the graveyard contained the remains of German SS troops—thereby giving the appearance that Reagan was honoring some of the war's worst aggressors. This episode is detailed

in Richard J. Jensen, *Reagan at Bergen-Belsen and Bitburg* (College Station: Texas A&M University Press, 2007).

48. After a thorough study of Carter's presidency, Erwin C. Hargrove wrote: "In both policy leadership and public leadership Carter did not want politics to drive policy. . . . Carter wanted policy objectives to drive politics." Hargrove, *Jimmy Carter as President: Leadership and the Politics of the Public Good* (Baton Rouge: Louisiana State University Press, 1988), 31.

49. At the time Rumsfeld was probably Ford's White House chief of staff.

50. Spencer's colorful account of his role in that campaign, and others, appears in the Stuart Spencer Interview, Miller Center, University of Virginia, Ronald Reagan Presidential Oral History Project, November 15–16, 2001.

51. On this trip, see "Southern Africa: Kissinger Starts a Final Crusade," *Time*, September 20, 1976, http://www.time.com/time/magazine/article/0,9171,946613-1,00.html (accessed November 16, 2010). Those interested in this story will also find fascinating detail in once-classified notes taken at a June 23, 1976, meeting between African leaders and Kissinger, with a number of other state department officials, in Germany. They can be found at http://geraldrfordfoundation.org/documents/memcons/1553485.pdf (accessed November 16, 2010).

52. Published accounts suggest otherwise: "Although [Rockefeller] publicly insisted that he jumped without having been shoved, privately he told friends, 'I didn't take myself off the ticket, you know—he [Ford] asked me to do it.'" Ford later expressed remorse at dissembling on this point. See Mark O. Hatfield, *Vice Presidents of the United States, 1789–1993* (Washington, D.C.: U.S. Government Printing Office, 1997), http://www.senate.gov/artandhistory/history/resources/pdf/nelson_rockefeller.pdf (accessed November 16, 2010).

53. In one of Ford's debates with Democratic nominee Jimmy Carter, he fumbled a question about Eastern Europe, leaving himself vulnerable to the charge that he did not understand the region was under the thumb of Soviet military oppression. Political aide Stuart Spencer recalls the episode: "[I] was sitting next to [National Security Adviser] Brent Scowcroft in the holding room watching this. I heard [Ford] say it, and I didn't think anything about it. Brent, in his style, punched me and said, 'You've got a problem.' I said, 'What's the problem?' He said, 'What Jerry just said about Poland. He means "emotionally."' . . . There are x-number of divisions in Poland.' . . . I said, 'How many is that?' He said, 'Some 240,000.' I go, 'Oh God, these are Russians, 240,000 Russians, and they don't have control of Poland?'

I go out. By this time, [White House Chief of Staff Dick] Cheney and I were spastic. We get back to the house. Henry [Kissinger] is already there, secretary of state. He's saying, 'You were wonderful, Mr. President. You did a wonderful job.' He gets through, and Dick and I say, 'Goddam, what are you talking about, Henry?'

We get on the plane the next morning, we're beating [Ford] up, and he says, 'What do you expect me to do, go out and say I was wrong?' We said, 'Yes.' . . . I think we came within two inches of getting canned, Cheney and I. . . . [Finally,] after two . . . news time frames, he came out and made some statement straightening the whole thing out." Quoted in the Stuart Spencer Interview, Reagan Oral History Project, 57.

54. Carter discusses the Kennedy challenge in *Keeping Faith*, episodically in pp. 441–578. Kennedy provided a brief account of this effort in Edward M. Kennedy, *True Compass: A Memoir* (New York: Twelve, 2009), ch. 18.

55. Kennedy's speech to the 1980 Democratic National Convention was one of his most celebrated, especially the peroration: "For all those whose cares have been our concern, the work goes on, the cause endures, the hope still lives, and the dream shall never die." The address appears on the website "American Rhetoric" as one of its Top 100 political speeches in the United States in the twentieth century. See http://www.americanrhetoric.com/speeches/tedkennedy1980dnc.htm (accessed November 16, 2010).

56. For a brief account of this part of the welfare reform debate, see John F. Harris, *The Survivor: Bill Clinton in the White House* (New York: Random House, 2005), ch. 22. Among those who resigned were Peter Edelman, a longtime friend and supporter of Bill Clinton, who had been serving as an assistant secretary in the department of health and human services.

57. Clinton's embrace of a free-trade agenda, which was one component of a larger positioning of himself as a New Democrat, placed him at odds with many of the party's core constituencies, who feared the adverse consequences of open trade on American laborers and the environment.

58. The Pentagon Papers were a vast collection of classified studies done for the Department of Defense examining the roots of the Vietnam War and American involvement in it. The portrait that emerged from these studies was not a flattering one, revealing patterns of deception to sustain public support in the United States for a flawed war effort. The papers were leaked to the *New York Times* by an internal consultant who worked on the project, Daniel Ellsberg. President Nixon subsequently authorized the creation of a team to stop the leaks—henceforth known as the Plumbers. Their involvement in the Watergate break-in ultimately led to the downfall of the Nixon presidency. For an insider account, see Ellsberg's *Secrets: A Memoir of Vietnam and the Pentagon Papers* (New York: Viking, 2002).

59. David Gergen is currently on the faculty of the Kennedy School of Government at Harvard, but he has extensive White House experience across the partisan divide. He was a Nixon speechwriter, communications director for Ford and Reagan, and, for a time, Bill Clinton's counselor. His first-hand account of these experiences, including comparative assessments of the presidents he served, is provided in Gergen, *Eyewitness to Power: The Essence of Leadership, Nixon to Clinton* (New York: Simon & Schuster, 2000).

60. Bryce Harlow (1916–1987) was a gray eminence of the Republican Party when he worked for Nixon both in the first and second terms, ultimately as counselor. He had helped to invent the permanent job of White House congressional liaison under

President Eisenhower. Clark McGregor (1922–2003) was a five-term member of Congress from Minnesota's 3rd congressional district, who went on to help lead the Nixon congressional liaison operation. He then chaired, in 1972, the Committee to Re-elect the President (CREEP), succeeding a disgraced John Mitchell.

61. P. Samuel Hughes (1917–2004) was a longtime assistant director of legislative reference for the Bureau of the Budget, later leading the Office of Federal Elections for the General Accounting Office. Dwight A. Ink served as a federal administrator and policymaker under presidents from Eisenhower to Reagan. Over those years his portfolio included such diverse assignments as the Atomic Energy Commission (as director), oil conservation (during the first oil shock of the 1970s), and major civil service reform (for President Carter).

62. Richard S. Beal held a number of mid-level staff positions in the Reagan White House, including senior director of the office of planning and evaluation and senior director of crisis management support and planning for the National Security Council. He died in 1984.

63. One of Richard E. Neustadt's principal concerns was the probability that those in the president's employ would find the temptation to pursue their own agendas irresistible. "Any aide who demonstrates to others that he has the President's consistent confidence and a consistent part in presidential business will acquire so much business on his own account that he becomes in some sense independent of his chief. Nothing in the Constitution keeps a well-placed aide from converting status into power of his own, usable in some degree even against the President." Neustadt, *Presidential Power and the Modern Presidents: The Politics of Leadership from Roosevelt to Reagan* (New York, Free Press, 1990), 36.

64. The precise extract from *Hamlet* reads, "Use every man after his desert, and who shall 'scape whipping?"

Chapter 10

Domestic Policymaking: Politics and History

Bruce Miroff

Compared to the ever-present imperatives of national security and economic management, domestic policymaking often takes the back seat in a president's journey. For some presidents—Richard Nixon and George H. W. Bush are recent examples—a preoccupation with foreign policy reduces even further the attention paid to domestic policy by the individual in the Oval Office. Yet the sprawl of issues that constitutes domestic policy can be neglected by the White House only at considerable risk. In domestic areas such as health care, education, welfare, the environment, and civil rights, the lives of ordinary Americans are deeply affected by major policy changes. Foreign policy and economic management may hinge on arcane details beyond the ken of most people, but domestic policies more often directly touch on popular hopes and fears. One need only recall the overheated and occasionally bizarre drama that marked the course of Barack Obama's health-care reform effort to observe the intense feelings that domestic policy proposals can evoke.

This volume presents one of the richest stores of information and insight into domestic policymaking that we possess. Based on the two-day symposium in June 2009 at the Miller Center of Public Affairs at the University of Virginia, it brings together domestic policy advisers from the administrations of Richard Nixon through George W. Bush with leading scholars on the presidency. By alternating transcripts in which domestic policy advisers share their experiences and perceptions with articles in which scholars probe their discussions and compare their perspectives to the findings in the academic literature of presidential studies, *Governing at Home* offers an unusual balance of practical wisdom and social scientific knowledge.

The domestic policy advisers who participated in the symposium were primarily concerned with how the substance of domestic policy proposals emerges, is fleshed out, and is promoted by the White House. Only in occasional references did they address another side of domestic policymaking, one

278

in which they were less directly involved: political considerations. Of course, presidents can insist that domestic policy formulation be driven by the requirements of "good policy," with political considerations kept at bay. However, the historical record suggests that separating policy from politics is not a formula for success, as the frustrations of Jimmy Carter's first year in office and Bill Clinton's health-care task force demonstrate. Hence, this concluding chapter seeks to add to the analytical balance between practical wisdom and social scientific knowledge a second balance between policy and politics.

The first part of the chapter summarizes the principal ideas found in the transcripts and scholarly articles that comprise the preceding chapters of this book. Specifically, my aim is to reduce their rich complexity to a manageable number of propositions about the making of domestic policy. For readers who want a summary of what they have encountered thus far or for scholars looking for hypotheses to guide further inquiry, this part endeavors to present the "take-away."

In the second part of the chapter, I turn to the political side of domestic policymaking. I consider the political units in the White House whose concerns about coalition politics interact with substantive considerations in the emergence, formulation, and selling of domestic policy. I also address the variability in the extent to which domestic policies reflect the president's own priorities and preferences.

In the final part of the chapter, I try to integrate considerations of policy and politics through an emphasis on historical context. Presidents vary from one another with respect not only to their personal interest in domestic policy but also to the opportunities and constraints that confront them when they take office. I approach the topic of historical context through a brief comparison of domestic policymaking by the three most recent Democratic presidents: Jimmy Carter, Bill Clinton, and Barack Obama.

Making Domestic Policy

The Miller Center symposium and this book, which emerged from it, break down domestic policymaking into four distinct albeit overlapping facets: the connection between campaigning and governing; the development of domestic policy in the White House; the selling of domestic policy; and the determination of success and failure. In each of these four areas, the symposium offered a profusion of observations, many of them fresh and arresting. These observations may be restated as propositions.

From Campaigning to Governing

1. *Campaign promises become the core of a president's initial domestic agenda.* Policy advisers from numerous administrations concurred that presidents take their own campaign promises very seriously. In the words of Clinton adviser Bruce Reed, "we treated the campaign promises as gospel. That was the only scripture to guide us."[1] Adhering closely once in office to promises uttered during the campaign is not only a matter of keeping faith. It also involves the danger that breaking those promises will be treated as shameful, even sinful. As Reed observes, "even in the transition, even before we'd taken office, whenever there was a hint that we were going to deviate in any possible way, it was front-page news." And if circumstances require the president to back away from a campaign pledge upon the receipt of new information, the political costs often run high, as Carter adviser Stuart Eizenstat observed with regard to an abandoned proposal for a fifty-dollar tax rebate.

2. *Campaign pressures that influence the making of promises can hinder the development of prudent domestic policy in the White House.* Precisely because the White House is committed on a number of issues by campaign promises, its initial domestic agenda has been constructed under less-than-ideal circumstances. Eizenstat notes that campaign promises "are made under suboptimum conditions for policymaking." Presidential candidates make promises that will substantially bind them before they have the time, staff resources, and structured processes that become available only when they are ensconced in the White House. Moreover, campaign promises tend to be phrased in ambiguous language—an advantage in leaving presidents wiggle room but a drawback when their staffs squabble over the correct interpretation.

3. *Once elected, presidents and their advisers must determine priorities and sequencing among their campaign proposals.* During the campaign, the presidential candidate has the luxury of making promises on a wide range of subjects. Once in office, however, the White House cannot move on all fronts at once. William Galston, a domestic policy adviser during Bill Clinton's first term, offers an instructive epigram: "Campaigning is about addition, and governing is about selection." A battle was waged inside the Clinton White House in 1993 over which campaign promise to address first: welfare reform or health-care reform. Some advisers believed that the wrong choice was made, with the more problematic initiative on

health care directly leading to Clinton's loss of his congressional majorities the following year.

4. *Once presidents enter office, unsettling realities, new issues, and public impatience further complicate the making of domestic policy.* Roger Porter, an adviser to presidents Ford, Reagan, and George H. W. Bush, says: "One of the things that presidents discover when they get into office is what might be called reality. Campaign promises are very valuable in setting a path and charting a course, but ultimately you have to deal with the situation in which you find yourself." Reality may expose some campaign promises as unlikely to be fulfilled; it may also compel a president to make commitments that were not previewed during the campaign, leaving members of Congress and the public to complain that they have been blindsided. Since certain campaign promises have to be placed on the back burner in order to make progress on others with a higher priority, some constituencies that have been wooed with pledges on the issues of greatest salience to them are likely to feel neglected or even betrayed. All of these complications were evident in the first year of the Obama presidency: Barack Obama had not campaigned with the expectation of a deep economic crisis, felt compelled once in office to propose unpopular bailouts of the financial services sector and auto manufacturers, and disappointed his union, Hispanic, and gay and lesbian supporters by not moving promptly on their issues.

5. *Campaign promises are essential for gaining a mandate to govern but tend to scatter White House attention and energies.* Pledges made during the campaign are "gospel" for voters as well as for presidents and their policy advisers. As Bruce Reed puts it: "You want to be in a situation where, when the president is elected, he is claiming a mandate that the country is actually aware of." Following through on—and, even better, fulfilling—campaign pledges are essential for a president's continuing public support. Yet because so many different promises are made to so many different groups of voters, White House domestic policy is likely to be disjointed. Andrew Busch points out in Chapter 2 that the complex structure of the executive branch, the fragmented character of American politics, and the vicissitude of events combine to make an integrated and comprehensive domestic policy unlikely. Among recent presidents, Busch suggests, only Ronald Reagan began with and continued to pursue a "coherent strategic vision."

Developing Domestic Policy in the White House

1. *Presidents will staff their administrations with personnel from the campaign in order to ensure commitment to their original promises, but these "keepers of the flame" should be balanced by the appointment of experienced Washington hands.* New presidents will bring top figures from their campaigns into the White House because these are their most trusted personal loyalists and ideological allies. Yet they are well advised also to bring into their inner circle individuals who stood apart from (or even opposed) their bid for the White House but have deeper knowledge of the levers of power. According to William Galston: "You do need keepers of the flame, loyalists who are prepared to remind the president and the people around the president . . . that the president stood for something during the campaign. . . . Pulling to some extent in the other direction: Experience matters, and very frequently, loyalists are inexperienced and the experienced are not too loyal." Jimmy Carter and Bill Clinton were presidents who paid a price for failing to grasp this lesson at the outset of their administrations, while Ronald Reagan exemplified its importance by making George H. W. Bush's campaign manager, James Baker, his top political strategist. Barack Obama appeared to have absorbed this lesson by placing both David Axelrod, his chief campaign strategist, and Rahm Emanuel, a veteran of both the White House and the Hill, at the apex of his staff at the start of his administration.

2. *The White House staff will predominate over the cabinet and the executive departments and agencies in the development of domestic policy.* Presidential appointees to the departments and agencies must gain Senate confirmation through a process that has, in the modern era of partisan polarization, become protracted. By contrast, White House staff can hit the ground running after Inauguration Day and, sometimes, even before, during the transition period. Thus, as Roger Porter observes, "There is a huge advantage that goes to people in the White House staffs, particularly during the first six months, arguably the first year, before you start filling out people in departments and agencies and they are then in a position to be a little more effective in countering what the White House is doing. But the initiative and drive always is coming from right out of the White House." The presence of so many campaign loyalists in the White House provides a second advantage that Bruce Reed notes: "White House aides by definition tend to know the president better, to know his preferences

better. They've been with him longer. Cabinet members often have a lot of catching up to do."

3. *There is no one best way of structuring the development of domestic policy in the White House, yet over time a general consensus has emerged about some aspects of what to do and especially what not to do.* Advisory structures in the White House vary with presidential personalities and priorities. Domestic policy itself is defined differently at different times, with some administrations (Reagan's and the elder Bush's) lumping it in with economic policy when organizing the White House staff. Yet here, as in other areas of White House policy development, the trend has been toward institutionalization and specialization. For four decades, Charles Walcott and Karen Hult show in Chapter 4, every administration has adopted some version of Nixon's Domestic Council. Since the third year of Carter's presidency, every president has abandoned the notion that advisory processes can be managed from the Oval Office and has relied on a chief of staff to coordinate policy development.

4. *The initial ideas for domestic policy come from many sources and the policy proposals hammered out in the White House are usually a collective product, averting the danger that a single adviser can sell the president on an ill-considered scheme.* Domestic policy is almost always, in Roger Porter's words, "the product of many hands." Whatever loss of coherence arises from compromise, the alternative is far worse. Citing two disastrous examples from the Ford administration in which he worked ("Whip Inflation Now" and the common-situs bill on union picketing), James M. Cannon III emphasizes that presidents must not become "a captive of one person. . . . Any issue, any development, any problem, any new initiative should be subjected internally to its natural enemy so that you make sure that you know everything that is wrong with this before you go public with it."

5. *Rationality in the process of developing domestic policy is hindered because the president's political needs and scarcity of time require advisers to face the tough choice of when to involve the president and when to make a decision on their own.* Because the White House operates on many fronts and under crushing time pressures, there is seldom an opportunity to subject domestic policy proposals to thorough scrutiny and analysis. As Walcott and Hult point out, the alternatives that are considered usually will be few and often well-worn; in familiar organizational language, administrations have to "satisfice" rather than "optimize" when developing policy. Limits on the time that presidents have to consider domestic issues lacking high

priority put their staff in a tough spot. "I suspect that everybody in a medium-to-high position in the White House," William Galston remarks, "ends up making a series of judgment calls on a daily basis as to what rises to the president's level and what you just have to take a deep breath and take responsibility for yourself. And you're going to get it wrong sometimes."

Selling Domestic Policy from the White House

1. *Presidential aides count on the "bully pulpit" to sell domestic policy to the public.* In the eyes of most of the advisers who served presidents from Nixon through George W. Bush, it is less the constitutional prerogatives than the communication advantages of the president that propel domestic policy proposals through the political process. As Stuart Eizenstat expresses this theme: "The president has very few real powers under the Constitution . . . besides being Commander in Chief. . . . The president's real power on the domestic side is his power to mobilize support, to use the bully pulpit of the presidency and to be, in effect, the salesman-in-chief, to rally the public and ultimately Congress behind his initiatives."

2. *To assist the president in the job of selling policy to the public, the White House has developed an elaborate apparatus for public relations.* No area of White House organization has mushroomed as much in recent decades as the extensive and specialized apparatus for presidential communication. Lawrence Jacobs writes in Chapter 6: "The political importance attached to public promotions has generated an institutional redesign of the presidency during the past half century. The modern presidency responded to the incoherence of the American system of government by developing an organizational infrastructure for public sales." Polling, press relations, and speechwriting are all geared to promoting the president's priorities to both general audiences and specific interest groups.

3. *Message discipline is essential for successful presidential sales.* Only by setting a small number of clear priorities and then deploying multiple spokespersons to make the case with carefully crafted "talking points" can presidential messages have their intended effect. Otherwise, administration spokespersons will step on one another's words and muddle the message from the White House. Eizenstat laments that in the first year of the Carter administration, "because there was no setting of priorities by the Chief of Staff, we had a multiplicity of priorities and the salesmanship

job therefore became more difficult." By contrast, Margaret Spellings, a White House aide during George W. Bush's first term (and a member of his cabinet in the second term) recalls proudly that "our watchword was discipline. I'll credit my colleague Karl Rove with thinking through and routinizing a calendar that had such discipline to it that really selling the president's policies was everybody's job in the White House."

4. *Although presidential aides believe in the power of the "bully pulpit," they are attuned to limits and risks in its usage.* Unlike some famous advertising gurus of the past, presidential aides recognize that the public will not buy just anything simply because the president is promoting it. Calls for sacrifice in peacetime, for example, or appeals to citizens to concern themselves with the long-term problems of the nation are more difficult to sell than promises of immediate benefits. As William Galston observes, "As adults we've all been living through a period where president after president has been unable to persuade the people and take the people toward certain fundamental truths that would deal with certain fundamental underlying problems. We may eventually, or soon, reap the whirlwind from that." Even when presidents push less daunting messages, they must calculate the dangers of failing to convince their audience. Carter aide Bertram Carp highlights the damage when "you undertake a big public promotional effort and it doesn't move the needle. . . . You take your life in your hands when you do these things. If you try and make it work, you can change the world. But if it doesn't work, you'll lose. You won't stay where you were; you'll slide backwards."

5. *Contrary to the beliefs of presidential advisers, political scientists who study presidential communication have concluded that the "bully pulpit" is mostly a myth.* Nowhere in this book is there as sharp a divergence between the perspectives of veteran White House hands and presidential scholars as over the power of the "bully pulpit." Lawrence Jacobs, drawing on his own research and that of other leading scholars on the public presidency, describes "the snare and delusion of presidential promotions." He emphasizes that "research on a wide range of cases of presidents making public appeals and attempting to trade on their popularity consistently demonstrates little effect on public opinion or congressional success." Presidents and their aides need to learn that while openings for presidential communication will sometimes appear and can be prudently exploited, over-reliance on the capacity of the White House to sell its policy wares will lead to over-reaching and spawn defeats.

Successes and Failures in Domestic Policymaking

1. *Conventional wisdom on presidential successes and failures is often wrong.* Advisers, particularly those who served presidents who generally are regarded as failures, find much to challenge in conventional judgments about successful and unsuccessful presidencies. Stuart Eizenstat concedes that the Carter administration was plagued, especially in its first year, by "self-inflicted wounds." Yet President Carter was also, Eizenstat notes, at the mercy of highly unfortunate external events—an inflationary surge and an Iranian Revolution—that battered his administration. Even more important to Eizenstat's argument is that Carter's well-publicized difficulties obscured his substantial accomplishments in the areas of energy, conservation, and deregulation: "President Carter had as many legislative successes as any first-term president and would equal those of most two-term presidents."

2. *A distinction needs to be drawn between effective presidential performance and perceptions of success.* Presidential advisers point out that success can have multiple definitions and dimensions, some of them contradictory. Several domestic policy advisers offer nuanced distinctions in place of blunt assessments. William Galston, focusing on the tension between "policy success and political success," says that "no president can be indifferent to sustained political support, but at the same time achieving sustained political support at the cost of doing what needs to be done is a hollow victory." Bruce Reed makes a similar point: "The definition of success is not what most of the political world thinks. It's not just winning elections. . . . The real definition of both policy and political progress is actual results, actual progress for the country." Nor should progress be measured merely in the moment: judgments on a president, Roger Porter insists, ought to wait on "the longer sweep of history."

3. *Although staff effectiveness is a critical contributor to presidential success, the conventional wisdom is right to credit or blame the president.* Presidential advisers have much to say about how staff performance influenced the development of domestic policy in the administrations in which they served. Yet they insist that presidents remain the prime movers, the individuals responsible for picking the right personnel, establishing effective advisory processes, and making intelligent choices. As Roger Porter puts it: "Ultimately, presidents make the decisions. I don't think it's fair for presidents to blame or give credit unnecessarily to staff. What staff

exists to do is to make sure that the president understands what his real choices are, and what are likely to be the pattern of costs and benefits associated with various courses of action."

4. *Presidents vary in the attention they pay to expertise and evidence, and although "reality-based policymaking" does not always bring political success, it serves the nation better than the alternatives.* Paul Quirk and Bruce Nesmith focus in Chapter 8 on the kinds of information and advisers to which presidents pay attention, distinguishing between executives who listen primarily to voices that echo their own ideological assumptions and goals and executives who seek "objective information." Quirk and Nesmith argue that Ronald Reagan and George W. Bush exemplify the ideological policymaker, while George H. W. Bush, Bill Clinton, and Barack Obama represent the evidence-based policymaker. They also suggest that the policy disasters of the George W. Bush presidency and the "reasonably positive early results" in Obama's presidency reflect the advantages of reality-based decisions over wishful thinking. Yet Quirk and Nesmith are sensitive to the widespread perception that for all their respect for expertise and evidence, the elder Bush and Clinton were not as successful as the ideological Reagan.

The Political Side of Domestic Policymaking

"I always divide the world into two real parties: hacks and wonks," remarks Bruce Reed. "We're all wonks." This gathering of "wonks"—policy specialists—naturally concentrated on the substance of what presidents can accomplish in domestic affairs. Lurking for the most part in the background of their discussions was the role that "hacks"—political strategists and tacticians—play in the making of domestic policy. Recalling the influence of Dick Morris, "one of the most breathtakingly cynical hacks in modern American history," in the Clinton administration, Reed laments that "wonks are always fighting an uphill battle." That battle was the source of the tradition that outgoing domestic policy advisers leave behind a bottle of whiskey for their successors. Reed quips "I think there is a reason that domestic policy advisers need to keep a bottle handy."

In this part of the chapter I consider the political side of domestic policymaking. One facet of the political side is the institutionalization within the White House of the "hacks"—a term that perhaps unduly derogates the value and legitimacy of those who raise political concerns in presidential decision making. Another facet is the relationship between the administration and external political interests—the place of coalition management and realignment in the making of domestic policy. Once policy and politics are considered together in analyzing the genesis of domestic policies, it becomes evident that major policies reflect different weightings of the two. Many domestic policies are genuine White House initiatives and represent presidents' own policy preferences. Some others are primarily products of politics, as presidents respond to pressures from their supporters or aim to neutralize the gambits of their opponents.

White House Political Units

The institutionalization of domestic policy advice in the modern White House has been paralleled by the institutionalization of political outreach and strategy. Presidents used to place their top political operatives in the cabinet position of Postmaster General, but in recent decades they have brought them into the Executive Office of the President. Just as President Nixon was the first to create a domestic policy unit in the White House, he was also the first to formalize White House relations with interest groups. Soon after, in the Ford administration, a clearly identifiable staff unit, the Office of Public Liaison, was created.[2] As with the domestic policy staff, the importance of the public liaison unit has waxed and waned with the varying policy concerns of succeeding administrations. Although Republican and Democratic administrations alike designate liaison staffers to serve as ambassadors to some of the same major groups in American society (such as African Americans and veterans), liaison assignments also vary by party. Thus, the Reagan White House was the first to provide liaison to evangelical Christians.[3]

Reagan was the first president to establish the Office of Political Affairs in the White House. Although the purview of this office is primarily elections rather than policy development, its staff members sensitize the White House inner circle to cross-currents in the political environment, including the potential effects of policy proposals on friendly and unfriendly interest groups as well as on larger demographic groupings.[4] Obama came under pressure after his election to abolish the office, which critics alleged was using taxpayer funds solely to promote partisan objectives, but he followed the practice of every president since Reagan in continuing it.[5]

A description of the specialized White House units devoted to politics does not do full justice to the place of political strategy in presidential deliberations about domestic policy. Recent presidents have placed close at hand "senior advisers" whose portfolios range freely over politics and policy. Dick Morris's brief and stormy tenure in the Clinton White House in 1995–1996 was the most notorious. Karl Rove's role in the George W. Bush administration and David Axelrod's in the Obama administration were nearly as prominent and, in Rove's case, controversial. The president's chief of staff is also involved in the integration of policy and politics.

Understanding the interplay between policy substance and political considerations in the making of domestic policy also requires attention to the personal role of the president. William Galston suggests that the "integration of the policy considerations and the political considerations is one of the president's highest responsibilities, and at the end of the day, that is a judgment that the president can't delegate, when it really matters." Some presidents have brought a strong policy background and commitments to at least a handful of major domestic issues. Yet it is important to recall that presidents are, by experience and training, professional politicians and not policy experts. No one reaches the highest office in the land by neglecting the political implications of the policy proposals they make.

It is difficult in most instances to unravel the ultimate mix of substantive and political considerations that underlie domestic policy proposals. Some administrations are accused of generally subordinating policy to politics.[6] Others have received praise for the substantive seriousness and rationality of their policy deliberations; many observers have regarded the Ford and Carter administrations in this light. Yet if an overall trend can be discerned, it seems to point in the direction of politics over policy. According to Karen Hult, "On one hand, like the U.S. political system as a whole, the presidency has grown far more open to members of the public and, especially, to interest groups. On the other hand, and over roughly the same period, the presidency has become less permeable to much of the expertise and experience available with the executive branch."[7]

Coalition Politics and Domestic Policy

Presidents need supportive coalitions not just to be elected and reelected, but also to mobilize political muscle for their policy initiatives. Partisanship supplies the essential continuity in presidential coalitions. Organized interests and demographic groups of various sorts typically align with either the Republicans or the Democrats. Yet presidents and their political advisers are alert for shifts in the coalitional landscape, sometimes trying to poach support from the opposition's coalition and at other times attempting to prevent allies from falling away in frustration. Domestic policy frequently is the linchpin in both endeavors.

Considerable but not complete overlap exists between presidents' electoral coalitions and their governing coalitions. When important domestic initiatives face uncertain fates in Congress, the White House, often through its public liaison unit, will aim to rouse its electoral allies for grassroots pressure and lobbying assistance. Yet on a few issues—trade legislation for Democratic presidents is a prime example—some electoral supporters will be antagonistic and presidents will need to find backing from electoral opponents. Alternatively, the White House will try to co-opt opposing interest groups through policy compromises to avert the danger that their potent opposition might sink a presidential initiative. Much to the dismay of his electoral backers, President Obama cut a deal with the giant pharmaceutical companies in order to break up a prospective coalition identical to the one that blocked President Clinton's proposed health-care reform.[8]

Coalition maintenance is a routine aspect of both campaigning and governing. Many of the campaign promises that presidential candidates make are directed to specific coalition members. Promises off-handedly delivered in the heat of a campaign can get a new president in hot water. Bill Clinton was driven off message at the outset of his first term because of a campaign pledge he had made to gays and lesbians to end the prohibition on their service in the armed forces. Promises to key coalitional supporters that presidents cannot turn into successful new legislation may have to be fulfilled in other ways. For example, George W. Bush, stymied on Capitol Hill, implemented "faith-based initiatives" by invoking his authority over the executive branch.[9]

Understood broadly, domestic policy as coalition maintenance can be pursued through multiple vehicles beyond new legislation: vetoes, executive orders, executive branch appointments, legal strategies, and judicial appointments. Running for president in 1980, Ronald Reagan championed a constitutional amendment to overturn the *Roe v. Wade* abortion rights decision, a powerful promise in his successful strategy of aligning pro-life forces with the Republican Party. Knowing that such an amendment had no chance of passing Congress, Reagan did not push hard for it during his administration. Yet he kept faith with—and maintained the backing of—pro-life supporters through other policy approaches: an executive order forbidding the expenditure of government funds on abortion counseling and a judicial strategy that endorsed restrictions on abortions by the states and placed anti-abortion judges on the federal bench.[10]

Coalition realignment requires more political art than coalition maintenance. Some presidents, particularly those whose party is in the minority, look to domestic policy to draw important electoral blocs away from their rival's coalition. Historic transformations in American politics may hinge on these efforts, as can be seen in the intertwined cases of Franklin D. Roosevelt and Richard Nixon.

During the first term of Franklin Roosevelt's administration, a majority of African Americans, who had voted Republican since the Civil War on the basis of historical memories and political patronage, began to identify with the Democratic Party. Blacks represented a target of opportunity for Roosevelt: they were poor relations in the Republican coalition, with little to show for their loyalty to "the party of Lincoln." To be sure, Roosevelt was constrained in his courtship of blacks because of the persisting power of the white South in his party. Acceding to southern pressures, he refused to back anti-lynching legislation in Congress, and his administration dropped its objective of universal coverage under the new Social Security Act and Fair Labor Standards Act, instead allowing southern congressmen to exclude occupations predominantly held by blacks from their provisions. Nonetheless, the economic relief that New Deal agencies offered to impoverished African Americans during the Great Depression, the appointment of blacks to lower-level federal offices (FDR's "Black Cabinet"), and the visible sympathy displayed by Eleanor Roosevelt and a few other leading New Dealers were sufficient to shift the allegiance of a majority of black voters by the time of the 1936 election. Once solidly Republican, no other group in American society would become as solidly Democratic as African Americans, particularly after two Democratic presidents, John F. Kennedy and Lyndon B. Johnson, responded to the civil-rights movement with landmark legislation.[11]

The acceleration of black alignment with the Democratic Party in the 1960s opened the door for a counter realignment pursued by Richard Nixon through his "southern strategy." Like FDR, Nixon could not openly embrace the new coalition members he was pursuing: the taint of racism was a risk in any legislative proposal that might appear anti-black. Yet Nixon used other policy vehicles to signal to the white South that the Republican Party was its friend. Nixon's Justice Department initially sought to slow down school desegregation in the South, and the White House seized on a judicial vacancy to try three times to put a southerner on the Supreme Court (the first two attempts failed). As his reelection bid neared in 1972, Nixon appealed to anti-civil rights forces South and North by proposing to Congress a moratorium on court-ordered busing for school desegregation. Sealed by the policies of the Reagan administration, the realignment of the white South into the Republican Party was the most important contributor to the party's ascendance over the next generation.[12]

A struggle over coalitional targets of opportunity has been very much in evidence in the domestic policies of George W. Bush and Barack Obama. As the loyalty of senior citizens to the party that gave them Social Security and Medicare began to fade over time, presidential candidates George W. Bush and Al Gore competed for the votes of the elderly in 2000 with rival proposals for prescription drugs through Medicare. Having narrowly won the election, Bush had to deliver on his campaign promise before the next presidential election or risk the loss of seniors' votes. The Bush White House and its allies in the congressional leadership muscled their prescription drug initiative into law in 2003, twisting the arms of some of their own partisans in the House of Representatives, who understandably regarded the new program as a large-scale federal entitlement contrary to their political philosophy.[13]

Illegal immigration is a significant social and economic issue in contemporary American public policy, but White House strategists are closely attuned to its political implications in an era when Hispanics are the fastest-growing group in the American electorate. Having done reasonably well with Latino voters in 2004, President Bush hoped that his administration's push for immigration reform in his second term would keep Republicans competitive with this critical voting bloc. To Bush's dismay, the Republican base, overwhelmingly conservative and white, denounced the president's plan as offering "amnesty" to lawbreakers, and congressional Republicans, concerned more with constituent sentiments than with the president's vision of the long-term good of their party, refused to support his legislative proposal. Sensitive to how economic hardships have exacerbated existing tensions over illegal immigration, President Obama and his political strategists handled the issue of immigration reform gingerly, waiting until the administration's second year to make a proposal similar to Bush's and not pushing the legislation with much vigor even then. Coupled with his Justice Department's opposition to a harsh immigration law in Arizona and his appointment of Sonia Sotomayor as the first Hispanic Supreme Court justice, however, Obama's endorsement of Hispanic interests in the face of mounting Republican opposition bodes well for the strength of his party's future coalition.[14]

Political Variations in Presidential Domestic Initiatives

Presidents get the lion's share of the credit when major domestic policies are enacted and implemented. At the end of a legislative session, or in a campaign for reelection, the White House will boast of its policy accomplishments. And in the longer run, as historians write textbook chapters and reference book entries, landmark laws will be listed under the president's name. In reality, not all of these laws reflect the intentions and priorities of the White House. A distinction can be drawn between three types of domestic initiatives: entrepreneurial initiation, responsiveness to coalition supporters, and competition for credit with rivals from the opposing party.

Entrepreneurial initiation most closely fits the image of presidential authorship of domestic reform. In this category are domestic policies that presidents supported before they ran for the White House and then promised during their campaigns. Once in office, presidents as policy entrepreneurs follow through on their pledges whether or not the external demand for action is strong. They launch a drive for policy innovation, remain largely in control of the process of policy development, and, despite the need to make compromises along the way, accomplish most of what they originally sought in the form of new legislation.

A recent example of successful entrepreneurial initiation is George W. Bush's No Child Left Behind reform in education policy. Bush developed a reputation as an education reformer while governor of Texas, promised during his 2000 campaign to advance the cause of educational standards, and began his administration by intensely focusing on the issue. "The very first week of the presidency we spent the entire week talking about education," recalled Bush domestic policy adviser Margaret Spellings. Unlike his other initial legislative priority, tax cuts, Bush promoted No Child Left Behind as a bipartisan undertaking. The president was willing to scrap his proposal for education vouchers and to increase education funding in order to attract Democratic support for the testing and accountability provisions that were closest to his heart. Roughly a year after Bush's inauguration, No Child Left Behind became the most significant educational reform enacted into law since the 1960s.[15]

Responsiveness to coalition supporters characterizes cases in which presidents are pushed to go considerably further in domestic policy than they originally intended because of pressure from key elements in their coalition. In this type of policy leadership, the White House initially supports modest policies that are favorable to a coalition group, but the issue is not a presidential priority and the group considers the administration's proposal to be inadequate. Often White House reluctance to satisfy such supporters stems from the controversial nature of the reform that they seek. If the group can raise the political stakes, impressing upon the White House that its agenda has broad support and that the president's reputation will suffer by sticking to timid incrementalism, the administration may respond with more substantial and significant reform proposals.

Several of the most historic achievements in domestic reform during the twentieth century followed this course, including the Wagner Act under Franklin D. Roosevelt, which labor unions insisted that he support, and the Civil Rights Act proposed by John F. Kennedy and signed into law by Lyndon B. Johnson. Kennedy was reluctant to champion civil rights legislation, fearing that to do so would turn powerful southern committee chairs in Congress against his entire domestic agenda. In place of a public push for civil rights, the Kennedy administration pursued quiet, modest advances through executive action and litigation. Impatient with these cautious calculations, the civil rights movement mounted increasingly militant campaigns, culminating with the Birmingham demonstrations in the spring of 1963. As the northern public reacted in horror to scenes of segregationist brutality, and as demonstrations spread rapidly to other cities in the South, Kennedy felt compelled to respond with a legislative proposal far more sweeping and forceful than anything his administration had previously contemplated.[16]

Competition for credit with rivals from the opposing party leads presidents to act against type by supporting domestic policies inconsistent with their own and their party's past commitments. In this variation, the president has either ignored the subject in the past or expressed antagonism to proposals for change. In most such cases, no commitments of any kind were made during the presidential campaign to move forward in this field of policy. Yet if the proposed reform becomes popular, and especially if prospective rivals for the presidency start to garner credit by championing it, a president may feel the need to enter this policy field and burnish his own reform credentials. In such cases, a telltale indicator that the president's heart was never really in his reform proposals is the lack of attention paid to the effectiveness of the policy once it is enacted.

Nixon aide Egil Krogh counts his administration's impressive list of environmental policies as "a great success." Krogh points out that the Nixon administration's development of environmental policy was the handiwork of "exceptionally talented people on the staff," and remarks that he was not sure the president "was ever terribly comfortable with what we were doing on environmental policy, but he signed all the bills." Krogh is correct about his boss's discomfort. Nixon did not discuss the environment during his 1968 campaign, but after he took office the environmental movement exploded in popularity and senators Edmund Muskie and Henry "Scoop" Jackson, both of them likely Democratic challengers to Nixon in 1972, emerged as leading environmental advocates.[17] In response, Nixon handed over environmental policy development to aide John Ehrlichman, telling him to "just keep me out of trouble on environmental issues."[18]

Abundant evidence from White House tapes and from the memoirs of aides shows that Nixon was never enthusiastic about environmental protection. Even at the height of his administration's policy activism, he hoped that "interest in this will recede."[19] He despised the environmental movement: its activists, he remarked to Ehrlichman, were "clowns" and their agenda was "crap."[20] Nixon was relieved once he sensed that momentum for environmental reform had ebbed. During the 1972 campaign, he announced at a private White House meeting that "people don't give a shit about the environment."[21] Feeling more electorally secure after the Democrats nominated George McGovern, Nixon vetoed the Federal Water Pollution Control Act in the fall of 1972. For the remainder of his presidency, he consistently sided with business interests and against environmental regulation.[22]

Historical Context and Domestic Policymaking

As noted above, the transcripts and essays in this volume point to important generalizations about domestic policymaking. Yet any such generalizations must be tempered with recognition of the influence of historical context—of how both substantive and political factors that affect domestic policymaking vary considerably from administration to administration. The importance of historical context can be illustrated by holding political party constant and examining variability in a succession of presidents. Because the public philosophy of the Democratic Party is generally more favorable to activism in domestic policymaking than the Republican approach, the trio of presidents briefly considered here consists of three Democrats: Jimmy Carter, Bill Clinton, and Barack Obama.

Jimmy Carter

Coming into office in 1977 as the last Democratic president elected "in the shadow of FDR," Jimmy Carter was the first to operate under the ideological cloud of liberalism-in-trouble.[23] The triumphs of the New Deal and Great Society had faded, and with a public backlash against liberalism in the areas of race and welfare, a mounting disenchantment with "big government," and the backdrop of a disastrous war in Southeast Asia, not much mileage remained in liberal political formulas. George McGovern's crushing defeat at the hands of Richard Nixon in 1972 had demonstrated the limited political appeal of full-throated liberalism, even as Nixon's resignation two years later amid the fires of the Watergate scandal subsequently opened the door for the Democrats to take back the White House. As Stuart Eizenstat emphasizes, the Jimmy Carter who was narrowly elected in 1976 "was, not coincidentally, a moderate Democrat. If he had been a liberal Democrat he wouldn't have gotten elected, even with Watergate."

President Carter had the apparent advantage of large Democratic majorities in Congress, but congressional Democrats were for the most part to his left ideologically and were more closely linked to liberal interest groups than to him. Carter did not endear himself to his party's members in Congress with his penchant for "good-government reforms" in domestic policy that were indifferent to the tasks of coalition maintenance: cuts in water projects, energy bills, hospital cost-containment, and a "zero-based-budgeting" scheme that squarely took aim at the bureaucracies that administered liberal programs of the past.[24] Even when Carter addressed welfare, an issue of central concern to liberal Democrats, his insistence that no new money accompany reform did not sit well with most members of his party, and his legislative proposal went nowhere.[25]

No other domestic issue so powerfully divided Carter from liberal Democrats as health-care reform. During the Nixon and Ford administrations, Senator Edward Kennedy, the leading champion of liberalism in Congress, had assembled a large coalition of Democrat-leaning interest groups behind a plan for national health insurance. In the course of the 1976 primary season,

Carter endorsed the Kennedy plan, mostly because it was a top priority of organized labor. Once in office, however, his administration delayed consideration of health-care reform until its second year and then proposed an incremental and fiscally cautious policy. Tense negotiations between Carter and Kennedy forces ended in failure, with Kennedy and AFL-CIO president George Meany publicly blistering the president for betraying his campaign pledge. Indeed, the rupture over health-care reform precipitated Kennedy's challenge to Carter for the 1980 Democratic presidential nomination, leaving a badly split party to face the onslaught of Reagan and his conservative agenda.[26]

Bill Clinton

Bill Clinton was elected after twelve years of Republican presidents, a period characterized by Stephen Skowronek as the creation and consolidation, at the hands of Ronald Reagan and George H. W. Bush, of a new conservative regime.[27] Republican ascendance in national politics was marked by the dominance of new terms of domestic policy discourse: hostility to "tax and spend" liberalism, enthusiasm about the wonders of cutting taxes, and a law-and-order mood in place of sympathy for minorities and the poor. Clinton was a self-proclaimed "New Democrat," intent on demonstrating that he had heard and responded to voters' complaints about the errors and excesses of past liberal programs. He pledged to "reinvent" rather than restore liberal-supported government agencies and to assuage middle-class fears about crime while serving middle-class economic and cultural interests.[28]

Clinton was also determined to avoid Carter's mistake of alienating the Democratic majority in Congress, whose domestic policy preferences were more liberal than his own. Consequently, his initial agenda sought to straddle the divide between liberal interests and New Democrat centrism, pursuing national health insurance, the major piece of unfinished business on the liberal agenda, while aligning his administration with centrist policy ideas on deficit reduction, crime, and "ending welfare as we know it." Clinton's budget measures and crime bill passed Congress while his health-care reform effort collapsed, but all three contributed to a public backlash that brought down the Democratic Congress in the midterm elections of 1994.[29]

Under the tutelage of political adviser Dick Morris, Clinton shifted to a strategy of "triangulation" in 1995, positioning himself midway between Democrats and Republicans in Congress. Paul Quirk and William Cunion have characterized this maneuver as "opportunistic centrism"—that is, oc-cupation of a political center defined by the popularity of proposals regard-less of their ideological provenance.[30] With its hopes dashed of moving large-scale domestic programs through Congress, the Clinton White House launched a steady stream of small-bore initiatives. Although Democratic lib-erals were disillusioned by the defensiveness and shrunken aspirations of Clinton's domestic policies, no disastrous party rupture occurred like the one that afflicted Carter. The absence of a liberal challenger with Kennedy's stature was one reason; even more important was the intensity of Republi-can opposition to Clinton despite his moderate approach. What ultimately led Democrats of all stripes to rally around the president was the Republi-cans' impeachment campaign of 1998–1999.[31]

Barack Obama

Barack Obama entered office in 2009 in what appeared to be a far more favorable historical context than had confronted either Jimmy Carter or Bill Clinton. Carter took office after Democratic liberalism had been indicted for both domestic disappointments and foreign-policy disasters, and Clinton was elected against the backdrop of a potent Republican realignment. In contrast, Obama's immediate context was marked by public unhappiness with the economic and global failures of his conservative Republican pre-decessor. As political analysts proclaimed the demise of the conservative regime, Obama benefited from public expectations of a historic transforma-tion of American politics. Unlike the early frontrunner for the Democratic presidential nomination, Hillary Clinton, Obama would not, he promised in his campaign, be another cautious Clinton in the White House.[32]

True to his campaign promises, on taking office Obama pursued the most ambitious and liberal domestic agenda of any recent Democratic president. Like Clinton, he sought national health insurance; like Carter, he tried to transform energy policy. In addition, Obama's domestic policy agenda included education reform, immigration reform, financial regulatory reform, and a host of other initiatives. Initially, Obama seemed blessed with critical advantages that his two Democratic predecessors lacked: a sizeable majority victory in the presidential election and policy preferences that he shared with most of his fellow partisans in Congress. Confronting an un-precedented near-unanimous opposition from congressional Republicans, made especially potent by routine deployment of Senate filibusters, Obama held together Democrats in Congress and secured the enactment of health-care reform legislation that had eluded Clinton. He achieved the same impressive result with financial regulatory reform and allowing gays and lesbians to serve openly in the military. Yet Obama's margin for error during his first two years in office was narrow, and a small number of defections by Senate Democrats from energy-producing states denied him cap-and-trade legislation and stalled his plans for a "green revolution" in alternative energy technologies.[33]

As public support for Obama began to decline more rapidly than anyone originally anticipated, the historic context he had inherited, it now appeared, had been double-edged rather than purely favorable. Bush left behind messes in the economy at home and in two wars abroad; these messes helped elect Obama, but once he was in office they became his problems. And since neither a crisis in jobs nor a seeming quagmire in Afghanistan allowed for prompt solutions, the public excitement that accompanied his inauguration soon succumbed to a sour national mood. Moreover, Obama's bold domestic agenda ran afoul of the longstanding mistrust of the national government, causing his historic success on health-care reform to diminish rather than boost his public standing. With Democratic liberals disheartened by the roadblocks their new president had encountered and the compromises he had made to move past them, and with Republican conservatives energized by the swift revival of their political fortunes, the Democrats lost control of the House in the 2010 midterm election, shifting the composition of Congress in an unfavorable direction for Obama.

Conclusion

The domestic policy advisers and political scientists who assembled at the Miller Center symposium offered an inside look at the genesis, development, and outcomes of White House domestic policymaking. Although advisers from different administrations did not always agree with each other, much less with the scholars, similarities of experience and insight over time and across party lines are broadly evident. From the beginning of the story—the presidential campaign—to its end in the historical evaluation of successes and failures, the symposium—and especially this volume—present much new information and many conclusions that depart from conventional understanding. Campaign promises, for example, are not political throwaways to be discarded after the inauguration, but instead loom large in setting the White House agenda and informing policy deliberations. Evaluations of what an administration has accomplished in domestic policy are poorly served by standard measures, particularly when popularity is conflated with effective performance.

This chapter has rounded out the perspective of what Bruce Reed dubs the "wonks" with discussions of the political side of domestic policymaking and the variations in historical context that affect the opportunities and constraints confronting presidents in the domestic sphere. Viewed from the perspective of substantive policy, the political perspective may seem crassly calculating and shortsighted, preoccupied far more with the next election than with the welfare of the nation. Yet politics is an integral part of crafting, enacting, and implementing domestic policies. It keeps the White House attuned to external constituencies whose concerns are not the same as those of the "wonks." To the policy expertise of the specialists in the White House, it adds representation for the values and views of organized interests and ordinary citizens.

If there is a single overarching lesson to be drawn from this volume, it might be that domestic policymaking is hard. Presidents are able, albeit with important exceptions, to put into place their basic foreign and economic policies, whether or not those policies ultimately prove effective. In the enactment of domestic policy, however, the principal initiatives undertaken by the White House are more frequently thwarted. Accurately weighing and balancing substantive and political considerations is difficult. An even harder challenge is to overcome resistance from passionate and well-organized opponents. Bill Clinton suffered his most consequential defeat with health-care reform, a political disaster that profoundly influenced the remainder of his tenure in office. George W. Bush found it easier to send troops into Iraq and to cut taxes than to alter Social Security or reform immigration policy. And even as he secured his historic victory in health-care reform, Barack Obama has learned just how arduous and costly domestic reform politics can be. Future domestic policy advisers are still likely to need that bottle of whiskey.

Notes

1. Unless otherwise noted, all quotations from domestic policy advisers are from the transcripts of the Miller Center symposium reported in chapters 3, 5, 7, and 9.

2. Joseph A. Pika, The White House Transition Project: The White House Office of Public Liaison, Report 2009-03 (2008), http://whitehousetransitionproject.org/re sources/briefing/WHTP-2009-03-Public%20Liaison.pdf (accessed November 1, 2010).

3. Pika, "White House Office," 6.

4. Committee on Oversight and Government Reform, U.S. House of Representatives, "The Activities of the White House Office of Political Affairs," (October 2008), 2–4.

5. Carol E. Lee, "White House Political Office Will Remain," *Politico*, November 21, 2008.

6. John DiIulio, who served as President George W. Bush's first director of the White House Office of Faith-Based and Community Initiatives, wrote that in his eight months at the White House, he "heard many, many staff discussions, but not three meaningful, substantive policy discussions." John DiIulio to Ron Suskind, October 24, 2002, *Esquire*, January 2003.

7. Karen Hult, "Strengthening Presidential Decision-Making Capacity," *Presidential Studies Quarterly* 30, no. 1 (March 2000): 28–29.

8. Jonathan Alter, *The Promise: President Obama, Year One* (New York: Simon and Schuster, 2010), 253–254.

9. Anne Farris, Richard P. Nathan, and David J. Wright, *The Expanding Administrative Presidency: George W. Bush and the Faith-Based Initiative* (Albany, N.Y.: Rockefeller Institute of Government, 2004).

10. On Reagan's alliance with the Christian right, see Daniel J. Tichenor, "The Presidency and Interest Groups: Allies, Adversaries, and Policy Leadership," in *The Presidency and the Political System*, 9th ed., ed. Michael Nelson (Washington, D.C.: CQ Press, 2010), 275–277.

11. See Nancy J. Weiss, *Farewell to the Party of Lincoln: Black Politics in the Age of FDR* (Princeton, N.J.: Princeton University Press, 1983).

12. Robert Mason, *Richard Nixon and the Quest for a New Majority* (Chapel Hill: University of North Carolina Press, 2004), 51–53, 144–150.

13. Barbara Sinclair, "Living (and Dying?) by the Sword: George W. Bush as Legislative Leader," in *The George W. Bush Legacy*, eds. Colin Campbell, Bert A. Rockman, and Andrew Rudalevige (Washington, D.C.: CQ Press, 2008), 177–179.

14. Ed Hornick, "What's Behind Obama's Immigration Reform Push?," *CNN Politics*, July 1, 2010.

15. Barbara Sinclair, "Context, Strategy, and Chance: George W. Bush and the 107th Congress," in *The George W. Bush Presidency: Appraisals and Prospects*, eds. Colin Campbell and Bert A. Rockman (Washington, D.C.: CQ Press, 2004), 115–117.

16. See Nick Bryant, *The Bystander: John F. Kennedy and the Struggle for Black Equality* (New York: Basic Books, 2006).

17. On the political context for Nixon's policies in this area, see J. Brooks Flippen, *Nixon and the Environment* (Albuquerque: University of New Mexico Press, 2000).

18. Quoted in Joan Hoff, *Nixon Reconsidered* (New York: Basic Books, 1994), 21.

19. Quoted in Rick Perlstein, *Nixonland: The Rise of a President and the Fracturing of America* (New York: Scribner, 2008), 460.

20. Quoted in Melvin Small, *The Presidency of Richard Nixon* (Lawrence: University Press of Kansas, 1999), 197.

21. Quoted in ibid.

22. See Flippen, *Nixon and the Environment*, 142, 179–183, 214.

23. William E. Leuchtenburg, *In the Shadow of FDR: From Harry Truman to George W. Bush* (Ithaca, N.Y.: Cornell University Press, 2001); Stephen Skowronek, *The Politics Presidents Make: Leadership from John Adams to Bill Clinton* (Cambridge, Mass.: Harvard University Press, 1997), 361–362.

24. See Burton I. Kaufman and Scott Kaufman, *The Presidency of James Earl Carter Jr.*, 2nd ed. (Lawrence: University Press of Kansas, 2006).

25. Laurence E. Lynn and David Whitman, *The President as Policymaker: Jimmy Carter and Welfare Reform* (Philadelphia: Temple University Press, 1981).

26. Timothy Stanley, *Kennedy vs. Carter: The 1980 Battle for the Democratic Party's Soul* (Lawrence: University Press of Kansas, 2010), 50–56.

27. Skowronek, *Politics Presidents Make*, 409–446.

28. See Kenneth S. Baer, *Reinventing Democrats: The Politics of Liberalism from Reagan to Clinton* (Lawrence: University Press of Kansas, 2000), 193–228.

29. Ibid.

30. Paul J. Quirk and William Cunion, "Clinton's Domestic Policy: The Lessons of a 'New Democrat,'" in *The Clinton Legacy*, eds. Colin Campbell and Bert A. Rockman (New York: Chatham House Publishers, 2000), 200–225.

31. See Bert A. Rockman, "Cutting with the Grain: Is There a Clinton Leadership Legacy?," in *Clinton Legacy*, eds. Campbell and Rockman, 274–294.

32. Stephen Skowronek, "Is Reconstructive Leadership Still Possible? Barack Obama in Political Time," paper delivered at the American Political Science Association Annual Meeting, Washington, D.C., September 2010.

33. Alter, *Promise*, 110–137, 395–434.

List of Contributors

Scholars

Andrew E. Busch

Andrew Busch is Professor of Government and Associate Dean of the Faculty at Claremont McKenna College, where he teaches courses on American politics, government, and public policy. He has also served as an Adjunct Fellow of the John M. Ashbrook Center for Public Affairs at Ashland University. He has written numerous articles on American politics for both the scholarly and popular press, and is the author or co-author of eleven books, including *Horses in Midstream: U.S. Midterm Elections and Their Consequences, 1894–1998; Ronald Reagan and the Politics of Freedom; The Constitution on the Campaign Trail: The Surprising Political Career of America's Founding Document;* and, most recently, *Epic Journey: The Elections of 2008 and American Politics.*

Karen M. Hult

Karen Hult is Professor of Political Science and an associated faculty member at the Center for Public Administration and Policy at Virginia Polytechnic Institute and State University. Before joining the Virginia Tech faculty in August 1990, she was an assistant and associate professor of government at Pomona College, where she also directed the Program in Public Policy Analysis from 1988 to 1990. She taught as well at the Claremont Graduate University. Hult has written numerous articles and four books: *Agency Merger and Bureaucratic Redesign; Governing Public Organizations,* co-authored with Charles Walcott; *Governing the White House: From Hoover through LBJ,* co-authored with Walcott (and winner of the 1996 Neustadt Award as the best book on the presidency published that year); and *Empowering the White House: Governance under Nixon, Ford, and Carter*, also co-authored with Walcott, and a 2005 *Choice* "Outstanding Academic Title."

Lawrence R. Jacobs

Lawrence Jacobs is Director of the Center for the Study of Politics and Governance in the Hubert H. Humphrey Institute at the University of Minnesota. He is the Walter F. and Joan Mondale Chair for Political Studies and Professor in the Department of Political Science. The Center for the Study of Politics and Governance sponsors nonpartisan independent analysis and forums that foster informed discussion of American politics and policy and contribute to designing practical solutions to the pressing problems of public life. Jacobs's research examines the nature of democratic governance and especially the system of political representation. He has published ten books including *Class War? What Americans Really Think about Economic Inequality* (with Benjamin Page); *The Private Abuse of the Public Interest* (with Lawrence Brown); *The Unsustainable State* (with Desmond King); and *Talking Together: Public Deliberation in America and the Search for Community* (with Fay Lomax Cook and Michael Delli Carpini).

Bruce Miroff

Bruce Miroff is Professor of Political Science at the University of Albany, State University of New York, where he has received the Excellence in Teaching Award and is a Collins Fellow. He teaches and writes on the American presidency, American political development, American political theory, and political leadership. Along with numerous articles and book chapters, he has authored or co-authored five books: *Pragmatic Illusions: The Presidential Politics of John F. Kennedy; Icons of Democracy: American Leaders as Heroes, Aristocrats, Dissenters, and Democrats; The Liberals' Moment: The McGovern Insurgency and the Identity Crisis of the Democratic Party; Debating Democracy: A Reader in American Politics* (6th ed.); and *The Democratic Debate: American Politics in an Age of Change* (5th ed.).

Michael Nelson

Michael Nelson is the Fulmer Professor of Political Science at Rhodes College and a nonresident senior fellow of the Miller Center of Public Affairs at the University of Virginia. A former editor of *The Washington Monthly*, more than fifty of his articles have been reprinted in anthologies of political science, history, sociology, and English composition, and he has won national writing awards for articles on music and baseball. His recent books include *The Presidency and the Political System* (9th ed.); *The Elections of 2008*; *The American Presidency: Origins and Development, 1776–2010* (with Sidney M. Milkis, 5th ed.); *The President's Words: Speeches and Speechwriting in the Modern White House* (with Russell L. Riley); and *How the South Joined the Gambling Nation: The Politics of State Policy Innovation* (with John Mason), which won the Southern Political Science Association's V.O. Key Award for the Outstanding Book on Southern Politics. He edits the American Presidential Elections book series for the University Press of Kansas and is currently working on books about the 1968 election and West Point.

Bruce Nesmith

Bruce Nesmith is Joan and Abbott Lipsky Professor of Political Science at Coe College. He teaches courses on American political institutions, religion and U.S. politics, and political philosophy. He is author of *The New Republican Coalition: The Reagan Campaigns and White Evangelicals*. His current research deals with policymaking by the president and Congress.

Paul J. Quirk

Paul Quirk holds the Phil Lind Chair in U.S. Politics and Representation at the University of British Columbia. He has held faculty appointments at several American universities and has published widely on the presidency, Congress, public opinion, and public policymaking. Among other awards, he received the Aaron Wildavsky Enduring Contribution Award of the Public Policy Section of the American Political Science Association and the Brownlow Book Award of the National Academy of Public Administration. He serves on the editorial boards of several scholarly journals, including the *American Political Science Review*. Among recent works, he is coeditor of *Institutions of American Democracy: The Legislative Branch* and coauthor of

Deliberative Choices: Debating Public Policy in Congress. He and Bruce Nesmith are working on a book-length study of the presidency and Congress as policymaking institutions.

Russell L. Riley

Russell Riley chairs the Presidential Oral History Program at the University of Virginia's Miller Center of Public Affairs, where he is an associate professor. His work with the center spans every presidential interview project from Carter to George W. Bush. He previously taught at Georgetown University and the University of Pennsylvania and was the founding director of Penn's Washington Semester Program. He also has been an academic program director of the Salzburg Seminar in American Studies, in Austria. He is the author of *The Presidency and the Politics of Racial Inequality: Nation-keeping from 1831 to 1965* and is editor of *Bridging the Constitutional Divide: Inside the White House Office of Legislative Affairs* and *The President's Words: Speeches and Speechwriting in the Modern White House* (with Michael Nelson).

Charles E. Walcott

Charles Walcott taught at the University of Minnesota for twenty-one years before coming to Virginia Tech in 1989. He has written or edited five books, including *Governing Public Organizations; Governing the White House: From Hoover through LBJ* (winner of a Neustadt Award as the best book on the presidency published that year) and *Empowering the White House: Nixon, Ford and Carter*, all co-authored with Karen M. Hult. He has also had numerous articles published in journals such as the *American Journal of Political Science, Polity, Policy Studies Journal, Presidential Studies Quarterly, Congress and the Presidency, Rhetoric and Public Affairs, International Interactions, Perspectives on Political Science*, and several edited volumes. "Organizational Design as Public Policy," by Hult and Walcott, received the Theodore Lowi Award from the Policy Studies Organization for the best article in the 1990 volume of the *Policy Studies Journal.*

White House Alumni

James M. Cannon III

From 1975 to 1977, James M. Cannon III worked directly with President Ford, Cabinet members, and senior White House staff as Assistant to the President for Domestic Affairs and Executive Director of the Domestic Council. He then served as chief of staff and a political consultant to Senate Majority Leader Howard H. Baker, Jr. In 1988, Mr. Cannon served as the executive director of American Agenda, a bipartisan policy committee headed by presidents Ford and Carter to assist the president-elect, George H. W. Bush. Since 1991, he has regularly worked as a writer, biographer, and political adviser. He has written or contributed to five books, including *Time and Chance: Gerald Ford's Appointment with History* and *Character Above All*. His current work-in-progress is entitled *A Time to Keep: The Presidency of Gerald R. Ford*. Earlier in his career, Cannon worked in journalism for a variety of publications, including the *Baltimore Sun, Time,* and *Newsweek,* and from 1969 to 1974 he was an assistant to New York Governor Nelson Rockefeller. From 1941 to 1946, Mr. Cannon served as a captain in the U.S. Army.

Bertram Carp

Bertram Carp was Deputy Assistant for Domestic Affairs to President Jimmy Carter and Legislative Counsel to Senator Walter F. Mondale. He served for ten years as Vice President for Government Affairs of Turner Broadcasting System, Inc., where he supervised the company's legislative and regulatory activities worldwide, and served on the company's executive committee. Earlier, he was Executive Vice President of the National Cable Television Association. Mr. Carp became a Principal of Williams & Jensen in 1997, and was elected Vice Chairman in 2007. His practice is general in nature, and includes telecommunications, intellectual property, mergers and acquisitions, and trade.

Stuart Eizenstat

Stuart Eizenstat has held a number of senior positions during a decade and a half of public service, including chief domestic policy adviser to President Jimmy Carter (1977–1981); and U.S. Ambassador to the European Union, Undersecretary of Commerce for International Trade, Undersecretary of

State for Economic, Business and Agricultural Affairs, and Deputy Secretary of the Treasury in the Clinton Administration (1993–2001). During the Clinton years, he had a prominent role in the development of several international initiatives, including the Transatlantic Agenda with the European Union; agreements with the European Union regarding the Helms-Burton Act and the Iran-Libya Sanctions Act; and the negotiation of the Kyoto Protocol, where he led the U.S. delegation. His articles on a variety of international and domestic topics appear in publications such as the *New York Times, Financial Times, Washington Post, Foreign Policy*, and *Foreign Affairs*. He also authored *Imperfect Justice: Looted Assets, Slave Labor, and the Unfinished Business of World War II*, detailing his experiences as Special Representative of the President and Secretary of State on Holocaust-Era Issues during the Clinton Administration.

William Galston

From 1993 until 1995, William Galston served as Deputy Assistant to President Clinton for Domestic Policy, where he had principal responsibility for education policy, among other assignments. His political activities include service as issues director for Walter Mondale's presidential campaign (1982–1984), as a senior advisor to Albert Gore, Jr.'s, run for the Democratic presidential nomination (1988), and again as a senior adviser to Gore's presidential campaign (1999–2000). Galston holds the Ezra Zilkha Chair in the Brookings Institution's Governance Studies Program, where he serves as a Senior Fellow. He is also College Park Professor at the University of Maryland. Prior to January 2006, he was Saul Stern Professor at the School of Public Policy, University of Maryland, director of the Institute for Philosophy and Public Policy, and founding director of the Center for Information and Research on Civic Learning and Engagement (CIRCLE). Galston is the author of 8 books and more than 100 articles in the fields of political theory, public policy, and American politics. In 2004 he was elected a Fellow of the American Academy of Arts and Sciences.

Egil Krogh

Egil "Bud" Krogh joined John Ehrlichman's staff as Assistant to the Counsel at the beginning of Richard Nixon's first term. During his time at the White House, his responsibilities included District of Columbia governmental affairs, work with the early Special Investigations Unit (eventually known as the "Plumbers"), law enforcement, and narcotics control policy. His final position in the federal government was Undersecretary of Transportation in 1973. As co-director of the White House "Plumbers," he approved a covert operation investigating the leak of the top secret Pentagon Papers to the *New York Times*. He later pleaded guilty to conspiracy and served four and a half months in prison. Between disbarment from law practice in 1975 and reinstatement in 1980, Krogh taught Ethics, Public Policy Analysis, and Administrative Law at Golden Gate University in San Francisco. After reinstatement, he focused his practice on mediation and energy issues in the Pacific Northwest and Canada. Krogh joined the Center for the Study of the Presidency and Congress in 2009 as a Senior Fellow on Leadership, Ethics, and Integrity. He is the author of *Integrity: Good People, Bad Choices, and Life Lessons from the White House.*

James Pinkerton

James Pinkerton worked in the White House domestic policy offices of presidents Ronald Reagan and George H. W. Bush, and for Republican candidates in the 1980, 1984, 1988, and 1992 presidential campaigns. In 2008 he served as a senior adviser to the Mike Huckabee for President campaign. Pinkerton is currently a senior research fellow in the American Strategy Program of the New America Foundation, a contributing editor to *The American Conservative*, and an adviser to the BMW Stiftung Herbert Quandt, the foundation of BMW. He has written for publications ranging from the *Wall Street Journal*, *New York Times*, *Washington Post*, *USA Today*, *National Review*, *New Republic*, *Foreign Affairs*, *Huffington Post*, and *Jerusalem Post*. He is also author of the book *What Comes Next: The End of Big Government–And the New Paradigm Ahead*. Pinkerton is a contributor to the Fox News Channel, a regular panelist on the Fox *News Watch* show, and a writer for FoxNews.com.

Roger Porter

Roger Porter served for more than a decade in senior economic policy positions in the White House, most recently as Assistant to the President for Economic and Domestic Policy for President George H. W. Bush from 1989 to 1993. He also served as Director of the White House Office of Policy Development in the Reagan Administration and as Executive Secretary of the President's Economic Policy Board during the Ford Administration. He joined the faculty of Harvard's Kennedy School of Government in 1977, and he is currently IBM Professor of Business and Government at Harvard, where he teaches courses on the American Presidency and the Business-Government Relationship in the United States. He is one of the nation's preeminent authorities on presidential advising and decision making and has authored numerous scholarly articles. His books include *Presidential Decision Making: The Economic Policy Board*, and *Efficiency, Equity and Legitimacy: The Multilateral Trading System at the Millennium*. Porter was a Rhodes Scholar at Oxford University, where he received his BPhil degree, and a White House Fellow from 1974 to 1975. He is also currently, with his wife, master of Dunster House.

Bruce Reed

Bruce Reed served for all eight years in the Clinton-Gore White House. As President Clinton's chief domestic policy adviser and director of the Domestic Policy Council, he helped write the landmark 1996 welfare reform law, create the 100,000 police program, and helped to enact the president's education agenda. In 1992, he served as deputy campaign manager for the Clinton-Gore campaign, supervising development of the domestic, economic, and foreign policy agenda. Earlier, Reed served as policy director of the Democratic Leadership Council (DLC) from 1990 to 1991, when Clinton was DLC chairman. He also was founding editor of the DLC magazine, *The New Democrat*. From 1985 to 1989, he served as chief speechwriter for Senator Al Gore. Reed, a Rhodes Scholar, was president of the DLC before leaving in January 2011 to become Vice President Joseph Biden's chief of staff. He also served in 2010 as Executive Director of President Obama's National Commission on Fiscal Responsibility and Reform. Reed's writing has appeared in the *New York Times, Washington Post, Wall Street Journal, USA Today, Los Angeles Times, New Republic, Economist,* and *Washington Monthly.*

Margaret Spellings

Margaret Spellings was White House Domestic Policy Adviser for President George W. Bush from 2001 to 2005. She managed the development of the president's domestic policy agenda, with oversight of education, health, transportation, justice, housing, and labor policy. Her achievements include the No Child Left Behind Act (NCLB), oversight of the development of the President's Emergency Plan for AIDS Relief, and the development of a comprehensive immigration plan. Spellings was subsequently named Secretary of Education, where she led implementation of NCLB, launched a national higher education action plan, and led the federal government's efforts to ensure access to student loans amidst turmoil in the credit markets. She initiated extensive international outreach and collaboration, overseeing education agreements with such countries as China, Russia, and the United Arab Emirates. Prior to her White House service, Spellings was Senior Adviser to Governor George W. Bush; led government relations efforts for the Texas Association of School Boards; and served in various leadership posts for the Texas legislature. She currently is the President and CEO of Margaret Spellings and Company.

Index

www.ingramcontent.com/pod-product-compliance
Lightning Source LLC
Chambersburg PA
CBHW051951270326
41929CB00015B/2613